Absence of the Buddha Image in Early Buddhist Art

Emerging Perceptions in Buddhist Studies

(ISSN 0971-9512)

1-2. An Encyclopaedia of Buddhist Deities, Demigods, Godlings, Saints & Demons — with Special Focus on Iconographic Attributes; by Fredrick W. Bunce. 2 Vols. (ISBN 978-81-246-0020-7; set)

3. Buddhism in Karnataka; by R.C. Hiremath; with a foreword by H.H. the Dalai Lama (ISBN 978-81-246-0013-9)

4-5. Pāli Language and Literature: A Systematic Survey and Historical Study; by Kanai Lal Hazra. 2 Vols. (ISBN 978-81-246-0004-7; set)

6. Maṇḍala and Landscape; by A.W. Macdonald (ISBN 978-81-246-0060-3)

7. The Future Buddha Maitreya: An Iconological Study; by Inchang Kim (ISBN 978-81-246-0082-5)

9. A Few Facts About Buddhism; by Gunnar Gällmo (ISBN 978-81-246-0099-3)

10. Buddhist Theory of Meaning and Literary Analysis; by Rajnish K. Mishra (ISBN 978-81-246-0118-1)

11. Buddhism as/in Performance; Analysis of Meditation and Theatrical Practice; by David E.R. George (ISBN 978-81-246-0123-5)

12. Buddhist Tantra and Buddhist Art by T.N. Mishra (ISBN 978-81-246-0141-9)

13. Buddhist Art in India and Sri Lanka: 3rd Century BC to 6th Century AD — A Critical Study; by Virender Kumar Dabral (ISBN 978-81-246-0162-4)

14. The Tibetan Iconography of Buddhas, Bodhisattvas and Other Deities: A Unique Pantheon; by Lokesh Chandra & Fredrick W. Bunce (ISBN 978-81-246-0178-5)

15. The Dalai Lamas: The Institution and Its History by Ardy Verhaegen; (ISBN 978-81-246-0202-7)

16. The Tibetan Tāntric Vision; by Krishna Ghosh Della Santina (ISBN 978-81-246-0227-0)

17. The Buddhist Art of Kauśāmbī: From 300 BC to AD 550; by Aruna Tripathi (ISBN 978-81-246-0226-3)

18. Mahāmudrā & Atiyoga; by Giuseppe Baroetto; Translated from Italian into English by Andrew Lukianowicz (ISBN 978-81-246-0322-2)

19. Theravāda Buddhist Devotionalism in Ceylon, Burma and Thailand; by V.V.S. Saibaba (ISBN 978-81-246-0327-7)

20. Faith and Devotion in Theravāda Buddhism; by V.V.S. Saibaba (ISBN 978-81-246-0329-1)

21. Sects in Tibetan Buddhism: Comparison of Practices Between Gelugpa and Nyingmapa Sects; by Vijay Kumar Singh (ISBN 978-81-246-0330-7)

22. Emptiness and Becoming: Integrating Mādhyamika Buddhism and Process Philosophy; by Peter Paul Kakol (ISBN 978-81-246-0519-6)

23. Buddhist Ethics in Impermanence; by M.V. Ram Kumar Ratnam, K. Srinivas (ISBN 978-81-246-0562-2)

Emerging Perceptions in Buddhist Studies, no. 8

Absence of the Buddha Image in Early Buddhist Art

— Toward its Significance in Comparative Religion —

Kanoko Tanaka

PRINTWORLD
Publishers of Indian Traditions

Cataloging in Publication Data — DK
[Courtesy: D.K. Agencies (P) Ltd. <docinfo@dkagencies.com>]

Tanaka, Kanoko, 1964-
Absence of the Buddha image in early Buddhist art.
(Emerging perceptions in Buddhist studies; no. 8).
Includes bibliographical references (p.).
Includes index.
ISBN 13: 9788124600900

1. Gautama Buddha — Art. 2. Art, Buddhist — India.
I. Title. II. Series: Emerging perceptions in Buddhist studies; no. 8.

ISBN 13: 978-81-246-0090-0
First Published in India in 1998
Second impression, 2014

Printed and published by:
D.K. Printworld (P) Ltd.
Regd. office : *Vedaśrī*, F-395, Sudarshan Park
(Metro Station: Ramesh Nagar)
New Delhi - 110 015
Phones : (011) 2545 3975, 2546 6019; *Fax*: (011) 2546 5926
e-mail : indology@dkprintworld.com
Web : www.dkprintworld.com

Preface

It was more than ten years ago that I came to know for the first time that there is no Buddha image in early Buddhist art. In those days, I was looking for a good theme for my research from various points of view. On discovering the 'absence of the Buddha image in early Buddhist art', I was inspired by the significance of this theme and so I made up my mind to search for its meanings. It was just like something voiceless out of ancient Buddhist sculptures forgotten by modern people had called out to me.

From the beginning, I had an intuition that a study of early Buddhist art would not end in dealing with fine arts but begin to create something valuable and worthy of the fine arts. But it took a long time before I set about working on such a theme. The reason was simple. It was necessary for me to go through the general process of studying the fine arts first of all.

The present work is the result — shall we say, 'fruit' — of my research on the 'absence of the Buddha image in early Buddhist art'. The fruit has ripened getting its sustenance from the soil, the water, and the sunlight of India. It may not taste sweet enough to satisfy everyone. But if the taste contains a sort of newness unknown to anyone before, it should be a joy for the cultivator who has been expecting a good harvest. Whether I get another 'fruit' in the near future depends on the manure and cultivation given to the same object of research.

My speciality has been comparative study of religions especially through the medium of fine arts. Therefore, I have tried in this research to look for a linkage between 'absence of the Buddha image in early Buddhist art' and other elements of non-Buddhist religious arts. The attempt might be seen as adventurous in the study of fine arts. But I do not feel so because in modern times different types of studies are expected to be inter-disciplinary. Both Buddhism and Buddhist art do not belong exclusively to Buddhist people any more. Each of them should be understood properly by everyone. For the purpose, it is necessary for a researcher to pursue new aspects and methods. In this context, the 'absence of the Buddha image in early Buddhist art' was quite an ideal theme because it continually inspired me by opening up new avenues of interest till the last.

Even in modern times, all the people in this world do not know that there is no Buddha image in early Buddhist art. It is natural that some of them will end their lives without knowing the fact because it is impossible to know everything in this world during one's lifetime. But some other people will have a chance to know about it and get some impression in their minds just as I have experienced.

It is important to remember that human beings always come to know about their cultural inheritance for the first time in their own lifetimes, although the inheritance itself becomes old year after year. As long as one is inspired by something of the past, one's research is worth carrying on. This is why the same object can be discussed by different people of all ages.

I hope that the subject of this book will be taken up by more researchers in the future so that their own religions and cultural backgrounds may be reflected in the results of their research.

Kanoko Tanaka

Acknowledgements

THIS research on 'Absence of the Buddha Image in Early Buddhist Art' in India is indebted to the scheme of the Indo-Japan Mixed Commission 1991-94 with the assistance of the Indian Council for Cultural Relations, the Government of India.

I am grateful to Professor K.K. Mittal, Professor Sanghasen Singh and Associate Professor Sudha Sengupta, Department of Buddhist Studies, University of Delhi, who aided me unhesitatingly throughout the course of my research.

My sincere gratitudes should be expressed towards Dr. K.T.S. Sarao, Head of the Department of Buddhist Studies, University of Delhi who cheered me up especially in the last stage of my work.

Since my first visit to Delhi in 1991, I have been maintaining friendship with Indian and foreign personalities of different religious faiths: Zoroastrian, Jewish, Christian, Islamic, Sikh, Hindū, Jain and Buddhist people. The knowledge and experience of each person has been a source of inspiration to me and I feel it has heightened the spirituality of my research work. I want to sincerely thank these people for their good wishes and blessings for me and for the successful publication of this book. May each of them be blessed with the grace of God/ Glory of the Eternal Truth!

Last but not the least, I want to express my heartfelt gratitude to my parents who have been understanding and supportive of my aspiration to constantly strive for greater learning and knowledge. Without their affection and cooperation, it would not have been possible for me to complete the work of this publication.

The only regret on this occasion is that I could not show this book to the late Professor Ryōichi Hayashi whose lecture at Komazawa University in 1986 gave me a chance to know about 'early Buddhist art' for the first time. He used to support my principle of discussing the spirituality of the fine arts. May his soul be in peace and know of my work in the life beyond.

I would also like to express my thanks to Mr. Susheel K. Mittal, Director of D.K. Printworld (P) Ltd., New Delhi, who is a good friend of mine and has been most helpful in the publication of this book.

Contents

Abbreviations

AN	*Aṅguttara-Nikāya*
ApDhS	*Āpastamba-Dharma-Sūtra*
Dhp	*Dhammapada*
DhpA	*Dhammapada-Aṭṭhakathā*
DN	*Dīgha-Nikāya*
Itiv.	*Itivuttaka*
Mhp.	*Mahāparinibbāna-suttanta*
MN	*Majjhima-Nikāya*
Mv.	*Mahāvastu*
Sn.	*Suttanipāta*
SN	*Saṃyutta-Nikāya*
Sum-vil	*Sumaṅgala-Vilāsinī*
Taishō	大正新脩大藏經 *Taisho Tr̥pitaka Edition*
Therag.	*Theragāthā*
Therig.	*Therīgāthā*
Udv.	*Udānavarga*

*****

Barua	Barua, *Bārhut Inscriptions,* 1926.
EI	*Epigraphia Indica.*
Hultzsch	Hultzsch, *Bharaut Inscriptions,* 1892.
Lüders	Lüders, *List of the Brāhmī Inscriptions,* 1910.

Majumdar	Cf. Marshall and Foucher, *The Monuments of Sāñchī*, vol. 1, 1982.
MS	Marshall and Foucher, *The Monuments of Sāñchī*, vols.1, 2, and 3, 1982.
P.T.S.	The Pali Text Society.
SBB	*Sacred Books of the Buddhists*, edited by Friedrich Max Müller
SBE	*The Sacred Books of the East*, edited by Friedrich Max Müller.
Vogel	Cf. *EI*, XX, 1929-30, pp. 1-37; XXI, 1931-32, pp. 61-71.

I

Introduction

THE absence of the Buddha image in early Buddhist art is a 'visible fact' that can be clearly seen in the archaeological discoveries of Buddhist art works. In other words, there was a long span of Buddhist life in India after the decease of the Buddha himself when the Buddha[1] was not seen through the Buddha image. This religious position of the ancient Buddhists is noteworthy because they were then free from accepting 'the Buddha' in its artistic sense. The freedom must have enabled them to behold the Buddha in their own minds just as they experienced him. The aim of this research is to rediscover their spiritual attitudes through the study of early Buddhist art.

On the contrary, 'the Buddha image', once it came into being, made an indelible impression in Buddhist minds. Its visual impact was overwhelming enough to take roots in the faiths and rituals of Buddhist people in later periods. Indeed, it might have been significant to the people to the extent that they could not see 'the Buddha' without remembering 'the Buddha image' in their minds. It was not easy for them to be conscious of this psychological bondage as long as they did not need to take an iconoclastic attitude toward their own reverence for 'the Buddha image'.

So far as we[2] know, there is nothing to prove that Buddhists have ever supported iconoclasm to destroy 'the Buddha image'. What is the reason? It is that the Buddhists have never doubted their faith in the fact that 'the Buddha image' portrays 'the Buddha' himself.

The legend of the first Buddha image in India is as follows.

According to the Chinese version of the *Aṅguttara Nikāya*[3], the first Buddha image was made by the order of King Udayana and King Prasenajit who missed the Buddha during his absence from this world for three months with a view to sermonizing Māyā, his mother in the *Trayastriṁśat*, the heaven of the Thirty-Three. After the sermon, the Buddha descended to Saṅkāśya by means of the triple-staircase and was welcomed by kings of many countries. Then King Udayana showed his Buddha image made of sandalwood to the Buddha himself. The Buddha is said to have preached the great virtue of making the Buddha image.

As far as the scene of Saṅkāśya is concerned, it is found in Bhārhut and Sāñcī sculptures in which Buddha images are not seen at all. In *Illust.* 11a-1 (second century, BC), the triple-staircase from the heaven to the earth is surrounded by noble people. *Illust.* 11a-2 (late first century AD) shows a variation in the simple staircase. Both these scenes do not present the Buddha's figure but try to only emphasise the Buddha's descent from the heaven in their depiction of the staircase.

On the other hand, the legend of the first Buddha image in India is not seen in Pāli texts, and its earliest example in sculpture from Gāndhāra[4] cannot be retroactive before the latter half of the third century AD.[5] In the sculptural scene, King Udayana holding the Buddha image in his arms is beside the Buddha himself who is in *dharmacakramudrā*. It is apparent that this scene is nothing but a creation after ages to authorize the origin of the Buddha image. However, the sculptor instead of regarding it as a creation might have believed it to be true to the Buddha's biography, because he must have been born in the period when everyone had already forgotten the following points:

1. There was a long time gap between the creation of the Buddha image in India for the first time, and the *Mahāparinirvāṇa* of the Buddha with his believers left behind.
2. The Buddha was one of the *śramaṇas*[6] in his days who took the tonsure (*muṇḍaka*)[7] without any kind of special sign[8] on his body just as seen in the Buddha image.

When the memory of (1) and (2) faded, one's way of seeing the Buddha image became devout enough to give rise to the belief that 'the Buddha image' portrays 'the Buddha' himself. It may be one of the most interesting phenomena in the history of religious arts. Such a tendency is seen at its best in Buddhist countries other than India.

For example, *Pl.* 16 is the image of *Śākyamuni* Buddha[9] brought from China to Japan in AD 986 by Chōnen (938?-1016), a Japanese Buddhist monk. Both in China and Japan, it was worshipped as the replica of the first Buddha image made under the orders of King Udayana. We can recognize the influence of Buddha images from India — the '*Gāndhāra Buddha*' — in its drapery covering both the shoulders, curved lines flowing down the standing posture, decorous looks, and the overall impression from its good proportions.[10] However, the evidence of Buddhist faith in 'the replica' is found in its internal rather than external appearance, as 'the replica' contains the models of internal organs which are formed by coloured pouches made in Japan. All of them are filled with the powder of fragrant wood, and the inter-connections of these organs have been found to be very accurate by the medical scientists of today.[11] This fact seems to show us the acme of Buddhist enthusiasm for the physical reproduction of *Śākyamuni* Buddha. Though *Śākyamuni* as the historical Buddha was not popular and influential in Japan as compared with the *Amitābha* Buddha of *Mahāyāna* Buddhism,[12] it is inferred that the legend of King Udayana must have stirred one's yearning toward India, the cradle of Buddhism, enough to make one press the palms together in prayer before 'the replica' with pure mind.

In this way, the Buddha image was welcome to the Buddhist countries and it became the centre of daily worship performed by the Buddhist people. This situation has formed an impression among the non-Buddhists that idols are worshipped in Buddhism.[13] It may be right in the sense that Buddhists treat the Buddha image just as the Buddha himself. But it must be wrong if the Buddhists' reverence for the Buddha image is regarded as essential to Buddhist faith. Indeed we cannot ignore its visual impact on Buddhist minds[14], but setting aside chronological questions, its origin was in the first century AD at the earliest. The Buddha image is a product of the historical process of Buddhist art. The Buddhist faith might have been coloured by 'the artistic product'. But if this 'colour' is removed, we would see the original form of Buddhist faith where no one ever relied on the Buddha image for the purpose of prayer. In other words, 'the Buddha image' developed out of the consciousness of those who produced early Buddhist art. They must have been really satisfied with the creation of their own fine arts; otherwise early Buddhist art would not have been able to make itself ripe in those days so that it could deserve one's appreciation.

There is no Buddha image in early Buddhist art. This visible fact should be accepted by everyone as a matter of course, and its significance should be considered independently of the origin of the Buddha image.

Scholars in the past have lacked these viewpoints as pointed out in the beginning of this Chapter. For the most part, they discuss positively as to how the Buddha image began to be made in India, and try to find the reason as to why 'the Buddha image' is not seen in early Buddhist art. The absence of the Buddha image looks so strange to their eyes that they cannot help referring to the problem. They never grasp the idea that early Buddhist art matures itself without 'the Buddha image', or rather, 'the absence of the Buddha image' is described as the negative expression of 'the presence of the Buddha image'.

The motive of our research originates in the criticism of such a theory — one that regards early Buddhist art as imperfect and immature fine arts for lack of the Buddha image. In this context the opinions of most of the scholars may be summed up as follows:

(a) There is no Buddha image in early Buddhist art, even in the biographical relief-scene where the Buddha should play a role of the central figure.

(b) Instead of the Buddha image, the motifs of the *stūpa*, the *dharmacakra*, the *āsana* under the *Bodhi*-tree, etc. symbolize the Buddha's presence.

(c) As the relief (belonging to the domain of fine arts) would seem to naturally visualize the Buddha's story (belonging to the domain of literature), there must be a reason why the Buddha was never represented in early Buddhist art.

(d) The reason is that there was probably a taboo against image-making among the Buddhists of those days. Therefore, ancient sculptors had to wrestle with the difficulty of depicting the biography of the Buddha without portraying the Buddha himself.

(e) Then, where did the taboo come from? Needless to say, from the scriptural accounts. It must be easy to find its philosophical source in Buddhist thought as found in the scriptures, because there must be a scriptural background (literature) in the tradition of religious art (fine arts).

If one feels satisfied with the logic given above, one has already lost the chance to appreciate the absence of the Buddha image in early Buddhist art.

First of all, in the historical process of Buddhist art, the Buddha image emerged on the way, came to play an important role in Buddhist faith and rituals, and evolved enough variation to form the Buddhist iconography. Accordingly, it is quite preconceptual for the scholars to observe early Buddhist art with the shadows of the Buddha image haunting before their eyes. As long as they do not try to remove those shadows and observe the absence of the Buddha image as it is, they cannot find the proper worth and significance peculiar to early Buddhist art.

The problem mentioned above seems to arise from the nature of human history where everyone cannot but accept new experiences one after another according to the current of the times. Sometimes, new experiences look more satisfactory than old experiences. But, at the same time, it is true that human beings tend to lose or forget something precious and memorable in old experiences once new experiences occupy their minds. The transition of history always leaves something behind and it is not easy to trace this back against the flow of time.

The emergence of the Buddha image was an epoch in the history of Buddhist art. But we should not lose sight of another epoch when the Buddha image had never occupied one's mind in Buddhist faith. There is a need to rediscover what is still unique in early Buddhist art.

Scholars tend to regard the fine arts as illustration of literary sources.[15] This standpoint is called 'literalism' which ignores the fact that 'fine arts' enabled sculptors to accomplish the style of early Buddhist art without the presence of the Buddha image, while 'literature' never realized a story of the Buddha without his presence. This points to an essential difference between the principles of fine arts and literature. A work of fine arts expresses itself according to the principle of fine arts. In the study of fine arts, therefore, researchers have to keep on observing the object until it naturally responds to their questions without difficulty, although it is also important to collect philological data.[16]

We should find out the principle of early Buddhist art as the basis of 'the absence of the Buddha image'. The principle must be different from any other principles of Buddhist art in later periods.

An enquiry into the absence of the Buddha image in early Buddhist art should not end in a disussion of the topics on Buddhist art. It is necessary to evolve its topical scope so that modernity may be found in all the discussions as a result. This is because a research work needs to cope with the existing current of public concerns. For this purpose, this study extracts the iconoclastic nature from the absence of the Buddha image in early Buddhist art and makes it significant in terms of a comparative study of religions, especially Zoroastrianism, Judaism, Christianity, Islām, and Sikhism.

These monotheistic religions are characteristic in their criticism of the act of idolatry. Above all, the Jewish, the Christian, and the Islamic peoples are still dominant and influential in the modern world. In this context, it is not meaningless to see a linkage between Buddhism and monotheism through the medium of early Buddhist art.

The methodology of this work is as follows:

(a) As long as we deal with the topic of fine arts, our research gives first priority to an observation of the visible facts in 'the absence of the Buddha image', from which the most reliable knowledge can be derived (Chapter II).

(b) Next, we start to interpret the object of our research, making reference to philological data in order that the visible facts may be given the spotlights from religious, artistic, and political aspects (Chapter III).

(c) After that, our research can afford to go ahead of the former methods from a philosophical point of view: 'The absence of the Buddha image' needs to become the topic of dialogues among different people of the world, and our research will not lose sight of the current of modern times (Chapter IV).

The order of (a), (b) and (c) is irreversible according to which all phases of discussion should gradually be evolved from the same object of our observation.

In the process of (a), (b) and (c), the nature of this research becomes more topical and less historical, or more philosophical and less philological.

Visual data: (1) Tables (2) Figures, (3) Illustrations and (4) Plates are the first and the last authorities in our research, because we place emphasis on knowledge and experience taken out of our own observations. The text of this book often makes reference to Tables, Figures, Illustrations and Plates in order to clarify what is being discussed.

(1) Tables are the analyses of visible objects.

(2) Figures are the drawings showing angles and viewpoints on the objects of observation.

(3) Illustrations are the monochromatic quotations from the plates of other publications.

(4) Plates are the coloured pictures to provide vivid impression of the visible objects.

Many Figures and Illustrations consist of a group of pictures in the same pages. For example, *Fig*. 8 has eight figures: a-1 ~ 4, b-1 ~ 3 and c. *Illust*. 1 is the collection of the plates: a, b and c-1 ~ 3.

Seeing is always a creative work. To show a way of seeing objects is one of the purposes of this book.

Literary sources are classified into Fine Arts, Art Philosophy, Philosophy, Scriptures, Religious Thoughts, and Religious Studies.

Now, let us return to the starting point of our research on early Buddhist art.

Try to imagine that we are standing on the hill of Sāñcī and looking at the silent sculptures of ancient India (cf. *Pls*. 2, 3 and 4).

Notes

1. In this book, 'the Buddha' mostly points to *Śākya-muni*, the sage of *Śākya*-clan.
2. 'We' refers to the author and the reader who will consider every chapter of this book in concert with the author's thinking process.
3. *Taishō* 2, 705b-706a.
4. Peshāwar Museum, No. 1534.

   cf. B. Rowland, 'A Note on the Invention of the Buddha Image', (*Harvard Journal of Asiatic Studies*, 1948, pp. 181-186, fig. 1); I. Lyons & H. Ingholt, *Gāndhāran Art in Pakistan*; New York, 1957, pp. 86-87, fig. 125
5. It is about one century earlier than the translation of the *Aṅguttara Nikāya* into Chinese.

6. The word *śramaṇa* means 'the person who practises asceticism with assiduity'. Whoever pursued an ascetic life instead of relying on the authority of Vedic scriptures was called *śramaṇa* in general.
7. Cf. *Sn*. 454, *Udv*. 11:13-14.
8. Cf. The *anuvyañjana* and the *mahāpuruṣa-lakṣaṇa* have been known in India from ancient times as the concepts of physical features peculiar to a great person.
9. It is called '*Seiryōji*-typed *Śākyamuni* image' in Japan. '*Seiryō-ji*' is the name of the temple in Kyōto built by Chōnen after his return to Japan.
10. Cf. *Illust*. 18 also seems to have these features.
11. Cf. *Journal of Japan Art History Society*, 15-16, the Japan Art History Society, 1955, pp. 112-13.
12. On the other hand, the *Śākyamuni* Buddha who appears in *Saddharmapuṇḍarīka-sūtra*, one of the most influential scriptures in *Mahāyāna* Buddhism, is the Eternal One who will sermonize the people for ever.
13. Cf. Chapter IV, 3, Note No. 92.
14. ex. In the *Amitāyur-dhyāna-sūtra* (『觀無量壽經』), the Buddha image is the object of one's meditation on the *Amitābha* Buddha for the purpose of seeing him at one's death.
15. This standpoint is called literalism.
16. This standpoint is often taken by '*the Vienna School*', one of the most eminent schools in the field of art-history, Austria. cf. Otto Pächt, *Methodisches zur kunsthistorichen Praxis. Ausgewählte Schriften,* München, 1977.

II

Visible Facts

1. The Role of 'Stūpa-Art' (Fine Arts dedicated to the Stūpa)

HOWEVER great one's deeds and personality may be, the memories of the person gradually fade away and finally vanish after one's death and with the deaths of those who remember him personally. This is universally true unless people take measures to bequeath his memories to the coming ages. In the case of the Buddha-*Śākyamuni*, his teachings were transmitted deliberately by his disciples who got together for the purpose of mutually reciting what they had heard from the Deceased One. The origin of Buddhist scriptures lies in such an effort to memorize the real words of the Buddha, although the real figure of the Buddha was not portrayed because his physical body should have been taken as a receptacle of the Enlightenment which is the real body of Buddhism as the source of his numerous acts and words.[1]

Then, where did Buddhist art originate? It may be said to have originated at the places associated with memorable events performed by the Buddha during his lifetime. According to the *Mahāparinibbāna-suttanta*, the Buddha himself referred to such places to impress pious pilgrims — consisting of monks, nuns, laymen and laywomen — with admiration: "*Tathāgata*[2] *was* born *here* (Lumbinī)", "*Tathāgata* attain*ed* the Perfect Enlightenment *here* (Bodh-Gayā)", "*Tathāgata began* to preach his sermon *here* (Migadāva)", and "*Tathāgata* enter*ed* into *parinirvāṇa*[3] without any remains of worldly attachment *here* (Kuśīnagara)."[4] These words full of emotion are told in the past tense, but they never end in mere remembrance; they rather begin to reproduce the past in the form of the events as if these were going on just in front of our own eyes. The act of such a reproduction can be successful by means of artistic creation to visualize what we are seeing through our minds. Therefore, the more the pilgrims of those days were moved by gazing at these places in rich imagination, the stronger was the motive for art-activity to depict their impressions or experiences; and eventually it might have created a style of *Buddhist art*.

Besides the four places mentioned above, there must have been many more sites connected with the missionary life of the Buddha. Some of these places must have been afterwards depicted artistically in the form of narrative scenes carved in wood and in stone.[5] This can be seen as the decorative part of a Buddhist edifice in the examples of early Buddhist art dedicated to the *stūpa*s at Bhārhut and Sāñcī.

Originally, from pre-Buddhist times in India, a *stūpa* meant 'a (relic) mount'.[6] However, it later came to have a special meaning as the container of the Buddha *śarīra*, as it was a historical evidence of *parinirvāṇa*. Besides preserving the symbolism of its components in terms of Indian mythology, it also preserves Buddhist ideas.[7] According to the *Mahāparinibbāna-suttanta*, the Buddha tells Ānanda that relic-worship should belong to laymen and laywomen who cremate the dead body of the Buddha and build *a stūpa* to preserve his bones and ashes. Thus, it is promised that *stūpa*-worshippers will improve their *karma* in this world and will be born in heaven after death.[8] But it seems to be undeniable that the act of *stūpa*-worship by Buddhists as a whole should contain a great longing for *nirvāṇa*. The reason for this is that the *stūpa* with its stable and semicircular appearance enables them to yearn for the perfect tranquillity not only of mind (*nirvāṇa*) but also of body (*parinirvāṇa*) as attained by the Buddha, beyond worldly passions as the source of human suffering, even if it is impossible for them to catch up with their Great Master in this life. Thus, it is not surprising at all that the inscriptions relating to *stūpa-art* refer to donors who wish to attain *nirvāṇa*[9] on the one hand, and hope to gain worldly prosperity on the other hand.[10] Following this logic, even monks and nuns enter their names as donors.

However, the idea of *nirvāṇa* should strike one's mind as the climax of religious experiences in the process of *stūpa*-worship. More active and familiar functions of the *stūpa* consist in providing more Buddhists and visitors from the outer world with a chance to call on the Deceased One personally or collectively with feelings of reverence, devotion and dedication, as they cannot meet him in person now. Additionally, it was popular to believe in the miraculous powers of his relics which were regarded as equal to the belief in the Buddha himself.[11] Therefore, devotional acts around the *stūpa* naturally come to be emotional and imaginative and include not only the cult of worship (*pūjā*) but also the art-activity to decorate railings and gateways with various reliefs in order to feel *as if* the Buddha were staying along with them. As it were, they enjoy pretending to be those who were alive in the Buddha's period by placing themselves in the world of fine arts.[12]

Moreover, it can be said that the *stūpa* becomes a source of prosperity in terms of the socio-economic phases of contemporary life when it is located in a point of traffic. The compatibility of secular and spiritual prosperities is essential for a ruler to reign over his land. In this context, it was quite reasonable that the Mauryan emperor Aśoka (*circa*

273-236 BC)[13] called *Dharmāśoka* (dharma-abiding Aśoka) after his conversion from '*Chandāśoka*' (ferocious Aśoka) decided to construct numerous *stūpas* all over his territory when he set about its unification, and established the *Dharma-Mahāmāttras*[14] to harmonize his people — the *Saṃgha* (Buddhist Community) and other religious communities of those days comprising *Brāhmaṇas*, *Ājīvikas*, and *Nirgranthas.*[15] The *stūpas* were closely associated with the activities of the *Saṃgha* and seem to have been surrounded by monasteries, some facilities for worship, and rest houses in order to welcome visitors coming from different cities and villages (cf. *Fig.* 1).

The only one example pointing out such circumstances is the *stūpa* remains on the hill of Sāñcī, the ancient *Saṅghārāma* situated at a distance of about nine kilometers southwest of Vidiśā, modern Besnagar in District Raisen of Madhya Pradesh, whose ancient names have been identified as Kākanāda, Chetiyagiri and Vidisāgiri in Pāli, etc. Both Vidiśā and the *Saṅghārāma* in themselves had nothing to do with the life of the Buddha, but they were the meeting points of the routes from Kauśāmbī and Śrāvastī in the north leading to Ujjayinī and Śūrpāraka in the south,[16] which should have been convenient for pilgrims to visit on the way from the main places where the Buddha had left the memory of his teachings and missionary life. Therefore, it may be said that the Sāñcī art had already contained a factor to reflect the experiences of pilgrimage when Aśoka built the original dome of bricks (*Stūpa* 1)[17] and erected a monolithic pillar with a royal decree against schism in *Saṃgha* (third century BC),[18] near the southern gateway first erected in the early period of Sātavāhana dynasty (early first century AD).

For King Aśoka, Vidiśā was not only the rich and populous city favoured with its mercantile community to fulfil any condition necessary for a Buddhist centre at Sāñcī, but also the memorable place where he fell in love with Devī (*Vidisādevī*), the daughter of a local banker, while he was on the way to Ujjayinī as a viceroy to his father King Bindusāra.[19]

Later, she became the mother of Mahendra and Saṁghamitrā who were tonsured at the advice of Moggaliputta Tissa, the teacher of King Aśoka and the leader of the Third Buddhist Council at Pāṭaliputra. The name of Moggaliputta Tissa has been discovered in the superscription of a relic-casket from *Stūpa* 2 at Sāñcī along with the names of nine other teachers.[20] Mahendra is well known as one of the missionaries dispatched to Śrī Laṅkā where the tradition of *Theravāda* Buddhism remains even to this day.

In this way, the hill of Sāñcī and its environments benefited from the beneficence of Vidiśā and the glorious power of King Aśoka. With the break-up of the Mauryan dynasty and the transference of power to the Śuṅgas, the Kāṅvas, and the Sātavāhanas, Vidiśā became the premier city in central India.[21] It seems that the rulers of these Brahmanical dynasties were generally generous and helpful to Buddhist activities.[22]

The only exception was Puṣyamitra (*circa* 184-148, BC), the founder of the Śuṅga dynasty, whose animosity towards Buddhism is said to have brought about the acts of destroying Buddhist monuments including the original brick dome of *Stūpa* 1 at Sāñcī.[23] We can see the royal generosity in the oldest example of Buddhist bas-reliefs on the eastern gateway at Bhārhut (*Fig.* 6) erected during the sovereignty of the Śuṅgas by a certain Rājā Dhanabhūti (*circa* 100-75 B.C.)[24] and in the workmanship of ivory workers from Vidiśā on the southern gateway of *Stūpa* 1 at Sāñcī under the patronage of Rāja Śrī-Sātakarṇi[25] who has been recently identified with the Sātavāhana King Śātakarṇi I (early first century AD).[26] In the background of this royal patronage to Buddhist art, there is the glorious memory of King Aśoka who stressed the concept of '*Dharma*' common to the political idea of the rulers in ancient India,[27] especially through the medium of his personal devotion to Buddhism. Its visible evidence can be found in many parts of the bas-reliefs on the four gateways of *Stūpa* 1 at Sāñcī.[28]

For those who made their pilgrimage to *Stūpa* 1, the historical situation stated above should have been almost as invisible as the breeze blowing on the hill of Sāñcī. From the moment of taking a glance at the shape of *Stūpa* 1 on the faraway hill-top, the act of pilgrimage increases in devoutness (*Pl.* 1).

When Vidiśā was a flourishing city, the main approach to *Stūpa* 1 came from the north-west (B and C of *Fig.* 1. A-C are the ancient passways),[29] and it is possible that pilgrims began to circumambulate it from the northern side (*Fig.* 2). In this case, the northern gateway naturally becomes both the entrance and the exit of *Stūpa* 1, because the two (higher and lower) paths for circumambulation (*pradakṣiṇa*) are joined by the steps on the southern side and pilgrims cannot help returning northward in order to finish going around the *Stūpa* at least three times after passing through the entrance. However, it is more probable that the southern side was originally a starting point of circumambulation from the facts that the Aśokan pillar had been still erected there and later the first gateway was placed beside it. If pilgrims had faced the southern gateway first (*Fig.* 3), they would have been able to return southward easily, or direct their steps northward naturally. Therefore, the northern gateway should have been required to be erected in the second place. In fact, it is known that the four gateways were placed in the chronological order, the southern, the northern, the eastern and western, within less than two or three decades.[30] After all the gateways were ready, pilgrims might have felt reverence for each direction of the *Stūpa* more than ever before, because they seem to have been guided from all directions by each gateway enriched with bas-reliefs.

Ascending the hill-top and getting closer to *Stūpa* 1 as the main object of pilgrimage (*Pls.* 1, 2, 3 and 4),[31] we reach its precinct and come across holy spaces around the *Stūpa* bounded by the stone railings (*vedikā*) whose basic structure (*Fig.* 5a) consists of plinth (*ālambana*), pillars (*stambhas*), cross-bars (*śūcīs*) and copings (*uṣṇīśa*). These are not confined to Buddhist edifices alone but form part of Indian architecture as a whole. In the case of Buddhist railings, they were decorated with many kinds of designs in the form of medallions and half-medallions, as well known in the Bhārhut *vedikā*[32] and on the *stambhas* around *Stūpa* 2 at Sāñcī (*Fig*. 5b). Above all, the Bhārhut *vedikā* is enriched with the panels depicting Buddhist legends as well as the medallions of lotus flowers.

A Rediscovery of 'Vedikā-Design'

On the railings of *Stūpa* 1 at Sāñcī, we cannot expect any kind of decorative art. But the design and the simplicity of the railings are quite important in enhancing the beauty of this semicircular dome (*aṇḍa*) and purifying the atmosphere of pilgrimage all around (*Fig*. 4). It seems that the artisans of those days recognized such a religious meaning of the railing so as to separate the sanctuary from the secular world. However, it never ended in abstract recognition, for they adopted this significant design of the railing (*Fig*. 5a) to separate every part (b-1,[33] b-2 and b-3 of *Fig*. 8) and scene (a-1, a-2, a-3, a-4 and c of *Fig*. 8) of the bas-reliefs on the gateways from one another (cf. *Pl*. 4), without any exception (cf. *Figs*. 4-5, 8-11, *Illusts*. 1-13). As a result, it may be said that the real railings around the *stūpa*[34] and the railing as design ('*vedikā-design*') on the gateways around the *stūpa* act in concert with each other for the purpose of protecting the same object of decoration from the outer world. In this respect, the '*vedikā-design*' carved in bas-relief is part of the quintessence of decorative art dedicated to the *stūpa*, that is to say, one of the keys to understanding the end and meaning of '*stūpa-art*'.[35] Therefore, it should be significant for us to enjoy seeing the harmonized '*vedikā-designs*' as a whole including the real *vedikā,* standing in front of the gateway (*Pl*. 4). *Fig*. 4 looks just like the '*vedikā-design*' extracted from the *stūpa*-components, which is nothing but one of the aims for drawing the Figure.

The design in itself is too simple to hold religious thoughts in its structure (*Fig*. 5-a). It might have been a popular style of the contemporary architecture in India; however, once adopted in the Buddhist sanctuary, its simplicity must have come to contain something religious for viewers who are conscious of staying inside the sanctuary's boundary, especially when they find Buddhist bas-reliefs carved on the structure, as seen in the Bhārhut *vedikā*.

Therefore, it is important to note that the '*vedikā-design*' is found in a wide range of early Buddhist art: it has been used to decorate *stūpas* at Bhārhut, Sāñcī, Mathurā, Bodh Gayā, Bhūtesar, Amarāvatī, Nāgārjuṇakoṇḍa, etc. and rock-cut caves of *caitya* and *vihāra* at Ajantā, Bedsā, Kārlā, Bhājā, etc. as if the design was essential to sanctify the space of those precincts (cf. *Pl*. 8).[36]

In the Bhārhut *vedikā*, it is found that *the 'vedikā-design'* to divide the square sections of relief-scenes on the pillars (*stambhas*) of *vedikā* results in decorating the real *vedikā-itself* (cf. *Figs*. 10-11, *Illusts*. 9, 10 and 11a-1). In *Illust*. 11a-1, we can see the back view of men whose half-lengths are concealed by the railing behind them although some of the worshippers are standing on the same railing. From this, it appears possible that the *'vedikā-design'* was also a device to suggest to viewers that some sacred event or important meaning is represented beyond the border (*vedikā*).

As it were, every scene depicted inside the frame (cf. *Fig*. 8) is underlined by the *'vedikā-design'* in order to draw one's attention to its own narration of something about the Buddha, his life-long deeds, or other elements of Buddhist faith familiar to everyone in those days. If we regard the *'vedikā-design'* as the stage of performing arts in which some role is played in front of the viewers, the meaning and significance of every scene depicted there can be derived easily from its own dramatic or theatrical aspect. Artistic expressions mean the act of creating and realizing some imagery by means of visual or audible elements so that the work of art may be accessible to everyone. For the purpose, there is always a necessity of producing some situation to embody the imagery, which brings about dramatization as an essence of art in a spontaneous manner. Therefore, any work of fine arts intrinsically produces a theatrical situation between the work and the viewer who appreciates the contents of the work, sitting or standing in front of it. The artistic value of the *'vedikā-design'* as pointed out above will be referred to again when we consider how to interpret the absence of the Buddha image in early Buddhist art (cf. Chapter III, 3).

The term *'stūpa-art'* has been coined and used here with a view to emphasising the meaning of 'fine arts dedicated to the *stūpa*'. This term seems to express the nature of early Buddhist art as known from the remains of *stūpas* in India more successfully than expressions like 'early Buddhist art'.

One of the most important elements of *stūpa-art* at Sāñcī recognizable on the gateways with the *stūpa* in the background (cf. *Fig* 4, *Pl*. 4) is the *'vedikā-design'*. On the other hand, it is important to observe various parts of the gateways more carefully in order to discover one more element which can be seen on the top lintels of all gateways as the motif depicting *'the stūpa'* itself (*Fig*. 7 and *Illusts*. 1-a, 13a1).

The Importance of 'Stūpa-Motif' in Stūpa-Art

It is worthy of notice that this *'stūpa-motif'* was adopted to decorate the front sides[37] of the top lintels so that pilgrims might ruminate upon the meaning of pilgrimage when they found their way to the *stūpa*.

Of course, as seen in *Fig*. 7, the *Bodhi Trees* of the seven *Mānuṣī Buddhas*[38] (whose orders from the *pāṭali* of *Vipaśyn*, the first of the *Mānuṣī Buddhas*, to the *aśvattha* of *Śākyamuni,* the seventh Buddha,[39] are written in numerals from 1 to 7. 8 means the *nāgapuṣpa* or *michelia champaka* of *Maitreya*)[40] behind the empty throne (cf. *Illust.* 1-c), the Wheel of the Law (*dharmacakra:*☸cf. *Illusts.* 1-b and 3) and the Nativity [: (N).[41] or, *Gaja-Lakṣmī*][42] are also important motifs not only in the bas-reliefs on gateways but also in terms of Buddhist iconography. However, in the background of '*Stūpa-art*', the following characteristics of '*stupa-motif*' need special attention.

(A) SIMPLICITY AND IMPERSONALITY OF 'STŪPA-MOTIF '

The '*stūpa-motif*' depicts the *stūpa*'s components, namely, the *aṇḍa*, the *harmikā*, the *chattra,* the *pradakṣiṇāpatha* and the *vedikā*. Its realistic depiction seems to reflect the feelings of attachment to the simplicity and impersonality of their own forms, apart from the efforts to depict the *stūpa*s of those days. On the top lintels of the four gateways (Fig. 7), '*stūpa*' alternates with '*Bodhi tree*' of the *Mānuṣī Buddhas* in order that there may be seven motifs in all. 'Seven'[43] is probably the number of the *Mānuṣī Buddhas*. But every '*stūpa*' is quite distinct from every '*Bodhi tree*' whose botanical features (cf. *Illust.* 1-c) easily remind one of the respective *Mānuṣī Buddha* who attained the Enlightenment under that tree.[44] The reason for this is that there is no device to discriminate '*stūpa*s' from one another (cf. *Illust.* 1-a) as long as we do not try to imagine the '*stūpa*s' as painted with seven different colours. According to the Aśokan inscription at *Nigālī Sāgar*,[45] the *stūpa* of *Kanakamuni* (Pāli: *Konāgamana*),[46] the fifth *Mānuṣī Buddha*, was enlarged by King Aśoka. Therefore, it is probable that every *stūpa* constructed by Buddhists in those days belonged to a specific Buddha of the past. Similarly, it is possible that every '*stūpa-motif*' was given a sort of distinct individuality as the people revered not only the *Śākyamuni* Buddha but also the six other Buddhas in the legend. However, it is not easy to find such an evidence from the discoloured appearance of the present. In any case, as far as the basic form common to '*stūpa-motif*' is concerned, it seems that its value and worth should lie in the amonymous nature which may suggest the perfect tranquillity (*parinirvāṇa*) beyond the Buddha's personality. The simple and impersonal body of '*stūpa*' transcends all kinds of other bodies in life depicted together with the '*stūpa*' (cf. *Illust.* 4-a and c). Its transcendency should have resulted in peace of mind and other religious or secular benefits for those who pressed their both hands together in prayer towards it (*Illust.* 4.)

(B) LACK OF LAMENTATION

In *stūpa-art* at Bhārhut and Sāñcī (*Figs.* 6-7), the *Śākyamuni* Buddha is treated as the last of the seven *Mānuṣī Buddhas* who had already passed away and could live only in one's memory or imagination. At first, the motive for the construction of a *stūpa* came from the recognition of his death, along with the sorrow of separation from the great Teacher. But it never ended in the ceremony of lamentation, but rather grew into an act of consolation or encouragement in the form of *stūpa*-worship. This became particularly important for those who were born after his death. Therefore, it is natural that there is no atmosphere of lamentation associated with the death of the Buddha around the '*stūpa*'. It is rather filled with joyous feelings of being there (cf. *Illust.* 1-a) and praising the deed of the Deceased One (*parinirvāṇa*, cf. *Illust.* 4-a) seen in other motifs of '*Bodhi-tree*' (enlightenment) and '*dharmacakra*' (the first sermon and sermons after that). Such a cheerful atmosphere among 'people' around the '*stūpa*' as depicted in the reliefs has been a good introduction to *stūpa*-worship as the most important act of Buddhist devotion in those days.

Accordingly, the *stūpa* of *stūpa-art* has nothing to do with the scene of *parinirvāna* in later periods where the dying Buddha is surrounded by men and animals crying beside themselves with grief. In this sense, the *stūpa-art* could transcend any element of human sorrow owing to its lack of the *Buddha image* and enabled one to be 'active' towards the '*stūpa*' in the same way as in case of matters concerning the real *stūpa* itself.

(C) ALWAYS WITH WORSHIPPERS

It is clear that the '*stūpa-motif*' plays a role of decoration as long as it is carved in some part of the building. However, it is not used merely as a decorative pattern without any exception, although '*Bodhi tree*' and '*dharmacakra*' are often depicted only for purposes of decoration without being accompanied by worshippers (*Fig.* 13-(4)b and (6)b, *Illusts.* 13b-1 and b-2) On the basis of this point, it is possible to conclude that the '*stūpa-motif*' is exceptional because of its priority over other motifs. So, what is the basis of its priority? It should be due to the matter that the *stūpa* contains the Buddha *śarīra*. Even around 'the motif' of *stūpa*, it was a matter of course that one should pay reverence to its sacred contents covered with the semicircular dome.

(D) NOTICE BOARDS OF DONATION

There are sixteen Brāhmī inscriptions carved on different parts of the four gateways around the *stūpa* 1 at Sāñci.[47] Most of them are found at inconspicuous parts. Only two examples (*Illusts.* 1-a and 4-a) are exceptional because each of them is inscribed on the '*stūpa-motif*' seen in the top and middle lintels (front faces) of the southern gateway first erected among the four (cf. *Fig.* 7). One of the inscriptions on the '*stūpa*' of the top lintel (*Illust.* 1-a) reads as "The gift of Ānaṁda, son of Vāsiṭhi (Vāsiṣṭhī), the foreman of the artisans of the Rājan Sirī Sātakaṇi (Śrī Sātakarṇi)."[48] The other inscription of the middle lintel depicting 'King Aśoka visiting the *Stūpa* of Rāmagrāma' (*Illust.* 4-a) reads as "The gift of Balamitra, a pupil of the Preacher of the Law, Aya-Cuḍa (Ārya-Cūḍa or Ārya

Kṣudra)".[49] These inscriptions are deeply carved in the bodies (*aṇḍa*) of '*stūpas*' which must have been conspicuous to pilgrims looking up at the gateway.

Probably both '*Ānaṁda*' and '*Balamitra*' were instrumental in producing the *stūpa-art* at Sāñcī as masters of art and religion in those days. '*Balamitra*' was also a donor of the right pillar of the western gateway last erected of the four.[50] It is worth considering whether 'the Preacher of the Law' (*dharma-kaṭhikā*) worked as the interpreter of bas-reliefs on the gateways and thinking of the concept of 'the Law' preached to the laymen.[51] Moreover, it is important to note that nuns and monks could participate in the task of donation for equipment around the *stūpa* such as railings, gateways and pavement slabs.[52] In any case, it is quite reasonable to suppose that '*stūpa-motif*' was selected in order to record the donations of '*Ānaṁda*' and '*Balamitra*' probably because such a selection was regarded as honourable among the Buddhists.

From the different phases of '*stūpa-motif*' as pointed out above, the '*stūpa-motif*' appears to be the core of *stūpa-art*. Towards this core, various acts of worship were performed collectively, rather than individually, just like the planets going around a fixed star. Collective performances naturally produce a festive mood (cf. *Illust*. 4-c— the scene is said to represent the *stūpa-festival* celebrated by the Mallas of Kuśinagara).[53] Originally, the *stūpa* was constructed on the premise that laymen would hold a festival around it.[54] In reliefs, every '*stūpa*' is embellished with garlands, encircled by railings or gateways, and surrounded by worshippers (cf. *Illust*. 4a-c), as if all of them were in harmony for the same purpose of holding a feast around the '*stūpa*'. Such a *stūpa* as seen in the relief reflects not only the actual circumstances of the *stūpa* itself but also the fact that the *stūpa-art* results in the formation of a link of festive acts as the fruit of artistic devotion to the *stūpa*.

In this way, several characteristics of *stūpa-art* (fine arts dedicated to the *stūpa*) can be found through general observation of the four gateways at Sāñcī. It is very important to consider them before discussing contents of relief-scenes decorating the gateways so that we may understand the role and meaning of every scene in the context of *stūpa-art*. In other words, a study of *stūpa-art* should start from a macroscopic aspect to grasp its characters and then shift to a microscopic aspect to analyze its contents, just as the foreman of the artisans should have made a plan of sculpture proper for the *stūpa-art*.

The characteristics of *stūpa*-art pointed out above (A) - (D) are mostly from the data of Sāñcī sculpture, especially of *Stūpa* 1 which is the only example of Buddhist remains showing the complete organization of fine arts surrounding a *stūpa*. Therefore, we cannot use the points (A) - (D) as a yardstick for other lost *stūpa-arts* at different places in India. For instance, the eastern gateway of Bhārhut *stūpa* (cf. *Fig*. 6) appears to have some different style and principle as compared with the gateways at Sāñcī. Nevertheless, it is certain that *Stūpa* 1 at Sāñcī and its surroundings, the railings and the four gateways, are the sole means for us to reproduce the experience of pilgrims around the *stūpa*. The only exception here is its discoloured appearance in modern times.

It is inferred that the dome of *Stūpa*1 was glaringly white, while the railings, the gateways, and the umbrellas on the summit were red.[55] The contrast of red and white colours appears bright even in our imagination. The white dome must have been embellished by colourful garlands and made all the more bright in contrast with the red surroundings. The sculpture on the gateways could have been clearer and much more realistic than it appears today. It is important to infer that the relief-scenes on the gateways produced a very clear and realistic impression, especially when the actual meaning of these scenes as a whole was considered. This is so as the coloured scenes should have emphasized the absence of the Buddha image and the presence of worshippers sitting or standing around the empty place — often expressed as the empty throne.[56] It may enable us to accept such a contrast of absence and presence as a matter of course, because colour has an equally emphatic and positive effect on all the coloured objects, as the final step to complete the work of sculpture. We have only to accept the result as it is, without having any doubts about the visible facts.[57] Moreover, it is necessary for us to imagine the red garishness of the four gateways around the white *stūpa* whenever we look at the respective relief-scenes since they are sculptured on the gateways.

2. The Basic Composition of Stūpa-Art

The basic elements of the relief-scenes in *stūpa-art* may be classified into the following four:

(a) unification of relief-frames (stage),

(b) role of Buddhist monuments (stage-setting),

(c) devotees performing on-stage (personage), and

(d) the atmosphere common to all the scenes (stage-effect), if we trace the process of composing the relief-scenes from the viewpoint of sculptors who were responsible for engraving Buddhist subjects upon railings and gateways around the *stūpa*.

When the sculptors set about engraving on the lintels (*Fig*. 8a-1), dies (*Fig*. 8a-2, a-3, a-4), pillars (*Fig*. 8c) and other parts of the gateway (*Fig*. 8b-1, b-2, b-3), they used to design the relief-frames first of all (*Figs*. 4, 8 and *Pl*. 4). — (a).

After setting the frames, the sculptors could have seen infinite possibilities of subjects to be engraved there. But in the context of *stūpa-art* and in accordance with the Buddhist faith of those days, they came up with a particular style of Buddhist art.

The composition of *stūpa-art* depended upon how Buddhist monuments should be placed in the relief-frames according to the meaning of various relief-scenes (*Figs*. 9, 10, 11) — (b).

Both (a) and (b) are the elements to produce a theatrical situation where every personage acts as a devotee (or as a devil, etc.) towards the Buddhist monuments (ex. *Fig*. 9b-2 → *Illust*. 12a-2, Fig. 9c-1 → *Illust*. 8c., *Fig*. 10 → *Illust*. 10 and *Fig*.11 → *Illust*. 9) — (c).

The performing arts on-stage, as a result of the composing process, produce the atmosphere common to all the scenes that we can grasp at the time of looking up at the gateway as a whole (cf. Pl. 4) — (d).

For understanding the *stūpa-art* and its meaning as a whole, a description from (a) to (d) is essential, because the value and the worth of any artistic work consists not only in the result after completion but also in the process — that convert 'nothing' to 'something' — imaginable as happening before us. If we omit or deny this fact, we will not be able to enjoy the visual art as it is, but will have to interpret it only in a logical way as if we are trying to read a pictograph with the help of philological clues, apart from appreciating the art itself, and finally should end in a question such as this: 'What is the reason that we cannot find any Buddha image in early Buddhist art?'

Very few concluded that it would be unhistorical to expect to see the presence of the Buddha image prior to its very advent. Then, what shall we expect in early Buddhist art? The answer will be revealed gradually in the process of our study.

The main object of our observation is derived from the reliefs describing various types of worship of the Buddhist monuments on the four gateways of *Stūpa* 1 at Sāñcī. However, we shall take some examples from the reliefs on the railing of Bhārhut *Stūpa*, etc. as there are some common points between the Sāñcī and Bhārhut sculptures.

(A) UNIFICATION OF RELIEF-FRAMES (STAGES)

Let us see *Fig*. 8. This is a sample of relief-frames taken from the main part of Sāñcī's gateways (cf. *Fig*. 4, *Pl*. 4): lintel (a-1), edge of lintel (b-2), pillar between the lintels (b-1), capital (b-3), die between the lintels (a-2, a-3), and pillar (a-4, c).[58] These frames are full of different reliefs (cf. *Illusts*. 1-8 and 11-13). While a-1, 2, 3, 4 and c contain some kind of narrative relief-scenes, b-1, 2, 3 deal with decorative motifs. We find that a-2 is supported by two octagonal pillars.[59] The walls of a-3 have a symmetrical design and a-4 is, as it were, a compromise between a-2 and a-3. We note that c uses its space to describe a multi-storeyed palace.[60] The pillars of a-2, a-4 and c show the Persian style common to that of Aśokan Pillars.

The top of every panel, except for a few examples, shows a kind of architectural design. Above all, a series of 'stepped-pyramidal' motifs appear in many cases (*Fig*. 8a-

1, a-2, *Illust*. 4b-2 and *Pl*. 7. cf. *Pl*. 8). What is the 'stepped-pyramid'? It is possible to trace its origin in the context of Indo-Iranian cultures.

First of all, the shape of 'stepped-pyramid' is the most similar to that of '*vedi*', the fire-altar of Brahmanical rituals on which offerings to a deity were placed or sacrificed. The rituals are called '*yajña*'. In *Pl*. 17, four devout servants are posing before the '*vedi*' as if they are about to offer the ashes to Agni, the deity of fire.

The shape of '*vedi*' can be found not only in a Hindu temple but also at many places of Indian daily life (*Pls*. 18, 19, 20). It is not certain whether architects and designers of modern India are aware of why they like to adopt the *vedi*-shaped motif. But *this* shape has been imprinted on the memory of the Indian people in the background of Brahmanical tradition.

Secondly, the 'stepped-pyramid' finds its relatives among the architectural motifs of Iranian culture. It is significant to find *this* shape from a fragment of a fire-holder (*Fig*. 12a) discovered at Pasargadae in the north of Pars, the capital city of Cyrus the Great (559-530 BC), founder of the Achaemenian dynasty. *Fig*. 12b is a restored image of the fire-holder designed to hold the sacred fire in whose presence Zoroastrians prayed to God, Ahura Mazdā. This holder has a three-stepped base to take a balance with a three-stepped top ("the number three is prominent throughout Zoroastrian observance").[61]

Fig. 12f can be explained as the 'crenellated' wall or the wall furnished with 'battlements' guarding the palace of Persepolis. It is interesting to see the raised portions on the wall take the shape of 'stepped-pyramids' and have their own loopholes, which seems to be a style peculiar to Persian battlements. *This* shape was also adopted as the ornamental motif to surround the Sasanian crowns (*Fig*. 12c, d, e). Is there any reason why Persian battlements have the 'stepped-pyramidal' projections? One of the most probable answers lies in a relationship between the shape of the fire-holder (*Fig*. 12a, b) and the royal sanctity (*Fig*. 12c-f) to be dignified by the sacred fire.

In *Fig*. 12g, a Soghdian sculptor has depicted a series of 'stepped-pyramids' above the scene of a sacred fire sustained by two priests (cf. *Pl*. 17). In this visible context of *Fig*. 12g, each motif of the 'stepped-pyramid' seems to originate from the shape of a fire-holder (*Fig*. 12a, b) and each hole of the pyramids looks like a hollow to hold the thick bed of hot ashes needed to sustain an ever-burning fire (*Fig*. 12a).

In any case, it is very certain that the Soghdian sculptor composed this sculpture with full religious consideration. There was no superfluous design in his mind. In the same way, we should regard the '*vedi*-shaped' motifs as meaningful to ancient Indians who composed Sāñcī sculpture. It is also significant to remember the fact that Indo-Iranian cultures can be traceable to an Āryan origin.

At the bottom of every panel, sculptors adopted the architectural design of '*vedikā*': the railing around the *stūpa* without any exception (cf. *Figs*. 5-11). At the bottom, the '*vedikā*-design' looks like the 'floor' or the 'stage' (*Fig*. 8a, c, *Figs*. 9 and 10) in contrast with the top as the 'ceiling' (cf. *Fig*. 8a) or the 'roof' (*Fig*. 8c) if we regard every panel as a sort of theatrical space.

The word '*vedikā*' has an old origin and means a kind of stage, chair, or holder.[62] As mentioned above, the '*vedi*' is the place for the flame-holder of *yajña*. Therefore, it is natural to infer that the '*vedikā*-design' was originally related to the place of Brahmanical rituals. In this respect, it is remarkable to find the fact that the '*vedi*-shaped motifs' always appear on the top of a panel as if they were in harmony with the '*vedikā*-design' (*Fig*. 8a-1, a-2, *Illust*. 4b-2, cf. *Pl*. 8).

The '*vedikā-design*' and its significance have already been discussed in the previous section, "1. The role of 'Stūpa-Art', A Rediscovery of 'Vedikā-Design' ". Here we have only to remember the sculptors' plan of decorating the *stūpa* with a unity of '*vedikā*-design' at *harmikā*, railings of *pradakṣiṇa patha* (procession path), main railings and at the bottom of every relief on *toraṇa* (Fig. 4, cf. Pl. 4).

The '*vedikā*-design' is the most important element to unify the relief-frames and spontaneously dramatize all the scenes inside their own frames. It guides the viewers to every relief-scene and makes them effectively hold on to its meaning. Moreover, it brings to the viewers a sense of psychological satisfaction which is necessary for those who have come all the way to the *stūpa* for the purpose of pilgrimage. No matter how many scenes the sculptors describe inside the relief-frames, they never fail to produce a clear-cut impression of each scene as long as the '*vedikā*-design' underlines its bottom[63] as if saying 'Look at this relief, and you will naturally remember and trace each of your experiences in the process of pilgrimage.'

(B) ROLE OF BUDDHIST MONUMENTS (STAGE-SETTING) — Motifs of early Buddhist Art—

How to put a Buddhist subject inside the relief-frame? There are various monuments like the *Bodhi-tree, dharmacakra, stūpa*, etc. that remind us of the Deeds of the Buddha in his lifetime.[64] How to recreate the Deeds of the Buddha and some Buddhist ideals through these monuments? It is here that the sculptors show their skill and expertise.

In *Fig*. 13, there are the samples of Buddhist monuments taken from the reliefs on the gateways of *Stūpa* 1 and *Stūpa* 2 at Sāñcī except for (1) A-a1, (1) A-a3, (5) a1, and (8)a2.[65]

Strictly speaking, most of the monuments (1)-(11) are not peculiar to Buddhist fine arts but common to the folklore and mythology of ancient India. So many scholars in the past have discussed their symbology in detail that we shall only focus attention on the Buddhist meaning of (1)-(11).[66]

(1) *Footprints, etc.*

(1)A; Of the main Buddhist monuments, the footprint (*pādukā, Buddha-pada*)[67] is the only one thing suggesting the physical existence of Buddha himself.

(1) A-a1 is seen in the relief on Bhārhut *vedikā* (middle of second century BC) depicting the *Deva-avatāra at Saṅkāśya*. Two footprints narrate the Buddha stepping on to the earth from the Heaven of Thirty Three gods by way of a staircase and going to take his seat under the tree (*Illust.* 11a-1).

(1) A-a2 is taken from the middle lintel of the eastern gateway at Sāñchī *Stūpa* 1 (end of first century BC) depicting *Mahābhiniṣkramaṇa* or 'Great Departure from the Castle of Kapilavastu' (*Illust.* 13a-2). The footprints under the umbrella are on the place where Prince Siddhārtha should bid farewell to his attendant, Chandaka and his horse, Kaṇthaka. Chandaka or someone playing the role of Chandaka is bending his knee before the footprints as if he has already foreseen the future of his master who would become the Buddha.

(1) A-a3 is seen in one of the fragments of the bas-relief decorating the Great *Stūpa* of Amarāvatī (middle of second century AD). Around the footprints on the throne, four female devotees are absorbed in their own worship.

(1) A-b decorates the east pillar (east face) of the northern gateway of Sāñcī *Stūpa* 1. It is placed in the lower part of the pillar as if we were allowed to touch the ten fingers. Above this motif, we can see the *triratna* on the top of the pillar [(7) b1]. (1) A-b seems to have been not only a decorative motif but also an object of worship that could be touched by pilgrims passing by the pillar every time they entered the gateway.

(1) B-a is a stage-setting of the '*Deva-avatāra* at *Saṅkāśya*' on the west pillar (front face) of northern gateway of Sāñcī *Stūpa* 1 (*Illust.* 11a-2). It enables us to imagine the Buddha going down a single (not a triple) staircase edged with two rails (cf. (1) A-a1, *Illust.* 11a-1).

The footprints are omitted here owing to the presence of two thrones under the trees.

(1) B-b is called *caṇkrama* as the path of Buddha's stroll and meditation. We can see it at several places of the scenes depicting some miracles of the Buddha, e.g. 'The Conversion of Kāśyapas', 'The Great Prodigy at Śrāvastī' (*Illust.* 8b-2), etc.[68] but there is no example where *caṇkrama* is used as an independent motif.

(2) *Umbrella*

Umbrella is *chattra,* used for protection against sunlight, etc. by a noble person in ancient times. It is used in the sense of reverence for the Buddha or his deeds, just as seen in (1) A-a2, (3), (4) a2, (5) a1, (6) a1 and (6) a2. Moreover, it has a decorative use just like (4) b and (6) b.

(3) *Stūpa*

It is made quite in the shape of the *stūpa* containing Buddha *śarīra* as the object of decoration of early Buddhist art. As it were, this *stūpa*-motif is 'the *stūpa* decorating the *stūpa*'. It is engraved elaborately and the sculptors must have enjoyed doing their work when they tried to portray the real *stūpa* built in those days.

It is remarkable that we cannot find even a single example where the *stūpa-motif* is used in place of the dying or dead Buddha, although the semicircular container of his relics can remind us of the end of his life, the *Mahāparinirvāṇa*. Each of them (*Illust.* 4) is an object of ritual worship. It produces a sort of festive atmosphere all around (cf. Illust. 4c) and describes the devotional attitudes of visitors towards the *stūpa* (cf. *Illusts.* 4a and b-2).

The *stūpa*-motif plays the most important role in the Buddhist monuments of early Buddhist art because of its portraying the *stūpa* itself.

(4) *Bodhi-Tree*

These are the *Bodhi-trees*, or the trees under which the Buddha must have preached his sermons. On these relief-motifs, we come across some expression of attachment to the trees which originated from the ritual of worshipping sacred trees. The depiction of their leaves and branches are vivid and lovable to observe. (4) a2 carved in the medallion of Bhārhut *vedikā* is specially beautiful for its elaboration. The tree motif is the only one that gives us a fresh breeze full of vitality. On the contrary, other motifs (1)-(3), (5)-(8) are rather idealistic than familiar to every viewer. We can recover our breath by turning our eyes to the tree (mostly above the empty throne) whenever we feel tired identifying the relief-scenes (*Illusts.* 1-13).

(4) a1 is encircled by the railing (cf. *Pl.* 22) which can be seen even in modern India (*Pl.* 21). (4) a1 as the *jambū*-tree suggests the 'First Meditation' of Prince Siddhārtha (*Illust.* 13a-2). However, its actual position is nothing but a memorial tree surrounded by devotees.

(4) a2 is a *Bodhi-tree* standing behind the *Buddhāsana*. This motif can be seen in all the top lintels of Sāñcī *Stūpa* 1 (*Fig.* 7). Numerals from 1 to 7 of *Fig.* 7 mean the *Bodhi-*

trees [(4) a2 of *Fig.* 13] of the seven *Mānuṣī Buddhas* (*Illust.* 1-c).[69]

Most of them appear alternately with the *stūpa-motifs* (*Illust.* 1a). This seems to suggest the importance of the Enlightenments (*Sambodhi*) and the Great Deceases (*Mahāparinirvāṇa*) of the *Mānuṣī Buddhas*. The *aśvattha* of the *Śākyamuni* Buddha (*Illust.* 1c-2) is naturally the most important among the *Bodhi-trees* (*Fig.* 7, *Illusts.* 8a-1 and c, 9, 12a-2, 13a-3).

(4) a2 reminds us primarily of the Enlightenment but it also suggests the Sermons in the lifetime of Buddha (cf. *Illusts.* 5 and 6).

(4) b is decorated by *chattras* in a symmetrical way [cf. (6)b, *Illust.* 13 b-1 and b-2.]

(5) *Empty Throne*

These are the monuments of the Buddha's sitting (*Buddhāsana*). They are always expressed in the form of the empty throne.

(5) a1 shows the flowers of *pūjā* and the umbrella is put on top [cf. (1) A-a1, *Illust.* 11b-1].

(5)a3 is placed in the rock-cave (*Illust.* 11b-2). Both (5) a1 and (5) a3 are seen in the scenes of 'Indra's Visit'.

Just as seen in (5) a2, the simplest form of *āsana* does not have many examples (cf. *Fig.* 6, *Illusts.* 5c-1 and 11b-2) but it may be said that its plain appearance is able to produce the purest religious experience of meditating or imagining the Buddha and his Sermons without being disturbed by any other kind of artificial forms, even by the images of the Buddha himself.

The significance of the empty space of *Buddhāsana* in early Buddhist art will be discussed in Chapter III, 2 and IV.

(6) *Wheel of Dharma*

These are the monuments of Buddha's Sermons (*dharmacakra-pravartana*).[70] In many cases, *dharmacakra*; Wheel of Dharma suggests the First Sermon (*dhamma-cakkappavattana*, Pāli) at *Mṛgadāva* near Benares. At the foot of (6) a2 (*Illust.* 3-b), we can see a herd of deer [(9)e of *Fig.* 13].

(6) a1 is one of the main motifs carved on the gateways of Sāñcī *Stūpas* (*Fig.* 7), as well as (3) and (4) a2. *Pl.* 13 (from Bhārhut *vedikā*) represents the Sermons at *vihāras*.

In (6) b, *dharmacakra* is placed on the pillar of Indo-Persian style with lion-shaped capital (just as the Aśokan pillar), and it shows a sort of completed style as the emblem to make propaganda for the *Buddha-dharma*. (6)b appears as the decorative motif of the pillars between two lintels, just as (4)b does (*Illust.* 13b-1 and b-2).

(3), (4) a2, and (6) a1 appear very often (cf. *Fig.* 7) as if they were the most popular in the actual scenes of Buddhist centres.[71]

(7) *Tri-Ratna*

These are the emblems of *Buddha, Dharma* and *Saṅgha* (*tri-ratna*), which are the most important motifs in early Buddhist art in the sense that they can symbolize the basic structure of the Buddhist order.[72]

Both (7) a1 and (7) a2 are seen on the *vajra-āsana* at the memorial temples of Sambodhi (*Illust.* 8a-1 and c). Each of the temple has the *aśvattha, the Bodhi-tree of Śākyamuni* Buddha in the inner space open to the sky (cf. *Illust.* 9).

The *Buddha*, the *Dharma*, and the *Saṅgha* are fully capable of being suggested by one *tri-ratna*, but three *tri-ratna*s should place emphasis on the symbolic authority of the three-fold essence of the Buddhist order. In *Illust.* 9 two *tri-ratna*s are standing symmetrically behind *the vajra-āsana*.

(7) b1 and (7) d are decorative. (7) b2[73] is practical in use, and (7) c is placed on the top of gateways (cf. *Pl.* 4 and Figs. 6-7) to have a demonstrative effect on the viewers.

(8) *Combination-motifs*

(8) a1 is the combination of *āsana, tri-ratna*, and *dharmacakra*.

(8) a2 is from one of the medallions decorating Amarāvatī *Stūpa* (second century AD). It is the combination of *Buddha-pada* on the stand [cf. (1) A-a3], *āsana*, and the column of fire surmounted by *dharmacakra*.

In (7)a1, (7)a2, (8)a1, and (8) a2, the *āsana* must be a place on which the Buddha should be seated. However, all the emblems on (or beside) the *āsana* tell not only about the Buddha himself but also about the strength of Buddhist faith to have survived after his death through the efforts of Buddhist people who could not help imagining the Buddha and his teachings in an idealistic way.

As far as *dharmacakra* is concerned, it may be possible to regard it as an expression of the Buddha as said by him in the *Samyutta Nikāya* (III. 120): "who sees dhamma sees me, who sees me sees dhamma". Nevertheless, in this context, the essence of the Buddha belongs to '*dhamma*' in itself. There would be no need to keep on seeing the Buddha in particular if one could see the '*dhamma*' as the omnipresent. In other words, the personality of Buddha *Śākyamuni* is already out of the question, and we cannot regard any emblem of early Buddhist art (*Fig.* 13) as a substitute for the Buddha image. Above all, it goes without saying that we cannot expect the (invisible) presence of the Buddha in the relief-scenes which place the *tri-ratnas* (*Illust.* 8a-1, c) on *āsana*.

(8) a2 is put in the scene depicting the Buddha's return to *Kapilavastu*, a product of the period in which the Buddha images had already appeared in the history of Buddhist art.

In *Illust.* 17, tonsured people as the disciples of the Buddha are gathered around the *Buddhāsana* (*Illust.* 17). Rāhula, the son of the Buddha, and his mother are closer to the *Buddhāsana* as if they are being called by the Master sitting on his throne. This scene is a perfect preparation — except for the absence of the Buddha image — for describing the story of the Buddha's return to his home. Therefore, (8) a2 must be considered as the emblem to suggest the presence of the Buddha whenever we expect some narrative scene in *Illust.* 17.

On the other hand, the monumental motifs of early Buddhist art are always surrounded only by laymen with their hands folded, which seems to express devotional attitude towards the Buddhist faith (cf. *Illusts.* 1-12a-1, a-2 and *Illust.* 13), rather than visualizing the stories of the Buddha who must play the leading role in any situation.

(8) a2 is devoid of the Buddha image on purpose but (4) a2, (5), (6) a1, (8) a1, (7) a1, and (7) a2 do not need the Buddha in human form because they are perfect as the Buddhist monuments used in every relief-scene. If the Buddha image had appeared there, all the scenes would have lost their beautiful order that maintains a sense of holy tensity between devotees and the objects of their worship.

(9) *Animals*

(9) a (elephant), b (bull), c (horse), and d (lion) are four holy animals related to the life of Buddha *Śākyamuni*.

(9) a is seen in the square panels of dies between the lintels [See (N) of *Fig.* 7].[74] There can be seen a goddess (*Gaja-Lakṣmī* or *Māyā*)[75] seated on a lotus sprouting out of a vase and being given a shower-bath by the two elephants. It is said that *Māyā* saw a dream of the white elephant (as the Bodhisattva who was descending from *Tuṣita* Heaven) entering her womb at the time of conception, and the elephant suggests the birth of the Buddha to be. On the gateways of Sāñcī *Stūpa*, the motifs of elephant are seen in: (1) Jātaka scenes, (2) scenes related to the life of Buddha, (3) capitals under the bottom lintel, and (4) dies between the lintels (cf. the bottom lintel of Bhārhut gateway, *Fig.* 6).

9 (b) is from the false-capitals of the top lintel of eastern gateway (front). The common name of Prince Siddhārtha was *Gotama* (supreme bull), and the word '*Gotama*' is often used in admiration of the Buddha.[76] But, in the decoration of gateways, the bull

is merely one of the animals on which noble men are seated. There is no example of the bull being worshipped by anybody. Even if the Buddha was called Gotama, the bull did not substitute Gotama or the Buddha himself.

(9) c can be seen in the *Mahābhiniṣkramaṇa* or 'Great Departure from the Castle of Kapilavastu' (*Illust.* 13a-2). This horse is well-known by the name of Kanthaka, which suggests Prince Siddhārtha's renunciation of the world.

(9) d; Lion is the king of animals. The Buddha *Śākyamuni*[77] is the supreme among men and gods (*devamanussaseṭṭha*).[78] Therefore, his facial features are termed '*siṃha-ketu*' and the atmosphere of his preaching is expressed as '*siṃha-nādin*'.[79] His seat is the '*siṃha-āsana*'.[80] The lion-shaped capital of Aśokan pillar is the oldest example of Indian art. On the gateways of Sāñcī *Stūpa*, the lion motifs are often seen as three-winged lions carved in the false capitals or as the lion-shaped capitals carved on the pillars between the two lintels (*Illust.* 13b-1 and b-2, cf. the middle lintel and the capitals of Bhārhut gateway, *Fig.* 6).

The lion motifs as well as the bull motifs do not suggest the Buddha himself. However, we can think of (9)a, (9)b, (9)c and (9)d as the motifs which were selected to decorate the capitals of Aśokan pillars as the effective means of propagating the *Dharma*, the ideal of Aśokan politics.

(9) e is from *Illust.* 3b. The deer can be found in Jātaka scenes and the scenes of *Mṛgadāva*, the place of the First Sermon (*Illust.* 1b). In the false capitals of southern and western gateways [81] at Sāñcī, deer is the vehicle of men.

(10) *Peacock*

It is a peacock (*mayūr, mora*), generally considered as the emblem of Mauryan dynasty. Two peacocks are shown in profile at the edges (front) of the bottom lintels of southern and eastern gateways (*Pl.* 4). The origin of Sāñcī *Stūpa*s dates back to the reign of King Aśoka and it is probable that the sculptors consciously selected the bird-emblem of the Mauryan dynasty as one of the decorative motifs.

(11) *Lotus Flowers*

Lotus flowers are blessed with their own pure nature (they beautifully come out of the bog) and their well-balanced shape is suitable for designing. Indians appear to have been deeply attached to this flower from ancient times. It would be no exaggeration to say that in early Buddhist art the lotus flower is the most excellent subject for pursuing the decorative patterns. Above all the Bhārhut *vedikā* is a treasury of lotus patterns showing a variety in decoration. Moreover, it is possible to say that the lotus-motif is the origin of the lotus-seat on which numerous images of the Buddhas and the Bodhisattvas have been shown seated in later periods.

Strictly speaking, (9), (10), and (11) are not Buddhist monuments but we cannot overlook any of them because of their animated role in the world of stony sculpture.[82]

Mostly a combination of more than two or three Buddhist monuments can be seen [cf. (1)-(8) of Fig. 13]. The nature of the monumentality of fine arts comes out most clearly when the Buddhist monuments are combined with the architectural plan just as seen in Fig. 9 (*Illust.* 8 a-1, b-1, c, *Illust.* 12a-2, *Illust.* 13a-3), *Fig.* 10 (*Illust.* 10), and *Fig.* 11 (*Illust.* 9). All of these relief-scenes invariably preserve some Buddhist significance based on the memories of the Buddha and his teachings, no matter whether the sculptors intended to describe a narrative scene or not.

For example, sculptors show us the variation of *Bodhi-maṇḍa* in memory of the *Sambodhi*, the Buddha's Enlightenment (*Fig.* 9b-1, b-2, c-1, c-2 and *Fig.* 11). There is no difference between *Fig.* 9b-1, b-2 and *Fig.* 11 as long as each of them reminds us of the same event in the lifetime of Buddha *Śākyamuni*. But once sculptors add some descriptive element to their work, the *Bodhi-maṇḍa* becomes a place where the Buddha should stay at the time of his Enlightenment (*Illust.* 12a-2). This is also the place where King Aśoka(?) pays reverence to the Deceased Buddha who attained his Enlightenment under the *aśvattha* tree (*Illust.* 13a-3) and where gods, angels and devotees show their admiration towards one of the Great Miracles in the life of the Buddha (*Illust.* 9).

In a word, the *Bodhi-maṇḍa* stands beyond the flow of time, being 'surrounded' by some kind of narrative scene to remind us of the significance of *Sambodhi*.

The facts stated above tell us that Buddhist monuments are too silent and impersonal to signify their own implication (cf. *Figs.* 9-11). Therefore, personages on the stage of relief-scenes are obliged to suggest the meaning and spirituality of Buddhist monuments by their own acts and attitudes towards them. It may be compared to the work of the pantomimist who aims at acting out something for the purpose of showing a situation to the spectators.

(C) DEVOTEES PERFORMING ON STAGE (PERSONAGE)

The first thing to observe about the personages on stage is that a majority of them have folded their hands (*aṅgulīhi*) towards the Buddhist monuments in sitting or standing postures (cf. *Illusts.* 1-11, 13). That is to say, their characters are unified by the attitude of the devotees rather than by the performance of actors or actresses playing specific roles in their own costumes. The devotees are acting collectively and cooperatively rather than in a personal and characteristic way. They are all laymen and we cannot find any tonsured people as the disciples of Buddha, or the Buddhist monks and nuns. It suggests that sculptors did not intend to reproduce a life story of the Buddha who used to itinerate with some of his disciples.[83] Devotees are mostly dressed in noble costumes,[84] all their simplicity covering their naked bodies.

Those who have human forms include gods as the Buddhist guardians (cf. *Illust.* 1-b), winged angels as the offerers holding garlands (cf. *Illust.* 9) and the family of *nāga-rājas* as the protectors of the *stūpa* (*Illust.* 4a). It may be said that a human being is a part of the creatures[85] and human form is treated as the medium of expressing both visible and invisible things of this world.

Generally, it is not easy to identify the exact meaning of every relief-scene because of its stereotyped situation crowded with devotees. For instance, *Illust.* 6a, b-1 and b-2 are quite similar to one another except for the difference in the trees standing there. Or, a group of the scenes containing *dharmacakra*s (*Illust.* 1b and *Illust.* 3) seems to show a variation based on the size of panels. In *Illusts.* 1b and 3b some scholars have identified the four noble men standing around the *dharmacakra* as the *dharmapāla*s (guardian gods of '*dharma*'), Brahmā, Indra, etc. admiring the First Sermon at Mṛgadāva. And the *dharmacakra* on the throne has been taken as the preaching Buddha. However, it is quite strange that sculptors have omitted the figures of the five monks who got a chance of listening to the First Sermon (cf. *Pl.* 13), if *Illusts.* 1b and 3b are put in the Buddha's period. A *dharmacakra* surmounted on the top of a pillar does not remind us of any image of the Buddha as a human being (*Illust.* 3b). Only the devotional postures and expressions of the deer and personages convey the greatness of the Buddha. But, it seems that even the great Buddha imagined by the viewer in his mind does not bring out a clear image of the Buddha himself in human form, or rather, the quintessence of his spirituality; the embodiment of *Buddha-Dharma* seems to be seen through the form of *dharmacakra*.

Devotees on stage are basically in stationary postures with a monumental atmosphere. On the other hand, some of them can be seen expressing their joyous feelings in a dynamical way — by flying in the sky, whistling with fingers, dancing (*Illust.* 9) and playing some instruments (*Illusts.* 4c and 5a). It seems that devotional feelings on stage can be classified into two kinds of emotion: *bhakti*[86] and *ānanda*.[87]

Now the question arises about the method of sculpture of human forms in early Buddhist art. Some influence of foreign cultures can be seen in the lion-motifs, decorative patterns of the lotus, etc. and only the modeling of human beings seems to follow the Indian style. It forms a pronounced contrast to the Greco-Roman modelings of copying the joints and muscles of the human body with anatomical accuracy.

Indian sculptors seem to have excelled in expressing abstract matters that are invisible to human eyes, for instance, as expressing the feelings of *bhakti* and *ānanda* through the medium of human forms rather than pursuing the beauty of nature as seen in human bodies. This reminds us of the philosophical background of India in which the Supreme Soul has a large number of incarnations (*avatāra*) with various names and forms (*nāma-rūpa*) of gods appearing before the human eyes.

Western scholars have been so much accustomed to observing Greco-Roman fine arts that they can see nothing but the naivety of modeling human bodies in ancient times: "In the time of Aśoka indigenous art was still in the rudimentary state, when the sculptor could not grasp more than one aspect of his subject at a time, when the law of 'frontality' was still blinding upon him, and when the 'memory picture' had not yet given place to direct observation of nature."[88]

However, both 'frontality' and 'memory picture' prove to be necessary to the monumentality of early Buddhist art (*stūpa-art*) whose most important role is to attract public attention as positively as possible. Even if sculptors were still blind to a style of carving, we should appreciate the blindness that was requisite for accomplishing the unique style of early Buddhist art.

It is very important to recognize the fact that an artistic work is always saturated with its own style in order to preserve its identity as distinct from any other styles.

Futhermore, we can evaluate the collective feelings of the devotees on stage who reflect the viewers of those days. The sculptors were not the artists who pursued 'beauty' itself, but they were the representatives of the masses who created what they experienced.[89] That is to say, they did not choose to imitate the outer world but described it through their own experiences. This represents the essence of Indian art through the ages as distinct from the Greco-Roman realism.

The description of experiences is influential in grasping the relief-scene as a whole. Viewers may not listen to the words of different personages but can grasp a religious atmosphere common to all even at a glance.

(D) THE ATMOSPHERE COMMON TO ALL THE SCENES (STAGE-EFFECT)

The atmosphere common to all the scenes consists of the feelings of *bhakti* and *ānanda*. This is true for everybody if the scenes are surveyed even once, as all the relief-scenes play the role of *stūpa-art* in one body. They do not visualize the stories of Buddha's life but dramatize the devotional feelings that were familiar to the Buddhist people of those times.

In passing, it may be mentioned that we cannot find any kind of tragic scene. Even the *stūpa-motif* which can suggest the death of the Buddha is one of the means to produce a festive mood among the devotees (cf. *Illust.* 1-a and *Illust.* 4).

It may be said that most of the relief-scenes depict the people who have their palms pressed together (*Illusts*. 1. 5-7, 10-11), or who are offering (*Illust*. 2), dancing or playing various instruments (*Illusts*. 4-c and 9). Such scenes can be witnessed in the Buddhist remains at Bodh Gayā, Sārnāth, Kuśinagara, etc. even in modern times.

Devotees in sitting (*Illust*. 5a, b-2, c-2 and *Illust*. 11b-1) and standing postures (*Illusts*. 6, 7, 8b-2, 11a-1 and a-2) around Buddhist monuments give us a similar impression irrelevant of the narrative situations. These scenes look like souvenir pictures taken of the groups of pilgrims in worshipping postures. It is almost impossible to identify each of them as a narrative scene. Even where an interpreter explains a story, the story is too unreasonable to aid in enjoying the scene itself.

However, if we put ourselves into the scene where the Buddha has already passed away, it must be natural for us to meditate on the Buddha and his lifetime. Here we can see a remarkable contrast between collective worshippers and the empty throne under the tree (*Illust*. 5), the crowd versus the emptiness, and the human forms versus the non-human forms. These contrasts place much emphasis on the absence of the Buddha. They are successful in directly expressing the practice of Buddhist meditation by those who lived in a period which did not have any custom of making and worshipping the Buddha images.

It is possible to say that the personages on stage produce a beautiful order through the scenes by facing the absence of the Buddha (cf. *Illusts*. 6, 7, 12a-2, 13a-3).

When the viewer turns his attention to the plain simplicity of the empty throne, he is sure to heave a sigh of relief despite the stuffy surroundings. If the Buddha were seated there, the Buddha's presence would not have helped in dividing the crowd into the right and left in order to show the viewer his whole body because any noble personage is not allowed to block the view of the Great Master with his figure (*Illust*. 12b).

In early Buddhist art, the absence of the Buddha becomes the most remarkable factor breathing life into all the relief-scenes. This is quite a paradox peculiar to plastic art. On the contrary, if Buddhist literature were without the appearance of the Buddha, they would lose their *raison d'être*.

In this way, (a) unification of relief-frames (stage), (b) roles of Buddhist monuments (stage-setting), (c) devotees performing on stage (personage), and (d) the atmosphere common to all the scenes (stage-effect) form a dramaturgy of the 'non-Buddha image' period. We cannot appreciate early Buddhist art until we discover this.

(E) SUPPLEMENT

Finally, it is necessary for us to point out several other visible facts which cannot be overlooked while interpreting the absence of the Buddha image in early Buddhist art.

(1) Jātaka scenes, one of the most important elements of early Buddhist art, depict the figures of Bodhisattva which can be regarded as the living beings (human beings, deer, monkey, elephant, etc.)[90] before becoming the Buddha who must have accumulated countless good deeds during his previous lives. Therefore, the appearance of such Boddhisattvas is comparable with the absence of the Buddha in the same stage of early Buddhist sculptures.

(2) Just as seen in the scene of the *Mahābhiniṣkramaṇa* or 'Great Departure from Kapilavastu' (*Illust.* 13a-2), not only the figure of Buddha *Śākyamuni* but also that of Prince Siddhārtha does not appear anywhere. It is also important to enquire into the absence of Prince Siddhārtha who can be called *Bodhisattva* seeking the true wisdom (*bodhi*) to save the living beings of this world.

(3) As mentioned before, there is no figure of Buddhist nuns and monks in the scenes where they must attend on the Buddha on his wanderings during his lifetime. On the other hand, we can find the figure of non-Buddhists such as a hermit living in a hermitage and Brāhmaṇas serving the sacred fire.[91]

This fact makes us wonder whether there is some special reason for the absence of those who had tonsured themselves to become Buddhist nuns and monks.

(4) In Bhārhut inscriptions, there can be found several explanations of what is depicted in the relief-scenes: "*A(jā)tasat(u) Bhagavato vaṃdate*"[92] (King Ajātaśatru pays reverence to the Blessed One), "*Erapato nāgarāja Bhagavato vadate*"[93] (Erapata, King of *Nāgas* pays reverence to the Blessed One), etc. We can see King Ajātaśatru or King Erapata with hands folded towards the empty throne. Scholars have been seeing the invisible Buddha there on the basis of references to the Buddha in the inscriptions. It is not futile to think about how to accept the whole meaning of the inscriptions when we interpret the absence of the Buddha image in early Buddhist art.

Before shifting to the last section of this chapter, it is important to classify and enumerate the contents of *Illusts.* 1 to 14 and 17 according to the identification done by Sir John Marshall, Alfred Foucher and other eminent scholars. It is not for defining what is described there but for reference at the time of directing spotlights upon the Plates from various aspects of interpretation. The classifications from Group 1 to Group 5 are based on the increasing decorative and monumental aspect of the scenes rather than their narrative and descriptive aspect.

Group 1 (Without devotees)

Decorative motifs of *Chattras*, *Bodhi-trees, Dharmacakras*, and octagonal pillars (*Illust.* 13b-1 and b-2).

Group 2 (With devotees)

a. Worshipping the *Bodhi-trees* (*Illust.* 7c)
b. Worshipping the *Dharmacakras* (*Illust.* 3a-1, a-2 and *Illust.* 7b)
c. Worshipping the *Stūpas* (*Illust.* 4b-1, b-2, c and *Illust.* 7 a)
d. Offering to the *Bodhi-trees* (*Illust.* 2a-1, a-2, b-1, b-2, b-3)
e. Bodhi-trees of seven *Mānuṣī Buddhas* (*Illust.* 1c-1, c-2, c-3)
f. *Stūpas* and *Bodhi-trees* of *Mānuṣī Buddhas* (*Illust.* 1a and *Illust.* 13a-1)

Group 3

a. Devotees and *Triratna* inside the *Bodhi-maṇḍa* (*Illust.* 8a-1, a-2, c)
b. Devotees at the *Bodhi-maṇḍa* (*Illust.* 9)

Group 4 (Narrative)

a. Worshipping the headdress (*cūḍā*) (*Illust.* 8a-3)
b. The *Mahābhiniṣkramaṇa* or 'Great Departure from Kapilavastu' (*Illust.* 5b-1, *Illust.* 13a-2 and *Illust.* 14b)
c. The temptation of *Māras* (*Illust.* 12a-1)
d. The *Sambodhi* or the Perfect Enlightenment after the struggle with the temptation of *Māras* (*Illust.* 5c-1, *Illust.* 12a-2, b)
e. The *Adhyeṣaṇa*, or the night's struggle before the Enlightenment (*Illust.* 6b-1)
f. Indra's Visit (*Illust.* 6b-2, *Illust.* 11b-1, b-2 and *Illust.* 14a)
g. The First Sermon at Mṛgadāva (*Illust.* 1b and *Illust.* 3b)[94]
h. Gift of the Jetavana (*Illust.* 8b-1)
i. The Monkey's Offering at Vaiśālī (*Illust.* 2c)
j. The Great Prodigy at Śrāvastī (*Illust.* 5a and *Illust.* 8b-2)
k. *Śākya* clan worshipping the Buddha, or the Buddha's return to his home (*Illust.* 5b-2, c-2, *Illust.* 6a and *Illust.* 17)
l. The *Deva-avatāra* at Saṅkāśya (*Illust.* 11a-1, a-2)
m. King Prasenajit visiting the Buddha (*Illust.* 10a-1)
n. King Viḍūḍabha visiting the Buddha? (*Illust.* 10a-2)

Group 5 (Aśokavadāna)

a. King Aśoka visiting the Rāmagrāma *stūpa* (*Illust.* 4a)
b. King Aśoka visiting the *Bodhi-tree* (*Illust.* 13a-3)

It goes without saying that these classifications are provisional and are meant to simply aid in the research work of enquiring into the absence of the Buddha image in early Buddhist art.

As mentioned before (cf. 1. The Role of *Stūpa-Art*), all the relief-scenes sculptured on the gateways and the railings were painted in one colour and not coloured differently according to the subjects described. It is not very clear whether ancient Buddhists needed to classify them just as we do at the time of viewing and appreciating them during the pilgrimage to the *stūpa*. Rather, they must have been accepted as a whole as a means to enhance one's religious experiences. Therefore, we should be careful not to be chained by our own convenient viewpoints at any time and see things as naturally as possible. For this purpose, we need to have a chance to be free from relying on technical knowledge necessary only for scholars.

The following section is also constructed on the basis of a conception such as stated here.

3. A Consideration of the Visible Facts

There are three basic points (A) ~ (C) for considering the visible facts of early Buddhist art in which the Buddha image cannot be seen at all.

(A) ITS ACCOMPLISHED SPATIALITY

The absence of the Buddha image in early Buddhist art does not mean any incompletion for lack of the Buddha image but rather shows the most essential element to complete the artistic style of those days. As long as we regard its lack of the Buddha image in a negative light, we cannot find anything meaningful in this ancient fine arts. However, once we accept the 'absence' as a matter of course, we can discover some artistic and religious values in different aspects which cannot be expected in the Buddhist art of later periods.

As pointed out while discussing (a) unification of relief-frames, (b) role of Buddist monuments, (c) devotees performing on-stage, and (d) the atmosphere common to all the scenes, those relief-scenes accomplish their own spatiality every time the personages on stage towards the Buddhist monuments succeed in reminding us of the Buddha and his Deeds. Here is only one visible order common to the spatial expression of all the relief-scenes. The order's simplicity satisfies the eyes of the viewer who has only to grasp a single essence from different scenes: the art of veneration towards the Deceased Buddha who is not here any more. This gives a sort of pleasure to those who appreciate early Buddhist art in the context of *stūpa-art* that originates from the Buddha's bodily absence.

(B) ITS FLEXIBLE TEMPORALITY

How to accept and appreciate the works of early Buddhist art? It depends on how the absence of the Buddha image is viewed.

The meaning of 'absence' can be understood in two ways.

(1) *The invisible presence of the Buddha image*

In this case, there is a preconception that the figure of the Buddha is not visualized in human form for some reason but suggested through something substitutive just like the empty throne under the tree. The invisible Buddha must be present in the relief-scenes narrating his Deed. Therefore, the scene must place itself in the Buddha's period, the ancient place where we cannot literally go back anyhow. It belongs to the past; we are the viewers in the present time. Of course, it is possible for us to look at the relief-scene as if it is occurring before our eyes, but still there remains a boundary between us — the viewers and the invisible Buddha placed in his own time.

(2) *The actual absence of the Buddha image*

The significance of 'absence' never ends in the manner stated above. Rather, it must be more creative and meaningful to regard 'the absence' as it is if we want to be faithful to our own eyes.

If the Buddha is really absent from the relief-scene referring to his Deed, how can his absence be appreciated? Can we expect to see him come back to the empty throne from elsewhere? Or has he already disappeared leaving his people behind?

Instead of answering these questions, we had better make a complete change in our point of view. It means that we should regard 'the absence' as a monumental space where the Buddha had ever stayed during his time. The monumental space is usually suggested by various Buddhist monuments. It must have been familiar to ancient Buddhists who had meditated on the Buddha and his Deeds without feeling any need for worshipping any Buddha image as the work of art. In their own minds, there must have been quite a rich oral-tradition about the life of the Buddha. Such a tradition would have tried to find some chance to describe itself.

As classified in the former section (Groups 1 to 5), we have already seen many narrative scenes (Groups 4 and 5) whose more archetypal work (Groups 2 and 3) can be found at other places. Where the ancient Buddhists are concerned, Groups 2 and 3 could have been most familiar to them. But, at the same time, they must have seen Groups 4 and 5 in the same way as they saw Groups 2 and 3, as they did not need to classify them into Groups but had only to appreciate all of them as a whole. Therefore, it may safely be said that all the relief-scenes are essentially filled with some imaginative vision of ancient Buddhists. In some of these scenes (*Illust.* 5c-1, *Illust.* 12a-1. a-2), there is an attempt to make them more narrative to describe what has been lost by the imagination. To modern people, however, it may look as if the ancient sculptors had difficulty in narrating 'the Buddha's' story without 'the Buddha image'. It is only a misunderstanding of those who do not understand how the ancient Buddhists could have enjoyed the relief-scenes relying on their own imaginative vision lingering around the absence of the Buddha.

Basically, the absence of the Buddha suggested by some monuments places itself in the 'present' of the viewers. But, at the same time, the absence contains the memory of the Buddha and his Deeds which are not imaginary but historical.

The Buddha *Śākyamuni* had already passed away in the time of early Buddhist art but there was an effort to call back something memorable and monumental from his life. As a result, ancient Buddhists managed to produce an artistic style of 'memory picture'[95] by way of leaving the absence of the Buddha where they had been accustomed to seeing it for quite a long time after his Death.

At this stage, the present time (of the viewer's world) and the past time (of the picture's world) co-exist in the same space of 'memory picture' and the two are inseparable from each other. In other words, there is no spiritual boundary between the viewers and the memory picture, the spectators and 'the personages on stage', where one finds a space of self-dramatization in one's own mind united with what one sees there. As far as this union is concerned, it is quite common as one of the most essential elements of ancient dramaturgy in not only Indian but also Greek and Roman worlds. The actors on stage, as the *dramatis personae*, reflected the spectators.

In this way, the absence of the Buddha produces a sort of flexible temporality according to one's way of seeing its vacancy. It transcends the flow of time which may have been forgotten by those who have become accustomed to living a life in accordance with the tempo of time on the clock. At least, it seems quite certain that ancient people could experience 'time' without subjecting it to the graduations on the clock's face.[96]

The points stated above should not be overlooked when observing ancient fine arts.

Once the Buddha image was created in the process of art history, nobody could obliterate it or stop its evolution. Rather, it must be natural that time erased the pre-history of the Buddha image from the minds of the Buddhist people. It is quite impossible to get back to the previous situation where everybody was satisfied without the Buddha image. The process of history is irreversible. Sometimes the older period of history is apt to be regarded as inferior to later historical developments. But we cannot deny the fact that it is fully possible to rediscover something worthy from ancient periods. It is indeed a re-search work.

(C) ITS ESSENTIAL MONUMENTALITY

We have already surveyed the characters of Buddhist monuments (*Fig.* 13). The most remarkable point is that they can suggest us some Buddhist meanings or the places where the Buddha is (was) seated, standing, and walking.[97] But they cannot substitute for the Buddha himself as the perfect and independent object of worship containing his own personality. We can only remember the Buddha's Deeds[98] by gazing at the monuments which are not equal to the Buddha. One may say, 'The motif (8)a2 of *Fig.* 13 can personalize the Buddha himself'. Yes, that is right, because it is a sole example in *Fig.* 13 that was created in the second century AD after the birth of the Buddha image (cf. *Illust.* 17).

In any case, it is almost impossible to expect some personal response from the Buddhist monuments even if one prays to them. They can just receive Buddhist reverence towards the Great Teacher and his Deeds, but never start talking themselves as long as the viewers do not positively imagine some situation around them. The passive character of Buddhist monuments is essentially different from the personalized character of the Buddha image which is always set up for the purpose of showing the way to salvation to worshippers.

To understand this nature of Buddhist monuments, it is necessary to come out of the world of Buddhist art and study a comparable aspect of this and another kind of religious art. Now, we will survey the main motifs of early Christian art in which people tried symbolizing Jesus Christ and his words, etc. in many ways without creating the Christ image.[99]

(D) A REFERENCE TO THE MOTIFS OF EARLY CHRISTIAN ART

The beginning of Christian art was in the period of Severus (Severus, Lucius Septiminus, AD 146-211) who reigned over the Roman Empire from AD193 to 211. His reign was specially tolerant of the religious activities of the Jewish people in the Empire. It was almost two hundred years after the crucifixion of Christ.

In those days, the Jewish people adopted fine arts for religious purpose earlier than the Christians.[100] They depicted the prophets of Israel on the inner wall of the synagogue (*Illust.* 20a-1, a-2). In the meantime, Christians had also begun to draw some Christian motifs around the baptistry, etc. Its only and oldest example (beginning of the third century AD) was discovered in *Dura-Europos* (its present name is Es-Salihiyeh) on the right bank of the Euphrates. Afterwards, the main centres of early Christian art came up in the *Catacombae* (Latin word, plural of *Catacomba* — 'sunken place'): the underground tombs of Christians who were persecuted by the paganish Emperors for hundred years until Constantinus I (Constantinus, Gaius Flavius Valerius, around AD 274-337, ruled from AD 324-337) authorized Christianity in AD 313.

Fig. 14 consists of the main motīfs of the Catacomb-paintings found along the highways of Roman suburbs. Let us see each of them.

1. *The signs regarded as equal to Jesus Christ*

(1) a1. Alpha and Omega.

It has a worth equal to Jesus according to his own words in The *New Testament*.

"I am the Alpha and the Omega, the First and the Last, the Beginning and End." (*Revelation* 22.13). Cf. *Revelation*. 1.8, 21.6, *Isaiah*. 41.4, 44.6, etc.

(1) b1. XP

This is the monogram of XP, the first two letters '*XPI*ΣΤΟΣ' (Christos) in Greek. The combination of these two letters readily gives the form of a cross.

(1) b2 is another form of (1) b1.

(1) c1 & (1) c2; IHS & IHC.

These letters are the first three letters of *Ihsus*, or *Ihcuc*, the name of Jesus in Greek. S and C are variant forms in the Greek alphabet.

(1) d. I.N.R.I.

This represents the four initial letters of the Latin words, '*Iesus Nazarenus Rex Iudaeorum*", meaning 'Jesus of Nazareth, King of the Jews'. After Christ had been crucified, Pilate wrote this title and put it on the cross. Cf. *John* 19.19.

(1) e IC XC NIKA

It was the ancient monogram symbolizing Christ the Conqueror. I and C are the first and last letters of the Greek word *Ihcuc* (Jesus); X and C are the first and last letters of *Xprictoc* (Christ); *Nika* is the Greek word for conqueror.

2. *Fish, the creature whose name is related to Jesus Christ*

The five initial letters of 'Jesus Christ, God's Son Saviour' form 'IXθUS' in Greek meaning 'fish'. As fish lives in water, it symbolizes baptism, too. Moreover, baptism in the early Church was performed by sinking one's whole body in water.

3. *Cross, the most direct symbol to signify Jesus Christ*

It reminds us of Christ's figure crucified. Its significance is in the Redemption and the Salvation by the name of Jesus Christ. The cross cannot be found before the fourth century AD. In passing, the first crucifix (in bas-relief) was made in the fifth century AD[101] and the earliest image of crucifix in the Church was made from the late tenth century AD.[102]

4. *Jesus Christ expressed in the form of metaphors in the New Testament*

(4) a1. Bread.

"I am the bread of life". [*John* 6. 35. Cf. (6)]

(4) a2. Grape.

"I am the true vine and my father is the gardener" (*John* 15.1). The motif of grape was liked as a decorative pattern, too.

(4) a3. Lamb

" . . . . . John saw Jesus coming toward him and said, "Look, the Lamb of God, who takes away the sin of the world!" (*John* 1. 29). Cf. *Revelation*. 14.1.

(4) a4 The Good Shepherd.

" . . . . And if he finds it, I tell you the truth, he is happier about that one sheep than about the ninety-nine that did not wander off." (*Matthew* 18.13).

The stray lamb found by the shepherd signifies the sinner who has been penitent. Cf. *Luke* 15.1-7.

5. *Orpheus and animals*

It means that Christians (animals) are listening to the words of Christ (the sounds of harp played by Orpheus). Or Orpheus can signify King David (cf. *The Book of Samuel* in *the Old Testament*).[103] Here is a sort of equality: 'Orpheus = David = Jesus Christ' (cf. *Matthew* 1.1-17). The illustration of (5) is seen in the Catacombs of Domitilla (third century AD).

6. *The animals signifying Jesus Christ*

(6) a. Bull

The bull sacrificed for the temple of Jerusalem signifies Jesus Christ who died in the Redemption.

(6) b. Pelican

It was said that the pelican raises her chickens by giving them her own blood, and it seems to have reminded Christians of Christ who sacrificed himself for the sinners, spilling blood on the cross.

7. *The symbols of Christian Faith*

According to a tradition that the flesh of peacock does not corrupt, the peacock became the symbol of immortality around the fourth century AD.

(7) b. Anchor

" . . . We have this hope as an anchor for the soul, firm and secure. It enters the inner sanctuary behind the curtain, where Jesus, who went before us, had entered on our behalf." (*Hebrews* 6. 19-20).

(7) c. Olive

It signifies the peace after death and the eternal life after resurrection. The motif of olive was often used for decorating epigraphs in the Roman Catacombs. Cf. *Genesis* 8. 11.

8. *Paradigma: the precedent examples of one's release from death by the grace of God*[104]

(8) a1. The sacrifice of Issac.

God prevents Abraham the righteous from sacrificing his only son Isaac by His own order. God gave Abraham a ram for sacrifice (*Genesis* 22. 1-13).

(8) a2. Three young men in the furnace

King Nebuchadnezzar commanded that three Jewish young men should be thrown into the burning furnace because they did not worship idols. The messenger from God (expressed in the form of an angel or a dove) saved those men (*Daniel* 3.8-30). (8) a2 is taken from the Catacombs of Priscilla (the middle of the third century AD).

(8) a3. Jonah and a great fish (or a whale)

Jonah tried to avoid his duty of prophecy in Nineveh as it was the town of pagans, but his ship was struck by storm. He regarded it as the fury of God and asked the mariners to cast him forth into the sea. The sea ceased her raging. God prepared a great fish to swallow up Jonah, and made it vomit him out upon dry land after three days (*Jonah* 1, 2).

Jonah is often considered as the archetype of Jesus Christ who had resurrected after three days and dispatched his disciples on mission to all nations (cf. *Luke* 24. 47).

(8) b. The resurrection of Lazarus

". . . Jesus called in a loud voice, 'Lazarus, come out!' The dead man came out, his hands and feet wrapped with strips of linen and a cloth around his face." (*John* 11. 43-44). 'The youth who works miracles with a staff' is one of the earliest motifs signifying Christ. Its example is seen in the Catacombs of Via Latina (fourth century AD), etc.

(9) *The sacrament of the Eucharist*

"This is my body given for you; do this in remembrance of me" (*Luke* 22.19). (9) is from the Catacombs of Callisto (third century AD).

(10) *Orans, the prayer*

The person who prays to God so that the soul of the dead may sleep in peace. Or, the personalized figure of the dead man's soul.

The motif is often seen in the reliefs on the stony coffin and the Catacomb-paintings.

(10) is from the Catacombs of Priscilla (middle of third century AD).

(11) *The portrayal of mother and her child, as the archetype of Madonna and her Holy Child*

It is more natural to see it as the portrayal of the dead. Some of its examples remind us of the holy dignity of St. Mary and Christ the Infant. It appeared after the second century AD. (11) is seen in the Catacombs of Coemeterium Majus (first half of fourth century AD).

(12) *The archetype of Christ image*

(12) a. The young philosopher (or teacher) surrounded by his disciples, or the Christ without beard.

(12) a is taken from the Catacombs of Domitilla (third century AD). The figure of the youth speaking with fervour towards his disciples. The basis of early Christ image took an ordinary human form.

(12) b. The man with Alpha & Omega, or the Christ with beard

(12) b is found in the Catacombs of Commodilla (middle of the fourth century AD). This is the portrayal of Christ with his nimbus, Alpha and Omega. The evolution of Christ images began in the fourth century AD. In the Eastern Church, the portrayal of Christ with beard was adopted in the icon of Christ and some characteristics of Christ's face (eyes, nose, mouth, beard, etc.) were taken over in other icons of later periods.

(1) symbolizes the mysterious and historical existence of Christ in the form of alphabets. (2)-(6) embody various aspects of the character of Christ. It may be said that the motifs from (1) to (6) are the symbols of Christ himself. Above all, (1) a1, (1) c1 or (1) c2, (3), (4)a3 were very often adopted as the essential motifs of Christian art even after Christianity had become the state religion of the Roman Empire in 392 [cf. *Illust*. 21 for (4) a3, *Illust*. 22 for (3)]. (1) cl, or (1) c2, (3), and (4) a3 were sometimes treated as independent objects of worship. For non-Christians, (3) must be the most popular symbol of Christianity. (11) and (12) are the first trials of expressing the mysterious nature of Christ and St. Mary in the figure of mother and her child, the youth, and the matured male.

In other words, (1)-(6) signify the presence of Christ and (7)-(10) express the expectations of people to be saved by Christ. A visual confirmation of some spiritual bonds can be found between Christ who has resurrected and the Christians including those who sleep in the Catacombs.

Now, let us compare *Fig*. 13 with *Fig*. 14. First, in *Fig*. 13, we cannot find any kind of motif equivalent to (1)-(6) of *Fig*. 14. There is no religious significance in (9)b and (9)d of Fig. 13 as compared with (4)a3 and (6)a of *Fig*. 14. (10) of *Fig*. 13 and (7)a of *Fig*. 14

deal with the same bird of peacock, but their respective usage is quite different from each other. (7) of *Fig.* 13 and (7)-(10) of *Fig.* 14 can find a point of contact in the sense that they have something to do with religious faiths.

Generally speaking, all the motifs of *Fig.* 13 except (9) and (10) are decorative and put somewhere as the Buddhist monuments. On the other hand, every motif of *Fig.* 14 is demonstrative in the sense that each can convey a specific meaning to the viewers even independently of any narrative scene [especially (1)-(4), (6), (7), (10)] and contains a sort of spiritual and mysterious power under the authority of Jesus Christ. In *Fig.* 13, is it possible to derive the personal dignity of the Buddha *Śākyamuni* or any other *Mānuṣī Buddha* from each of the Buddhist monuments? Probably not. *Fig.* 13 represents the characteristic of Buddhism based on the impersonality of *Dharma* rather than pursuing salvation in the personal authority of the Buddha.

In this way, a comparative survey of *Fig.* 13 (early Buddhist art) and *Fig.* 14 (early Christian art) reflects each religious characteristic, and the differences between the two are made clear.

Let us see how the motif of early Buddhist art was adopted in later periods (*Pl.* 13). This is the most representative example of the Buddha image in the Gupta Dynasty (fifth century AD, Sārnāth). Its artistic quality had already attained maturity in this period. The Buddha image in the *dharmacakra-mudrā* is seated on the place where only the monument of *dharmacakra* was seen [*Fig.* 13; (6) a1, *Illust.* 1b].

The scene of the First Sermon can be seen as the bas-relief on the pedestal. Five disciples of the Buddha (according to the legend), the donor and her child, and two deer are all together beside the *dharmacakra*. However, they seem to lack vital appearances as compared with *Illust.* 1b. The worshippers of *Pl.* 13 look like dummies. Futhermore, the *dharmacakra* turns its face (the nave) toward those dummies and has no power of talking to us as the viewers. These observations seem to suggest that the early style of Buddhist worship without the Buddha image could not attract people's attention any longer in those days. *Pl.* 13 symbolizes a big turning point in the history of Buddhist art — from the stage of non-Buddha image to the evolution of Buddha images.

On the contrary, the motifs of early Christian art play an important role in *Illust.* 21. This is the ceiling painting of the tomb of saints in the Catacombs of SS. Pietro e Marcellino (end of the fourth century AD). The scene of this painting is divided into two parts.

The upper part represents Jesus Christ surrounded by his greatest disciples, St. Petrus (right) and St. Paulus (left). Christ has a nimbus with Alpha & Omega [*Fig.* 14 (1)a1] and his right hand is blessing the viewers.

The lower part depicts (from the left) St. Gorgonius, St. Petrus, St. Marcellinus, and St. Tiburtius praising the Lamb of God [*Fig*. 14 (4)a3] on the hill from where four Heavenly Rivers are flowing down. Names of these saints are recorded in Latin beside their heads in this painting. They are crowned with the title of St. (Saint) as the martyrs who died "because of their testimony for Jesus and because of the word of God" (*Revelation* 20.4).

The centre of this painting is occupied by the Lamb of God (lower) and its true form, Jesus Christ (upper) who are praised by the saints gathered around them.

Here we can see a sort of hierarchy:

1. Christ and his apostles, and
2. the symbolic Christ and the devout Christians.

This is one of the most important subjects adopted in the later Christian art (cf. *Illust*. 23, 'The Last Judgement', twelfth century AD.; *Illust*. 24, 'The Dispute On the Eucharist', fifteenth century AD).[105]

Illust. 21 was painted soon after the Roman Empire ceased persecuting Christians in AD 313, but it may be said that *Illust*. 21 is one of the greatest works in the history of Christian art because of its beautiful way of expressing the spiritual intercourse between Christ as the visible God in human form and those who are blessed with the Christ's grace. In Christian art, the incarnation of Christ is the most important element to give a human dignity to every person to be painted and sculptured.

Let us view *Pl*. 13 again. It can be clearly stated that there is great difference in the artistic expression of the Buddha and his disciples. In the history of Buddhism, the Buddha's disciples were not specially sanctified and worshipped by Buddhist devotees. For example, Mahā-Moggallāna, one of the greatest disciples of the Buddha, as well as Sāriputta is said to have been persecuted by those who had a hatred for the fame of the Buddha and his disciples. But we do not know any example of Mahā-Moggallāna ever being enshrined as a martyr. It is well known that the *Stūpa* 3 at Sāñcī enshrined the relics of Sāriputta and Mahā-Moggallāna. However, in early Buddhist art, we cannot find any narrative relief-scene describing the episodes of these great disciples of the Buddha. As we have already seen, the motifs of early Buddhist art enable us to meditate on the Deceased Buddha and his Deeds. There is no space even for his greatest disciples to occupy any position.

What does this mean? At least, it means that the essence of Buddhism depends on the contents of the *Sambodhi* or the True Wisdom manifested by the person who can be called 'the Buddha', 'the Enlightened One'. If the Buddha had behaved as the only Son of God just like the Christ, the early Buddhist art would have expressed the personal existence of the Buddha much more positively.

Moreover, 'the personages on stage' of the relief-scenes could not have sat cross-legged in the presence of the Buddha (*Illust.* 5a, b-1, c-2, *Illust.* 11b-1 and *Illust.* 12a-1), felt relaxed (*Illust.* 1a, Illust. 2a-1, a-2, etc.) and looked down at the Buddha's seat (*Illust.* 5c-1).

It is not too much to say that Buddhist art had placed great emphasis on the religious experience of the Buddha rather than on the Buddha himself from the beginning. But then, what about the Buddha image and the Bodhisattva image in the later periods? Those images also personalize the wisdom and the grace of the Buddha and the Bodhisattva, none of which are the portrayals of any historical persons. By the period of Gupta dynasty, the physical characteristics peculiar to the Buddha and the Bodhisattva had already been defined in the pattern book of Buddhist iconography. According to those models, painters and sculptors created various images of the Buddha and the Bodhisattva for the purpose of expressing many kinds of Buddhist virtues. It seems to signify the symbolical nature of Buddhist art that tries to represent something abstract and profound in the Buddhist context through the medium of human forms. *Illust.* 1b and *Pl.* 13 show us two ways of expressing the First Sermon in their own artistic styles.

As compared with *Fig.* 14, *Fig.* 13 makes a silent and contemplative impression. Above all, the motifs from (3) to (8) look like hieroglyphic epitaphs if one remembers the Buddha as the Deceased One. We again find that the *Bodhi tree* of *Śākyamuni* Buddha stands in a row of other *Bodhi trees* of *Mānuṣī Buddhas* who had already passed away and only left their memories. That is, the early Buddhist art is motivated by the Deceased Buddha whose relics are enshrined in the *stūpa* as the first object of Buddhist art. On the other hand, *Fig.* 14 originates from the spiritual presence of Christ who had already risen from death.

In Christianity, death is 'the last enemy' (*I Corinthians* 15:26) that will perish when Christ comes on the last day of this world (*I Corinthians* 15:23-24). Christians believe in the eternal life after death. But in Buddhism, death, as well as birth, old age, and sickness, belong to one of the Laws of Nature from which nobody can escape. Not only human beings but also other living beings have to undergo rebirth in accordance with their own deeds (*karma*) in this life. However, those who have released themselves from the bonds of *kārmic* life (*arahā, arhat*) do not undergo rebirth any more.[106] This life is the last for such people. The *arhat*'s death is the perfect peace and it is praised by others, as the *Mahāparinirvāṇa*.

The essential monumentality of Buddhist motifs (*Fig.* 13) and relief-scenes (*Illusts.* 1-12a-2 and *Illust.* 13) also reflects the basic nature of *Theravāda* Buddhism of those days.[107]

In this chapter, we have described the visible facts as plainly as possible apart from tracing the results of other scholars' works. As a result, we have come up with some findings on the basis of our own observations. They contain several suggestive points to interpret the absence of the Buddha image in early Buddhist art.

Notes

1. Cf. *ye māṃ rūpeṇa pāmiṃsu*
   ye ca ghoseṇa anvagā
   chanda-rāga-vasupetā
   na maṃ janenti te janā (*Theragāthā*, 469).
   This verse is equivalent to *Udanavarga* 22.12, and its spirit can be found in *Vajracchedikā Prajñāpāramitā* 26a (cf. ed. and tr. by Edward Conze with introduction and glossary. Serie Orientale Roma XIII. Roma, Is. M.E.O. 1957).
2. This is a rare example referring to the Buddha as '*Tathāgatha*' in the context of *Mhp*. Its meaning seems to be 'the person who has completed his practice'. The concept was common to *śramaṇas* of other new religions of the Buddha's period such as *Nirgrantha* and *Ajīvika*, although it contains a special meaning to suggest some superhuman power of the Buddha. However, the Buddha was usually called '*bhante*' (lord or sir) by his disciples and was referred to as '*Bhagavā*' (the Exalted One).
3. '*Parinirvāṇa*' is the ultimate state of '*nirvāṇa*' completed by death, the extinction of human body as the physical attachment to this world. Originally, '*nirvāṇa*' points to a practical state of mind in which the flames of worldly passions have been blown out as compared with the ontological concept of '*parinirvāṇa*'.
4. *Mhp* Ch. 5.8, cf. T.W. Rhys Davids and J. Estlin Carpenter (ed.) *The Dīgha Nikāya*, Vol. II, London, The Pali Text Society, reprint, 1947.
5. Sir John Marshall and Alfred Foucher, *The Monuments of Sāñchī*. Vol. I; (*MS*, I), Swati Publications, Delhi, 1982, p. 93.
6. Cf. B.M. Barua, *Bhārhut Aspects of Life and Art, Fine Arts Series Book 1. Stone as Story-Teller*, Calcutta, 1934, p. 80.
7. Peter Harvey, "Venerated Objects and Symbols of Early Buddhism", pp. 83-100, Karel Werner (ed.) *Symbols in Art and Religion*, Motilal Banarsidass Publishers, Delhi, 1991.
8. *Mhp*. Ch. 5, 10-12 (D.N. II, 141-3).
9. D.R. Sahni Vogel, *Catalogue of the Archaeological Museum at Mathurā*, 1910, C2 "*nivāṇa-saṁpati-saṁpādake*" (. . . hoping to acquire the bliss of *nirvāṇa* [of my own]) from the stone pillar of Nāgārjunakoṇḍa *stūpa*. Cf. Vogel, *ibid*., B4, B5, C3, C4, C5, E.
10. Cf. Vogel, *ibid*., B4, "*apono ubhaya-loka-hita-sukha-nivāṇathanāya*". In this way, the word '*nirvāṇa*' is often mentioned along with '*sukha*' (the ease and benefit in this world and the next world after rebirth).
11. *Mahāvaṁsa* XXXI 97-100.
12. In this respect, we can recognize a dramatical or theatrical nature of early Buddhist art in which the figures of devotees play active roles. Cf. Chapter III, 3.

13. K. Krishna Murthy, *Material Culture of Sāñchī*, Sundeep Prakashan, Delhi, 1983, p. 3.
14. The Fourteen Rock Edicts, Ch. 5. Cf. Radhakumud Mookerji, *Aśoka*, Motilal Banarsidass, 1989, p. 139.
15. The Seven Pillar Edicts, Ch. 7. of Mookerji, *ibid.*, p. 190.
16. Cf. A.L. Srivastava, *Life in Sāñchī Sculpture*, Abhinav Publications, New Delhi, 1983, p. 4.
17. Sir John Marshall, *A Guide to Sāñchī*, 3rd ed., The Government of India Press, Calcutta, 1955, p. 33.
18. The Minor Pillar Edicts at Kauśambī, Sāñcī, and Sārnāth. Cf. Mookerji, *op. cit.*, pp. 193-200.
19. Cf. Murthy, *op. cit.*, p. 11, Srivastava, *op. cit.*, p. 5.
20. *MS*, I., pp. 81, 287, 289.
21. Cf. B.C. Sinha, *Glorious Art of the Śuṅga Age*, Durga Publications, Delhi, 1985, p. 64.
22. *MS*, I., p. 3.
23. *Ibid.*, pp. 23-24.
24. *MS*, I., p. 295.
25. *Ibid.*, p. 342. Inscription No. 398.
26. Akira Miyaji, *Indo Bujutsushi* (History of Indian Art), Yoshikawa Kobunkan, Tokyo, 1984, p. 42.
27. According to the Minor Rock Edicts, Ch. 2, it is found that Aśoka adopted a nature of *'porānā pakiti'* (the moral principles of human life from ancient times) in his concept of *'Dharma'*.
28. Cf. Chapter III, 2.
29. *MS*, I., pp. 12-13.
30. *MS*, I., p. 37.
31. It is inferred that *Stūpa* 1 was constructed as the container of the *Buddha śarīra* (cf. Alexander Cunningham, *Bhilsa Topes or Buddhist Monuments of Central India*, London, 1854). In this connection, *Stūpa 2* contained the relics of ten Buddhist Teachers of Aśokan period and *Stūpa 3* enshrined the relics of Sāriputta and Mahāmogallāna, two of the greatest disciples of the Buddha, cf. *MS*, I., p. 32, pp. 44-45, 296.
32. Cf. Satish Chandra Kala, *Bhārhut Vedikā*. Municipal Museum, Allahabad, 1951.
33. Cf. *Fig.* 13 (4)b, (6)b, and *Illust.* 13b-1, b-2.
34. On the top, we can find the railing of *harmikā* surrounding three umbrellas.
35. As far as the studies of early Buddhist art are concerned, there are very few scholars who have ever referred to this *'vedikā-design'* which I have named so for convenience and the significance of which I have discussed in terms of the *stūpa-art*. In this sense, we can find out a precious example from Srivastava, *op. cit.*, p. 56. The author takes notice of "the design of this railing in every storey of the buildings depicted on the Sāñchī toraṇas" which "has directly been adopted from the ground railing of the Great Stūpa erected sometime during the Śuṅga period."
36. In Buddhist *Saṃgha*, nuns and monks fixed the boundaries in an appointed place so that they may observe their order and precept not to commit errors. In this sense, it may be

possible to think that the *'vedikā-design'* of Buddhist rock-cut caves stress the meaning of *'sīmābandha'* (holy boundaries) towards the inhabitants of *vihāra*.

37. The top-bottom lintels of southern gateway and the middle-bottom lintels of western gateway have been put back with the face reversed during restoration in the last century (*MS*, I, *Pls*. 10, 54, 60). Their original appearances are drawn in our *Fig*. 7.
38. Cf. *Therag*. 491. *Therag*. 490 refers to the names of the *Mānuṣī Buddhas*, *Vipaśyin, Sikhin, Viśvabhū, Krakucchanda, Kanakamuni* and *Kāśyapa* who had passed through the way of Truth before *'Gotama'* Buddha traced the same.
39. *Therag* 1276 calls the Buddha *Śākyamuni 'isisattama'* (the seventh saint).
40. Marshall and Foucher, *op.cit.*, Vol. II, Pls. 46, 56.
41. Marshall. *op.cit.*, p. 44, Foucher, "On Iconography of Buddha's Nativity", *Memoirs of Archaeological Survey of India*, No. 46, New Delhi, 1934, p. 3.
42. Cf. Srivastava, *op.cit.*, pp. 120-21. However, at the same time, it may be possible to regard *Gaja-Lakṣmī* as the design of praising the Nativity because it should include a Buddhist meaning within the frame of Buddhist art.
43. Cf. *Ṛg-Veda*, Vol. X, 130.7. 'Seven' is also a sacred number for the Buddhists.
44. In *Illust*. 1, from right to left (C-3, C-1 and C-2), we can see the *Bodhi trees:* 1. the *pātali (bignonia)* of *Vipaśyin,* 2. the fig tree (unspecified) of *Sikhin,* 3. the *sāla (shorea robusta)* of *Viśvabhū*, 4. the *sirīsha (acacia sirissa)* of *Krakucchanda,* 5. the *udumbara (ficus glomerata)* of *Kanakamuni*, 6. the *nyagrodha (ficus indica)* of *Kāśyapa,* and 7. the *aśvattha (ficus religiosa)* of *Śākya-muni*.
45. The Minor Pillar Edicts at Nigālī Sāgar, cf. Mookerji, *op.cit.*, p. 205.
46. In *Therig.*, 518, a nun recollects her previous life that she donated a monastery when the honourable Teacher *'Konāgamana'* lived in his new dwelling of the monastery.
47. *MS*, I, pp. 340-342, Nos. 389-404.
48. *Ibid.*, p. 342, No. 398.
49. *Ibid.*, p. 342, No. 399.
50. *MS*, I, p. 342, No. 402.
51. Chapter III, 2 deals with the importance of 'the Law' (*dharma*) in early Buddhist art.
52. *MS*, I, pp. 301-361 (Nos. 15-630); cf. *Mhp* Ch. 5. 10.
53. *MS*, I, II, Pl. 36-c 1.
54. *Mhp* Ch. 5. 10, Ch. 6. 24-28.
55. *MS*, I., p. 36.
56. Cf. Chapter IV.
57. It naturally raises some points for research which have been taken up in Chapter III especially sections 2 and 3.
58. Cf. *MS*, II, Pls. 27, 38, 46, 49, 51 and 62.
59. This designing technique of putting pillars on both sides of some narrative scene is common to the tradition of Greco-Roman paintings as seen from the period of Hellenism (323 BC-31 BC).

60. Cf. *MS*, II, *Pl.* 49-a. The palace expresses various stages of Heaven as the residence of Yama, *Lokapāla*, and *Trayastriṁśat* (Thirty-Three gods), etc.

    Cf. Coomaraswamy, A.K., *La Sculpture de Bhārhut* (Bibliotheque D'Art Nouvelle Série; VI) Paris, 1956, Pls. VIII, XI.

61. See *Illust.* 4b-2. They can be seen clearly.

    Cf. A. Ghosh, (ed.) *Indian Archaeology 1955-56—A Review;* Department of Archaeology, Government of India, New Delhi 1956, p. 72, Pl. LXXVII.

62. The word, *'vedikā'* sometimes means a kind of stage, chair or holder. In passing, *'vedi'* means the place for the flame-holder of *yajña*. It is possible to infer that *'vedikā-design'* is originally related to the place of Brahmanical rituals. Cf. J.M. van Gelder, *The Mānava Śrautasūtra*, New Delhi, 1963, pp. 44-45, M. Winternitz, *A History of Indian Literature*, Vol. 1, Calcutta, 1959, p. 180.

63. Some photographers often cut and omit taking a picture of the *'vedikā-design'* when they work at Bhārhut and Sāñcī. We can see such an example used as a plate in the publication of Buddhist art. It means that both the authors and the photographers overlooked the importance of *'vedikā-design'* in early Buddhist art.

64. In the works of Bodh Gayā sculpture, some examples managing their narrative scenes have been found without these monuments. Cf. R. Mitra, *Buddha Gayā*, Calcutta, 1878; A. Cunningham, *Mahābodhi*, London, 1892; B. Barua, *Gayā and Buddha-Gayā*, 2 vols., Calcutta, 1931 and 1934; K. Coomaraswamy, *La sculpture de Bodhgayā*, Paris, 1935.

65. (1) A-a1 (Bhārhut), (1) A-a2 (40), (1) A-a3 (Amarāvatī), (1) A-b (37), (1) B-a (34c), (1) B-b (19C, 34a-3, 36c-3, 50-a, 51a, b), (2) (51), (3) (60, 63), (4) a1 (40), (4) a2 (46), (4)b (23), (5) a1 (Bhārhut), (5) a2 (35B, 51b, 65bl, cf. 52a), (5) a3 (35), (6) a1 (60, etc.), (6) a2 (18), (6)b (22, cf. 27), (7) a1 (51), (7) a2 (18), (7) b1 (37), (7) b2 (42), (7)c (XXXVIII), (7)d (Stūpa 2, 31-b, 80), (8) a1 (*Stūpa* 2, 71.1c, 94-4), (8) a2 (Amarāvatī), (9)a (44), (9)b (43), (9)c (40), (9)d (44), (9)e (18), (10) (44), (11) (23b).

    Numerals inside the second parentheses ( ) are Plate nos. of *MS*, II (for *Stūpa* I) and *MS*, III (for *Stūpa* 2).

66. (ex) Karel Werner (ed.) *Symbols in Art and Religion*, Motilal Banarsidass Publishers Pvt. Ltd., Delhi, 1991, pp. 68-102.

67. Cf. *AN*, II, pp. 37-38. On the other hand, the hand-print (*pañcāṅgula, pañca-aṅgulika*) is also often seen. It is a charm to protect against evil eyes.

68. *MS*, II, Pls. 34a3 and 51b.

69. Cf. Notes No. 44 (Chapter II, 1).

70. Cf. *Sn*. 684, 693, etc.

71. It is interesting to note that these motifs were actually used as mascots by Buddhist pilgrims.

    Cf. A. Foucher, *Les débuts de l'art bouddhique*, (JA, 1911, pp. 64f., Eng. tr. in *The Beginnings of Buddhist Art*, 1917, pp. 11f).

72. Cf. *Sn*. 457, *Dhp* 296-298.

73. It is called *'aṅkuśa'*, a kind of banner. Cf. *MS*, II, Pl. 42.

74. Cf. *MS*, II, Pl. 41.
75. A. Foucher, *On the Iconography of the Buddha's Nativity*, MASI, No. 46, Delhi, 1934.
76. Cf. *Sn*. 684, 690, etc.
77. '*Śākyasiṃha*'
78. *Itiv*. 100 G; *AN*, II, p. 9G cf. '*sadevakassa lokassa aggo*' (*AN*, II, p. 17G); '*lokajeṭṭha*' (*Therig*. 154), etc.
79. Cf. *Sn*. 562, 684.
80. Cf. *Therag*., 1095.
81. *MS*, II, Pls., 13 and 63.
82. On Bhārhut Gateway (Fig. 6), lions and elephants appear very often other than the motifs of *stūpa*, throne, and *Bodhi-tree*. Both edges of lintels are decorated with *makara*, the sea-monster having a crocodile's head.
83. Does it have something to do with the fact that the Buddha entrusted lay-believers with all the rituals of his *stūpa*? Cf. *DN*, II, 5(10), p. 141.
84. Cf. K.K. Murthy, *Material Culture of Sāñchī*. Sundeep Prakashan, Delhi, 1983, pp. 34-115 (Costume, Personal Ornaments, Coiffure and Head-dress).
85. Cf. B.C. Sinha, *Glorious Art of the Śuṅga Age*, Durga Publications, Delhi, 1985, p. 52.
86. The devotional feelings of ancient Buddhists toward their Lord are closely related to the *bhakti* movement whose origin dates back to the *Upaniṣadic* period of *MN*, I, 472; *Bhagavat-Gītā* II, 48, 57, IX 26, 27.
87. A feeling of delight is incidental to an act of devotion because one detaches oneself from earthly passions and desires even while simply folding one's hands towards one's Lord. In these ancient sculptures, we can see those who are purified by *ānanda* filling the spirit of *bhakti* in their own minds.
88. Marshall, *A Guide to Sāñchī*, pp. 10, 11, 8-13. The best example of frontality can be seen in the wall-paintings of Ancient Egypt, cf. *MS*, I, p. 104.
89. Cf. A.K. Coomaraswamy, *Introduction to Indian Art*, 2nd ed., Munshiram Manoharlal, Delhi, 1969, p. 78.
90. Cf. *MS*, II, Pl. 29. 1, 3, Pl. 36. c2, etc.
91. *Ibid*., Pls. 51b, 52a2, etc.
92. Cf. Hultzsch, no. 77; Lüders List, no. 774. Barua, no. 167; Majumdar, no. 184; Lüders, Bhārhut, no. B 40.
93. Cf. Hultzsch, no. 61; Lüders List, no. 753; Barua, no. 180; Majumdar, no 265b, Lüders, Bhārhut, no. B37.
94. Provisionally, these scenes can be regarded as narrative. The presence of deer suggests Mṛgadāva where the Buddha revealed his teaching for the first time. The designs of *Illust*. 1b (lintel), *Illust*. 3a-1, a-2 (dies), *Illust*. 3b and *Illust*. 7b (pillars) and *Illust*. 13b-1, b-2 (decorative pillars) seem to depend on the size of architectural space.
95. Cf. Notes No. 88.
96. For instance, it often occurs that one story is divided into several processes which are

described within the same scene. The viewers can grasp those processes at once or look at each of them free from a temporal order. This flexible temporality exists in ancient fine arts. Ex. *MS*, II, Pls. 29, (*Viśvantara-jātaka*), 64a (*Mahākapi-Jātaka*), 65b1 (*Māra's getaway* and *the Sambodhi*), etc.

97. They are called *'caitya'* in *DN*, II, 140-141. The word of *'caitya'* origninates from the root of a verb $\sqrt{ci}$ meaning 'pile up' or 'accumulate'. Therefore, it seems to signify *'cayana, citya'* as the fire altar made of bricks or stones. But, on the other hand, it is also thinkable that *'caitya'* is a derivative of $\sqrt{cint}$ meaning 'remind' or 'memorize'. It also signifies 'the place to be memorized'. In Buddhist meaning, *'caitya'*, is a place of pilgrimage (*caitya-cārikā*) where the Buddha was born, and finally reached the Perfect Decease, etc. It seems that the Buddhist monuments of relief-scenes show various types of *'caitya'* in ancient India.

98. It is notable that Grünwedel interprets Buddhist monuments as 'the signs of his activity', 'the symbols of his miracles', and 'the symbol of his doctrine', not as the symbol of the Buddha himself. Cf. *Buddhist Art in India*, Delhi, 1974, p. 67.

99. Grünwedel refers to the similarity between early stages of Buddhist and Christian arts. Gründedel, *op.cit.*, 1974, pp. 42, 68.

100. Cf. Kanoko Tanaka, "On the Early Motifs in Buddhist and Christian Arts", *Journal of Religious Studies,* No. 14, Komazawa University Religious Study Institute, Tokyo, 1988, p. 48.

101. It is carved on the wooden door of St. Sabina Church, Roma.

102. The crucifix of Gero the arch-bishop, the Köln Cathedral, AD 969-971.

103. The word 'the Old Testament' is used only by Christian people who regard the Gospels as the true Books of Salvation. Here we dare use it for convenience.

104. Cf. *'Ordo commendationis animae'* (The prayer of entrusting one's soul to God). *The Rituale Romanum* enumerates many examples of those whose lives were saved with the help from God.

105. The invisible presence of Christ is symbolized by the empty throne with the Cross and the Book of Life (*Illust.* 23), and the altar set for the Eucharist (*Illust.* 24).

106. Cf. *DN*, II, p. 68; *Sn*. p. 16, SN, I. p. 140, AN, II, p. 211, etc.

107. Cf. *MS*, I, p. 155; "The particular sect established at Sāñchī appears to have been the old and generally orthodox *Theravādin*, closely connected, among others, with the *Sthaviras* or *Haimavatas* and *Sarvāstivādins*, and it is likely enough that rival sects, such as the *Mahāsāṅghikas*, did not share their progressive ideas in regard to figurative arts."

III

Possible Interpretations

In this chapter, we will develop the meaning of 'the absence' on the basis of

1. The Religious Aspects
2. The Artistic Aspects
3. The Political Aspects

The purpose of these interpretations is understanding what early Buddhist art means to us in modern times rather than trying to look for a single answer to the worn-out question: 'Why the Buddha was not represented in early Buddhist art?'

1. The Religious Aspects

(A) IN THE CONTEXT OF STŪPA-ART

In the period of early Buddhist art, the climax and the final goal of Buddhist pilgrimage (*caitya-cārikā*)[1] was the visit to the *stūpa*. As discussed in Chapter II, it is very important for us to note that early Buddhist art was the fine arts dedicated to the *stūpa* when we interpret the absence of the Buddha image.

Even in modern times, '*caitya*', the place to be visited by the Buddhist people where the Buddha must have stayed a long time ago, is nothing but the ruins' vacancy surrounded by its natural environment, except for the remains of the Buddhists' own making. A visitor cannot help imagining and meditating on the actual occurrence that took place in ancient times. He sees the visionary Buddha only in his mind no matter where he visits even though the Buddha image is present before his eyes (*Pl.* 11). This is because his purpose is to carry himself to the historical reality that the Buddha had ever lived a life in this very world. For pilgrims, the vacancy of '*caitya*' (*Pl.* 10) is much more significant than the presence of the Buddha image (*Pls.* 11 and 12). Before the reality that nothing remains there except for one's reverence for the Buddha, any kind of artificiality looks extra and additional. In other words, an iconic medium should not disturb one's contemplation (*smṛti,* or *samjñā*) to be pure and spiritual.

In this sense, the *stūpa* must be superior to any other '*caitya*', because it contains the historical evidence of the Buddha (*Buddha śarīra*) and its semicircular appearance has no element for disturbing one's spiritual silence, beyond all kinds of mundane figures. It is very natural that the *stūpa-art* positively expressed the contemplative space (the absence of the Buddha) for the pilgrims of those days. There was no space for adding the Buddha image or anything else. At least, ancient Buddhists could appreciate such a kind of fine arts as a matter of course.[2] This interpretation may be the most conscientious to the psychological conditions of *caitya-cārikā*.

(B) THE ANICONIC SITUATION OF VEDIC RITUALS

If there was no necessity to worship the Buddha image, it may have been partly due to the aniconic situation of Vedic rituals in which a Brāhmaṇa called the invisible gods (the deified natural phenomena) above the altar as often as he needed to perform a rite. It was unnecessary to build a permanent sanctuary to put some image of god inside. Early Brahmanism used a complicated system of signs and symbols, an 'iconography without icons'[3] for the purpose of keeping its esoteric nature consisting of a highly developed ritual of sacrifices (*yajñā*).

It is not impossible to imagine that this Indo-Āryan religious custom influenced the aniconic attitude of early Buddhist art,[4] but at the same time, there remains a problem of placing 'the absence of the Buddha' and 'the invisible presence of Vedic gods' in the same category. The former leans on historical evidence that the Buddha existed in human form (or as a human being). On the other hand, the latter belongs to the idealistic world beyond historical time. In other words, there is an essential difference between the two: a historical person who left memorable words and deeds during his lifetime and natural phenomena deified in a rhetorical way.[5]

If it is necessary to interpret 'the absence of the Buddha' from religious viewpoints, they should be taken out of the Buddhistic context.

(C) GENERAL INTERPRETATIONS ON THE USAGE OF BUDDHIST MONUMENTS

Generally speaking, the Buddhist monuments seen in the old aniconic reliefs have been regarded as the symbolic images suggesting the noble 'presence' of the Buddha who was "believed to be everywhere, in all the lotuses, beside all the wheels, on all the thrones, under all the trees".[6]

"The profound nature of a Buddha could not be adequately conveyed by a mere human form",[7] but be suggestively expressed by some aniconic and impersonal symbol which might be a manifestation of the transcendental essence of the Buddha 'above men and gods'.

However, even if the concept of a Buddha's nature (*buddhatā*) had already developed in those days, everyone would have known that the Buddha had lived a life among men as one of them: a tonsured *śramaṇa*, with his disciples.[8] Then, why his transcendency 'above men and gods'? Many scholars have referred to the following paragraphs taken out of early Buddhist scriptures.

(D) The *Dīgha Nikāya (Brahma-Jāla Sutta,* 73*)*

> The outward form, brethren, of him who has won the truth, stands before you, but that which binds it to rebirth is cut in twain. So long as his body shall last, so long do gods and men behold him. One the dissolution of the body, beyond the end of his life, neither gods nor men shall see him.[9]

For the person who has won the truth (*Tathāgatha*), there is no fear of rebirth after death, because he is perfectly free from all kinds of sensations causing an adherence to future lives.[10] The outward form of him is truly the last body before his eternal extinction from this world. On the dissolution of the body — it can be called the perfect decease or the *Mahāparinirvāṇa* —, beyond the end of his life, he ceases his existence, and never disappears into 'a realm of invisibility'[11] just as Jesus Christ is believed to have ascended to the invisible Kingdom of God after his resurrection.[12] Not only in Buddhism but also in Jainism and other contemporary religions of India, the extinction of one's existence was the ultimate salvation in ontological sense, which only the Blessed One could attain successfully. Being born in this world was essentially nothing but a suffering for every living being even though one could be born in the world of gods. Both men and gods have to continue their own lives endlessly. Therefore, "neither gods nor men shall see him" shows a clear-cut contrast between the Deceased Buddha and others left behind.

This relationship between the two reminds us of the *stūpa* and *stūpa*-worshippers; or 'the absence of the Buddha' and 'devotees on stage' in the world of fine arts. As long as we interpret the 'absence of the Buddha image in early Buddhist art' as the monumental space where the Buddha is not actually present any more, that paragraph of the *Dīgha Nikāya* referred to above may be effective.

However, the interpretations of the same paragraph by Vincent A. Smith and O.C. Gangoly are quite different from ours.

Smith thinks that it prevented ancient sculptors from giving a human form to the Buddha who had entered into *parinirvāṇa* and that they must have been satisfied to substitute symbols for his spiritual existence.[13] But he gives no explanation as to why such symbols signifying the 'spiritual existence' after *parinirvāṇa* are used in the biographical scenes where the Buddha's body still lasts. How to solve this gap between his 'spiritual existence' through the medium of symbols and his presence in biographical stories? Smith seems to overlook the importance of "so long as his body shall last, so long do gods and men behold him". If ancient sculptors had known this paragraph, they might have been encouraged to express the Buddha in human form.

Gangoly positively regards it (*Brahma-Jāla Sutta* 73) as a law forbidding image-making.[14] That is, he confidently believes that Buddhist scriptures must have been influential in creating Buddhist art more than Smith does. However, it is obvious that the paragraph cannot be interpreted as forbidding image-making, but it may well emphasize the ontological contrast between the Deceased Buddha and his devotees.

Both Smith and Gangoly seem to expect the spiritual presence of the Buddha. But was his soul released from his body after death? Never! We should remember that Buddhism denies any kind of substantial existence including one's own soul. This is quite a different situation as compared to Christ who sent Holy Spirits to Christians after he had ascended to the Heaven.[15] If the Buddha promised to exist in an invisible way after his death, what would have happened to the Buddhist community? At least, it seems that *Mahāyāna* Buddhism prepared the eternal Buddhas[16] who exist beyond the ages for the purpose of making up for the historical death of *Śākyamuni* Buddha.

But it is impossible to infer that early Buddhist art contains such a *Mahāyāna* Buddhist thought. Rather, it must be remembered again that *Śākyamuni* is treated as one of the seven *Mānuṣī Buddhas* whose *Bodhi-trees* are memorized together (Pls. 3, 4c). He is still an object of Buddhist remembrance, even if devotees would like to feel as if the Buddha manifests himself on the empty throne under the tree (Pl. 10).

(E) The *Sutta-Nipāta (*1069, 1073, 1075*)*

> "Having in view nothingness, being thoughtful, O Upasiva," — so said Bhagavat, — "by the reflection of nothing existing shalt thou cross the stream, having abandoned sensual pleasures, being loath of doubts, thou shalt regard the extinction of craving (i.e. Nibbāna), both day and night." (1069).
>
> "As a flame blown about by the violence of the wind, O Upasiva," — so said Bhagavat, — "goes out, cannot be reckoned (as existing), even so a Muni, delivered from name and body, disappears, and cannot be reckoned (as existing)." (1073).

> "For him who has disappeared there is no form, O Upasiva," — so said Bhagavat, — "that by which they say his is, exists for him no longer, when all things (dhamma) have been cut off, all (kinds of) dispute are also cut off" (1075).[17]

The paragraph of the *Dīgha Nikāya* quoted above had an ontological implication. On the other hand, those given above offer an existential confession of the Buddha who has completed "the extinction of craving (i.e. *nibbāna*), both day and night" as if a flame were blown out by a blast of wind (i.e. *nibbāna*). He is already free from all kinds of sensual sorrows[18] and pleasures and actually out of his name and body (*nāma-rūpa*) causing rebirth (*saṃsāra*). Only in this sense it is allowed to say that he cannot be reckoned as existing (like other men and gods who are in bondage of earthly sensations) even while he is still alive in this world. The last paragraph (1075) has a very internal and empirical meaning understandable properly only by the *Bhagavat* himself.

Nevertheless, "so long as his body shall last",[19] a state of '*nibbāna*' is incomplete. The '*parinibbāna*' is attainable by the extinction of his body, although it is out of dispute whether such an extinction makes any sense to the person concerned.

Heinrich Zimmer refers to (E) and interprets that *Ārhat,* the perfect sage, can only be described as being in a state of 'nothingness' (*akiṃcana*).[20] He thinks much of the essence of '*nibbāna*' inexpressible in the form of *kārmic* body, and infers that Buddhist monks might have taught sculptors that it is useless to visualize the Buddha in human form.

David L. Snellgrove also comments on (E) and comes to the conclusion that "the reluctance to depict the Buddha in human form, therefore, is not simply the outcome of a universally valid principle of aniconism or of a law forbidding image-making, but finds its explanation in the philosophically radical doctrine concerning his true Nirvāṇa essence, inconceivable in visual form and human shape."[21]

As far as 'his true *nirvāṇa* essence' is concerned, it may be significant to think that its inexpressible nature could not help being expressed in a non-artistic way, just like 'the absence' of the Buddha image in early Buddhist art.

The clear contrast between 'the absence' and the devotees folding their both hands towards it seems to emphasize the essence of *nirvāṇa*. Moreover, devotees do not include Buddhist nuns and monks but consist of laymen only. This fact may suggest that early Buddhist art makes distinction between '*gṛhin*' (lay-believer)[22] and '*pravrajita*' (nun or monk who has renounced a home life to concentrate on the way of Buddha);[23] '*laukika*' (a state of mind or world which suffers from afflictions of this world)[24] and '*lokottara*' (a state of mind or world which has conquered mundane afflictions);[25] or '*saṃsāra*' (wheel of rebirth, worldly existence, phenomenal life) and '*vimokṣa*' (release from *saṃsāra*).

The viewer comes across the empty space surrounded by worshippers (ex. *Illusts.* 5a and 6). The emptiness may be a relief to his eyes after he has looked at some other crowded descriptions. When he directs his eyes towards the emptiness, it may communicate to him its religious implications as stated above. At least, it is true that ancient Buddhists were seeing something venerable in the empty space. We can infer it not only from Buddhist attitudes in the world of relief-scenes but also from those in the real world of modern times (Pl. 11).

Then, how to explain Prince Siddhārtha's absence from the relief-scenes (*Illusts.* 5b-1 and 13a-2)? He would still be far from a state of *nirvāṇa*. However, even before becoming a Buddha, he proves to be 'transcendental' when he is seen as a Bodhisattva who will attain the Enlightenment in the last stage of his bodily existence after passing through many births. In *Illust.* 13a-2, footprints (*Buddha-pada*) are placed with solemnity. *Dharmacakra*s are seen inside, as if Prince Siddhārtha had been already promised that he would become a Buddha, or as if one is trying to imagine Prince Siddārtha with reverence for the Buddha to be.

Osamu Takata points out that *Śākyamuni* does not appear all through his life, from birth to death, and supposes that it was forbidden to express the Buddha in human form because the last stage of his bodily existence must have been deified irrespective of whether he had already attained the Enlightenment or not.[26]

But in Buddhist scriptures, there is no evidence of such a taboo on image-making.[27]

Takata refers to some paragraphs of the *Anguttara Nikāya* for the purpose of demonstrating his theory on the taboo against image-making.

(F) The *Aṅguttara Nikāya* (in Chinese Version; *Taishō.*, Vol. 2, pp. 657, 664).

> The body of *Tathāgata* is pure and breathing celestial aurae, which is too mysterious to regard the body as artificial . . . Therefore, the body of *Tathāgata* cannot be made. It is beyond the ability of gods . . . the body of *Tathāgata* cannot be measured. It is impossible to regard it as long nor short. In this way, the stage of Buddha is mysterious.[28]

> (The body of *Tathāgata*) is supreme and the most venerable in the carnal world. It trancends all the class of gods and contains the seven riches of Law, which is beyond the stages of men, gods, and other natural living beings, and cannot be made in image."[29]

These paragraphs show a type of Buddhist literature that praises 'the stage of Buddha' in a rhetorical way. Both the paragraphs are found only in the Chinese version, and their Pāli texts are not available. The *Anguttara Nikāya* itself consists of newer strata of Buddhist thoughts as compared with other *Nikāyas*. Therefore, it cannot be authentic as long as its original thought is not traced in the oldest strata of Pāli *Nikāyas*. But we do not find it anywhere else. Or rather, it is quite possible to imagine that the Buddha image had already been made when the *Anguttara Nikāya* was written by a Buddhist who was an expert in praising the Lord. The artistic expressions of fine arts (Buddha images) and literature (Buddhist scripture) are intrinsically different from each other. The former cannot help expressing its object in form and colour as positively as possible. But the latter can praise its object with negative expressions such as 'inexpressible'; 'indescribable' (「不可造作」;「不可像貌」) and 'unmeasured' (「不可模則」).[30] However, it is questionable whether such literary rhetoric has anything to do with 'a taboo' against image-making in the history of Buddhist art.

The taboo theory must be necessary especially to those who have never discussed the origin of the Buddha image because it enables them to consider the emergence of the Mathurā and Gāndhāra Buddhas as the actual day-break of Buddhist art that was freed from the old tradition where the creation of the Buddha image had been forbidden for centuries.

(G) GENERAL COMMENTS ON THE INTERPRETATIONS OF (D), (E) AND (F).

Not only Takata but also many other scholars seem to have a preconception that ancient sculptors had to wrestle with the difficulty of showing the biography of the Buddha without portraying the Buddha himself.[31] That is, all of them believe that the biographical relief-scenes (fine-arts) must reflect and visualize the biographical sources of Buddhist scriptures (literature).[32] Therefore, they mostly concentrate on how the relief-scenes should be identified on the basis of literature, but naturally face the problem of rationalizing 'the absence' of the Buddha, Prince Siddhārtha, Buddhist nuns and monks in early Buddhist art. Nevertheless, they persist in relying on literature and manage to extract some paragraphs from the scriptures just as seen in the above examples. However, such a paragraph cannot give a satisfactory explanation of early Buddhist art as it was not written for the purpose of teaching Buddhists how to create their fine arts.[33]

However, some important points have been duscussed above that may be true in the case of a pious person who venerates the Buddha too much to look him in the face. But it should be remembered that "we have no literary or other evidence to confirm this".[34]

It is strange that no scholar in the past has ever tried to find the key to the problem in early Buddhist art itself. For he would find one solution, at least, by simply turning his eyes to what is there, because it is 'a complete work of those days' to which there is no need to add any eleborate explanation in order to satisfy modern viewers. We should not rationalize any problem of early Buddhist art even if the situation does not satisfy our eyes simply because the familiar Buddha image of later times is not to be found.

It may be appropriate to conclude this section with the following remark of a historian:

"This visitor, standing on the hill of Sāñchī on a sunny winter day, when the wild peacocks walk among the ruins and the great plain shimmers in the hazy distance, gets the overriding impression that this is the work of a contented people at one with itself."[35]

It may not be out of place here to discuss the religious condition of those who had participated in the construction of *stūpa* including its decorative arts because it would keep us from deviating from possible interpretations on early Buddhist art.

The Brāhmī inscriptions of Bhārhut, Sāñci, and Bodh Gayā (second century BC-first century AD) record numerous names of donors — Indians and foreigners, lay-believers and nuns and monks, upper classes and lower classes — who supported the construction of *stūpas*, *toraṇas*, *vedikās* and other parts of Buddhist architecture. However, to our regret, these people did not express any words of prayer and religious vow. Thus it may be said that there is no direct data on the religious situation that produced early Buddhist art.

If it is allowed to make reference to the inscriptions of Amarāvatī (second-third centuries AD) and Nāgārjunakoṇḍa (third century AD), we can analogize the religious background of early Buddhist art.

It goes without saying that the Buddha image had already been popular among the Buddhists of those days. But, at the same time, it is well known that they still adopted the aniconic motifs to suggest the presence of the Buddha[36] till the latter half of the second century AD[37] at least (cf. *Illusts.* 15 and 17).

Illust. 15 is the bas-relief depicting a typical *stūpa* of South India (Amarāvatī) characterized by *Āyāka Khambha*, five angular-pillars, on which offerings are said to have been placed. There are three empty thrones under the two pillars surmounted by big *dharmacakras* at the right and the left ends of this relief, and inside the niche of this *stūpa*. Each of them is being worshipped by devotees with reverence (cf. *Illust.* 17) in spite of the fact that the Buddha images can be seen at other places in the same space of this relief. It seems that these devotees are still maintaining a spirit of early Buddhist faith, although a vision of the Buddha image might have been haunting their eyes.

Illust. 16 is from Nagārjunakoṇḍa of the third century AD. It gives the impression that some mysterious power of the empty throne (*Illust.* 15) has realized the resurrection of the Buddha. This relief-scene is filled with rapture because of his emergence. At the feet of the devotees, there are two water jars (*Pūrṇa ghaṭa*) which have symbolized a source of vital power from ancient periods. Moreover, the *stūpa* is also often called '*aṇḍa*' (egg) or '*garbha*' (womb) containing '*bīja*' (seed), the Buddha *śarīra*. Therefore, it may not be strange to imagine that the Buddha has appeared from his *stūpa* after a long period of incubation just as seen in one of the most dramatic scenes of the *Saddharmapuṇḍarīka Sūtra*[38] (*Stūpasaṁdarśana*) where *Tathāgata* shows himself in his *stūpa* containing relics of the whole body. But such a bold illusion vanishes when we survey the data of inscriptions as follows although it is still interesting that *Illust*. 16 has a premonitory atmosphere to remind us of the *Mahāyāna* Buddhist thought.[39]

(1) From the inscriptions carved on slabs, pillars, and railings of the Amarāvatī *Stūpa*, we come to know that some Buddhist people contributed '*padukapaṭa*' (a slab of *Buddhapada*),[40] '*dhammacaka*' (a monument of *dharmacakra*),[41] and '*sihaṭhāna*' (a lion's seat, *siṃhāsana*)[42] to show their reverence towards '*bhagavata mahācetiya*' (the great *stūpa* of the world-honoured One).

It was only the Buddha *Śākyamuni* who was the centre of devotion. Devotees seem to have been uttering the words, "*Namo Bhagavato Savasatutamasa Buddhasa*" (I adore Thee Thou Buddha as the world-honoured One; the best of all living beings),[43] "*Namo bhagapato lāgaticasa*" (I adore Thee Thou the world-honoured One as the sun of this world),[44] "(*Namo savasa*) *tutamasa Naravasabhasamasaṁbudhādicasa*" (I adore Thee Thou the person who attained the supreme Enlightenment; the best of all living beings; the most superior man; the lord of human beings; and the sun).[45]

From these confessions, it may look as if the Buddha were present even spiritually. But, they originally belong to one's own religious experience inexpressible in form and colour. The contribution of '*pādukāpada*', '*dhammacaka*' and '*sihaṭhāna*' seems to suggest that donors still liked to produce a meditative space where they could contemplate in their own minds in the presence of the Deceased One whose relics were enshrined in '*mahācetiya*', although they must have ever folded their both hands towards the Buddha image.

In fact, a setting of '*pādukāpada*' or other Buddhist monuments must have been much more realistic for the purpose of expressing the Deceased One with dignity (cf. *Illust*. 15) than any good-looking image created by those who had never met the Buddha himself. In this sense, it is certain that the *stūpa-art* of those days was more religious than artistic.

(2) From the inscriptions carved on pillars of the Nāgārjunakoṇḍa Stūpa, it is not difficult to understand the main motives of donation. One of the most helpful

inscriptions belongs to *Mahātalavari Cā(ṁ)tisiri* who was a younger sister of King Vāsiṭhiputa Siri-Cātamūla of Ikhāku (Ikṣvāku) dynasty.[46] Her inscription consists of four kinds of prayer (a-d):[47]

(a) *apano ubhaya-kulasa atichitam-anāgata-vaṭamānakānaṁ parināmetunaṁ* (To transfer the virtues of this donation towards those who belong to both of her clans in the past, in the present and in the future),

(b) *ubhaya-loka-hita-sukh-āvahathanāya* (.... so that her clans may be provided with complete welfare and happiness both in this world and the next),

(c) *atano ca nivāṇa-saṁpati-saṁpādake* (.... and so that she may obtain the bliss of *nirvāṇa*),

(d) *sava-loka-hita-sukh-āvahathanāya ca* (. . . . and wishing that all world may be provided with complete welfare and happiness),

(e) ... she set up this pillar (*khaṁbha*) at the Great *Stūpa* (*mahācetiya*).

(a) uses the word of '*pariṇāma*' (transfer of one's virtures to someone else) which is often found in the scriptures of early *Mahāyāna* Buddhism. It seems that other Buddhist inscriptions do not use it, except for those of Nāgārjunakoṇḍa.

Prayers (b) and (d) remind us of the phrases of the Aśokan edicts.[48]

Prayer (c) seems to confess her own faith in Buddhism, although it is not certain if she embraced only the Buddhist religion because it is known that her elder brother, the King of Ikṣvāku had held the '*aśvamedha*' as the greatest rite of Brahmanical dynasty.[49]

In other inscriptions of the same royal family, we often see a combination of (b) and (c); "*atano ubhaya-loka-hita-sukha-nivāṇaṭhaya*"[50] (. . . . Wishing that she may be provided with complete welfare, happiness, and *nirvāṇa* both in this world and the next).

In this context, the word '*nirvāṇa*' seems to signify 'the best religious stage of one's mind in life', not 'the stage of *ārhat* who has conquered all the desires of this world and does not take rebirth any more'.

It was impossible for royal donors to abandon their positions, earthly welfare and happiness, but on the other hand, they must have longed for '*nirvāṇa*' which sounds too peaceful to be forgotten easily. It may be said that '*nirvāṇa*' was the ultimate goal of prayers common to those who felt reverence for the Great *Stūpa* (*mahācetiya*).

Such a craving for '*nirvāṇa*' is reflected in the following inscription:

'*(Deya)-dharmmam = ida (ma)ṁ = kr̥tvā yat = puṇyam samupārjjitaṁ (tam) / te (na) puṇyeṅa (na) loko = yaṁ nir(vv)āṇam = adhigacchatu* / /'[51] (No matter what kind of virtues are attainable by this donation, may the virtues let the world attain *nirvāṇa*).

These phrases also begin with the word '*sidhaṁ*' (May it come true), and so do many other inscriptions.[52] It is interesting to imagine that the *stūpa* was alive with the voices of '*sidhaṁ*!' sounding around it all day long as if the semicircular dome had contained a magical power to fulfil any prayer of the devotees.

It seems that the Buddhist communities of Amarāvatī[53] and Nāgārjunakoṇḍa[54] had nothing to do with any kind of *Mahāyānic* thought[55] and their religious situation was not much different from that of Sāñcī, Bhārhut, and Bodh Gayā. Therefore, it is possible to see a single stream of Buddhist consciousness between *Illust.* 4 and *Illusts.* 15-16.

When we turn our eyes from *Illusts.* 15-16 to *Illust.* 4, its simplicity looks more attractive than ever before and the attitudes of the devotees look more significant in contrast with the profound silence of the *stūpa*s. There is no decorative magnificence in the appearance of Buddhist monuments described in early Buddhist art (cf. *Illusts.* 1-12a-2 and *Illust.* 13) as compared with the later works of South Indian art (cf. *Illusts.* 15-17). Therefore, the whole unity of a relief-scene should be all the more important. Our eyes naturally appreciate the relief-scene as a whole, as if we are seeing a performance on stage. Its theatrical situation is already complete (cf. Chapter II, 2). There is no need for adding any other elements. We have only to accept it just as ancient Buddhists must have done.

One may ask, 'Then, how to accept it? Is it possible for you to appreciate early Buddhist art where you cannot but recognize the absence of the Buddha image?'

The answer is: 'Let us enjoy seeing it together, and we will be able to discover something lacking or forgotten in our study. For the purpose, our eyes should see things in an artistic or aesthetic way, because it enables us to liberate ourselves from the bondage of philosophical knowledge on fine arts so that we may derive some knowledge directly from the fine arts. This is the reason why we will have 'the artistic aspects' of the absence of the Buddha image in early Buddhist art as follows.

2. The Artistic Aspects

(A) STŪPA-ART AS ONE OF THE BUDDHIST RITUALS

When the Buddha *Śākyamuni* was alive in this world, he was the centre of a religious circle which was to be known as a Buddhist *Saṃgha* in later periods. Wherever he was, a circle of devotees would have been around their teacher. If we had been there, we would have been quite impressed to see him preaching in his own voice. His teachings were accepted by those who gathered around him and memorized by them. They must have been willing to serve him whenever he needed food, water or some place to take a rest. In this way, there was physical contact between the Buddha and his devotees when the Buddha lived amongst the people.

However, after the Buddha ceased to exist anywhere, there came a sort of vacancy in the circle of his devotees. How to make up for his absence? One of the best ways was the construction of a *stūpa* containing his relics, because the *stūpa* enabled them to bring offerings and behave as servants of the Deceased One — as if he were still there and alive. Their behaviour around the *stūpa* was, as it were, a devotional play or performance.[56] Devotees knew very well that they pretended to serve the Buddha himself. Even if they did not see him in person, they could have enjoyed being the offerers and the worshippers, which can be confirmed from the relief-scenes of early Buddhist art (ex. Illusts. 1, 2 and 4). In this context, it is fully natural to think that both the *stūpa* and its fine arts (the *stūpa-art*) were made for the purpose of satisfying those who were left behind after the death of their Master (cf. Illust. 4c). Both of them belong to the earliest and the most primitive style of Buddhist rituals inseparable from the memory of the historical Buddha.

(B) ITS DRAMATIC ESSENCE

The *stūpa-art* retains its historical sense by describing 'the absence' of the Buddha who is actually absent in modern times. But, at the same time, some of the memorable events of his missionary life — the Enlightenment, the First Sermon and other miracles — are dominant in what is depicted in relief-scenes. Then, is it contradictory to put 'his absence' into such a situation so as to demand 'his presence'? It was out of question at least for ancient sculptors who completed their works successfully in spite of 'his absence'. Then how is it possible? It depends on how 'his absence' is understood. How to appreciate it? The most positive way is to find its theatrical effects on the devotees on stage and other constructive elements of the relief-scenes (cf. Chapter II, 2).

In fact, most of the devotees do not play any specific role but express their reverence towards the Buddhist monuments. The attitude makes their figures indistinguishable in the same atmosphere.... Nevertheless, it is not difficult for the viewers to read a story from what is described there. What is the reason? First, the relief-scene as a whole lays down minimum conditions to suggest a story to the viewers, by a tree (*Illust.* 6), a ladder (*Illust.* 11a-1, a-2), and other non-human figures (cf. *Illust.* 12a-1, a-2 and *Illust.* 5c-1). Secondly, even a minimum suggestion is enough for the viewers who have ever ruminated over the story in their own minds. Therefore, the relief-scene itself is not 'a story-teller'.[57] Or rather, the viewers are invited to enjoy a story well known to them. It means that the relief-scene leaves its narrative climax unsaid so that the viewers may describe it in their own imagination.

In other words, the relief-scene is not an illustration of a story but a sort of open space towards the outer world where the viewers live. The value of such a work of fine arts can be recognized when we find a possibility of interaction between the viewer and the work of art. It does not produce the silence of an art gallery, but the lively air of a theatre.

The relief-scene is usually seen as a piece of plates prepared for the purpose of discussing some topic on the fine arts, and we are apt to overlook its actual utility appreciated by ancient people. However, we cannot but recognize a theatrical situation when looking at the *stūpa-art* as a whole unifying all the pieces of the relief-scenes engraved on railings and gateways (cf. *Pl.* 4).

The point mentioned above can be reconsidered as follows.

For example, there is a theory on the formation of Buddhist paintings in India.[58] It points out one possibility of inferring that a sort of specialists in interpreting religious pictures painted on cloth (*paṭa*) had been active at least since the post-Vedic period.[59] In the context of early Buddhist art, 'the picture showmen' might have contributed towards drawing some religious effect from the *stūpa-art*. Their sketches must have been drawn in pictures before the sculptors began to work.

There is no archaeological evidence to suggest that 'the picture showmen' used a picture characterized by the absence of the Buddha image. But it is probable that such a picture was suitable for allowing them to make a version of their interpretation, depending on the response of the audience who were rich in imagination about how the Buddha had been greater than others, etc. His absence must have prevented them from feeling unsatisfied with an imperfect modelling of the most venerable One. The space of his absence is silent and inactive in any case, and its surroundings are naturally made active and creative, as if they are trying to harmonize with the profound silence of his absence.

Sometimes, they produce a kind of humorous effect by acting towards the absent space (the empty throne) just as a pantomimist tries to suggest a narrative situation (cf.

Illust. 5c-1). On the other hand, they make '*a tableau vivant*'[60] with their stationary postures as if they were taking a memorial picture, disguising themselves as the personages on stage (cf. *Illust.* 5a, b-2, c-2, etc.).

In any case, the absence of the Buddha enables a sort of play or performance in the surroundings and allows much more freedom than possible in his presence. Just as seen in *Illust.* 5, personages are allowed to look down at the Buddha's throne (c-1) from its rear and sit down closely before the throne.

On the other hand, sculptors have to make enough space to dignify the Buddha's figure once they start creating his image (*Illust.* 12b). Personages become much more subordinate to the Buddha whose figure is made differently from men and gods or any other living beings of this world. They are naturally made to appear modest in the presence of the Buddha and can never look down at him nor block his niew with their own figures. Futhermore, their role on stage is defined properly in relation to the Buddha and their characters are clearly recognizable. Therefore, scholars should not find any difficulty in identifying the scene described there. As we are quite used to seeing this kind of scene, some of us may naturally feel a sense of incompatibility when seeing the absence of the Buddha image in early Buddhist art.

However, we should try to see it as if it were the newest and the most familiar to our eyes just as ancient people accepted it as a matter of course. For the purpose, it is necessary to recognize the advantages of the Buddha's absence.

First, the personages coming together around 'his absence' (cf. *Illusts.* 2, 7, 11) make themselves anonymous rather than characteristic, which is suitable for producing a devotional atmosphere in the relief-scene.

Secondly, such an atmosphere can evoke the direct sympathy of the viewers as devotees without separating them from the world of relief-scenes.

Finally, the viewers naturally get the freedom to appreciate 'his absence', for instance, some pilgrims offer flowers on the throne and others meditate on what occurred there long ago (cf. *Pl.* 11, *Illust.* 2). In other words, the viewers recognize from the beginning that the Buddha does not exist on the throne. It depends on their imagination whether he is regarded as present there or not. His presence is not actual and realistic but visionary and idealistic.

Therefore, in case the picture showmen had a chance to interpret the *stūpa-art* for pilgrims, the interpretation could have focused on dogmatic matters rather than narrative elements. It may mean that the *stūpa-art* had a suggestive role as a cue to talk about what was taught in the Buddhist scriptures, especially if we take into consideration its missionary effect on the pilgrims. In this sense, it is understandable that scholars have been trying to interpret the relief-scenes by means of scriptural sources.

In passing, it may not be out of context to refer to the fact that Bhārhut and Sāñcī inscriptions record the profession of '*bhāṇaka*' i.e. 'a reciter of text' who recited the scriptures to devotees in the precincts of the *stūpa*.[61] It is well known that the reciters were respectable Buddhist monks entitled '*bhadanta*'[62] who sometimes became '*navakamika*' to supervise the construction of a *stūpa*. It may be worth considering whether they had something to do with the *stūpa-art* although there is no direct data to testify it.

It is well known that many of the Bhārhut inscriptions suggest the contents of the relief-scenes. For instance, "*A(jā)tasat(u) Bhagavato vaṃdate*" (King Ajātaśatru pays reverence to the Blessed One)[63] requests the viewers to regard the scene as narrative in the absence of the Blessed One. "*Indraśāla*" (*Idasāla*)[64] suggests that Indra came to the cave to hold an interview with the Buddha (*Illust.* 11b-1, b-2). In *Illust.* 11b-1 and b-2, only one person turns his back upon the viewers and attracts the attention of his company as if the cave echoed back his voice (*Illust.* 11b-1). In this case, the viewers may have felt that they were listening to an interpreter who could reproduce 'his voice'. As compared with *Illust.* 14a, the role of personages is more suitable for a dialogue with the Buddha in spite of his absence.

In this way, the inscriptions might have suggested how to enjoy seeing the relief-scenes. Then, who would have read them for the majority of the illiterate people?[65] The sculptors, the picture-showmen, the reciters of texts, or any other specialists? In any case, it is necessary to note that even such inscriptions cannot change the essence of what is described in the absence of the Buddha. Even if someone could interpret the scene vividly, the audience would have still returned to the actual situation where they cannot find the Buddha's figure. It means that the relief-scenes are much more eloquent and significant than their inscription.

It must be regrettable if one cannot enjoy a work of art without relying on its title. In modern times, we often see the people who take more time to read the title-plate than enjoy looking at the painting itself when we visit museums and art galleries. Most of them pass by the painting soon after reading its title and explanation. However, this kind of tragedy must not have occurred among the ancient visitors who were welcome to look at the *stūpa-art* as a whole before understanding what was described in each position of the railings and the gateways. Moreover, the way in which they viewed the relief-scenes seems to have been rather flexible because the stage-settings depend on the Buddhist monuments similar to one another. For example, *Illust.* 12a-2 (The Enlightenment and the Māra's Army) and *Illust.* 13a-3, *Illust.* 10a-1 (King Prasenajit visiting the Buddha) and *Illust.* 10a-2 (King Viḍūḍabha visiting the Buddha) have the same kind of stage-setting. But the personages on stage suggest different stories. If all of them were to vanish from the spot, then only the Buddhist monuments would remain there just as seen in *Fig.* 9 a, b-1 and b-2, *Fig.* 10a-1 and a-2. It may be safe to think that sculptors portrayed the actual scenes of Buddhist edifices of the post-Mauryan period. The edifices could have become the stage where a sort of Buddhist play was shown to the visitors.

Let us see *Fig.* 11. This is a typical *Bodhi-maṇḍa* encircling the *Bodhi-tree of Śākyamuni* Buddha (cf. *Fig.* 9c-1, c-2). It tells us how ancient Buddhists tried decorating the *Bodhi-tree* under which the Enlightenment was attained by the Blessed One. On the roof of this edifice, there is an inscription which reads: "*bhagavato Sakamunino bodho*". Most of the scholars have interpreted it as 'The Enlightenment of *Śākyamuni* the Blessed One' where the invisible '*bhagavato*' should be seated on the throne. But there is another possibility of reading it as 'The *Bodhi-maṇḍa* of *Śākyamuni* the Blessed One'[66] where the devotees are paying reverence around the empty throne. Which of the two inscriptions is more acceptable? Though this depends on what the viewer wants to see, the latter appears to be more natural because of its stage-setting.

Now let us turn our eyes to *Illust.* 9. We see the winged-angels and the whistling gods praising the event of *Sambodhi*, the Enlightenment. Their feelings of rapture seem to be transmitted to the posture (*āṅgika*) of the girl dancing beside the devotees. She must be a '*devadāsī*'[67] who belongs to the temple for the purpose of performing a dance-drama (*nāṭya*) in front of the visitors.

The empty throne is strewn with flowers. Who strewed them? It was a duty of the *devadāsī* for the success of her play to kneel down and offer flowers at the altar in the centre of the stage, according to the *Nāṭyaśāstra.*[68] If the dancing girl had strewed flowers before her performance, some dance-drama should be still going on in this relief-scene, although it is not clear whether the other male devotees are playing any part with their both hands folded firmly. In any case, this scene tries to share its joyful atmosphere (*rasa*) with the viewers. It fully suggests that ancient Buddhists enjoyed a dance-drama (*nāṭya*) in the precincts of their sanctuary on the occasion of a festival. If the actors and the actresses followed the traditional rules of Indian dramaturgy, they would have made the most use of pantomime (*nṛtya*) and spoken in the style of retitativo (*pāṭya*).[69] Furthermore, the stage (*raṅga*) was often set inside the edifice so that the voices of players and the sound of music could be heard clearly even on a windy day.[70] Thus it is probable that such an indoor stage was preferred for convenience even though a drama-scene had to represent an outdoor situation.

If the sculptors had a chance to make reference to the contemporary drama-stage, they could have incorporated more creative elements into a relief-scene, free from the scriptural sources. Its uniqueness may be unfamiliar to our eyes but it is not impossible for us to interpret the subject-matter with the help of visible facts. In the next section, we will try to reproduce a Buddhist drama in *Illust.* 10a-2. As long as it is an interpretation, it must include something of our own creation apart from the historical truth. Nevertheless, it is never futile to find more possibilities of interpreting the same object of observation as the effort not only contributes to a study of early Buddhist art but also develops our sense of appreciation. In any case, it is a happy and pleasant experience to appreciate the worth of things from different angles.

(C) AN EXAMPLE OF THEATRICAL INTERPRETATION: A DRAMA IN MEMORY OF 'BHAGAVATO DHAMACAKAṂ' — A CONVERSION OF KING VIḌŪḌABHA —

1. *A Survey of the Interpretations in the Past*

(1) *Identification*: Let us see (1), (14), and (15) of 'A Table of the Theories on *Illust.* 10a-2' [(1), (2) and (3)].

The interpretations of *Illust.* 10a-2 in the past appear to be divided into two: (1) Lüders and (2) Barua, Coomaraswamy, Lippe, Craven, depending on the rendering of the fragmentary inscription and based on the analogy with another relief-scene (*Illust.* 10a-1) belonging to the same railing of Bhārhut *Stūpa*. Every scholar infers a successive relation between *Illust.* 10a-1 and a-2.[71]

Illust. 10a-1 has the inscriptions, *"Rājā Pasenaji Kosalo"* (King Prasenajit of Kosala) and *"Bhagavato Dhamacakaṃ"* (The *Dharmacakra* of the World-Honoured One). Barua identified *Illust.* 10a-1 as the scene of 'King Prasenajit's last interview with the Buddha'.[72]

In the Buddhist texts, it is well known that Prasenajit, king of Kosala very often went to Jetavana in his territory and discussed his administrative affairs with the Buddha.

When Prasenajit wanted to see the Master at Ulumpa, a country town of the *Śākya*s, he was in a state of remorse and had no piece of mind, and felt no joy in being king,[73] because of his murder of the innocent Bandhula, the commander-in-chief of Kosala.[74]

The king reached Ulumpa and went to the perfumed chamber (*gandhakuṭi*) with a few attendants including Dīrgha Kārāyana, Bandhula's nephew, the new commander-in-chief who nurtured a sense of revenge in his mind against the king's treatment of his uncle.

King Prasenajit handed the five symbols of royalty (*pāca rāja-kakudhabhaṇḍāni*)[75] to Kārāyana and alone entered the chamber where the Buddha was staying. It was a fatal moment for the king who was never to return to his throne. Kārāyana took those symbols of royalty and put Prince Viḍūḍabha on the throne.

When Prasenajit came out of the chamber after a pleasant interview with the Master, one horse and a serving woman left behind for him signified what had been done during his absence. He set out for Rājagṛha, the capital city of Magadha, in order to capture his son with the help of his nephew, King Ajātaśatru. But the city-gates were already shut and he had to lie down in a shed, exhausted by exposure to wind and sunshine. He is said to have died there.[76]

In *Illust.* 10a-1, King Prasenajit is saluting the viewers by raising a hand on the chariot (with four horses) outside and joining his palms with an attendant inside the hall as if he were perfectly innocent of his pathetic end, although the worshippers are so similar to each other that we cannot distinguish the king from his attendant. This is contradictory to the account that the king entered the chamber alone. Two of the symbols of royalty, the parasol and the yak-tall are seen, but the crown cannot be seen on his head even before his getting down from the vehicle. The heads of horses are coming out of the arch and it may proceed to the next scene, the king on his chariot. On the left side, someone is walking up to the hall, and another is coming down from the same on the other side where an elephant's head is recognizable. Therefore, the narrative proceedings of *Illust.* 10a-1 may be in a right-handed revolution. It is a typical way of describing several stages of a story in the same narrative scene.

It may safely be said that *Illust.* 10a-1 represents one of the stories of King Prasenajit of Kosala. However, it is not sure whether *Illust.* 10a-1 intends to describe King Prasenajit's last interview with the Buddha' based on the accounts of Buddhist scriptures and their commentaries.

The inscription of "*Bhagavato Dhamacakaṃ*" seems to suggest that *Illust.* 10a-1 had a role in telling as to what the Venerable One taught the king as if the wheel of Truth had been turned round beautifully.[77] Two devotees in the hall are standing together symmetrically and look as if they are listening to the sound of the wheel. At least, these persons would have shared the same feelings with the viewers of those days by knowing what is described in the relief-scene.

Illust. 10a-1 belongs to a collection of narrative scenes thought out for the purpose of preaching the Buddhist doctrines by medium of a sculptural dramaturgy (cf. next section 'A Possibility of New Interpretation'). In early Buddhist art, all the narrative scenes do not make a continuous series describing the teachings of the Buddha although a scroll of such narrative series was made in later periods with the evolution of the Buddha image.

However, as far as *Illust.* 10a-1 and *Illust.* 10a-2 are concerned, most of the scholars ['Table' (1), (2) and (3)] see a successive relation between the two according to the *Bhaddasāla-jātaka* (No. 465) and the *Dhammapada-Aṭṭhakathā*. The pieces of Buddhist literature show an episode preceding the massacre of *Śākya* clan of Kapilavastu by King Viḍūḍabha who ascended the throne by conspiring with the commander-in-chief, Dirgha Kārāyana, as mentioned before.

It was on the way to Kapilavastu. The new king of Kosala, Viḍūḍabha was hurriedly marching towards the capital city with revengeful feelings against the Śākya clan as his maternal relatives.

The beginning of this tragedy can be found in a request of King Prasenajit to the Śākyas. The king wanted a *Śākyan* daughter to be his queen in order to gain nearness to the Buddha and get the confidence of Buddhist monks who should have been welcome to Kosala. However, the *Śākya*s were too proud of their own pedigree to offer any daughter of noble birth in marriage to the king although their country was a dependency of Kosala. Mahānāma, the chief of *Śākya*s, played a trick by sending his daughter, Vāsabhakhattiyā whose mother was a slave-woman,[78] Nāgamuṇḍā.

It was after the birth of Prince Viḍūḍabha that King Prasenajit came to know everything about the trick of the *Śākya*s. Prasenajit withdrew all the patronage to Viḍūḍabha and his mother together with the status he had granted them, but both of them were later restored to their respective positions at the intercession of the Buddha.[79]

Prince Viḍūḍabha was destined to be insulted by those who felt an antipathy to his birth. When he was sixteen years old, he had a chance to visit Kapilavastu. The young Prince found that none of the *Śākya*s paid homage to him. Soon after his departure from Kapilavastu, one of his armed men returned there to fetch the weapon left behind and happened to hear the words of a slave-woman who was washing the seat, which Viḍūḍabha had used in the resthouse, with milk-water: "Here is the seat where sat the son of Vāsabhakhattiyā, the slave girl". The soldier asked the meaning of these words and was told about the whole conspiracy of the *Śākya*s. Prince Viḍūḍabha was informed of this matter and he was very much enraged at the insult done by the *Śākya* clan. He is said to have registered a vow, "Let them pour milk-water over the seat, I sat in, to wash it. When I will be king, I will wash the place with their heart's blood."

On the way to Kapilavastu, King Viḍūḍabha was recalling his bitter experiences and in a hurry to take revenge against the *Śākya*s. The Buddha saw destruction threatening his kin and thought "I must help my kindred". In the evening time, the sage of *Śākya* clan went to a spot near Kapilavastu and sat beneath a tree that gave scanty shade. [80]

Hard by that place, a huge and shady banyan tree stood on the boundary of

Viḍāḍabha's realms. Viḍūḍabha seeing the Master approached him and, saluting him, said,

"Why, Sir, are you sitting under so thin a tree in all this heat? Sit beneath this shady banyan, Sir." He replied,

"Let be, O King! the shade of my kindred keeps me cool."

— "The Master", thought the other, "must have come here to protect his clansmen." So he saluted the Master and returned to Śrāvastī.

Likewise it happened on the second and third time. This episode shows us the true and human sentiment of the Buddha not as the Enlightened One but as one of the members of the *Śākyas*. Furthermore, it is also a fine anecdote of King Viḍūḍabha who could be restrained thrice from marching on to Kapilavastu. On the fourth occasion, the Buddha did not intervene any more, because of the great sin committed by the *Śākya*s in poisoning a river.

In this way, the revenge of Viḍūḍabha against the *Śākya*s was carried out as he had made a vow in his boyhood. Within seven days after the massacre of the *Śākyas*, Viḍūḍabha and most of his army are said to have been washed away into the waters by the floods of the river Achirāvatī. [81]

In spite of the bloody story concerning the fate of the *Śākya*s, there still remains a moving and moralistic impression in the episode of the Master and King Viḍūḍabha in a dialogue at a spot near Kapilavastu. In case *Illust.* 10a-2 is identified as 'King Viḍūḍabha visiting the Buddha', the episode is always taken into consideration. On the other hand, the inscription of *Illust.* 10a-2 (sculptured on 'the roof of the *caitya-hall*') has been regarded as a paragraph saying that the kinsmen of the Buddha do not take the lives of others, even of the army of Kosala, even when they be dying themselves. Though there is a contradiction between the episode to be expected in *Illust.* 10a-2 and its inscription, [82] most of the scholars seem to follow the former theories uncritically [cf. 'Table' (1), (2) and (3)].

The biggest problems in identification of *Illust.* 10a-2 are as follows:

(a) The stage-setting of *Illust.* 10a-2 does not describe what the Buddha was sitting beneath a tree that gave scanty shade.

(b) It is doubtful whether the inscription describes its tragic implication in the narrative scene of *Illust.* 10a-2.

These two points have been neglected so far. It seems to suggest some peculiarity in the artistic style of *Illust.* 10a-2, and makes us doubt properly interpreting some fragments of inscription.

If we do not take the inscription into consideration, it is possible to regard *Illust.* 10a-2 as the variation of *Illust.* 10a-2 ['Table' (2) Lüders] because of the similarity between the two. At any rate, it is necessary for us to clarify the meaning of each part of *Illust.* 10a-2 ['Table' (2) - (13)] in order to identify its theme.

(2) *Theories on the components of Illust. 10a-2:* 'A Table of the Theories on *Illust.* 10a-2' [(1), (2) and (3)] shows that every scholar has a respective opinion, being influenced by the former theory of (2) (4) (6) (10) and (13) . The common point is found in (8) ; the *dharmacakra* is regarded as the preaching Buddha and some narrative scene is expected inside the hall.

On the contrary, there is no scholar who can explain the mutual relations among the components [(2) - (13)] in order to clarify the narrative meaning of *Illust.* 10a-2 as a whole. Above all, the relationship between the subject (1) and the left scene [(2), (3), (4)] is not clear as compared with the case of the right side [(9) - (13)]. As a matter of fact, it seems to be the most important problem common to all the theories in the past.

2. *A Possibility of New Interpretation*

It is time for us to reconsider *Illust.* 10a-2 as a theatrical stage on the basis of the view that some element of the relief-scene should reflect the reality of those days when sculptors were working there.

The archetype of the *caitya-hall* in *Illust.* 10a-2 can be seen in another relief, *Illust.* 8b-1 (cf. 'Table' Coomaraswamy, Lippe).[83] The detailed depiction seems to suggest that this kind of hall was actually built in ancient times. In fact, it is not difficult to find a similar style of architecture in the early Buddhist *caitya-hall* at Bedusā (first century BC) and other places in India.

If the scenery inside the *caitya-hall* reflects the scene of worship familiar to ancient Buddhists, it is not necessary to make a connection with some narrative meaning. It seems that the setting of personages in a symmetrical way (cf. *Illust.* 9 and *Illust.* 10a-1) was a well-known device of composition. The worshippers gaze at the happenings in the scene of *Illust.* 10a-2 together with the viewers. Such an inseparable situation between the viewers and the personages on stage is one of the most important elements of ancient dramaturgy.

(1) *The tragic elements wiped out of Illust. 10a-2:* In the context of the Bhārhut sculptures that are filled with praise for the Buddha and his Deeds, it is difficult to expect any tragic element in *Illust.* 10a-2, even though it has something to do with the story of the *Śākyas* mentioned earlier.

The first notable point is found in the right scene. Two noble men are approaching the viewers' side by chariot. The person under the umbrella appears to be a king. He puts his left hand on the shoulder of his charioteer in order to give some command. The right hand is raised solemnly to indicate his intention (cf. *Illust.* 10a-1). From his meek attitude, it is imaginable that he has directs the charioteer to restrain the motion of the chariot [cf. 'Table' Barua (10)]. Two animals with raised hooves are still at a fast trot [cf. 'Table' Craven (13)]. Most of the scholars regard these animals as horses ['Table' (13)]. But their curved horns and massive bodies indicate that they are bullocks, that is to say, 'the king' is on the chariot drawn by bullocks.

According to the *Arthaśāstra*,[84] the king's army consists of infantrymen, cavalrymen, chariots, and elephant corps.[85] The chariot was always drawn by horses. In case they did not have enough horses to organize a corps, bullocks were used together with horses.[86] The main force was the elephant corps.[87] The vehicle of the king in the forefront of his army[88] was an elephant with cavalrymen, or a chariot.[89] However, there is no reference to the role of the chariot drawn by bullocks, and even to the meaning of the king mounted on such a chariot. In any case, it is clear that there is no intention to fight once the king mounts the bullocks' chariot.

On the other hand, the left scene describes the rear of the passing through the arch and the mahout refraining his elephant from breaking a branch.

After viewing both the sides of *Illust.* 10a-2, it seems that the sculptor is showing us the turning of three kinds of animals: a horse, an elephant, and two bullocks. Therefore, a story of *Illust.* 10a-2 may narrate itself in a right-handed rotation (*Illust.* 10a-1).

From the above observation, it is still possible to identify *Illust.* 10a-2 as 'King Viḍūḍabha visiting the Buddha' because 'the king on the bullocks' chariot' can play a role of King Viḍūḍabha who gave up marching on Kapilavastu; besides, the meaning of the horse and the mahout is made clear *vis-à-vis* the act of King Viḍūḍabha.

As referred to in the earlier section [1. (1)] 'King Viḍūḍabha visiting the Buddha' tells about the virtue of the Buddha who tried to protect his own kinsmen against the enemy. *Bhaddasālajātaka* no. 465 (*Jātakaṭṭhaṇṇanā*) introduces this episode as one of the narratives of '*ñātatthacariyā*' (good deeds towards the kinsmen).[90] Even King Viḍūḍabha is treated as a hero who could refrain from invading Kapilavastu. The narrative scene leads itself to a happy end in spite of the fact that it is a prelude to the massacre of the *Śākyas*.

If this interpretation is true of *Illust.* 10a-2, it may be said that we are blessed with a good chance to see a precious scenery of early Buddhist art. In the illustrations of Buddhist literature in later periods, we cannot find any example dealing with the same subject as this illustration.

(2) *An experiment on stage:* The narrative scenes of early Buddhist art are based on

the scenes of worship at Buddhist places. Even the narrative elements are suggestive because of depicting some Buddhist monuments as the main objects of sculpture. Therefore, the scene itself is not 'a story-teller' but 'a technician' who is good at making the viewers tell a story in their own words. It enables us to realize the reason why *Illust.* 10a-2 can produce several interpretations. In other words, the value of *Illust.* 10a-2 largely depends upon how the viewers see it rather than anything special in the scene itself.

First, the hall of *dharmacakra* draws one's attention. Inside of it, the preaching of Buddha (Pāli: *dhammacakkavattana*) is recalled and praised by worshippers. It is the scene outside the hall that informs about the circumstances of his preaching.

a) The left side: Both the horse and the elephant are useful animals for battle. It is possible for both to represent a state of mind of King Viḍūḍabha who was hurriedly marching towards Kapilavastu because of his grudge against the *Śākya* clan. The king on the chariot drawn by 'the horse' catches sight of the Buddha under 'the tree' and approaches there (the horse passing through the entrance of the *caitya-hall*). The Buddha soothes his furious feelings of revenging upon the *Śākya*s with the words of worrying about the kinsmen, and the king loses fighting spirit. The psychological process has been expressed successfully by 'the elephant' whose intent to break a branch from the tree is restrained because of the mahout's training. According to the *Dhammapada* 326, this act is comparable to the restraint on one's mind: "This mind of mine went formerly wandering about as it liked, as it listed, as it pleased; but I shall now hold it in thoroughly, as the rider who holds the hook holds in the furious elephant".[91]

As far as 'the tree' is concerned, it is said to have been 'the tree that gave scanty shade'. But we cannot know what kind of tree was standing there, although the trees of *Nyagrodha* can be found near the tree.

The tree in *Illust.* 10a-2 is not the *Nyagrodha.* It may be the tree of *Pāṭali* (with purple flowers) or *Aśoka* (with red flowers), if the foliation is observed carefully. However, it is not easy to infer the colour from its present condition.

Anyway, the scene on the left side is impressed by the vigorous motions of the mahout and his elephant. It is certain that there is some significance in the suggestive expression.

b) The right side: The chariot drawn by the bullocks indicates that King Viḍūḍabha gallantly gave up invading Kapilavastu. He is on his way to his kingdom after shifting to the bullock's vehicle. In passing, it may be pointed out that the personal name of the Buddha *Śākyamuni* was *'Gotama'* (the best of the bulls). Two bullocks in *Illust.* 10a-2 have big pompons on their heads. Is it thinkable that the ornaments decorate the virtue of the Buddha who tried protecting his kinsmen against the enemy, or praise the courage of King Viḍūḍabha who was considerate of the Buddha's mind? It is not difficult to regard the details even like those prompons as meaningful for those who describe the story of 'King Viḍūḍabha visiting the Buddha' in their own minds.

King Viḍūḍabha is notorious in Buddhist accounts for the massacre of the *Śākyas*, but at least in *Illust.* 10a-2 he is treated as a sympathetic person. His right hand raised up with confidence looks as if it were a response towards the viewers of *Illust.* 10a-2 who were satisfied with the happy end of its narration.

(c) The centre: The eyes of the viewers are naturally led to the centre again after wandering over the left and right sides of *Illust.* 10a-2. Here is the space inside the *caitya-hall* open to one's liberal thoughts about the narrative scene. Time is not flowing away because of one ruminating the narration. The viewers are given the experience of visiting the hall and racalling the story of *Illust.* 10a-2 in their own minds. Therefore, it is natural that there are various interpretations regarding the men and the women with folded hands who are around the *dharmacakra* on the throne [Table ⑧].

The empty throne is strewn with the flowers of auspice. The large central wheel is embellished with a fine garland, under the umbrella festooned with flowers. Even on the wheel, the design of flowers is seen clearly.

What is the meaning of the floral designs? For one of the possible interpretations, we can refer to the story of 'King Viḍūḍabha Visiting the Buddha' which is introduced as one of the commentary narrations on *Dhammapada* 47: "Death carries off a man who is gathering flowers, and whose mind is distracted, as flood carries off a sleeping village."[92] This passage reminds us of the end of King Viḍūḍabha who was washed away by the flood waters of the river Achirāvatī. The king's mind must have been quite distracted soon after the massacre of the *Śākyas*.

Furthermore, *Dhammapada* 53 says, "As many kinds of wreaths can be made from a heap of flowers, so many good things may be achieved by a mortal when once he is born."[93] If the similes of flowers in the Scripture were familiar to ancient Buddhists, the floral designs must have been significant in the context of stage-settings, as found in *Illust.* 10a-2.

And if it is allowed to regard the two women kneeling down at the throne as '*devadāsīs*' (cf. earlier section '(B) Its Dramatic Essence'), the flowers on the empty throne must have been scattered by their hands at the beginning of a dance-drama for the purpose of praying for the success of their performances. If this interpretation is pertinent to *Illust.* 10a-2, there should remain the reality of the absence of the Buddha who is expected to be seated on the throne. The personages on stage would be able to show us what is happening in the scene of *Illust.* 10a-2 if they could move and speak their own parts. However, to our regret, we cannot see their 'next movement' because they are always made motionless in the world of stone-works. Nevertheless, it is very important to give sufficient attention to the postures maintained by the personages as they give us much information about the cultural and religious elements of ancient India.

3. *A Comment on the Interpretation from the Artistic Aspects.*

If we try to interpret all the narrative scenes of early Buddhist art in the same way as done in the case of *Illust.* 10a-2, we would experience some hesitation in touching various meanings of the ancient works of art unfamiliar to us in modern times. Actually, it is almost impossible to appreciate the ancient work just as the ancient people gazed at it. Then, what is the significance of our study? We have only to study it from our own point of view and the way we want to. In the case of early Buddhist art, the most notable point to be discussed is the absence of the Buddha image, because it must look strange to those who take it for granted that the Buddha image is present in the works of Buddhist art.

How to make the modern people accept 'the absence of the Buddha image' as naturally as possible? One way is interpretation from the artistic point of view especially as a theatrical situation peculiar to early Buddhist art. A theatrical interpretation relieves our mind of the thought that the Buddha must be present in the narrative scene even in a symbolic or invisible way because the narrative belongs to the Buddha's period.

In the theatre, a drama can go on without the actual presence of the Buddha. If there is a good device to produce a narrative situation without any Buddha figures, it should be enough to entertain the audience, and it must be much more realistic and suggestive as the performing art.

When we see the drama on stage in the relief-scenes of early Buddhist art, time flows into our side out of the world of ancient stone-work. Our consciousness of 'the drama' must be different from that of ancient people. But, at least, the stone-work can give us the same visual impact on human minds beyond the flow of time. Accepting an experience out of the impact as it is, is the best way for us to appreciate 'the absence of the Buddha image' in as lively a manner as possible. If we can enjoy seeing the drama there, we will be very close to the ancient Buddhists ignorant of portraying the Buddha himself. It may end in a simulation to satisfy ourselves. Any kind of trial is useful as long as we wish to approach the truth from various aspects including our own experiences in observing the object of study.

An approach to the 'absence of the Buddha image' in the theatrical way is not only an interpretation but also a result of finding out the theatre-like composition of relief-scenes discussed in Chapter II, 2.

So long as 'the absence of the Buddha image' belongs to a part of artistic works, it is impossible to understand it separately from the context of artistic expression.

The artistic expression does not always reproduce a historical or scriptural account, or rather it often prefers to deviate from reality. The preference produces various works on the same subject. The evolution of the fine arts is intrinsically a result of this.

Therefore, it is necessary for us to derive an artistic effect of 'the absence of the Buddha image' on the whole relief-scene from the facts to be seen there. What becomes possible and effective by the 'absence of the Buddha image'? This question should be recalled whenever we enquire into its meaning. Where the artistic aspects are concerned, it is possible to answer as follows:

(a) The absence of the Buddha image enables the viewers to concentrate on the narrative significance without being distracted by the solemn presence of the Buddha image. In other words, the sculptors can focus on the cream of a narrative instead of trying to authorize the figure of the Buddha in keeping with the surroundings.

(b) Because of (a), the absence of the Buddha image is effective on those who want to read something religious in the narrative scene. It may sound paradoxical that the narrative scene becomes more religious for lack of 'the Buddha'. But if someone wants to know about the teaching of the Buddha, he must listen to the words of the Buddha rather than looking at the Buddha's figure. In the case of fine arts, the words of the Buddha can be expressed by borrowing narrative scenes. In early Buddhist art, the narrative scenes do not depict the Buddha's figure just as the Buddha had never described his physical characteristics. In this sense, 'the absence of the Buddha image' can be evaluated not only artistically but also religiously.

Furthermore, (a) and (b) do not end in the answers given above. Each of them gives us a hint to interpret 'the absence of the Buddha image' from the political aspects in the following section. We will make reference to the Aśokan inscriptions as the source of knowing about the basic policy of King Aśoka who must have been a great patron of early Buddhist art.

3. The Political Aspects

After the death of Buddha *Śākyamuni,* his teaching (*Buddha-dharma*) was preserved by his disciples and his relics (*Buddha-śarīra*) were entrusted to the lay-believers. In the period of the Mauryan dynasty, a genius in politics became a devout Buddhist after conquering a region of Eastern India. For the governor, the *stūpa*, the container of *Buddha-śarīra,* did not just symbolize the reconstruction of the physical body of the Buddha; it also represented *'Dharma',* the political ideal of his empire. In this context, it is imaginable that the *stūpa* came to include a governmental role in the society of ancient India. The act of *stūpa*-worship mostly belonged to Buddhist people, but its social effect on other religious peoples must have been considerable for those who had to maintain public order to govern so many regions of the empire.

It is well known that King Aśoka, the third ruler of the Mauryan dynasty, is said to have built eighty-four thousand *stūpas* (or *vihāras*).[94] He went on a pilgrimage with the elder Upagupta to honour all the places where the Buddha had lived and to set up a *caitya*, a commemorative monument, at each of the places. It was not only for himself but as a favour to future pilgrims so that they might retrace and remember the events of the Buddha's life. The pilgrimage was named *'dhaṃmayattā'*, etc.[95] in his edicts; however this *'dhaṃma'* does not indicate the *Buddha-dharma* exactly but means the moral of Indian society from the ancient times (*porāna pakiti*).[96] The *Buddha-dharma* might have been not only his personal faith but also a good aid to constituting his policy (*dhamma*). But, the thoughts of his edicts were not Buddhistic but common to various peoples in the territory of his empire.

As one of the unique administrative reform of King Aśoka, it is interesting to refer to the establishment of *'Dhaṃmamahāmātta'*[97] (Skt. *Dharmamahā-mātra*), one of whose duties was the administration of religious orders: of (Buddhist) *Saṃgha*, *Babhana* (Brāhmaṇa), *Ājīvika, Nigaṃtha* (Jain), etc. The concord [98] of these orders was indispensable to grasp the public because a person must have belonged to one of these religious sects in those days. The *Dhaṃmamahāmātta* in charge of Buddhist *Saṃgha* administered the meeting of Buddhists (*uposatha*), accompanied by a lay-believer (*upāsaka*), for the purpose of confirming whether the edict was well-observed by them.[99] The edict warns nuns and monks not to break up the *Saṃgha*.

The duty of the *Dhaṃmamahāmātta* was to proclaim religious messages[100] of King Aśoka to the people of his empire. It is notable that the animal-shaped capitals of the Aśokan pillars are the oldest example of Indian art related to the beginning of Buddhist art. Some of them were erected in Buddhist centres: Rummindei (Lumbinī), Sārnāth, Sāncī, and Amarāvatī. It is not difficult to imagine the Buddhist people listening to the Aśokan edicts proclaimed by the *Dhaṃmamahāmātta* with their both hands folded firmly, which reminds us of the relief-scenes of early Buddhist art (cf. *Illusts*. 3b, 7b).

If each of the relief-scenes had depicted a Buddha image, their significance would have been Buddhistic only. But in fact, there is no figure of the Buddha anywhere. It makes early Buddhist art universal in appeal — that is, significant to any kind of people and country.

In the edicts, King Aśoka often desires that his peoples may be provided with complete welfare and happiness both in this world and the next.[101] How to achieve both?

He commands his people to observe any moral act: cessation of slaughter of animals; non-violence towards living beings; proper treatment of relatives, of Brāhmaṇas and *Śramaṇas*; obedience to mother and father and to the seniors.[102] These acts and such others are called *Dharma-maṁgalas,* the ceremonial of *Dharma*.[103] Other kinds of ceremonies are all of doubtful effect, but the *Dharma-maṁgalas* will produce endless merit in the world beyond even if one does not achieve the object in this world. The *Dharma-maṁgalas* is not of time.[104] It is adaptable to all religions having the views of the other world beyond one's lifetime, i.e., even foreign religions, Judaism and Zoroastrianism.[105]

It is interesting to note a reference to the idea of the Last Judgement in one of the Aramaic edicts: ". . . And of people who are devoted to duty (*dharmayuta*), there is certainly no judgement (*vicāraṇa*) (awaiting them) in the other world (*paratra*)".[106] From a political viewpoint, the reference to 'the other world' is very suitable to grasp the public feeling. King Aśoka shows his genius in policy here. Moreover he states that the obedience to *Dharma* is for the hereafter[107] and in order that everyone may be free from confinement (or bondage, viz., sin)[108] of this world. In other words, his edicts expect the people to practice '*Dharma*' in order to produce the greatest fruit in the world beyond. It is impossible even for the emperor to peep into the next world. But it is helpful for his policy to command his people to do good deeds for the afterlife, as it enables him to govern a lot of districts of his empire without forcing the people to observe his policy under his personal name, Aśoka.

King Aśoka gives a name to himself, "*Devānaṃpriya priyadassi rāja*"[109] (the king who is loved by gods and has kind features). The name of *Devānaṃpriya* is suitable for the king whose edicts command obedience to *Dharma* for the hereafter.

In the context of Indian religions, enjoyment in the world of heaven as a result of one's good deeds[110] has its origin in the thoughts of Brahmanism. The merits of good deeds are the support for people in the next world.[111] This thought can also be found easily in some of the oldest Buddhist scriptures and in the inscriptions of Buddhist donors who were concerned with the construction of *stūpas*, etc. To take rebirth in heaven (*sadgatiḥ*)[112] was the goal of life for those who believed in the world of *saṃsāra.*

In the edicts, King Aśoka refers to the fact that he visited the *Saṁgha* to exert himself sincerely as a lay-disciple (*upāsaka*). During his exertion, what was going on in the land of India? He states with confidence: " . . . Thus during this time the people in *Jambudvīpa* who had remained unassociated with the gods became associated with the gods."[113] This passage has many interpretations, but the most probable ones are (1) Indian people who lacked faith in gods had become religious, or worshippers of gods, and (2) the strife of gods and their worshippers (because of the discord among sects) had ceased in India.[114] Both the interpretations are eventually suggesting that King Aśoka's closer ties with the Buddhist *Saṁgha* had become a great stimulation for religious minds in India. Therefore, his visit to the *Saṁgha* included a sort of propaganda for the policy of his *Dharma,* apart from his personal faith in Buddhism.

In early Buddhist art, the physical features of men and god are hard to distinguish. For example, *Illust.* 13a-2 and a-3 may represent figures of gods as well as men according to their narrative sources. There is no device to establish the figures of gods. Men and gods are always mingled with each other to praise the great deeds of the Buddha who had already deceased long ago. In every relief-scene, human figures seem to express that men are associated with gods in this world. At least, this visible fact is not contrary to the Aśokan policy.

King Aśoka was not only a genius in politics but also a great propagator of religious festivals. The edicts tell us that he exhibited various performances to the people: "the sight of the cars of the gods, of elephants, masses of fire and other heavenly shows."[115] It is told that "the sound of the war drum has become the call (not to arms but) to Dharma."[116]

It reminds us of the relief-scenes of Bhārhut and Sāñcī depicting gods (?) beating the drums (*Illust.* 11a-2), whistling (*Illust.* 9) and playing on musical instruments (*Illust.* 4c). Heavenly scenes are often found here and there.[117] The celestial spectacles both in festivals and fine arts must have been very influential in demonstrating that the practice of morality in this world will produce great merits in heaven, the world beyond.

Thus some of the characteristics of early Buddhist art are in keeping with the Aśokan policy of viewing obedience to *Dharma* as the morality of Indian society. But this political viewpoint does not end in a mere inference, because there are several examples to show that the memory of King Aśoka remains clearly in early Buddhist art. We can see some of them in the Sāñcī sculptures.

(a) First, let us see *Illust.* 4a, King Aśoka visiting the *Rāmagrāma stūpa*. According to the *Aśokāvadāna,* this relief-scene should narrate as follows: King Aśoka went to the *Rāmagrāma stūpa* being worshipped by the *nāgas*[118] in order that he might take *Buddha śarīra* from the *stūpa* to build more *stūpa*s in his territory. The *nāga*s escorted the king to their palace to show him the treasures but never surrendered the *Buddha śarīra* to him, because they wanted to continue honouring their *stūpa*. Understanding what was in their minds, King Aśoka departed from Rāmagrāma empty-handed.[119]

In *Illust*. 4a it appears that the figure of King Aśoka occurs twice: on the chariot and on the left side of the *stūpa*. It is a well-known device of ancient fine arts to make the same person appear more than twice for the purpose of describing a process of time. King

Aśoka bows his head in reverence for the Deceased One whose relics are enshrined in the *stūpa*. The family members of *nāga-rāja* are watching this scene in a modest way. It is important to take note of the authority of the *stūpa* that makes even the Mauryan emperor bow his head. The emperor's humility may transfer his dignity to the *stūpa*, but as a result, he comes to receive all the merits of public peace and order produced by the religious acts of *stūpa*-worship. It is quite an ingenious idea for any ruler who wants to rule his people without using force.

Let us turn our eyes to *Illust.* 13a-3 where King Aśoka is worshipping the Bodhi tree. The king dismounts from the elephant and joins his both hands towards the *Bodhi-maṇḍa* where the *Bodhi* tree is encircled by the *caitya-hall*. It is known that King Aśoka regarded the *Bodhi-tree* as the Buddha himself.

"When I looked at the king of trees, I knew that even now I was looking at the Self-Existent Master."[120]

After the king had finished marking and honouring all the places of pilgrimage, he returned to Bodh Gayā where his faith was aroused by the Bodhi tree. As he treated it just like he did the queen, the real queen Tiṣyarakṣitā had even tried killing the '*Bodhi*' out of jealousy. When the '*Bodhi*' was drying up, the king is said to have declared that he should expire as if he were the '*Bodhi*'.[121]

Thus the Bodhi tree was not only like the Buddha but also like the king himself. According to the *Mahāvaṃsa*, Aśoka bestowed his own kingship upon the Bodhi tree.[122] Though the kingship might be bestowed upon the tree ceremoniously, it goes without saying that Aśoka exercised kingship 'on behalf of the tree'. The tree stood at the site of the Buddha's Enlightenment and so it can symbolize the *Buddha-dharma*. As Aśoka exercised the *Bodhi* tree's kingship, it is reasonable to assume that he had an epithet, '*dharmarāja*'. The same logic is applicable to the relation between Aśoka and the eighty-four thousand *stūpa*s most commonly called *dharmarājikā*s,[123] i.e., '(monuments) pertaining to the King of *Dharma*'.

(b) Secondly, we shall see *Illust.* 13a-2, 'The Great Departure of Prince Siddhārtha from Kapilavastu'. According to the previous interpretations, the invisible Prince is on horseback under the royal umbrella and he dismounts (at the right end of the lintel). His attendant, Chandaka worships the Prince at his feet and goes back to Kapilavastu with the horse Kaṇṭhaka. The figure of the horse raised up by the hands of people can be recognized five times: from the gate (*toraṇa*) to the footprints (*Buddhapada*). The last horse is not raised up any more as the Prince had already left the horseback.

The *dharmacakra*s are engraved on the large footprints, although the Prince has not attained the Enlightenment. For the people in later periods, even the footprints of Prince

Siddhārtha could be taken as the *Buddhapada*. In the centre, there is a *jambū* tree under which the Prince experienced the First Meditation before the Great Departure. It is surrounded by devotees with familiarity. From the balconies of the palace, many people seem to be enjoying seeing this procession of 'the Great Departure'.

As far as the visible facts are concerned, it is much more natural to view *Illust.* 13a-2 representing a scene of the festival in connection with the Great Departure. In this case, we can point out its political significance on the analogy of a curious festival held by Harṣa, a north Indian emperor of the seventh century. The process of this festival is described by the Chinese pilgrim Hsüan-tsang.[124]

In the period of King Harṣa, the great quinquennial festival (*pañcavārṣika*) was celebrated as well as Aśoka had done in order to outdo him at *dāna* (alms; offering) in honour of the Buddhist *Saṃgha*. The story of the Great Departure, in which Prince Siddhārtha divests himself of the accoutrements of royalty, "became a model for the Buddhist ordination ceremony, with its ritual forsaking of royal symbols at the moment of the candidate's entrance into the monkhood. Unlike the Buddha, however (and unlike most *bhikṣus*), Harṣa does not remain a monk; he instead reacquires the royal garments and ornaments, is recrowned, and becomes once again a great *dhamarāja-cakravartin*".[125] It was a large-scale performance of the king's self-dramatization to renew and re-emphasize his kingship before the eyes of the people.

During the performance the King could have enjoyed two types of experiences: (1) a sacred devotion for the *Saṃgha* by his own entrance into monkhood, and (2) a secular ecstasy in being recrowned as a great *dharmarāja-cakravartin.* (1) can accumulate a great virtue in preparation for (2), and (2) can authorize the *Saṃgha* from the side of kingship. Thus (1) and (2) are reciprocal to each other. As a result, the ceremony of the Great Departure is nothing but one of the political rituals to impress the divine right of the King on those who come to see the Buddhistic drama performed by the King himself.

Let us see *Illust.* 13a-2 once again. There is no figure of the king who should play a part of Prince Siddhārtha. Therefore, it may be impossible to regard *Illust.*13a-2 as the scene of the royal ceremony as mentioned above. Nevertheless, the part of Chandaka as the attendant of Prince Siddhārtha can be performed by the King to show his adoration to the *Buddha*, the *Dharma* and the *Samgha*. In this case, Chandaka is the person who faithfully attends on his Master on horseback. At the place where the Prince enters into monkhood, Chandaka becomes the first person who pays reverence to his Master as the Buddha to be. The posture of Chandaka bending himself towards the footprints seems to express the same emotion as the King in *Illust.* 4a. Moreover, it is also important to find *Illust.* 13a-2 just above *Illust.* 13a-3 describing King Aśoka visiting the *Bodhi-maṇḍa* where the former Prince of *Śākyas* became the Buddha after six or seven years since he had experienced the Great Departure. This is not accidental but intentional. In this context, it is fully possible to see King Aśoka in the image of Chandaka of *Illust.* 13a-2.

It seems that *Illust.* 4a, *Illust.* 13a-2 and *Illust.* 13a-3 include a sort of political significance which is more explicit here than in other relief-scenes.

(c) Finally, the memory of King Aśoka can be found in several decorative motifs of peacock (*mayūra*) and pillar (Aśokan pillar?).

The peacock is the dynastic symbol of the Mauryas.[126] The peacock motif is seen in both the edges of the bottom lintels of southern and eastern gateways.

The pillar's motifs appear independently as the decoration on the pillars (*Illust.* 7b, *Illust.* 13b-1, *Illust.* 13b-2). Those pillars are surmounted by the capitals of lions and *dharmacakras*. It suggests that the Aśokan pillar still had some social effect in the period of the Sātavāhana king Śātakarṇi-I who patronized the Sāñcī sculpture.The Aśokan politics must have been helpful for other rulers in later periods because of its moral universality. In this sense, even the motif of *triratna*, the symbol of the *Buddha*, the *Dharma* and the *Saṃgha*, seems to symbolize the social order of those days, although King Aśoka, as an *upāsaka*, had confessed his faith in the *triratna*.[127] It is interesting to find the figures of the king and his queens, etc. (*Illust.* 8a-2) just below the scene of the *Bodhi-maṇḍa* whose inside is authorized by the presence of *triratna* on the throne (*Illust.* 8a-1). It is not easy to identify the king (Aśoka, or one of the other rulers?) but it is clear that the Buddhist faith was formally approved by the royal authority.

From the issues raised in this section, it can be seen that the emphasis on *Dharma* in Aśokan edicts was influential in early Buddhist art. As for its relation with the absence of the Buddha image, it may be said: at least, for the ruler's eyes, the absence of the Buddha image naturally emphasized the impersonal essence of *Dharma*, not the personal presence of the Buddha. This situation was more helpful for his policy to be carried out beyond the people's preference for different religious leaders.

However, once the Buddha image began to be worshipped by devotees as if it were alive and merciful to worshippers, the ruler could not expect the people to medidate on *Dharma* only. As the ruler could not stop their doing so any more, or rather, he began to think how to make good use of the people's devotional acts before the Buddha image. In the case of King Harṣa, he set up an image of the Buddha in a thatched temple on the first day of the Great Quinquennial Festival, and the largest quantity of precious goods were given away as alms. But he had to install other images of the god *Āditya* (Viṣṇu) and the god *Īśvara* (Śiva) day after day in order to renew his act of almsgiving.[128] It means that the King needed to show those who belonged to different religious faiths that their respective images were being worshipped.

Therefore, the absence of the Buddha image is much more flexible to be approached and dealt with by any ruler who wants to refer to the *Buddha-dharma* for political purposes.

King Aśoka did not erect his own tomb (*stūpa*) but constructed a number of *stūpa*s of *Buddha-śarīra* not only for the Buddhists but also for those who prompted the growth of their own faith[129] by associating with those *stūpa*s as the '*dharmarājikā*s'. The early Buddhist art characterized by the absence of the Buddha image seems to have taken over the Aśokan spirit of offering the *stūpa*s and their decorative arts for benefit of the people. The absence of the Buddha image had been fully accepted and enjoyed by both the rulers and their people for a long time until the birth of the Buddha image, because of its ability to convey the *Dharma* itself (as the social rule) without any specific image in human form — which tends to divert one's eyes from the *Dharma* to be focused on.

The absence of the Buddha image itself is a sort of abstract and transparent space recognizable in the relief-scene as a whole. But the most orthodox expression of the Buddha's absence is 'the empty throne', usually represented together with *Bodhi-trees* (ex. *Illust.* 6), *dharmacakras* (ex. *Illust.* 3a-1, a-2) and *triratnas* (ex. *Illust.* 8a-1, c). The throne means the ruler's seat both in the secular and the religious world. The ruler is the centre of his people gathering around him. In the world of religions, the ruler does not always show himself in a visible manner especially if he belongs to something divine beyond human ideas. His throne may look empty to human eyes, but it has some sacred significance. In the case of the Buddhist world, what is the meaning of 'the empty throne'? How about the other religious worlds? Are there any categories of 'the empty throne' in Comparative Religion? Is it possible to point out the modernity of 'the empty throne' in early Buddhist art in order that modern people may discover a possibility of peaceful dialogue between Buddhism and other religions warning against idol worship (idolatry)? The next chapter deals with these questions. It is important for us to tackle each one of them especially for the purpose of showing that 'an enquiry into the absence of the Buddha image in early Buddhist art' is not limited only to the field of Buddhist studies.

Notes

1. Cf. *DN*, II, pp. 140-41.
2. Foucher has much to say about the early Buddhist situation where nobody had a custom to make and worship the Buddha image. But, he regards such a custom as the "long habit" which "always prevented them from breaking openly with traditional usage and showing the Buddha otherwise than symbolically". He thinks that "the old methods . . . no longer

met the requirement of the new generations" (*MS*, I, p. 193), and never tries to think that "the old methods" must have been significant enough to satisfy the spiritual life of ancient Buddhists.

Cf. Foucher, *Les débuts de l'art bouddhique*, (JA, 1911, p. 61; Eng. tr. in *The Beginnings of Buddhist Art*, London, 1914. p. 7), Foucher, *L'art greco-bouddhique du Gāndhāra*, II-1, Paris, 1918, p. 364.

3. Coomaraswamy, *The Origin of the Buddha Image*, Art Bulletin, Vol. 9, no. 4 (1926-27); reprint (New Delhi, 1972), p. 7.

   In later periods, some religious images of serpent divinities (*nāga, nāgin*) and tree-spirits (*yakṣa, yakṣinī*) in human forms appeared in the history of Indian art, which are to be seen in early Buddhist art, as well as Indra and Brahmā. They are treated as the guardians of Buddhism (*dharmapāla*). Above all, the image of a *yakṣa* is said to be connected with the origin of the Buddha image. Cf. Coomaraswamy, *Yakṣa,* 2 parts, Washington, 1928, 1931.

   Cf. J.N. Banerjea, *The Development of Hindu Iconography,* (2nd ed., Calcutta. 1956, pp. 36ff) tells about the appearance of various god images in post-Vedic periods. K.C. Chatterji, *Patañjali's Mahābhāṣya,* Calcutta, 1957, Preface p. 2, and B.N. Puri, *Indian in the time of Patanjali*, Bombay, 1957, p. 182 tell that the image of god (*arcā*) had already been made and sold in the period of Mauryan dynasty.

4. Cf. Sinha, B.C., *Glorious Art of the Śuṅga Age*, Durga Publications, Delhi, 1985, p. 54.
5. Cf. *Ṛg veda.*
6. *MS*, I, p. 248.
7. Peter Harvey, "Venerated Objects and Symbols of Early Buddhism", p. 68 (*Symbols in Art and Religion,* ed. by Karel Werner, Motilal Banarsidass Publishers, Delhi, 1991).
8. *Sn*. 454, *Udv*. 11. 13-14, etc.
9. Translated by Rev. Daniel Gogerly, Wesleyan missionary in Ceylon, in 1846. *Sacred Books of the Buddhists* Vol. II, ed. by F. Max Müller, the Pali Text Society, Oxford, 1992, p. 54.
10. Cf. *Brahma-Jāla Sutta,* 71.
11. Benjamin Rowland interprets '*parinirvāṇa*' as 'disappearance into a realm of invisibility' (*Encyclopedia of World Art,* Vol. II, 1971, p. 711).
12. Cf. Acts 1.9.
13. Vincent A. Smith, *A History of Fine Art in India and Ceylon*, Oxford, 1911, p. 79.
14. Gangoly, O.C., *The Antiquity of Buddha Image; The Cult of the Buddha,* OZ, 1938, pp. 43-44.
15. Acts 2. 1-4.
16. Ex. *Amitābha* Buddha of the *Sukhāvatī-Vyūha* (Western Paradise of the Buddha *Amitābha*) and *Śākyamuni* Buddha of the *Saddharmapuṇḍarīkasūtra*.
17. Translated by V. Fausböll, *The Sacred Books of the East,* Vol. 10, Part II, *Sutta-Nipāta* (V. *Pārāyanavagga,* 7. *Upasīvamānavapukkhā*), Motilal Banarsidass, Delhi, 1992, pp. 189-190.

18. Cf. *DN* [*Brahma-Jāla Sutta* 71(44)], p. 53 '. . . from rebirth comes death, and grief, lamentation, pain, sorrow, and despair.'
19. *DN* (*Brahma-Jāla Sutta*, 73).
20. Zimmer, *The Art of Indian Asia*, Vol. 1, New York, 1955, pp. 61-62.
21. Snellgrove (ed.) *The Image of the Buddha*, UNESCO, Vikas Publishing House, New Delhi, 1978, p. 24.
22. Cf. *MN*, II, p. 197.
23. Cf. *Dhp* 184.
24. Cf. *Madhyāntavibhāga-bhāṣya*.
25. Cf. *MN*, III, p. 72, '*loka-uttara*'.
26. Takata, *The Origin of the Buddha Image* (*Butsuzō no Kigen*, in Japanese edition), Iwanami Shoten, Tokyo, 1967, pp. 44, 62.
27. It is interesting to compare it with Exodus 20.4 and Deuteronomy 4.16, 5.8, etc.
28. *Taishō*, Vol. 2, p. 657. Translated by the author.
    「如來身者清淨無穢、 受諸天気、 為是人所造耶、 此亦不可思議 . . . 所以然者、 如來身者不可造作、

    非諸天所及 . . . 如來身不可模則、 不可言長言短、 如是佛境界不可思議」。
29. Ibid., p. 664. Translated by the author.
    「於欲界中最尊第一、 天中之上、 七財具足、 諸天人自然梵生、 亦無与等、 亦不可像貌」。
30. 「不可」 means 'impossible'.
31. Cf. *MS*, I, p. 193.
32. This kind of thinking is called 'literalism'.
33. The *Vinayapiṭaka* tells about what kind of motif is desirable to be painted on the wall of the monastery. The motifs of '*mālākamma*' (garland), '*latākamma*' (arabesque), and '*pañcapaṭṭhika*' (five-lined ribbons?), etc. are allowed to be depicted, but the mundane and sensual motifs like '*mithuna*' (a pair of man and woman) seem to be forbidden. However, there is no reference to whether they should portray the Buddha or not. It is inferred that the *Vinayapiṭaka* refers to the wall painting of early Buddhist monastery in the beginning of the post-Mauryan period at the latest. Cf. H. Oldenberg (ed.), *The Vinayapiṭaka*, London, 1879-83, Vol. II, p. 152.
34. A.L. Basham, *The Wonder That Was India*, Rupa & Co., New Delhi, 1967, p. 369.
35. Basham, *op. cit.*, p. 368.
36. Cf. "The early Buddhist attitude was essentially religious not artistic. But as time wore on, the emotional and sensuous of the pre-Aryan Southerner got the better of the religious and rational of the Aryan Northerner and eventually transformed these symbols into human form vibrant with life." B.C. Sinha, *op. cit.*, p. 54.
37. Cf. "The northern and mid-Indian plastic tradition was carried to Amaravati and the Deccan caves where considerable mastery of sculpture was achieved by about the second century, AD" D.N. Jha, *Ancient India — An Introductory Outline —*, Pratul Lahiri for

Peoples Publishing House (P) Ltd., New Delhi, 1977, p. 92.

38. Cf. *Saddharmapuṇḍarīka,* ed. by H. Kern and B. Nanjiō, St. Petersbourg, 1912 (*Bibliotheca Buddhica* X).
39. Cf. Kanoko Tanaka, "The View of Buddha Observed in the Stūpa Carved in Stone" (*Journal of Religious Studies.*, No. 15, Komazawa University Religious Study Institute, Tokyo, 1989), p. 47.
40 *Lüders* 1209, 1217, 1219 and 1286.
41. *Ibid.*, 1248.
42. *Ibid.*,1223.
43. *Ibid.*,1234.
44. *Ibid.*,1271.
45. *Ibid.*,1239.
46. Vogel C3.
47. English translations are done by the author.
48. Ex. The Fourteen Rock Edicts VI, IX, The Kalinga Rock Edicts I and II, The Seven Pillar Edicts I, III, and VI.
49. Vogel B2.
50. Vogel C5. Cf. Vogel B4.
51. D.C. Sircar, EI, XXXV, pp. 11-13, No. 4. This inscription records that a Buddha image was set up at the monastery.
52. Ex. Vogel A2, A3, A4, B3, B4, B5, C1, C3, D2, D4, X, Vogel H, D.C. Sircar, EI, XXXIII (1959-60), p. 250 (Site 38).
53. '*Cetiyavaṁdaka*' Lüders 1248, 1223, 1250.
54. '*Aparaseliya*' (Vogel C1), '*Bhahusitīya; Bhahuśrutīya*' (Vogel G2). Cf. '*Mahāsāṁghika (?)*' (Vogel C1).
55. Cf. The *Mahāvastu* (*Mv.*), belonging to the *Lokottaravāda*', one of the sects of *Mahāsāṁghika*, is notable because of its reference to the *stūpa*-worship showing a *Mahāyānic* tendency just as: "The person who removes withered flowers at the *stūpa* will become a Buddha; a caravan-leader or this world (in some of the future lives)", *Mv.* ii. 393. 14-15. Some *stūpa*-worshippers are called '*bodhim-abhiprasthita*' (a person who wishes to attain '*bodha, bodhi*') *Mv.* ii. 367, 21-22; 368. 2-3, 4-5, etc. Moreover, it is interesting that there is no reference to the Buddha image in any context. On the basis of its linguistic style of composition, *Mv.* is said to have been written as early as the first or the second century BC.

    The *Mahāsānghikas* "lived mostly at Vaiśāli and Pātaliputra, and migrated, in course of time, to Amarāvatī and Nāgārjunakoṇda in the Guntur district of Āndra State". P.V. Bapat, *2500 Years of Buddhism,* Publications Division, Ministry of Information and Broadcasting, Government of India, 1956, p. 128.
56. Cf. Chapter 1 ('The essence and the meaning of play as the cultural phenomenon') of John Huizinga, *Homo Ludens — Proeve eener bepaling van het spel - element der cultuur;* Tjeenk Willink & Zoon, Haarlem, 1958.

57. Cf. Benimadhab Baura adds a sub-title 'Stone As A Story-Teller' for his book, *Bhārhut Book 1*, The Indian Research Institute, Calcutta, 1934, but the actual composition does not act as a story-teller.
58. Cf. Keiji Sadakane, "The Formation of Buddhist Painting in India — The Relationship between Buddhism and Painting in Early Ancient Times —"(*BIGAKU: Aesthetics* 160, Vol. 40, No. 4, The Japanese Society for Aesthetics, Tokyo, 1990, pp. 47-59).
59. H. Lüders, "*Die Śaubhikas*",. *Philologica Indica,* Göttingen, 1940, p. 414; A.K. Coomaraswamy, "Picture Showmen", *The Indian Historical Quarterly,* Vol. V, 1929, p. 183.
60. The French word '*tableau vivant*' means a picture composed by means of living human beings. It is a kind of show to represent a famous scene of literary works or historical stories and imitate a masterpiece of painting by placing personages in the framed stage just as in a painting. In a *tableau vivant,* personages must take stationary postures.
61. Cf. Bharhut; Lüders 738, 773, 789, 804, 833, Sāñcī; Majumdar 529, Lüders 602, etc.
62. Lüders 773.
63. *Ibid.,* 774.
64. *Ibid.,* 805.
65. A work of religious fine arts is often used as 'the Bible for the illiterate'.

    In Christian art, there are so many kinds of reliefs and paintings illustrating the life of Christ according to the *New Testament.* Especially, the Gospels of SS. Matthew, Mark, Luke and John have been offering rich subjects to sculptors and painters, for the four Gospels are the versions of Christ's life-story.

    On the other hand, the Buddhist scriptures have been dogmatic and not biographic from the beginning. Originally, they are, as it were, the collection of words of the Buddha whose lifestyle had already been established when he attained the Enlightenment. Therefore, it is reasonable to assume that early Buddhist art mainly focuses on the events related to the Buddhist *Dharma*, just as the Enlightenment, the First Sermon, and the *Mahāparinirvāṇa.*
66. H. Lüders (ed.), *Bhārhut Inscriptions,* Ootacamund, 1963, pp. 94-96.
67. Cf. *Arthaśāstra,* 2, 23, 2.
68. Bharata, *Nāṭyaśāstra* 5, 16-30. Cf. Alain Daniélou, *Bharata nātyam. Der klassische Tanz Indiens,* Berlin, 1970, S. 16.
69. Cf. Walter Kaufmann, *Musikgeschichte in Bildern Altindien*, VEB Deutscher Verlag für Musik, Leipzig, 1981 (Japanese version, Tokyo, 1986, p. 29).
70. *Nātyaśāstra*, 2, 82-83.
71. Other fragmentary remarks on *Illust.* 10a-2 are as follows: cf. Cunningham, *The Stūpa of Bhārhut,* London, 1879, p. xxxi, 2. ['Table' ⑥]: "Objects of worship: Dharma Chaka", ['Table' ⑭]: "sa danam Atenā Charata". Coomaraswamy, *Elements of Buddhist Iconography,* 1935, Plate V, Figure 18, ['Table' ①]: "Cult of the Buddha as Dharmacakra, Principal Wheel, i.e., as Supernal, Sun."
72. Barua, *Bhārhut Book II*, 1934, Pl. XIII, Scene 52, pp. 46-48, cf. *Dhammacetiya-sutta, MN*,

II, pp. 118f, No. 89.

73. *Introduction to the Bhaddasāla Jātaka*, No. 465, Cowell's ed., Vol. IV, pp. 95-96.
74. *Ibid.*, Fausbölls' ed., Vol. IV, pp. 145 ff.
75. The King's crown, his parasol, his sword, his jewelled yak-tall, and his richly embroidered shoes. Cf. Rockhill, *The Life of the Buddha,* Trubner & Co., London, 1884, p. 113.
76. *Dhammapada-Aṭṭhakathā* I, 356, *Bhaddasālajātaka* No. 465, 151-52.
77. Cf. The expression of praising the Buddha's sermon; *Saṃyutta-nikāya (Sagātha-vagga)* III, p. 97.
78. Introduction to *Jātaka* No. 7.
79. According to the *Dharmaśāstra* (Chapter X, Section 9), a child born of a kṣatriya to a śūdra is called *'Ugra'* who likes cruel and atrocious acts, similar to those of a kṣatriya and a śūdra (cf. Chapter III, sections 14, 15, 19).
80. The following accounts are from Cowell (ed.) *The Jātaka or Stories of the Buddha's Former Births,* Vol. IV, Cambridge University Press, 1901, p. 96.
81. G.P. Malasekera *Dictionary of Pāli Proper Names*, Vol. II, Indian Text Series, London, 1937-38, pp. 876-77.
82. *DhpA*, I, 358: *"sammāsambuddhassa pana ñatakā asattughātaka nāma attanā marantāpi pare jīvitā na voropenti"* (The relations of the completely enlightened one, however, are such who do not kill the enemies. Being put to death themselves, they do not deprive others of their life). Cf. Lüders, *Bhārhut Inscriptions (Corpus Inscriptionum Indicarum)* Vol. II, Part II, Government Epigraphist for India, Ootacamund, 1963, p. 56.
    Lüders clearly denies the relations between *Illust.* 10a-2 and its inscription.
83. Cf. "The original gandhakuti is represented and labelled as such in another Bhārhut relief where it is a simple one-storey hut." Lippe, A., *The Freer Indian Sculptures* (Oriental Studies No. 8), Freer Gallery of Art, Smithsonian Institution, Washington, D.C., 1970, pp. 8-9.
84. The author is Kauṭilya, the Brāhmaṇa who served Chandragupta, the founder of Mauryan dynasty, the grandfather of King Aśoka who contributed to the development of Buddhist art.
85. *Arthaśāstra* 10, 4, 1. In. *Pl.* 13 a-1, we can see a procession of the cavalrymen, the infantry-men (left side), the king's chariot (middle), and the elephant corps (right side); cf. Lippe, *op. cit.*, p. 7.
86. *Ibid.*, 10, 5, 18.
87. *Ibid.*, 10, 3, 5.
88. *Ibid.*, 10, 3, 42.
89. *Ibid.*, 10, 3, 40.
90. *Bhaddasāla Jātaka* No. 465, 144, 153, 157, cf. *Jātaka* Nos. 22, 140, 407.
91. F. Max Müller (tr.) *The Sacred Books of the East* Vol. 10,(Part I *Dhammapada*), Motilal Banarsidass, Delhi, 1992, p. 79, cf. *Udv*. 31. 5, *Therag.*, 77, 1130.
92. F. Max Müller, *op. cit.*, p. 18.

93. F. Max Müller, *op. cit.*, p. 18.
94. Wilhelm Geiger (ed). *The Mahāvaṃsa*, Orig. pub., 1908; reprinted, London; Luzac and Co., 1958, p. 32.
95. The Fourteen Rock Edicts, Chapter 8.
96. The Minor Rock Edicts, Chapter 2.
97. The Fourteen Rock Edicts, Chapter 5.
98. *Ibid.*, Chapter 12.
99. The Minor Pillar Edicts, Sārnāth.
100. The Seven Pillar Edicts, Chapter 7.
101. The Kalinga Rock Edicts, Chapters 1 and 2, The Seven Pillars Edicts Chapter 1. Cf. Mookerji, *Aśoka*, Motilal Banarsidass, Delhi, 1989, p. 121.
102. The Fourteen Rock Edicts, Chapter 4.
103. *Ibid.*, Chapter 9.
104. Mookerji, *op. cit.*, pp. 155-56.
105. In Aśokan period, both Judaism and Zoroastrianism had already established their own views of the present life and the life to come, which later reflected on Christian thought. Cf. *I Timothy* 4. 8-9.
106. The Minor Rock Edicts, Chapter 4, Mookerji, *op. cit.*, p. 283.
107. The Fourteen Rock Edicts, Chapter 10.
108. Mookerji, *op. cit.*, 156-57.
109. The Fourteen Rock Edicts, Chapter I, etc.
110. Cf. *devalokasmiṃ modanti* (*Itiv.* 107G); *modeta viṣṭape* (*ApDhS* XXII, 8).

    The Fourteen Rock Edicts, Chapter 6; *savaggaṃ ārādhayaṃtu* [to make people attain heaven (in the world beyond)].
111. *Udv.* Chapter 5, 22, etc.
112. *Ibid.*, 25, etc.
113. The Minor Rock Edicts, Chapter 1, Mookerji, *op. cit.*, p. 110.
114. Mookerji, *op. cit.,* p. 111.
115. Mookerji, *op. cit.*, pp. 136-37. The Fourteen Rock Edicts, Chapter 4, cf. J. Bloch, *Les inscriptions d'Aśoka*, Paris, 1950, pp. 97-98.
116. Mookerji, *op. cit.*, p. 136.
117. Ex. *MS*, II, Plates 34c, 49a, 64c, etc.
118. Cf. "These Nāgas were not serpents but Kṣatriyas of the Nāgakula, the descendants of Rāma, governing at Rāmagrāma." V. Pathak, *History of Kośala,* Motilal Banarsidass, Delhi, 1983, p. 269.
119. Cf. Sujitkumar Mukhopadhyaya, ed., *The Aśokāvadāna,* New Delhi, Sahitya Akademi, 1963, p. 52.
120. Mukhopadhyaya, *op. cit.*, p, 93.
121. *Ibid.*, p. 93.

122. Wilhelm Geiger (tr.), *op. cit.*, p. 125, John S. Strong, *The Legend of King Aśoka,* Motilal Banarsidass, Delhi, 1989, p. 126.
123. Strong, *op. cit.*, p. 109.
124. Cf. Strong, *op. cit.*, pp. 92-95.
125. *Ibid.*, pp. 94-95.
126. V. Pathak, *op. cit.*, p. 271.
127. The Minor Rock Edicts, Chapter 3 (The Bhabru or Bhairāt No. 2).
128. Strong, *op. cit.*, p. 92.
129. Cf. The Fourteen Rock Edicts, Chapter 12.

IV

The Concept of the Empty Throne

1. Its Meaning for Buddhist People

For those who had actually seen the Buddha *Śākyamuni* sitting under the tree or in the *vihāra* preaching before his disciples, lay-believers and others, the Buddha's seat or place must have become venerable and commemorative even when he was no longer there. However, at the same time, its empty space made devotees lonely and eager to see their Master.[1]

Originally, the *śramaṇa* including the Buddha *Śākyamuni* and his disciples preferred to stay at the foot of the tree,[2] the place where corpses were buried or left behind (*sītavana; sīvathika*),[3] the caves in the mountains, and the quiet place where nobody else was seen.[4] But what about the seat? They used to fold their robes (*saṃghāṭi*)[5] and placed them on the ground, or the rugs were used in the same way.[6] When somebody invited them to his residence, they sat on the seats prepared in advance.[7]

In any case, the places where the Buddha had been seated were uncountable and even his devotees could not remember all of them. There was no need for anyone to long for these places too much, at least, while the Master was alive.

But, once he was deceased, his old seats were left empty for ever. A sense of emptiness prevailed in the minds of his devotees. No one could occupy these seats on his behalf, although his teaching was taken over by some of his leading disciples.[8]

The seats of the Buddha (*Buddhāsana*) were memorized in later periods. They were made of stone and placed at many pilgrimage sites so that visitors might meditate and perform *pūjā* there. The seats were washed with water[9] and strewn with flowers just as seen even in modern times (*Pl.* 10, cf. *Illusts*. 9, 10a-2, 11b-1).

Above all, the seat in memory of the *Sambodhi* at *Bodh Gayā* (*vajrāsana*) was the most sacred and left together with the *Bodhi*-tree. It was treated as the throne on which the king should be seated.

In the period of early Buddhist art, Buddhists seem to have worshipped not only the throne of *Śākyamuni* Buddha but also the thrones of six other *Mānuṣī Buddhas* who had attained the Enlightenment under different sacred trees (*Illust.* 1 c-1. c-2 and c-3); probably, the throne of *Maitreya* Buddha who would come to this world after *Śākyamuni* Buddha has gone beyond[10] was also added to the Buddhist monuments.

It is important to note that the Buddha *Śākyamuni* was treated as one of the seven *Mānuṣī Buddhas*, and not as the divinity whose spiritual presence should be recognizable. In other words, he was the person who had already passed away in historical time. After the moment of his death, his existence had become a great memory which was deserving of the creation of its monument. It goes without saying that the greatest monument was the *stūpa* containing his own relics. But its semicircular dome stands aloof from this world especially when it reminds one of the *Mahāparinirvāṇa* — the stage where one does not take rebirth any more and does not wish to be born even in the world of gods.[11] Therefore, the *stūpa* tends to put a period to one's recollection of the Buddha's career.

On the other hand, the empty throne is more practical and flexible in reminding one of the Buddhas of the past periods and their careers. Even the Buddha to come in the near future can be expected there.[12] It means that the empty throne can accept the Buddha's memories through the ages because those who have attained the Enlightenment are called 'the Buddha' in the logic of Buddhism.

But in reality, the empty throne originates from the absence of Buddha *Śākyamuni* as a result of his death. The emptiness on the throne can preserve the historical truth that the Buddha had been alive in this world where we live now in the most realistic way. The emptiness is, as it were, the afterimage of his historical existence. It may sound paradoxical. But it is proved to be true when we realise that the emptiness is much more realistic than any other thing made by human hands, any elaborate image of the Buddha as the product of human imagination. The Buddha images went on increasing in variety and number as a result of the evolution of artistic activities, apart from the historical Buddha. It may be said that the Buddha images are also able to partly express his nature enough to impress the visitors and worshippers. But, at the same time, the Buddha images cannot help including creation and artificiality, because they do not portray the historical Buddha but try to represent the ideal body to be owned by the Buddha. It is known to us from the earliest Buddhist scriptures that the Buddha was one of the greatest *śramaṇas* of his times who tonsured himself (*muṇḍaka*)[13] and put on simple robes patched with rags.

If we want to look for his real image, it would be better to see a monk meditate under a tree (*Pl.* 9). We will find only the shade of the tree after the monk leaves. But a sort of invigorating air should be felt under the tree, because we remember seeing the monk in meditation there. Or, we can expect a monk to be seated under the tree and see the vision of his figure even before he comes there. This is the origin and the essence of the empty throne as the memory of the Buddha. The Buddha left his seat for ever after death (*Pl.* 10) but his image has come back there in the historical process of Buddhist art after quite a long interval (*Pl.* 13).

Those who were born after the Buddha image came into being must have worshipped it just as the Buddha himself. But those people were not free from its artistic expression once they had been accustomed to seeing and feeling reverence for the Buddha through his image. It may be imagined that they could not turn their eyes back to the empty throne or the vacancy under the tree for the purpose of recalling the Deceased One. However, it is also observed that Buddhists had even left his seat empty without placing any Buddha image there. It means that Buddhists still preserved the old monument (the empty throne) and memorized its history.

According to a record of Buddhistic Kingdoms by Fa-hsien (fifth century AD), there were the seats of four *Mānuṣī Buddhas* (*Krakucchanda, Kanakamuni, Kāśyapa and Śākyamuni*) in front of one of the caves of *Gṛdhrakūṭa.*[14] Fa-hsien must have seen those seats reverently kept for pilgrims. We are told that at the *Saptaparṇiguhā* where the first Congregation was held by five hundred disciples (*ārhats*) after the death of the Buddha, three empty thrones of the Buddha (centre), Sāriputra (left), and Mahāmaudgalyāyana (right) were set up and decorated with solemnity at the time of taking out the *sūtras*.[15] Fa-hsien refers to this ritual as if it were actually held by the direct disciples of the Buddha. But in reality, the *sūtras* of those days were always recited and learnt by heart without being recorded in writing. This situation was important for the disciples to take the responsibility of revising the *sūtras* according to their own memories of the Buddha's teaching. Therefore, Fa-hsien seems to have seen those empty thrones or heard of the legend mentioned above.

It is also interesting to know that Fa-hsien saw many memorial *stūpas* at every places where the Buddha had preached, sat and walked in meditation.[16] 'The Buddha' means not only *Śākyamuni* but also other *Mānuṣī Buddhas*, *Krakucchanda, Kanakamuṇi,* and *Kāśyapa,* just as seen in the top lintel of the southern gateway (front) of Sāñcī *Stūpa* 1 (*Fig.* 7).

Thus, Fa-hsien recorded the presence of the empty throne in India in the fifth century AD. But, at the same time, he believed the legend of the first Buddha image made by King Prasenajit.[17] It is said that King Prasenajit put the Buddha image on the seat of the Buddha who was absent from this world in order to preach to his mother in heaven. Needless to say, the seat had been kept empty for the Buddha. The Buddha image was on that very place till the Buddha came back from the heaven. The image itself came down from the seat to welcome the Buddha, but the Buddha is said to have made his image return there by saying, "You may go back to the seat, and I will allow you to become the model for my disciples (*bhikkhu, bhikkhunī*) and lay-believers (*upāsaka, upāsikā*) after the death of mine (*parinirvāṇa*)." Then the Buddha image returned to the seat granted by the Buddha himself. Furthermore, it is interesting that the Buddha kept himself apart from his image by shifting to another small *vihāra*. For us who are focusing on the history of Buddhist art, this shifting seems to symbolize the historical gap between the Buddha and his image. The legend dared to create the situation where the Buddha had even seen his image, but did not say that they had stayed together at the same place. At least in the world of this legend, Buddhists must not have paid the highest reverence to the Buddha image as long as the Buddha was alive and active.

In the seventh century AD when Hsüan-tsang visited the Buddhist remains of India, there were many monumental seats in honour of the last four *Mānuṣī Buddhas* mentioned above.[18] Under the *Bodhi-tree* outside the fort of Gāndhāra, Hsüan-tsang saw the seated statues of those Buddhas who were believed to have sat there. He says that nine hundred and ninety six Buddhas should sit there in the future during the period of *bhadra-kalpa*.[19] Besides these monuments of *Mānuṣī Buddhas*, there were innumerable *stūpas* in memory of the previous lives of *Śākyamuni*[20] and the events of his last life in this world. Most of them were said to have been built by King Aśoka of the Mauryan dynasty. But Hsüan-tsang does not mention about the empty thrones at the caves of *Gṛdhrakūṭa* and *Saptaparṇiguhā* which Fa-hsien saw around two hundred years before,[21] or rather he records the fact that a life-size statue of the preaching Buddha was placed in the brick *vihāra* built on a cliff of Gṛdhrakūṭa.[22] In passing, it is interesting that this Chinese monk believed that the Buddha preached the *Saddharmapuṇḍarīka-sūtra,* one of the most important *Mahāyānistic* scriptures, on this peak.[23]

Hsüan-tsang also refers to the legend of the first Buddha image made in the Buddha's time by King Udayana of Kośāmbī. The king asked Mahāmaudgalyāyana to take a sculptor to the heaven where the Buddha was preaching to his mother. The sculptor copied the exact features of the Buddha and completed a statue in sandalwood. Hsüan-tsang reports that he saw the statue at the *mahāvihāra* in the fort of Kośāmbī and heard of its miraculous effect on the people in later periods.[24] It is true in the history of Buddhist art that this statue was copied by foreign Buddhists and one of the replicas was brought to Japan by way of China. *Pl.* 16 is the most famous example in Japan sanctified by the legend of King Udayana. As the Buddhist people did not hesitate in paying reverence to 'the Buddha image' as a copy of the Buddha himself, it is natural that 'the empty throne' was eventually forgotten even in India. Hsüan-tsang during his stay in India saw many kinds of Buddha images describing famous events of the Buddha's life. To his eyes, those images might have been more impressive than the impersonal appearance of the empty thrones, especially if he needed to approach the visible Buddha accepted by Indian people from ancient times.

Nevertheless, it is notable that the empty throne had remained as one of the Buddhist monuments in India since it was made in the period of early Buddhist art. It is a historical phenomenon peculiar to the region of India where the Buddha had lived a life. Therefore, the empty throne is not expected to be found in foreign Buddhist countries where the Buddha image did not exist from the beginning. The empty throne is, as it were, a native monument just as seen under the *Bodhi-tree* of Bodh Gayā (Pl. 10).

Paradoxically, it is possible to say that the empty throne survived in later periods as the pedestal of various Buddha images. The images occupied their own thrones and never vanished once they had been placed there as long as Buddhists could take care to preserve them. However, each of the images was nothing but an artistic expression. There is no ideal and final image to visualize the Buddha because the visualization itself is an act of creation. In other words, many Buddha images of different kinds on the thrones are like the visionary Buddhas described in human minds, which emerge for a while and change their styles one after another in response to the people's needs through ages. The Buddha images are, as it were, the visions on the empty throne. Visualizing each of the visions elaborately was the work of numerous and nameless artists.

At first sight, the Buddha images seem to predominate over their thrones (cf. *Pls*. 12 and 13). But, it is only the throne that would remain in any period even if the Buddha image is lost or broken for some reason (cf. *Pl.* 15).

One may dislike or criticize the Buddha image because of its artificial work, but who can dare to hate the empty throne where nobody stays any more? We have never heard that the empty throne was destroyed by Muslim invaders who had cut many heads of the Buddha images (cf. *Illust*. 18) probably because it looked so simple and plain that Muslims could not regard it as the product of idolatry. It suggests that any kind of visible image essentially fails to appeal to different religions of the world but the empty throne, on the other hand, can appeal to any kind of people beyond their likes and dislikes. In this respect, 'the empty throne' deserves to be chosen from the history of Buddhist art in order to promote mutual understanding between Buddhists and other religious peoples.

As far as the empty throne of early Buddhist art is concerned, it is only the perfect and complete expression of the historical reality that the Buddha attained the Enlightenment, the wisdom of Truth, and preached it before the people at many places in India. The empty throne may not look empty when another Buddhist monument (*dharmacakra* or *triratna*) is placed on it (cf. *Illust.* 1b and 8a-1); however there is no change in the essential realization that the Buddha is not there in fact but only reminds one of his presence in one's own imagination. What does it mean? It means that the empty throne has the open space where one can bring offerings (*Pl.* 10), fold one's hands and think of the Deceased One (*Pl.* 11), and see the vision of the Buddha idealized by one's faith in Buddhism (*Pl.* 12). What one does or thinks around the empty throne depends on one's own will. No one is forced to do anything there. Thus the empty throne can accept one's spiritual freedom spontaneously. In the context of the history of Buddhist art, the freedom was the source of the creative energy that produced innumerable images to be worshipped by the Buddhist devotees. In other words, the images that emerged in later periods should not have been created if early Buddhist art had not prepared the empty throne in advance.

Taking all the things pointed out in this section into consideration, it becomes easier to realize the value of the 'absence of the Buddha image in early Buddhist art'. However, this recognition belongs to us in modern times, because it is attainable only when one can look back to the whole history of Buddhist art by means of all kinds of literary and achaeological data. On the other hand, ancient people could appreciate only the thing that was present before their eyes without any historical survey. They could concentrate themselves on 'the present time' much more easily than can be done nowadays.

Therefore, a study of the empty throne here is just a discovery of its modernity tfor the benefit of the people of today although at the same time it is also a re-search work on early Buddhist art.

2. Its Categories in Comparative Religion

The representation of God, gods, and other divine beings in religious arts has shown an infinite diversity of forms, colours, styles, and designs, etc. from times immemorial. In other words, the human desire to grasp the presence of God and other divinities has been making a contribution to the history of art. Such a desire, however, could not help reaching the limits of man's representation of the Divinity, so that finally the holiest place (sanctuary) was left empty, unseen, and inexpressible. The sanctuary is also a place arranged by human hands. But at least, the human beings in the sanctuary know how to concentrate themselves on the Supreme Being that is the almighty and trustworthy. The concentration enables them to get peace of mind and find a refuge there beyond the order of this world.

In this section, the empty, unseen and inexpressive essence of the sanctuary is the most important concept to make a linkage between Buddhism and five other monotheistic religions: Zoroastrianism, Judaism, Christianity, Islām and Sikhism.

In the case of Buddhism, it is necessary to define its sanctuary as 'the empty throne' of early Buddhist art because the Buddhist sanctuary in later periods was occupied by the Buddha image (cf. *Pl.* 13). Looking back on how the Buddha image emerged on 'the throne' (cf. *Illusts.* 1b, 3, and *Pl.* 13), it proves that 'the Buddha image' is nothing but a symbolic expression of the *Dharma* which takes the form of the human body. For Buddhists, the Buddha image is not a physical and historical object of worship but a spiritual and idealistic medium of meditation. 'The throne' (the pedestal of the Buddha image) is nothing but a place where various forms of the Buddha image emerge, remain and disappear into the streams of art-history. Nevertheless, in reality, 'the Buddha image' always occupies 'the throne', and not only non-Buddhists but also Buddhists themselves do not see the symbolism of 'the Buddha image' on 'the throne'. Therefore we omit this fact from the discussion of this section.

On the other hand, the Zoroastrian, Jewish, Christian, Islamic and Sikh sanctuaries are essentially aniconic because of the invisibility of God, with the exception that they use some symbols to represent the Divinity: "the Fire, Son of Ahura Mazdā, . . . of the Royal Glory created by Ahura Mazdā . . . who is seated in the hearts of kings" (*Ātarš Nyāišn,* 20, etc.); the Menorah, seven-branched candelabrum made by order of Yahweh (*Exodus* 25 : 31-40); the Cross signifying the Redemption of Jesus Christ (*Philippians* 2 : 6-11, etc.); "the name of Allāh, the Beneficent, the Merciful" (the first line of the *Sūrahs* of the *Qur'ān*); and the *Ādi Granth* (or the *Śrī Guru Granth Sahib*) as the biblical witness of monotheism: 'Ik Oṅkār' (the first two words of the *Jap-jī Sahib*).

At least for the proper understanding of Buddhism whose essence can be seen in 'the empty throne' rather than any other idolatrous work of art, it is worth while introducing the concept of 'the empty throne' and finding a common ground that can lead to a dialogue between Buddhism and monotheism.

According to the theory mentioned above, a comparative study of religions can be realized by a series of questions:

(1) What is the holiest space (sanctuary) that is symbolized by the concept of 'the empty throne'?

(2) What is the emptiness of the throne?

(3) What (or who) is enthroned there?

(4) Who pays reverence to 'the empty throne'?

(5) What is performed on, before or around 'the empty throne'?

These questions contain the topics of (1) religious art, (2) & (3) dogma or theology, (4) religious community, and (5) religious rituals (1) ~ (5) form the identity of each religion and offer us many subjects of Comparative Religion. In most cases, (1) ~ (5) are individually discussed on different occasions. It is a microscopical observation of the religious world. To understand the entire meaning of religions, we should join the fragments of (1) ~ (5) with the paste of 'a common concept'. For the purpose, we present the concept of 'the empty throne' to construct 'A Table of the Key-Concepts in Chapter IV, 2'.

The monotheistic religions of 'A Table ~' can be classified into three groups.

(1) Zoroastrianism is the oldest of the revealed religions.[25] It was around 1,500 century BC that Zarathuštra became the Prophet who followed the Will of Ahura Mazdā, the Lord of Wisdom. God's Wisdom suggested the seeing of His Image through the medium of Fire from the very beginning of the first Revelation. Since then, Fire is only one symbol of God authorized by God Himself. Accordingly, Zoroastrians have never invented the graven or painted image of God to install it in the sanctuary all through their long history.

The reverence for the sacred Fire signifies the fact that Zoroastrianism originates from the same religio-cultural background as the Vedic religion where the fire-god (Agni) was enshrined at the altar (*vedi*). In earlier times, the two branches of Āryans, the Indo-Āryans and the Iranian Āryans, had the common concept of 'gods' with different names and natures. One of the most sacred gods was worshipped through fire. Both Āryans separated from each other around 2,000 century BC. The Indians developed their polytheism, suggesting "They call Him (one God) Indra, Mitra, Agni, and He is heavenly able winged Garutman. Are Rāma, Kr̥śna, Śiva and Viṣṇu so many Names of One?" (Ṛg-veda I, 164.46). The Iranians, on the other hand, were revealed a prophetical religion where God could be worshipped in the form of His own seven attributes (cf. (B) The Empty Throne in Zoroastrianism). In this way, two tribes of same origin finally formed different types of religion. Among the prophetical religions, only Zoroastrianism is not Semitic but Indo-Iranian in origin, which makes it a unique monotheism in the history of world religions.

(2) Sikhism is a monotheistic religion where the only one God (*Wāhegurū*) does not reveal Himself through one's prophecy but can be recognized by the tradition of Guruhood, from Guru Nānak (1469-1539) to the tenth Guru Gobind Singh (1666 - 1708);[26] the words and acts of the ten spiritual leaders (Gurus); and the holy Scripture, the *Ādi Granth*. Since the decease of Guru Gobind Singh, the Scripture has become the symbol of Guruhood and has been given the title of '*Śrī Guru Granth Sahib*'.

Guru Nānak, the founder of Sikhism, was born as a son of Hindū parents in Puñjāb, the north-west of India in the fifteenth century. It was under the reign of the Mughals, Muslim rulers who needed to control the Hindū society, the majority of Indians. The

Hindūs, on the other hand, had to make an effort to get along with the rulers to maintain their faith and culture. However, in reality, both did not try to understand each other but had a tendency for adhering to ritualism without embodying the spirituality of their own religions. In such a situation, Nānak became the Guru, the spiritual leader standing in the line of Guru-disciple tradition of India.[27] The word 'Sikh' is derived from '*Śiṣya*' meaning 'the followers (of Guru)'. He was neither a prophet nor an *avatāra* (an incarnate divinity), but a meditator who attained the Enlightenment, "There are no Hindus or Muslims" and "All are the children of one God."[28] Proclaiming the equality and universal brotherhood of human beings. Guru Nānak taught "both Hindus and Muslims to practice their own faiths with a view to strict moral life and social service without caring much for rituals and external observances".[29] For his own followers (Sikhs), he did away with some elements of Hindu tradition such as caste system and idol-worship in order to realize the Sikh community, where everyone, free from the chains of birth, race and creed, is welcome to dine and work together in the unity of devotional service towards one God, the true Guru of mankind.

Accordingly, Sikhs did not develop any kind of visual art to represent the image of God, but only devoted themselves to enshrining the Scripture as the eleventh and eternal Guru at the sanctuary of their temple called 'Gurdwārā', meaning 'the gateway to the Guru'.[30]

Among the monotheistic religions, Sikhism is in a unique position to have a linkage with both Islām and Hinduism. Therefore, it is worthwhile introducing the Sikh sanctuary in this section.

(3) Judaism, Christianity, and Islām belong to a group of Semitic monotheism, although they approach only one God in different ways. According to the *Qur'ān*, those who embrace these religions can be called *'ahl al-kitāb'*[31] (the peoples of the Books revealed by God). The Books, *Taurāt* (*Tôrâ*; the five Books of Moses), *Zabūr* (Psalm), *Indjīl* (Gospels), and *Qur'ān* (Koran) are all critical and prohibitory of idolatry.

Above all, it is well known that the *Qur'ān* has been strictest in observing monotheism and destroying the idols of non-Muslims including the Buddha image (cf. *Illust*. 18). In this sense, Islām may be the first religion to be welcomed to a dialogue with Buddhism under the comparative study of 'the empty throne'.

On the contrary, Christianity has another situation where the Christ image deserves to be paid reverence, as long as it is believed that Christ lived a life in this world as the incarnate God, the visible God in the form of human being.[32] It was one of the most important doctrines for the theologists who protested against iconoclasm that had taken place in Byzantium in the eighth-ninth centuries AD possibly under the influence of Judaism and Islām,[33] and in a political background of the Empire.[34] As a result, the

Eastern Church had restored the veneration of icons depicting Christ, St. Mary and other saints, but the use of graven images was prohibited because it could be connected directly with idolatry. On the other hand, the Western Church (Catholicism) took a more liberal attitude toward religious arts by utilizing the aesthetic effects of paintings and graven images on those who should arouse their reverent feelings. Therefore, the Christian art in the West has a variety of Christ images in every period, in contrast with the icons of the Eastern Church that observed the traditional canon in order to portray the Christ in historical reality.[35]

As a whole, the Christian arts both in the East and the West can play a decorative role in the inner space of the Church whose sanctuary; the altar's place must be kept simplest in awe of God. Originally, the early Church, fearful of idolatry, was consistently opposed to the making and veneration of portraits of Christ and saints, just as we have already seen in the main motifs of early Christian art (*Fig*. 14) in Chapter II, 2. This stoicism is still taken over at the altar where man stands before God.

As compared to the Eastern and Western Churches, Protestantism does not use any work of fine arts positively, except for the simple cross without the Christ image in crucifixion. For Protestants, the Bible is the most important in their daily lives and the Church is the assembly hall where they come together around their leader (parson). He is not a priest who is allowed to forgive one's sin on behalf of Christ but a preacher who should make an effort to evangelize his listeners. Thus the Protestant Church has no place sanctified by the medium of the priest, but the sanctuary still remains there as long as Protestantism also relies on the role of the Church to embody the Holy Spirit.

Finally, it is important to pick up several types of the sanctuary from the history of Israel, because they are the archetypes of Christian and Islamic sanctuaries in the context of monotheistic history.

Yahwism is the religion of Yahweh, the only God who called Abraham to make a contact with him and his posterity (nineteenth century BC)[36], and made Moses take the tribes of Israel out of Egypt in order that they might be given Canaan, the Land of Promise[37] (thirteenth century BC).

Abraham is called *Ibrāhīm* in Arabic. In Islām, he is idealized as *ḥanīf*,[38] the person who had a pure and genuine faith in God. Muḥammad believed that Islām had to revive the 'religion of Abraham' (*dīn Ibrāhim*)[39] in opposition to Judaism and Christianity.

In this sense, it may be said that Islām can be familiar with Yahwism, the religion before its institutionalization by the Jewish community on the basis of the house of the Lord in Jerusalem (tenth century BC-AD 70) and the Synagogue[40] (AD 70 —).

Generally, the word 'Judaism' tends to mean the religion institutionalized by the

Law of Moses.[41] In Judaism, Moses is respected as the prophet who received the Law directly from God.

The priest had become more central and powerful than ever before especially after King Solomon built the house of the Lord in Jerusalem for the first time (tenth century BC). It means that Yahwism had come to take the form of 'Judaism of the Priest'.[42]

The house of the Lord seemed to be perpetual in those days. But it was destroyed by Babylonians (BC 586) and Romans (AD 70). There after, the rabbi, as the expert in the Law, became the leader of the Jewish community. It was the beginning of 'Judaism of the Rabbi' or 'Rabbinic Judaism'which lasts in modern times.

In this way, Yahwism/Judaism has quite a long history and contains the reason why there are found a variety of sanctuaries. Furthermore, it is very interesting to find some different points between Islām and Yahwism/Judaism on the same basis of the only God (*Yahweh/Allāh*), as seen in 3, 4, and 5 of 'A Table of the key-Concepts in Chapter IV, 2'.

For these reasons, Yahwism/Judaism, Christianity and Islām should be taken as a series of monotheistic religions and it is impossible to omit even one of them when we want to try a comparative study of the sanctuaries under the concept of 'the empty throne'.

In this chapter, (1), (2) and (5) of 'A Table ~' mentioned above will be explained in order to clarify the meaning of 'the empty throne' and its role in each religion. It is very important to compare the visual data (cf. *Illusts.* 1b and c, 2, 3a, 5,6,7c, 8a and c, 9, 10, 11,12a, 13a-3, *Illusts.* 19-20, *Illusts.*22-24, *Illusts.* 25, and *Pls.* 24-32) because we need to see the religious situation where 'the empty throne' is placed. Above all, the work of fine arts can visualize a miraculous scene around it.

We cannot become a believer of all religions who has all kinds of religious experiences, but can only observe others' faiths as an outsider. Nevertheless, as far as 'the empty thrones' are concerned, they can convey their significance through the same dimension of 'emptiness'. If only we grasp the essence of every religion beyond the horizon of 'the empty throne', we may be able to understand and respect others' faiths and lives. This kind of effort should be tried with courage and perseverance if we wish to make preparations for a dialogue among the religions of the world. The effort to be made in this chapter is nothing but one possibility out of many others.

'A Table of the Key-Concepts in Chapter IV, 2' has five sections. (3) and (4). are important for confirming the relationship between man and God/Buddha under the situation of 'the empty throne'. (1) chooses various sanctuaries in order to prepare the basis of comparison by means of the concept of 'the empty throne'. (1) explains the nature of (3) with the reality of (2). (1) and (5) are necessary to know how 'the empty throne' [(1)] can be accepted [(5)] by the believers [(4)]. It suggests that (3) is the receiver of (5). (2) should always be made clear by referring to (1), because (1) has already contained the factor to define (2). (2) and (4) are the basic conditions of (5). (5) can be done not only at 'the empty throne' but also at some other places where the people should confess their faiths by thoughts, words, and deeds. In this way, (1) ~ (5) closely connect with each other.

We will make reference to 'A Table ~' and discuss the meaning of 'the empty throne' in Buddhism and other religions. How to appreciate the space of 'emptiness' common to all the religious sanctuaries? This is the last section of Chapter IV, '3. A Discovery of its Modernity'.

(A) THE EMPTY THRONE IN BUDDHISM

In Buddhism, those who have become the Buddhas will never take rebirth any more. After death, they neither remain spiritual in this world nor disappear into the invisible world. Because the cause of rebirth, the result of bad and good deeds (*karma*), has been dissolved by the power of *Sambodhi* (the right wisdom about this world, the Enlightenment) in the lifetime. The physical body, as the last product of *karma*, has to remain during the time. But it is finally extinguished by death, the real end of *kārmic* life. This is the ultimate stage of salvation in ontological sense, *Mahāparinirvāṇa* [(1)]. It is not attainable by ordinary people, but its greatness can become a reliable authority to enable them to have a pure faith in the teachings of the Buddha. Though they know well that the Deceased One will never come back to the empty throne [(1)], the place is necessary for them to retrace and believe what the Buddha taught till the time of his death [(2)].

In early Buddhist art, those who look towards the empty throne are all lay-believers (*upāsaka* and *upāsikā*). But in fact, nuns (*bhikkhunī*) and monks (*bhikkhu*) must pay reverence to the place as the members of the *Saṅgha* [(4)]. The Buddhists do not offer a sacrifice to the Deceased Teacher, different from the Vedic religion (cf. Yahwism/ Judaism). They bring flowers (*Pl.* 10, *Illusts.* 2 and 9), light (*Pl.* 11), incense (*Pls.* 10 and 11), water (*Illust.* 2a-1), etc. as if they are visiting a grave to recollect the dead. The prayer is performed by folding both hands together before the chest (*Illust.* 5, 6, 7c, 9). The monument of *triratna* (*Illusts.* 8a-1, c, 9) suggests that the prayer includes the confession of faith in the Buddha, the *Dharma* and the *Saṁgha*, and it is reasonable to imagine that the *Sūtras*, as the Teachings of the Buddha, are read or recited on behalf of the Buddha himself who should have sat on his seat and preached there [(5)]. In this way, the Buddhist performances around the empty throne try to recall the Deceased One in order to keep the life of Buddhism. But the Buddhists neither try asking the Buddha to respond to their prayers nor expect any spiritual contact with him. Because it is the principle that he is not God but a human being no matter how he lived a great life (cf. Christianity).

In *Mahāyāna* Buddhism, the Buddhas (just as the *Śākyamuni* Buddha of the *Saddharmapuṇḍarīka-sūtra* and the *Amitābha* Buddha of the *Sukhāvatī Vyūha*) and even Bodhisattvas (just as the *Avalokiteśvara*) are almost deified and perpetuated as the Buddhist saviours, and they belong to the Buddhist pantheon. Nevertheless, if we carefully study the Buddhist scriptures, all these Buddhas and Bodhisattvas are seen to be modeled upon the historical Buddha born as the Prince of the *Śakya* clan.

The *Mahāyānistic* Buddhas are also preaching in their respective Lands, and the listeners are following the Teachers in order to ultimately attain the *Bodhi* (to become the Buddha) in the future. Therefore, here is the relationship between the Teacher and His disciple, basically. It is essentially different from the clear contrast between man (creature) and God (Creator). In this respect, Buddhism and other monotheistic religions have to draw a line of demarcation between the two.

But if we turn our eye to the empty throne and its emptiness, there comes out a possibility of finding the greatest common measure of every religion's sanctuary. Here we should remember the impersonal nature of the empty throne in early Buddhist art in contrast with its surroundings, the animals and those who are expressed in human forms including *nāgas, yakṣas, yakṣinīs, devas,* etc. (*Illusts.* 1b, c, 5, 6, 9, 11b, 12a, 13a-3). The empty throne transcends all these transitory lives and places itself there in the eternal stability. Even if the throne disappeared on the spot, there would not be any change in the quintessence of its emptiness. The emptiness seems to transcend even the Deceased One. Then, where is the transcendent emptiness coming from? Those who embrace monotheistic religions may say that it should come from the only God. However, the Buddhists can only answer, "It is certain that it comes from the profound that the Buddha saw in his own experiences, which urged him to preach for others." It may be permissible for us to identify the profound with the *Dharma* on which his teachings were founded.

The *Dharma* itself does not start talking to the human beings because of its impersonality. Only the Buddha can interpret it successfully by words. Once it is made clear, it remains through the ages, beyond the lifetime of Buddha.

It may look as if the Buddhists worship the Buddha just as their god or saviour. But basically, they should see the *Dharma* through the Buddha. In other words, the Buddha is nothing but the container of the *Dharma.* For example, the Buddha image in *dharmacakra-mudrā* seems to personify the *Dharma* elaborately (*Pl.* 13). But it cannot possibly attain the perfection as long as the impersonal *Dharma* tries to be expressed in human form. The Buddha images are generally devised for characterizing the great qualities of the Buddha (*mahāpuruṣa-lakṣaṇa*). Nevertheless, any kind of device does not amount to much when compared with the impersonal emptiness on the throne. The empty throne is more suitable for expressing the *Dharma* rather than the Buddha.

It is impossible to identify the impersonal *Dharma* with God who has His own personality. But as long as both of them show the guiding principles in life to the human beings of this world, there must be a common ground between the two. The commonality seems to be visible through the emptiness suggested by 'the empty throne', especially when we remember the moral aspects of religions. Eventually, every religion concerns the pursuit of good in human life. For those who practice the good in this life, it does not matter whether their respective religions deal with the afterlife or not. The most important thing is to spend the present time well.

In this respect, the present time common to every human life can be seen and felt on 'the empty throne' where the hearts of the religions must be present. The emptiness on the throne can absorb the eyes of any people tying to see the profound meaning of this lifetime and the eternity lying behind. 'Looking at the empty throne' can be equal to 'thinking about the most essential matters of this life'. Above all, the empty throne in Buddhism is totally concerned with this real world where one should not waste time on laziness.[43] There is no vision of hell and heaven where God should send the human beings after His judgement. Therefore, it may be possible to regard it as the starting point in Comparative Religion. If something else is added there, the category of the empty throne will increase naturally (Zoroastrianism,Yahwism/Judaism, Christianity, Islām and Sikhism).

(B) THE EMPTY THRONE IN ZOROASTRIANISM

Candles and lamps are alight in all the world and cast their rays over the most holiest places. The still flames penetrate through the most solemn moments of prayer.

From ancient times, fire has always been purifying religious sanctuaries where God/ divine beings are believed to manifest Himself/themselves. Towards the sanctuary, people still like to offer the fire lit on a candle or lamp even in modern times when one's daily life relies on electric light.

We usually have an experience of staying in darkness owing to the stoppage of power supply. Someone among us scrapes a match into flame to light a candle. It is the only chance to see the fire lit up in the dark night all around us. Some people may recall the fact that fire is the closest guard of mankind in the darkness of the night. Other people, especially in a mountain hut or a cabin on a stormy night, must feel that their own lives also are burning as fire against the menace of death.

Fire becomes a sacred symbol in the process of finding the dignity of one's precious life. Candles and lamps will always be lit by each offerer in various sanctuaries of the world, as long as fire suggests vital force and holiness to reflect them upon human spirit. Among the burning fires of the sanctuaries, Zoroastrian fire has the oldest history behind it.

We cannot establish fixed dates for the life of Prophet Zarathuštra who lived in pehistoric times; but there is archaeological evidence to suggest that "he flourished when the Stone Age was giving way for the Iranians to the Bronze Age, possibly, that is, between about 1,700 and 1, 500 BC."[44] In those days, the ancestors of both the Iranians and the Indians were going to drift apart from each other, but still lived in the common religio-cultural background. Iranian priests, as well as Indian brāhmaṇas, served the deity of fire and water, etc. and performed the rituals called '*yasna*' (Skt. *yajña*) with animal sacrifice.[45] Above these gods and goddesses of natural phenomena, three gods, Mithra, Varuna, and Mazdā occupied the highest status of '*Ahura*' (Skt. *Asura*,'the Lord') as the guardian of '*Aša*' (Skt. *Ṛta,* 'order', 'righteousness' and 'justice'). These Lords, however, were merely the objects of warriors' worship to gain a mighty power on the battlefield of pillage. The Bronze Age enabled man to invent chariots and other weapons. Priests were still at the level of magicians who tried to control gods' will with the power of rituals and incantations. The fame of warriors' victory has to be paid for with the death of the weak and unprotected, and the sufferings of the defeated. God still kept silence in the dark age, at the latest, till the time of the Prophet.

Zarathuštra (*Zarathushtra* = *Zara*: golden + *thush*: shining + *stra*: star)[46] actually illuminated the world where he was born as a son of the Spitama family, a priest class of those days. In the history of monotheistic religions, he is the only person who was both priest and prophet. According to tradition, he condemned his father Pourušāspa for following in the wake of evil-magicians and finally left his birthplace.

The young priest was wandering from one village to another to witness acts of warriors and devil-worshippers who destroyed peaceful communities. He became filled with a strong longing for the response of the Ahuras[47] who would never pass over the injustice.

At the age of thirty, revelation finally came to Zarathuštra on the bank of the River Daiti.[48] He, as a priest, went at dawn to the river to fetch water from midstream for a spring festival. When he returned to the bank, he saw there a radiant Being, who revealed Itself as (1) *Vohū Manah* (Good Mind/Purpose) and led him into the presence of five other shining Beings to reveal the entire attributes of Ahura Mazdā, the Lord of Wisdom; (2) *Aša Vahišta* (Best Righteousness), (3) *Spenta Ārmaiti* (Holy Love and Devotion dedicated to what is good and just), (4) *Khšathra Vairya* (Desirable Dominion to realize the Kingdom of God), (5) *Haurvatāt* (Health and Perfection), and (6) *Ameretāt* (Long Life and Immortality). Ahura Mazdā Himself is (7) *Spenta Mainyu* (Bounteous Spirit)[49] whose nature is entirely good. (1) ~ (6) are just like the rays from His ever-shining domain. From the revelation of (1) ~ (7), the seven 'Bounteous Immortals' (*Ameša Spentas*), Zarathuštra was given his prophecy to proclaim that Ahura Mazdā is "the one uncreated God, existing eternally, and Creator of all else that is good, including all other beneficent divinities".[50]

In the history of monotheistic religions, Zoroastrianism, '*Mazdāyasni Dīn*' (Religion of Mazdā-worshippers) is unique in the sense that God can be worshipped as the isolated Beings [(1) ~ (7)]. Other divinities too, are not denied as non-existing idols[51] of pre-Zoroastrian religion. If a divinity is good and beneficent, it proves to be the creation of Ahura Mazdā and His co-worker in the struggle with the Hostile Spirit, *Angra Mainyu*, equally uncreated, but entirely evil. Prophet Zarathuštra, in his vision, beheld the clear-cut contrast between good and evil from the very beginning of the Universe.

> And now when these Two-Spirits together
> did-foregather, they created first-of-all
> LIFE and NOT-LIFE;
> and thus Creation's purpose shall-be-(fulfilled), —
> the worst for-the-followers-of Untruth,
> but for-the-follower-of-Truth the Best (state of) Mind
>
> (*Yasna* 30, 4)[52]

Yasna 30, 4 reveals that 'Two-Spirits' at first created LIFE and NOT-LIFE when they encountered for the first time. Which 'Spirit' is the Creator of LIFE? Obviously, it is the 'good' Spirit, *Spenta Mainyu* as the essence of Ahura Mazdā. Here we can see the LIFE-centred ethics to proclaim that 'LIFE is good' and 'Evil is the Deceiver or Destroyer of LIFE (NOT-LIFE) and its doings; lie, idleness, ignorance, or violence and killing, etc.' The criterion of 'good' and 'evil' can be always defined from the side of LIFE. Nobody dares to deny this because we ourselves are the LIFE, and our vitality is convinced that 'the Lord of LIFE' (*Yasna* 30, 9) should be 'good'.[53]

From the beginning of *Yasna* 30, one of the most important chapters of the *Avestā*, Ahura Mazdā expects that Man should choose His path to the time of retribution when 'good' wins the final victory over 'evil' (*Yasna* 30, 8-11). LIFE will be prosperous for ever without being on the verge of NOT-LIFE. The time is called '*Frašō-kereti*' (Healing or Renovation) as the ideal world of LIFE. All through the times of '*Bundahišn*' (Creation of spiritual/immaterial beings[54] and physical/material beings),[55] '*Gumēzišn*' (Mixture, a blend of good and evil) and '*Wizārišn*' (Separation of good from evil), Ahura Mazdā continues to improve His creation to make the perfection of LIFE. In Zoroastrian context, LIFE is the supreme good beyond all ages and places of the world that dominates over any other kind of good values.

Among the attributes of Ahura Mazdā, the '*Aša*', the nucleus of 'the Divine Law, Truth, Justice, Righteousness and Holiness'[56] is the best protector of LIFE. Because '*Aša*' rules over good thoughts (*Humata*), good words (*Hukhta*), and good deeds (*Hvaršta*) that finally lead to the eternal LIFE. From the day of the initiation ceremony called *Navjōte* ('New Initiates'), a Zoroastrian child recites '*Ašəm Vohū*' (*Aša* is good) along with other prayers (*Padyap-Kušti*) five times a day:[57]

> In righteousness (Ashoi) lies real happiness,
> for it is God's finest gift; happiness is his
> who is righteous for true righteousness' sake.[58]

At the very moment of the first revelation from Ahura Mazdā, Zarathuštra imaged the *Aša* as the ever-shining flame of the Divinity that expels the darkness of evil in the world.

> As the Holy One I recognized Thee, O Wise Lord,
> When He came to me as Good Mind (Vohū Manah).
> To His question: "To whom wilt thou address thy worship?"
> I made reply: "To Thy Fire ! While I offer up my veneration to it,
> I will think of the Right (Asha) to the utmost of my power.
> (*Yasna* 43, 9)[59]

Thus the Prophet raised an altar for the sacred Fire of Ahura Mazdā and made it His sanctuary.

Fire is the image of God made by His own hands, "incomparably more sublime than any image graven by human hands".[60] It reflects His living reality upon the heart of a prayer whose life comes from His Life itself.

It is notable that the sacred Fire (*Ātarš*) is often addressed as: "O Fire, son of Ahura Mazdā, the universal purifier, grant me a full life, full of happiness, ever-increasing wisdom, a tongue that convinces,[61] and strength that is manly" (The *Ātarš Niyāišn*)[62]. The Son of God is considered as "the King"[63] enthroned on the altar.

In this context, it is possible to see the Fire-altar (*Khuān*) as 'the empty throne' of Zoroastrianism. Through the medium of His image (Fire), the invisible God represents Himself. Priests have a duty to hold the ever-lasting Fire. They perform the Boi-ceremony[64] five times a day in order to renew 'the throne' (altar) by placing frankincense (*Lobān*) and six pieces of sandalwood over the Fire. Pieces of sandalwood are sometimes used for making a symbolic-throne over the burning embers.[65]

Let us see *Pl*. 24. On the left side, King Lohrāsp is standing as the representative of royal patronage to the Prophet Zarathuštra and Zoroastrians in later periods. Another figure with a halo is the Prophet himself. Over the heads of these personalities, *Fravašis*, the guiding spirits, are flying with solemnity. The divine radiance on the altar is called '*Ātarš Bahrām*' in the highest rank of Zoroastrian sacred Fires.[66] In ancient Persia where the rulers embraced the Zoroastrian religion, there was the tradition of enthroning a sacred Fire on a stone pillar-altar (cf. *Fig.* 12-b). In *Pl.* 24, however, the painter does not reproduce the historical fact. The Fire is kept in the *Afarganyu*, a huge metal container used originally to hold glowing embers during the act of worship. In the fifteenth century, the Parsis, the Zoroastrians of India,[67] began to use this metal vessel to hold the *Ātarš Bahrām*.[68] In modern times, the *Afarganyus* are used at every Fire Temple of the world. *Pl.* 24 is the frontispiece of the book published in Bombay[69] whose Parsi population is the largest in India [cf. Visuals; Plates]. Therefore, *Pl.* 24 may show that the Parsi tradition is authorized by the figures of 'Kai Lohrāsp' and 'Ratu Zarathuštra'.

Pl. 25 is the Temple to hold the Fire called '*Dar-e-Meher*'. '*Meher*' (*Mihr*) is a Pahlavi word meaning the origin of light and the rays of the sun.[70] '*Meher*' is one of the most important '*Yazads*' (worthy of worship) among the divine beings created by Ahura Mazdā. Where the people embrace His light, there is no room for darkness.[71] It enables them to battle with *Angra Mainyu* (Pahlavi: *Ahriman*[72]) who unleashes his evil powers: deceit, decay, disease, death, and destruction, etc. The illuminator of "the sacred Fire" in the dark night (*Pl.* 25)[73] proclaims that the invisible God can be watched through the Flames of the Fire not only by Zoroastrians as long as one seeks for His Glory in this world.

Fire makes a linkage with every religion because of its symbolism of Life, Purity, and Justice, etc., which means the very fact that religions have the one purpose of realizing one ideal world for mankind and other living beings.

Though Zoroastrianism is a religion of Indo-Iranian origin, it proves to be monotheistic because Zarathuštra was the first prophet who taught "the doctrines of an individual judgement, Heaven and Hell, the future resurrection of the body, the general Last Judgement, and life everlasting for the reunited soul and body",[74] all of which can be realized by only one God.

(C) THE EMPTY THRONE IN YAHWISM/JUDAISM

God is the invisible Being whose symbolical name Y H W H must not be pronounced by Jewish people.[75] As He is invisible, He manifests Himself in many ways towards human beings.

When God appeared before the eyes of Abraham, He was taking the form of 'three men'.[76] When He talked to Moses for the first time, His presence was in a flame of fire out of the midst of a bush (*Exodus* 3 : 4).[77] Or, He went before the tribes of Israel "by day in a pillar of a cloud, to lead them the way; and by night in a pillar of fire, to give them light; to go by day and night"[78] when they were wandering in the wilderness away from Egypt.

God can manifest Himself everywhere at His own will. But when the human beings need to offer their prayers and sacrifices, they cannot help preparing some holy place where they should turn their faces toward God. God also needs to place Himself at the human level whenever He expresses His will towards the human beings as the best of His creatures.[79]

When there was no house built unto the name of the Lord, "only the people sacrificed in high places".[80] The people made the altars of earth and stone in open air under the guidance of God Himself.[81] It goes without saying that God prohibited them from making and worshipping any kind of idols[82] because He is the living God[83] who has entered into a moral contract with the human beings, especially in His selection of the Israel as the blessed people.

It was after Moses was given the Law of God on the top of the mount Si'nai that the people began to need their own sanctuary where "two tables of stone"[84] should be placed in peace. During the Exodus, the tables of stone on which God wrote the words of Law had been put into the ark of the covenant[85] and placed in "the tabernacle of the tent of the congregation".[86] The tabernacle was filled with the glory of the Lord and even Moses could not enter into the sanctuary .[87] Whoever sees God's face directly can live no more.[88] For the purpose of entering the holy place, the priest had to bring "a young bullock for a sin offering, and a ram for a burnt offering",[89] etc. God appeared "in the cloud upon the mercy seat"[90] and accepted the offerings and the prayers of His people.

In passing, the altar of burnt offering[91] had the horns on the four corners of it. The priest used to "take of the blood of the bullock, and of the blood of the goat, and put it upon the horns of the altar round about".[92] The horns were sometimes grasped by hands when someone pleaded for his life in the midst of crisis.[93] From this example, it is not difficult to infer that the tabernacle of the Lord, especially the altar of offering, was also a refuge against some danger. Originally, the concept of 'sanctuary' contains the meaning of 'refuge' free from the secular world. The refuge gives peace and safety to everyone whenever one needs.

Both the altar set in the open air and the tent of the congregation with the ark of the covenant were made under the supervision of God. Therefore, those were the proper places where God should be present. It is an invisible presence. When the people stood towards God, they must have appeared as if they were looking toward the empty space because of His invisibility. Both the altar and the tent can be regarded as the God's thrones where He should manifest His supreme authority. His orders are absolute for the human beings, for they are all His creatures. In this context peculiar to religion, there is no possibility for them to revolt against His kingship.

This irresistible kingship of God was symbolized in the greatest way when King Solomon built "the house of the Lord".[94] After its construction, the elders of Israel "brought up the ark of the Lord, and the tabernacle of the congregation, and all the holy vessels that were in the tabernacle".[95] "And the priests brought in the ark of the covenant of the Lord unto his place, into the oracle of the house, to the most holy place, even under the wings of the cherubims."[96]

"King Solomon stood before the altar of the Lord in the presence of all the congregation of Israel, and spread forth his hand toward heaven."[97] ". . . will God indeed dwell on the earth? behold, the heaven of heavens cannot contain thee; how much less this house that I have builded?/ Yet have thou respect unto the prayer of thy servant, and to his supplication, O Lord my God, to hearken unto the cry and to the prayer, which thy servant prayeth before thee today: / That thine eyes may be open toward this house night and day, even toward the place of which thou hast said, My name shall be there: that thou mayest hearken unto the prayer which thy servant shall make toward this place."[98]

'Thy servant'[99] includes not only a member of Israel but also a stranger who comes from a far off country for the great name of God so that all people of the earth may know His name.[100] It is a cosmopolitan phase of Yahwism making linkage with other monotheistic religions.

Thus, the house of the Lord had existed in the history of Israel at least until it was destroyed twice by Babylonians (586 BC) and Romans (AD 70). The glory of the Lord had filled there[101] and God was actually enthroned upon the sanctuary, which looked like 'the empty throne' in visual sense.

However, even after the destruction of the Lord's House, the ark of the covenant has been occupying the sanctuary of the Jewish people, the niche for the ark in the synagogue. In the synagogue, they used to read and think about the Law of God (*Tôrâ*), study the commentary on the *Tôrâ* (*Midrasch*), offer the nineteen prayers (*t^{e}fillā*) in standing posture (*^{a}mīdā*) and confess their faith in God according to the thirteen creeds edited by Moses Mimonides (1135-1204), etc. Though the synagogue is basically an assembly hall of the Jewish community, the niche for the ark still symbolizes the presence of invisible God and His living Word.

From several categories of the empty throne in Yahwism/Judaism [cf. 'A Table of the Key-Concepts in Chapter IV, 2' (1)] it is proved that each of their existences originates from the word of God which we can find in the *Tôrâ*. In other words, none of them are artificial nor idolatrous even though the human beings make performances around the sanctuary in their own ways. It is necessary for the Jewish people to keep the sanctuary in order to observe the orthodoxy of their monotheism. In this context, they may look as if they refused all kinds of artistic activities for expressing their religious faith because of the dangers of idolatry. But the history of religious art shows many examples of Jewish art professing the faith successfully.

Let us see *Illust*. 19. This is the wall-painting with representations of the *menorah* (seven-branched candlestick), the *etrog* (fruit), and the ark of the covenant (or the house of the Lord in Jerusalem), between the late second century AD and the early third century AD, discovered from Jewish Catacombs of Villa Torlonia, Rome. The *menorah* was one of the instruments belonging to the tabernacle elaborately made under the direct instruction of God Himself.[102] When the tabernacle is lit up by the *menorah*, it signifies the presence of the invisible God. The ark of the covenant symbolizes His living Word. In the upper side of this painting, the sun, the moon, the stars, and the veil (or the curtain) as the symbol of the heavens are recognizable. *Illust*. 19 as a whole is nothing more than an indication that the tomb belongs to a Jewish family, but it must be interesting for us to know about Jewish iconography apparently different from the fine arts of other religions. The house-shaped symbol between two candlesticks (*Illust*. 19) seems to contain the mystery of God and, at the same time, reveal that only the empty space lies inside the house. Just as the saying of King Solomon,[103] even the heaven of heavens cannot contain God. Nevertheless, there comes a necessity of expressing His presence by any means as long as the human beings need to confirm it by their own eyes. It may be that "blessed are those who have not seen and yet have believed" (*John* 20: 29).[104] But it is also a reality that the invisibility can be impressed by visible signs and symbols, etc. Here we can see a paradoxical significance of religious arts.

Now let us turn to *Illust*. 20a-1. This is the oldest example of Jewish art of the synagogues, from the fresco-paintings of *Dura-Europos* (cf. Chapter II, 3). When we survey each scene according to the Biblical accounts, it becomes quite clear that this wall-painting collects some of the most important subjects of the Jewish faith.

a. The niche to place the ark of the covenant.

b. (From the left) the *menorah*, the Lords' house, and the sacrifice of Isaac.[105]

c. The big tree of grape, Orpheus (or David) and animals.

d. Jacob blessings his sons, Joseph, Manasseh and Ephraim, the sons of Joseph;[106] One person sitting on the throne.

e. Moses called by God in a flame of fire out of the midst of a bush.[107]

f. Moses receiving the Law of God on the top of the mount Si'nai.[108]

g. Ezra (or Moses?).

h. Abraham (or Joshua, or Moses?).

i. The twelve tribes of Israel before crossing the Red Sea. [109]

j. The Egyptians being drowned in the midst of the sea.[110]

k. The Israels walking upon dry land in the midst of the sea.[111]

l. The well in the wilderness; The water flowing out of the central well toward the houses of the twelve tribes of Israel.[112]

m. The tabernacle of Aaron, the High Priest.[113]

n. The shrine left alone.[114]

o. The Dagon's house punished for the guilt of having captured the ark of the covenant.[115]

p. Elijah who revives the son of the widow woman.[116]

q. The victory of Mordecai.[117]

r. The elders of Israel who anoint David king over Israel.[118]

s. The childhood of Moses; the baby Moses drawn out of the river by the daughter of Pharaoh.[119]

(a) is the holiest place where the Law of God is enshrined. The Law's spirit, the God's Will can be symbolized by the motifs of 'b'. The *menorah* is found in other scenes ['l', 'm'] also. The sacrifice of Isaac promises the genuine dovotion for God of Abraham, the father of Israels. 'c' is the common subject to one of the main motifs of early Christian art.[120] Christians regarded Orpheus as Christ preaching the Gospel to the people but for the Jews, Orpheus reminded them of the King David who was good at playing the harp.

It seems that all of the scenes from 'd' to 's' try to remind the viewers of the historical bond between God and the tribes of Israel. If the viewers were Jews, they would be able to confirm their own faith in God through the blessings and the miracles of God depicted here. Needless to say, God is never pictured anywhere. But, in spite of the fact, there can be felt a sort of tension in the presence of God. It is as if the personages of this wall-painting were the mirrors reflecting the image of God.[121] In other words, the personages are looking towards the invisible God, just as they attend upon the empty throne.

In synagogue, the Ark of the Covenant (Oron Hakodesh) can be regarded as 'the empty throne'[122] where God's Will is present. *Pl.* 27 is an example of the sanctuary in the synagogue of modern times. The holy Ark is behind the Poroches (curtain), toward which the cantors or readers stand at the Omud (reading stand) to lead the congregation in prayer. "Frequently, a decorative legend is inscribed on the Omud, reading 'Know Before Whom You Stand'. Another phrase is often inscribed on the Ark itself or on the Omud: 'I Place The Lord Constantly Before Me'."[123]

Illust. 20a-2 is a part of *Illust.* 20a-1 ('h'). He is identified as Abraham, or one of other important prophets like Joshua and Moses. In any case, we can enter into his devout feelings for God. He is standing firm on the earth under the sky strewn with stars, the sun and the moon, with his hands crossed in solemnity. His eyes are looking up at the sky as if he is seeing some vision there. There is a black square in the backside of his face, which emphasizes the absorption in his prayer to God and the strong-minded character peculiar to a prophet. It might have been quite a bold device for the painter to have painted the black square behind the prophet's face.

Or, it has something to do with the Biblical account that Moses had ever put a veil on his face when he came down from the mount Si'nai in order to convey the Word of God?[124] What was the reason? It was because the skin of his face had been shining since "he went in before the Lord to speak with Him".[125] In case *Illust.* 20a-2 is the portrayal of Moses, the meaning of the black square may be made clear, although it is not a veil on the face but a screen behind it.

We cannot overlook the fact that this prophet (*Illust.* 20a-2) is standing with his back to the infinite space of the sky signifying the greatness of God beyond imagination. Nobody can recognize God visually, but His presence looks through the figure of a prophet who has a dialogue with Him under the sky just as the throne of the Invisible.

In the context of our study dealing with the concepts of the empty throne, *Illust.* 20a-2 seems to show us the prototype of the particular situation which cannot but set up something visible (the altar, the tabernacle, etc.) for the purpose of setting one's face towards God as the Invisible.

Judaism is one of the strictest religions of this world, as well as Islām, which has been taking caution against the danger of confining 'God' to the level of human concepts and imaginations. Therefore, it can be said that Illust. 20a-1 as a whole represents the spirit of monotheism with the historical scenes of Israel. Those who saw this painting at the time of their visit to the synagogue might have felt the same way as we have described in this section. Or, they might have recalled a religious passion peculiar to the Jewish people who had been yearning for the Land of Promise, which is unknown to non-Israel. The racial enthusiasm is unique as compared with other kinds of religious passions in Zoroastrianism, Christianity, Islām and Sikhism which are also focused on their respective sanctuaries or 'the empty throne'.

(D) THE EMPTY THRONE IN CHRISTIANITY

In Christianity, Christ is "the image of the incarnate God who appeared on earth in the flesh, and who, in his ineffable goodness, lived with human beings and assumed the nature, the thickness, the shape and the colour of the flesh."[126] It is a series of the Christian faith that Christ lived a life in this world, died by crucifixion, lay in the tomb, resurrected, appeared before his disciples, ascended to the heaven,[127] and God sent them the Holy Spirit on the day of Pentecost[128] in the name of Christ,[129] and Christ will come to this world on the day of the Last Judgement. This process suggests several categories of 'the empty throne' in Christianity as follows.

(1) *The empty tomb of Christ*

It is proof of Christ's resurrection. The Roman Emperor, Constantinus I (274?-337) constructed the Christian Church in Jerusalem. It was the edifice in memory of three places: the Christ's tomb carved in the rock-cave, the site of crucifixion on the hill of Golgotha and the place where Helena (250?-330?), the mother of Constantinus I, is said to have discovered the holy Cross.[130] The cross crucified Christ, but it becomes the Cross of Victory[131] because of his resurrection. It was quite reasonable for the Emperor to have commemorated the resurrection in the form of the empty tomb.

When we consider the empty tomb just as the empty throne, what does it mean? It is certain that Christ is not present there any more.[132] He will not come back to his tomb. Therefore, 'this empty throne' signifies his eternal absence from the death. In other words, it may become the throne in memory of the victory over death. Here Christians can confirm their faith in Christ and hope that they will be given the same grace of resurrection as the eternal life.[133]

As Christ takes human forms, the places where he should stay, walk, preach and leave for somewhere else can recall each visible scene to be described, too. Christianity is basically regarded as one of the monotheistic religions.[134] But it is unique as compared with Zoroastrianism, Judaism, Islām, and Sikhism in the sense that the whole nature of God is believed to be condensed into the personality of Christ who had lived as a devout Jew, 'Jesus of Nazareth'.[135] In Christianity, the people gather around Christ because of his personality equal to the Divinity to be worshipped. If they do not worship God through his presence, it is not Christianity any more.

In this sense, Christianity seems to be nearer to Buddhism in which the people gather around the Buddha because of his virtue based on the *Dharma*. It means that both the Buddhist art and the Christian art could produce similar situations where the human beings look towards something which is the holiest symbolized by the empty throne.

(2). *The empty throne to be occupied by Christ at the end of this world*

Let us see *Illust.* 22, a part of 'The Last Judgement' (*Illust.* 23) made of Mosaic in the twelfth century AD in the Cathedral of Torcello, near Venice. It can be regarded as the genuine 'empty throne' because Christ is not yet seated there but certainly will be enthroned as the Judge on the last day of this world.

This empty throne is represented along with the Cross and the Book of Life.[136] Two seraphims are flying aside.[137] And the archangels are standing behind a man and a woman as if they are beckoning these humans to come nearer. Both the man and the woman look very afraid of the Lord of the empty throne even before His advent, because the human beings should be judged according to what they have done in their lifetimes as recorded in the Book of Life. These two persons can only plead for their lives not to be pronounced a death on the day of Judgement.[138] This situation is true of all the Christians conscious of time flowing towards the end of this world. *Illust.* 23 represents the Christian eschatology with five horizontal bands one above the other, peculiar to the Byzantine art.[139]

a. The resurrection of Christ or His descent into limbo (the *Anastasis*). Christ is taking the hand of Elijah the prophet out of the limbo.

b. The Second Coming of Christ, or coming of Christ in judgement (the *Parousia*). Christ is surrounded by the Virgin Mary and St. John the Baptist interceding for sinners (the *Deësis*), twelve apostles sitting in the seats of jurymen and many other saints. Beside the nimbus of Christ, the monograms of IC . XC are seen [*Fig.* 14 (1)e].

c. The preparation of the throne for the Last Judgement.[140] It is called *'Hetoimasia tōu thronou'* (the preparation of the throne) in Greek. The angels are blowing horns to awaken the dead and they rise from the tomb on both sides of *'Hetoimasia'*.

The depictions in 'b' and 'c' are united in this eschatological context. It is also possible to identify the symbology of 'c' with the scene of 'b', if the invisible presence of Christ is recognizable on the empty throne.

In 'd' and 'e' is shown the separation of the righteous 'd' from the wicked 'e', after the resurrection of the dead. The righteous are praising the Christ but the wicked are tormented with the retribution. The skulls at the feet of their naked bodies symbolize the second death.[141]

'f' is a sort of the *Deësis* (cf. b) where only the Virgin Mary is raising her hands and interceding with Christ the Judge for sinners. Her posture can find its prototype in some of the motifs of early Christian art [Fig. 14 (10) and (11)].

This mosaic-painting as a whole produces the tense air in waiting for the Last Judgement. It cannot but urge the viewers to repent of their sins and confess faith in Christ (*Credo*). Above all, 'c' (*Illust.* 22) expresses the tense air in the most effective way because of its emptiness full of mystery.

Originally, the Christian Church had the altar as its sanctuary where a priest administered the sacrament in remembrance of Christ[142] and as the new covenant with God.[143] It has been necessary for Christians to take bread and wine as the body and the blood of Christ in order that they may be invigorated day by day in spiritual life. Though the inner wall of the Church is often decorated with paintings and sculptures, the altar is invariably the simplest and without any images on it, except the cross-shaped instrument. The reason is that the Eucharist, through the reception of bread and wine, must experience the spiritual presence of Christ during his absence from the earth. Christians can appreciate it with the help of the Holy Spirit.[144]

Let us see *Illust.* 24 painted by Raffaello Sanzio (1483-1520), one of the greatest artists of the Italian Renaissance. The theme is '*Disputà*', the Dispute on the Eucharist whether Christ is present spiritually in the sacramental wafer and wine. Many priests are around the altar discussing this subject. On the other hand, Christ himself and his twelve disciples are sitting together on their respective thrones. God the Father (the figure of the old man), Christ and the Holy Spirit (the figure of the dove) symbolize the Trinity, at the same time. The scene of heaven testifies that the Eucharist on earth (at the altar) certainly manifests the spiritual presence of Christ (cf. *Pl.* 26).

Therefore, it may be said that the altar can be treated as the throne where Christians attend on their Lord the Christ to get closer to God.[145] Furthermore, the emptiness on the throne must be full of the Holy Spirit owing to its invisibility.

The altar in Christianity is, as it were, the peephole through which can be seen the presence of God by the medium of Christ according to his words[146]: "Anyone who has seen me has seen the Father." It is quite a Christian situation where Christ is the sole support of one's spiritual life, as compared with the fact that the Buddha *Śākyamuni* is one of the Buddhas (cf. *Illust.* 4c-1, c-2 and c-3). In Christian faith, the Lord (of the altar; the empty throne) is only Jesus Christ. Christians are the gathering of those who have been called by God in the name of Jesus Christ (*Ecclesia*).[147]

In the context of symbology, the altar means not only the throne, as stated above, but also others including the tomb (of Christ), the table of the Last Supper,[148] or the manger[149] and the Church.[150] It signifies that the altar is the main object to remind Christians of many biographical details of Christ's life.

In the case of Christ, it is natural for him to be recognized in human form because of his incarnation, and each of his absence and his presence makes a clear impression on one's mind.[151] Such an experience is familiar to us in human relationships, too. On the contrary, strict monotheism observes the invisibility and omnipresence of God. Above all, Islām seems to recognize His transcendency and expresses the awe towards Him in the clearest of terms.

(E) THE EMPTY THRONE IN ISLĀM

The word 'Islām' means that a human being (creature) surrenders himself/herself to God (Creator). The surrender is absolute and unconditional. There is a relationship between the Lord *(rabb)* and his slave *(ʿabd)*.[152] This treatment may look quite disgraceful to human eyes. But if human beings accept God as the Creator and the only one Being who rules over the universe, then their slavery should be felt proud of and blessed under His authority.

As God acts on human beings in an ethical way, their good deeds should be rewarded in the present lifetime and in the afterlife. In this respect, we can find a common point between Islām on the one hand and Judaism and Christianity on the other. However, the difference between the two in relation to the hell for the unfaithful[153] and the heaven for the faithful[154] is very vivid and severe. This is particularly so as in the *Qur'ān*, because God speaks to Muḥammad in direct narration. Both the *Tôrâ* in Judaism and the Gospels in Chistianity are descriptive and lack power as compared with the *Qur'ān*.

Through the *Qur'ān*, Allāh (God) confirms many times that the only true religion is Islām, one's perfect surrender can be only to Allāh,[155] and that Muḥammad is the last prophet of God *(khātam al-nābīyīna)*[156] standing in a row of prophets of the past including Abraham, Moses, David & Solomon, and Jesus as the son of Mary, etc.[157] The *Tôrâ* *(Taurāt)* and the Psalm *(Zabūr)* of Jewish people,[158] the Gospels *(Indjīl)* of Christian people[159] and the *Qur'ān* of Islamic people are regarded as the four greatest Holy Books revealed by Allāh.

Therefore, the name of Islām does not point to one of the specific religions but means the religion dedicated to only one God. The Arabic name of God (Allāh) also does not have any special implication just as Jews do not pronounce YHWH (the symbolic initials of God Yahweh),[160] or rather., the name of Allāh should be called repeatedly whenever the human beings praise Him.[161]

In the pre-Islamic period (called *jāhilīyah*[162] by Muslims), Allāh was the name of the chief god whose idol was placed in the *Kāʿba* of Mecca, together with many other idol-gods worshipped by Arabic tribes.[163] In 630 when Muḥammad entered the city of Mecca in triumph after the conflict with the citizens, he destroyed hundreds of idols standing around the *Kāʿba* and declared the equality of all the people in the contract with only one God, beyond social ranks, lineage, race, and many other worldly restrictions.

Formerly, Allāh had been called 'the Lord of *Mecca*' (*Rabb Makkah*), 'the Lord of the *Kā'ba* (*Rabb al-Kā'ba*), and 'the Lord of the House' (*Rabb al-Bait*), as the supreme god above other tribal gods. However, since the Islamic period, Allāh had become the name of only one God[164] and other gods had been thoroughly denied their own existences as the products of human imagination.[165]

At the same time, the *Kā'ba* had become the House of Allāh[166] constructed as the base of Islamic rituals,[167] as the place of Allāh's blessing and guidance for living beings,[168] and as the asylum of security for men.[169] From these functions, it follows naturally that the *Kā'ba* is the sanctuary of Islām.

Furthermore, it was proper for Muḥammad to have decided that Muslims should offer prayer (*ṣalāt*) in the direction of Mecca, the place of the *Kā'ba*.[170] This direction of prayer (*ḳibla*) is important in the sense that Islām is independent of other prophetical religions (Judaism and Christianity) in spite of its inheritance from the tradition of monotheism.

If Islām is independent of Judaism and Christianity as the former monotheistic religions, what is the proper nature of Islām? According to the *Qur'ān*, it is explained by the Semitic idea of *'dīn Ibrāhīm'* (the religion of Abraham).[171]

"Abraham was not a Jew, nor yet a Christian; but he was an upright man who had surrendered (to Allāh), and he was not of the idolaters."[172]

The person who is upright and all for Allāh is called *'ḥanīf'* (pl. *ḥunafā'*).[173] Islām is the religion of *ḥanif* (*dīn al-ḥanīf*). And the ideal of *ḥanīf* is Abraham (*Ibrāhīm*) who accepted and bequeathed his faith to his descendants, Isaac, Jacob, Ismāīl, etc.

> "When his Lord said unto him:
> Surrender! he said: I have surrendered to the Lord of the Worlds".[174]

The genuine devotion all for the Lord[175] is praised the most from the standpoint of Islām trying to revive the purest type of monotheism.

That is why Abraham appears with Ismāīl in the *Qur'ān,* as the founders of the *Kā'ba* that is "the first Sanctuary appointed for mankind".[176] Furthermore, these prophets are said to have prayed to the Lord:

> Our Lord! And raise up in their midst a messenger from among them who shall recite unto them Thy revelations, and shall instruct them in Scripture and in wisdom and shall make them grow. Lo! Thou, only Thou, art the Mighty, Wise.

> And who forsaketh the religion of Abraham save him who befooleth himself? Verily We chose him in the world, and lo! in the Hereafter he is among the righteous.[177]

According to these passages, Abraham and Ismāīl hoped that God would send 'a messenger' to instruct His people 'in the Scripture' after ages, which is nothing but a reference to the fact that Muḥammad would appear as the last prophet who should convey God's message in the form of the *Qur'ān*. Therefore, in the Islamic context, it may be said that 'the religion of Abraham' had prepared the way for the last prophet and made the path straight for him.[178]

In this respect, it is very reasonable that *'Maqām Ibrāhīm'* (the place where Abraham stood up to pray)[179] inside the precinct of the *Kā'ba* is one of the plain memorials of Allāh's guidance. The legend says that Abraham was standing there during the construction of the *Kā'ba*.

From the Islamic viewpoint, there must be revived the true tradition of monotheism (the religion of Abraham) when Muḥammad recaptured the *Kā'ba* from the Arabic tribes who had been keeping their idol-gods.[180] The tradition is eternal and immutable.[181]

All these accounts mentioned above clearly point out that the *Kā'ba* is the sanctuary of Islām and can be given the concept of the empty throne. The cube-like appearance (the plan is an irregular rectangle in reality) should remind us of the throne without difficulty. It goes without saying that there is no idol but the holy emptiness inside the *Kā'ba*. There "are three wooden pillars, which support the roof, to which a ladder leads up. The only furnishing is the numerous golden and silver lamps suspended. On the inner walls there are many building inscriptions. The floor is covered with slabs of marbles."[182]

Its inner space is, as it were, a focus of the prayer's direction (*ḳibla*) for all the Muslims, the community of Islām (*Ummah*). When Muslims gather around the *Kā'ba*, saying loudly, *'Labbaika, Allāhumma! Labbaika!. . .'* (we are going toward the presence of Allāh), it seems to convey their religious enthusiasm for the sanctuary. The pilgrims perform the *ṭawāf* round the holy house, going around it left-handedly for seven times. At the end,[183] they sacrifice sheep, goats, camels, and oxen, etc. at their own camps in celebration of the success of their pilgrimage, as a token of thanks to Allāh. The sacrifice of animals for God is one of the devotional acts in Islām,[184] but it is unlike 'the case in the Lord's House of Jerusalem (cf. 'A Table of the Key-Concepts in Chapter IV, 2'; Yahwism/Judaism) because blood is not allowed to flow in the *ḥaram,* the sacred zone around the *Kā'ba*. "Muḥammad left the *Kā'ba* as a building unaltered."[185]

The common act of Muslims in their daily lives is the *ṣalāt* including the confessions of one's faith in Allāh and His apostle (*rasūl*), Muḥammad. No matter where they stay in this world, this prayer is performed on time towards the same direction (*ḳibla*). In the *Masjid* (the Mosque), the *miḥrāb*[186] usually shows the *ḳibla* with its semicircular niche. The niche holds its own empty space inside. It should not be paid special reverence because of its role of pointing to the *ḳibla* in the inside of the *Masjid* as the assembly hall of prayers. Nevertheless, the emptiness of the *miḥrāb* niche seems to symbolize the invisibility of God and the strict prohibition against image-making. From this point of view, it is possible for us to treat the *miḥrāb* niche just as the empty throne and consider its meaning by observing one of the examples to relate the nature of the *miḥrāb*.

Let us see *Pl*. 28. This is the titled *miḥrāb* in the *Masjid* of Sokullu Mehmet Pasha, Istanbul; designed by Sinan for an independent patron in 1571-72. As a sort of chandelier is hanging down from the ceiling, it is hard to observe the polygonal part of the *miḥrāb* whose design was originally developed by the Turkish people and brought by the Seldjūḳs to Asia Minor.[187] This *miḥrāb* shows not only the beauty of Muslim decorative art but also the fact that its place forms the culminating point in the whole equipment of the *Masjid*. We can point it out from the Arabic scripts written in calligraphy.[188]

a. There is no God but Allāh who is the King, true and incomparable.[189]

b. Muḥammad is the prophet of Allāh. He is of true promise and trustworthines.[190]

c. In the name of Allāh, the Beneficent, the Merciful.

Say: He is Allāh, the One!
Allāh the eternally Besought of all!
He begetteth not nor was begotten.
And there is none comparable unto Him.[191]

d. (And her Lord accepted her with full acceptance and vouchsafed to her a goodly growth; and made Zachariah her guardian). Whenever Zachariah visited her in the sanctuary (he found that she had food. He said : O Mary! Whence cometh unto thee this (food)? She answered: It is from Allāh. Allāh giveth without stinct to whom He will:).[192]

e. I witness that there is only one God.

He is alone and has no partner. [cf. 'a'].

f. I witness that Muḥammad is His slave and His prophet [cf. 'b'].

What is given as 'c' here is the whole of *Sūrah* CXII named *Al-Tauḥīd* (The Unity) which has been regarded as the essence of the *Qur'ān*. 'a' and 'e' seem to derive from 'c'.

As Arabic scripts are written from right to left, it is proper to read from 'a' to 'b', and from 'e' to 'f'. 'a' and 'e' (right side) are monotheistic; 'b' and 'f' (left side) are peculiar to Islām. Both of them, ['a' and 'e', 'b' and 'f'] are echoing each other from their own sides of the *miḥrāb*. Futhermore, we can see the scripts of 'Allāh' (right side) and 'Muḥammad' (left side) written on the tops of two decorative poles standing beside the *miḥrāb*.

For those who remember the words of the *Qur'ān* at the time of their prayer (*ṣalāt*), the scripts of 'a', 'b', 'e', and 'f' are the best indications to help in concentrating on what they do in front of the *miḥrāb*. (c) written inside the circle is just like the seal put on the sanctuary authorized by Allāh Himself. As a whole, all of these seem to express the principle to maintain the *ummah muslimah,* the community of Islām which has been laying itself under the guidance of Muḥammad as the last prophet of Allāh. It is reasonable that 'a, c, e' are placed side by side with 'b, c, f'. Then, what is the meaning of 'd' in the centre of other passages? Why is it seen there?

'd' is quite interesting especially for us to interpret the *miḥrāb* niche as the empty throne, because this passage tells about the sanctuary where Allāh's grace is given to whom He will. In the *Qur'ānic* accounts, Zachariah, the father of John the Baptist, took care of Mary who would become the Mother of Jesus in the future.[193] After Zachariah saw the sign from Allāh, "the angels called to him as he stood praying in the sanctuary: Allāh giveth thee glad tidings of (a son whose name is) John (*Yahya*), (who cometh) to confirm a word from Allāh, lordly, chaste, a prophet of the righteous".[194]

These accounts suggest that Allāh had ever given His blessing and good news for the purpose of informing that prophets (John and Jesus) would appear in this world, just in the situation of the sanctuary. In Christianity, Jesus is the Christ, the only Son of God. But in Islām he is standing in a row of other prophets, and the Seal of the prophets (*khātam al nābīyīna*) is none other than Muḥammad.[195]

Accordingly, 'd' expresses how the sanctuary is blessed by Allāh and His blessing fills it till now, backed up by the Islamic truth of 'a, b, c, e, and f'. The *miḥrāb* niche itself is not the sanctuary but indicates the direction of the *Kā'ba*. However, it should be naturally sanctified as long as the *ṣalāt* is performed in the *Masjid*, out of Mecca. It should not end in a sign of *ḳibla* but develop into the sub-sanctuary on which the eyes of the faithful are focused all the time. The niche's inner space may look as if it were the dent made by accepting the eyes of countless prayers for a long time.[196]

"The *miḥrāb* niche has been given a twofold origin by Orientalists and historians of art: from the Christian apsis and the Buddhist niche."[197] The semicircular shape is similar to them (cf. *Pl.* 15), but its significance is very Islamic in the sense that the inner space refuses to accept any kind of artificiality, to say nothing of idols. In other words, it can accept only the true faith of Islām. "It is not righteousness that ye turn your faces to the East and the West; but righteous is he who believeth in Allāh and the Last Day and the angels and the Scripture and the Prophets."[198]

If it is allowed to say furthermore, the true sanctuary is where the true faith is: "the true *Kā'ba* is nothing other than our own being".[199] In this context, our empty throne should be shifted into our inner sides which only God can see through and talk to. The prayers cannot help peeping into the cavity of their own minds, turning their eyes towards the *miḥrāb* or the *Kā'ba*.

The inner space of the *Masjid* (*Illust.* 25) seems to suggest that God is omnipresent but man is allowed to see the Infinite inside the edifice under its architectural effect. The vast cavity over the heads of the prayers fills in the interior with divine purity. Nothing should be added there any more. Only the names of the *khalīfah* (the deputy of Allāh) after Muḥammad: (from the left) Abū Bakr, Ali, Hussain, Ḥassan, Osman, and 'Umar are decorative elements. Their calligraphies inside the medallions look like the eyes watching the divine purity all the time. *Illust.* 25 is a good example to grasp the concept of 'the empty throne' in Islām.

(F) THE EMPTY THRONE IN SIKHISM

Whoever visits a Sikh temple (Gurdwārā) finds himself/herself in the stream of reciting and singing voices from the *sanctum sanctorum,* where the Holy Scripture (the *Ādi Granth*) is enshrined on the throne (*Āsana*). The throne is always supported by a wooden stand with a roof called *'Pālkī'* (Pl. 29). Devotees stand in front of the throne, kneel down towards it in prayer, and stand up again to right-handedly go around the sanctuary. This process is given the name of 'Pārikarma', a completed act of 'Godward' (Gurumukh)-worship. Each devotee looks as if he/she has joined the stream of 'the words of the Gurus' (*Gurbānī*) recited and sung continuously. After the act of 'Pārikarma', the devotees seat themselves on the floor and listen to the *Gurbānī* in meditation.

In the early morning, the custodian of a Gurdwārā or another Sikh (*Granthī*)[200] begins his daily routine (*Nitnēm*) by bringing out the *Ādi Granth* from the *Sukhāsana*, the rest room (cf. on the right side of *Pl.* 30) where the Scripture is enshrined overnight, and placing it under the *Pālkī*. The *Nitnēm* starts with the recitation of the *Japjī*, the words of Guru Nānak:

> *Ik Oṅkār*
> *Sat(i) nām(u) Kartā-purakh(u)*
> *Nirbhau Nirvair(u)*
> *Akāl-mūrat (i) Ajūnī*
> *Saibhaṅg Gur-prasād(i)*
> *Jap(u).*[201]

This is the opening words of every Sikh recitation, meaning: "God is only One./His name is True. He is the Creator./ He is without fear. He is inimical to none./ He never dies. He is beyond births and deaths./ He is self-illuminated. He is realised by the kindness of the True Guru./ Repeat His Name."[202]

The first two words *'Ik Onkār'* are one of the most important symbols of Sikhism. Its Puñjābī scripts ੴ are usually made as an ornament and placed beside the *Āsana* (cf. *Pls*. 29, 30, and 32). In Sikhism, God reveals Himself only through the *Gurbānī* and His name, *'Wāhegurū'*[203] meaning 'Wondrous Master'. The repetition of the Sikh mantra *'Wāheguru'* is an invocation of God's Holy Spirit. A Sikh life without 'Nām Simran' (the remembrance of 'The Name', invoking the Holy Spirit) is barren and meaningless.[204] The sound of *'Wāhegurū'* actually inspires every Sikh who repeats it. Their inspired and vigorous attitudes remind us of the occasion of Pentecost where the people were filled with the Holy Spirit.[205] Sikhs pray and chant only in Puñjābī and other languages spoken in India, not in foreign tongues. But we can observe here how the Name of God enhances the spirit of devotees.

After the *Japjī* is finished to recite at the *Āsana,* the *Kīrtan* (singing of the optional verses from the *Ādi Granth*) is performed by three trained musicians called *'Rāgī'*[206] (cf. two of them can be seen in *Pl*. 29). Two Rāgīs usually play the Harmoniums and another Rāgī beats the Drum (*Tablā*). It is essential to note that the *Gurbānī*, the spirit of the *Ādi Granth* or the *Śrī Guru Granth Sāhib* is always appreciated as the combination of poetry and music. Both have come together to touch and awaken the soul of listeners from the time of Guru Nānak. He used to sing his hymns to the accompaniment of a *Rabāb*, an instrument played by his follower, Bhāī Mardānā.

The melody lines of the *Gurbānī* continuously shower upon the people in the Gurdwārā. It is compared to the raindrops of Nectar (Amṛt):

Bāṇi Gurū, Gurū hai Bāṇī, vich(i) Bāṇī Anmrit (u) sāre.

"*Bāṇī* is the Guru and Guru is the *Bāṇī*, which is full of Nectar."[207] *'Bāṇī'*, the Divine Word, comes from God through the meditation of the Gurus. To the listeners of the *Bāṇī*, God in the Gurus pervades their words (*Gurbānī*), and the Gurus reflect the image of God.[208] Thus the Sikh Gurus can be treated as the living Word of God and the only Way to know Him.[209] The following *Gurbānī* is *"jhim jhim varse, amṛt dharā"*, one of the most popular verses sung with different tunes:

In gentle showers is *amṛta*-rain falling;
By the Guru's guidance, the Guru's guidance truly,
has the Beloved Lord come within sight.
By the loved Name Divine is the world saved;
by the Name Divine is attained exaltation.[210]

The word *'Amṛt'* symbolizes the sweet Grace of God to liberate one's soul from the continuous births and deaths (*saṃsāra*) in the law of *Karma*.[211] In Sikhism, "God is the Creator of the first *Karma*, the origin of the universe, and destroyer of *Karma*":[212] One's deeds in this life cannot be effaced but they would be recorded by God.[213] He is the sole authority to implement the reward or the punishment in the cycle of *saṃsāra*. "Whatever one sows, he reaps. (Satguru) Nānak (says), man takes birth and dies by God's order", until he attains the God-realization,[214] the perfect unity with God. This shows that Sikhism subscribes to the fourfold principles of Hinduism, *Karma-Saṃsāra-Jñāna-Mukti*, but surrenders them to 'the Will of God' (*Hukam*)[215] at the same time. According to Sikhism, all past *Karma* can be erased through the association with saints,[216] and meditation on "the Name", [217] because of the Grace of God.

As the *Amṛt* tastes sweet, Sikhs dissolve sugar in drinking water for the Baptism (*Amṛt Chhakana*), and distribute a sweet dish (*Karāh Prasād*)[218] to all attending the service in a Gurdwārā irrespective of birth (caste), race and creed.

When the daily routine is going to be finished in the evening, the *Śrī Guru Granth Sāhib* returns to the rest-room, '*Sukhāsana*'. The climax of the Sikh ritual comes when the *Granthī* holds the Scripture on his head (*Pl.* 30), goes around the sanctuary at the head of a procession of the followers (*Pl.* 31), and enters into the *Sukhāsana* (*Pl.* 32). The Scripture is placed there overnight, but it is said "never to take a rest and sleep" according to the Sikh tradition.[219]

After the procession of the *Śrī Guru Granth Sāhib,* the members of the *Sangat* (congregation) begin to clean the *Pālkī* and the *Āsana*, chanting '*Sat Nām Wāhegurū*' [True Name (is) Wondrous Master] all together. Both the acts of this cleaning work and the *Pārikarma* around the sanctuary aim at purifying one's soul to offer God oneself as the instrument of His Will.

In Sikhism God has "no particular name"[220] except for the titles of 'Wondrous Master' (*Wāheguru*), 'Creator' (*Kartār*), 'Eternal' (Akāl), 'True Name' (*Sat-nāma*), and 'Lord' (*Sāhib*), etc. But He can also be called by the names of Allāh, Rāma, Gopāl, Śiva, Viṣṇu, Brahmā, Pārvatī, Lakṣmī, Sarasvatī, etc. because the Gurus and their followers have a faith that Hindus, Muslims and other people worship one God by different names. In addition to the theory of Karma, Sikhism takes over an Indian traditional thought of God from the *Ṛg-vedạ* (cf. Pl. 23). Moreover, Sikhs, as well as Buddhists and Jains, use the concept of '*Dharma*' for the eternal Truth/Law. These are unique and exceptional among other monotheistic religions of the world.

Because of the catholicity towards other faiths, the Sikh scripture contains not only the verses and hymns of the Sikh Gurus, but also those of Hindu devotees (*Bhaktas*) and Muslim mystics (*Sūfis*), with expressions from Puñjābī, Western Hindī, Prākṛt, Persian, and Arabic, etc. This suggests the spirituality of Guru Nānak, the founder of Sikhism, who widely travelled over Indian and foreign sacred places including Mecca in order to exchange views with those who had different faiths. After he expired, his Hindū and Muslim disciples developed a serious dispute about whether his mortal remains should be consigned to fire or must be buried. However, on the next day, they could only find his coffin filled with flowers. There was no mortal body any more.[221] This story describes well the essence of the Sikh sanctuary where the *'Srī Guru Granth Sāhib'* is enshrined; that is to say, the Scripture is the spiritual remains of the ten Gurus and other saints, but the Sikhs should not adhere to their sacred memories and authority.

> In the body God is present,
> The body is His temple,
> In the body is the place of pilgrimage,
> Of which I am the pilgrim.[222]

The religious awakening and practice ultimately depend upon one's own self. A server of God should enshrine Him in his own being, first of all. The presence of the Scripture on the throne is an instrument to turn the people Godward (*Gurmukh*). In this very respect, Sikhism finds a way of dialogue with other religions beyond doctrinal differences.

Thus the Sikh sanctuary is also regarded as 'the empty throne' whose essence belongs to the invisible Being. Through the transperancy of the 'emptiness', we should find the underlying reality in all religions that is much more important than differences in religious characteristics. When can we see the day when human beings would cease from the fighting among themselves over the names of religions and other creeds?

3. A Discovery of its Modernity

From the discussion so far, it is clear that the concept of 'the empty throne' can contain various meanings depending on the characteristics of respective religions. A common point is that all kinds of 'the empty thrones' express the highest and purest value to be adored by human beings. 'It' is invisible and dignifies 'the throne' as the sanctuary. What is 'It'? It is possible to recognize the presence of God according to the tradition of monotheism. Or, there can be seen the everlasting Truth or Law. In any case, human beings cannot live without orbiting around their Supreme Authority.

It is necessary to point out the fact that all 'the empty thrones' witness not only the prayers and the reading of holy scriptures but also the repentance for one's sin and the confession of faith. What is the meaning of these religious actions? It means that the religious sanctuaries set their faces towards 'this world' full of troubles and sufferings. At the very places of 'the empty thrones', the people can find common problems to be solved in cooperation with each other. For the purpose, they need to revere others' sanctuaries to understand others' humanity and ways of life. In this respect, the concept of 'the empty throne' finds its modernity that enables us to reach the heart of the problems beyond the difference of religious faiths. The author has arranged 'A Table of the Key-Concepts in Chapter IV, 2' in order to discuss the different religions, but finally would like to remove the partition of the 'Table' as there is no border of Humanity in the religious world.

In spite of various theories of the world beyond, nobody can know about the afterlife. 'The empty throne' (the religious sanctuary) is silent about it and takes us back to the reality of 'this world'. From the height of the skies, the earth satellite sees one world on the planet where quite a number of peoples are alive and co-existent with each other. The satellite's lens do not find Heaven and Hell anywhere in the universe, but gives us a vision of the religious world where the people offer the prayers at their own sanctuaries. All the vectors of the prayers will finally unite to form one stream towards the ocean of the Universe. In this vision, the earth itself can become 'the empty throne' floating in the cosmic emptiness.

In this way, the concept of 'the empty throne' brings forth a macroscopical view of this world. It proves that 'the empty throne' becomes the key-concept to discuss the common object of human reverence in modern times. Because of its transparency to reflect the Invisible Divinity/Truth, 'the empty throne' does not concern itself with the act of idolatry to be condemned in case it causes immorality.[223]

The philosophical vision as shown above is not in vain when we turn our eyes back to 'the empty throne' as one of the motifs of early Buddhist Art, especially if we pursue the modernity of its 'emptiness' (cf. *Pl.* 10).

It is apparent that the history of Buddhist art is almost full of the Buddha images with various styles and makings. As mentioned before in Chapter I, Buddhist people did not concern themselves with why the first Buddha image had been made during the lifetime of the Buddha himself. They just accepted it as a matter of course. There was no possibility of bringing about any iconoclastic movement from the side of Buddhists.

However, from the viewpoint of non-Buddhists who believe in God, such a reverence for the Buddha image is nothing other than idolatry. It is well known that Muslims destroyed the Buddha statue in the stone-cave of Bāmiyān. The broken face (*Illust.* 18) seems to signify one's hostility towards others caused by misunderstanding in ignorance of the other faiths.

Marco Polo (1254?-1324), one of the greatest travellers, refers to numerous idols and idolators in Buddhist countries. One of the most famous accounts is the Ceylonese story of '*Sogamoni Borcan*'[224] (*Śākyamuni* Buddha).[225]

According to the legend, '*Sogamoni Borcan*' was the first sage whose portrayal (idol) had been made for the first time in this world. He was born as a Prince but finished his life as a sage in quest of God, the Eternity and the Creator. The king lamented the death of his son and made the idol of '*Sogamoni Borcan*'. Polo mentions that all the idols in later periods stem from this sage. We can admit it to be true from our knowledge of Buddhist art. But he is different from the historical Buddha *Śākyamuni* in the sense that he did not bring others any salvation but satisfied himself in his own ascetic life. Therefore, this Ceylonese sage can be regarded as the *pratyekabuddha* in Buddhist context. Needless to say, Polo did not have any proper knowledge of Buddhism. Nevetheless, his comment on the biography of '*Sogamoni Borcan*' is remarkable, "If he (*Sogamoni Borcan*) had been a Christian, he must have become a great saint equivalent to my Lord, Jesus Christ". Our interest lies in the fact that '*Sogamoni Borcan*' is praised because of his sacred life, apart from idolatry in later periods. Though Polo was a Catholic coming from Italy, he could objectively recognize the true nature of '*Sogamoni Borcan*' from which idol-worship must have originated. It may be that Polo remembered the Christ image (the Crucifixion, etc.) of the Catholic Church when he heard of the 'Borcan' image (the Buddha image) of Ceylon. But, at the same time, it must be inevitable that the Buddha image had to become 'an idol' as long as he had a Christian faith that only God deserves to be worshipped properly.[226]

To our regret, there is no account that Polo found any monument of 'the empty throne' (cf. *Pl.* 10) in the Buddhist art of Ceylon. If he had seen it there, the nature of '*Sogamoni Borcan*' could have been heightened all the more. Because 'the empty throne' reaches the height of spiritualism with the paradoxical aesthetics that the emptiness is most eloquent of the Lord on the throne. It is quite regrettable that Polo did not have a chance to know about early Buddhist art without the Buddha images (idols).

The quotation from *The Travels of Marco Polo* may at least suggest that one recognizes Buddhist idolatry as a by-product of the artistic activities in the evolution of Buddhism, especially if Polo had known something about the nature of Buddhism or the Buddha *Śākyamuni* even in the form of legend. This recognition should remove one's prejudice or misunderstanding that Buddhism is idolatrous.

Now the question arises: If non-Buddhists do not regard Buddhism as 'idolatrous' to be condemned, what is the basis of criticism against 'idolatry'?

Originally, the idea of idolatry belongs to a series of monotheistic traditions of Zoroastrianism, Judaism, Christianity, Islām and Sikhism. Each of these religions has its own history of conflict with those who worship idol-gods as the inheritance of their ancestors.[227] The basis of criticism of idolatry can be classified into several levels of conception as follows:

(1) Human beings must revere and worship only one God as the Creator and the

Creator of the Universe. God is only one and any other gods are all vanities.[228]

(2) Only God deserves to be worshipped. Therefore, not only gods but also the sun, the moon, the planets, all the host of heaven[229] and other natural phenomena must not be worshipped,[230] even though they look divine to human eyes.

(3) God is alive and active (In God, the human beings live and move and have their being).[231] The human beings "should not think that the divine being is like gold or stone — an image made by man's design and skill".[232]

In other words, an idol is made by the craftsmen "according to their own understanding".[233] It is artificial, powerless and unable to save anybody.[234]

(4) Idolatry, the act of worshipping something other than God, is often connected with the concepts of misconduct: adultery,[235] false oath,[236] indulgence in drink[237] and the sacrifice of one's child for the sake of the idol-god.[238] All of these acts themselves can be called idolatry in contravention of the Word of God.[239]

God is moral and not impersonal. If one is against God's morality, one must set up an idol in one's heart.[240] The idol is invisible but harmful for one's heart to observe loyalty to only one God.

Additionally, the indulgence in great matters, or in things too high for the human beings[241] can become idolatry if one keeps them in one's heart according to one's own imagination. For instance, when one yearns for Paradise so much that one cannot live a life of this world properly, even Paradise is nothing more than an idol.[242]

In this way, idols include both the abstract and the concrete, the material being and the spiritual being. In any case, idolatry should be criticized because of its temptation to divert one's heart from only one God. Blessed are those who love God and keep His commandments.[243] But betrayers are out of His mercy and blessing as long as they do not repent their sins. This is a basis of monotheism under the contract between man and God.

To sum up, all kinds of arguments against idolatry are made for the purpose of taking man back to the pure faith in only one God[244] whose ethical orders are absolute. As God hates idolatry, it is reasonable that each sanctuary of monotheistic religions has no idol but keeps a sort of emptiness where man may stand before God in awe of His dignity (cf. *Illust.* 20a-2). The emptiness is not artificial but realistic to express the invisibility of God. Even any kind of artistic maturity and perfection has its own limitations and cannot reach the infinite expressed by the emptiness of the sanctuary.

Now another question arises: 'Is it possible for us to introduce the empty throne (cf. *Pl.* 10) of early Buddhist art to monotheistic peoples in order that they may not misunderstand Buddhist people as idolaters?'

We have already discussed the main motifs of early Buddhist art in Chapter II (cf. *Fig.* 13) and found some elements of revering the Buddha because of his great deeds, the Enlightenment, the First Sermon, and the Perfect Decease, etc. [cf. *Fig.* 13 (3), (4) a2, (6) a1]. But, at the same time, it is clear that the reason for Buddhist reverence for their Master lies in the great nature of the *Dharma* behind Him [cf. *Fig.* 13 (8) a1, (7) a1, (7) a2, (7) c]. The *Dharma* is abstract and impersonal in itself as long as it is unexpressed by words.

If it is allowed to see the nature of the *Dharma* by the medium of 'the empty throne' (cf. *Pl.* 10, *Illusts.* 1c, 3a, 6, 8a-1, 8c, 9, 12a-2, 13a-3), Buddhist faith may not become the focus of monotheistic criticism even though Buddhists join their both hands towards 'the empty throne' (cf. *Pl.* 11, *Illusts.* 5, 6, 9, etc.).

Furthermore, it goes without saying that no immoral situations can be produced on, before, and around 'the empty throne', as there is no idol at the mercy of human rituals. The human beings can only stay beside 'the empty throne' respectfully.

Up to this point of our discussion, it seems possible to take up 'the empty throne' for promotion of dialogues between the Buddhists and the monotheists. And it is important to point out the modernity of 'the empty throne' as one of the motifs of early Buddhist art, especially because even modern Buddhist people should not be satisfied with the Buddha images which are often treated as curious and cultural assets before the eyes of non-Buddhist people.

Where the Buddhists' own experiences are concerned, a Buddha image is not an idol as long as one sees something virtuous, merciful, and meditative symbolized in the form of the Buddha image. However, it is also a reality that one's reverent attitude towards the Buddha image 'looks like' idol worship. If the insiders (Buddhists) and the outsiders (non-Buddhists) could realize each other's way of seeing the Buddha image, there might be no possibility of creating a misunderstanding between the two. But in reality, it must be normal for everyone to be satisfied by knowing only about one's own thought, experience, and circumstances during one's lifetime.

Accordingly, it is proved that we had better look for something else without any doubt about idolatry. Here we have a reason why the concept of 'the empty throne' should figure in the last stage of our discussions on the 'absence of the Buddha image in early Buddhist art'.

For the present, it is not yet universally admitted that 'the empty throne' of early Buddhist art is notable as the medium of dialogues between Buddhism and other religions, above all, monotheism. But if more and more people see the necessity for understanding others' religions, it may be expected that 'the empty throne' of early Buddhist art would attract their attention sometime. The modernity in the concept of 'the empty throne' consists in our expectation of the future. When the concept is used for Comparative Religion, there should come some methodological problem because the system and the condition of every religion is not simple in reality. Nevertheless, at least for our eyes (cf. A Table of the Key-Concepts in Chapter IV, 2), 'the empty throne' can become the greatest common concept among different religions.

We will be able to think about the absence of the Buddha image in early Buddhist art all the more, after going through the trial process just as seen in this chapter.

Notes

1. *SN*, IX (*Sambulā*) 4. (*Sagātha-vagga*), p. 199.
2. Ex. *Sn*, 708, *Udv*., 33. 53.
3. Ex. *SN*, X. 8 (*Sudatta*), p. 211, *Therig*., 19, 82, *Therag.,* 854.
4. Ex. *Sn*., 925, 958, *Therag.,* 1169.
5. Ex. *Mhp*., chapter 4, 21.
6. Ex. *Mhp*., chapter 3, 1, *Sum-vil*, p. 554.
7. Ex. *SN*, VII (*Saṅghārava*), p. 183.
8. Ex. *Sn*. 556-557, *Therag.,* 827, *SN*, VIII (*Pavāraṇā*), p. 191.
9. Ex. *Sum-vil,* p. 582.
10. Cf. *MS*, II, Pl. 56, 1.
11. Ex. *Therig*., 32, 455, 476.
12. Ex. *Udv*., chapter 21, 11-12.
13. Cf. *Sn*., 454, *Udv*., 11. 13-14, 33. 9-12, *Therag*., 998, *Therig*., 32.
14. *Taishō* 51, 862c.
15. *Ibid*., 863a.
16. *Ibid*., 860a, 860b.
17. *Ibid*., 860b.
18. Ex. *Ibid*., 890b.
19. *Ibid*., 879c.
20. *Ibid*., 882c-883b, etc.
21. *Ibid*., 862c, 863a.
22. *Ibid*., 921 a-b.
23. *Ibid*., 921b.
24. *Ibid*., 898a.
25. Mary Boyce, *Zoroastrianism — Their Religious Beliefs and Practices,* Routledge & Kegan Paul, London, 1979, p.1.
26. The chronology of the ten Gurus is:

    1. Guru Nānak (1469-1539), 2. Guru Angad (1504-1552), 3. Guru Amar Das (1479-1574) whose nephew's spouse was the daughter of Guru Angad, 4. Guru Ram Das (1479-1574),

5. Guru Arjan Dev (1563-1606), the son of Guru Ram Das, 6. Guru Hargobind (1595-1644), the son of Guru Arjan Dev, 7. Guru Hari Rai (1630-1661), the grandson of Guru Hargobind, 8. Guru Hari Kishan (1656-1664), the son of Guru Hari Rai, 9. Guru Teg Bahadur (1621-1674), the son of Guru Hargobind, and 10. Guru Gobind Singh (1666-1708), the son of Guru Teg Bahadur.

Since Jehangir, the Mughal Emperor, executed the fifth Guru for a political reason, the following Gurus had solidified the blood relation to cope with the rulers, and became both '*Piri*' (Saint) and '*Miri*' (Soldier).

27. In India, the concept of 'Guru' is ancient, popular and universal among different religious traditions, Hinduism, Jainism, and Buddhism. Indians usually call their sages and spiritual leaders 'Guru-ji' and 'Gurudev' in reverence. The people like to have a Guru's guidance (*Darśan*), no matter whether the Guru belongs to their own religion. In Indian society, the Guru's speech and action is almost absolute and very influential to his own disciples and others. For example, Mahatma Gandhi (1869-1948) can be regarded as one of the greatest Gurus of the twentieth century. In addition, it is interesting to make a reference to the author's information that Indian Christians sometimes call Christ by the name of '*Saccā Guru*' (True Master) in their hymns sung in the church.
28. H.S. Singha, *Sikh Studies*, Hemkunt Press, New Delhi, 1991, p. 6.
29. Y. Masih, *A Comparative Study of Religions,* Motilal Banarsidass, New Delhi, 1990, p. 261.
30. H.S. Singha, *Mini Encyclopaedia of Sikhism* (Illustrated), Hemkunt Press, New Delhi, 1989, p. 43.
31. *Qur'ān* (*Sūrah*) III 64-75, 110, 199, V 44-48, 68-69 (cf. II 62), etc. *The Meaning of the Holy Qur'ān* (tr.) by Muḥammad Marmaduke Pickthall, Crescent Publishing Company, Delhi, 1985.
32. *Philippians* 2. 6-11, John Meyendorff, *Christ in Eastern Christian Thought,* St. Vladimir's Seminary Press, New York, 1975, pp. 178-79.
33. *Encyclopedia Britannica* Vol. II, William Benton, Publisher, 1965, p. 1056.
34. Cf. Arnold Hauser, *Sozialgeschichte der Kunst und Literature*, 2 Bde., München, 1953.
35. As suggested by Fr. Yasuyuki Takahashi of the Russian Orthodox Church in Tokyo, Japan.
36. *Genesis* 17. 1-8.
37. *Ibid.* 17. 8.
38. *Sūrah* II 135, III 67, IV 125.
39. *Ibid.* II 130.
40. A synagogue is the assembly hall of Jewish people.
41. The Five Books of Moses: *Genesis, Exodus, Leviticus, Numbers,* and *Deuteronomy*.
42. It may be remembered that Christianity originates from a reformationary of this Judaism.
43. *Therig.*, 95, *Therag.*, 452, 1004.
44. Mary Boyce. *op. cit.*, p. 2.

45. Regarding the rituals towards the sacred Fire, there is a significant linkage between Vedic and Avestan religions. In Zoroastrian rituals, however, animal sacrifice is forbidden. Priests (Mobeds) deal with only water, plants, fruits and bread, etc. On the other hand, Hindu altar (*vedi*) of post-Vedic periods came to require goats and buffaloes, etc. killed by the hands of Brāhmaṇas.

46. Dastūr Khurshed S. Dabu, *Zarathushtra and His Teachings (A Manual for Young Students)*, Bombay, 1966, p. 2. 'Dastūr' means the High Priest.

    The word 'Zarathuštra' (: Avestan) got corrupted into 'Zoroastres' (: Greek), which is usually written as 'Zoroaster' in English.

47. Among the three Ahuras, Mazdā was supreme.

48. Framoz Rustomjee, *The Life of Holy Zarathushtra*, Bombay, 1984, pp. 30-33.

49. Cf. *Genesis* 1 : 2, *Psalms* 104:30, etc.

50. Mary Boyce, *op. cit.*, pp. 19-20.

51. Cf. *I Kings* 16:13, *I Corinthians* 8:4, 10:19-20, etc.

52. Irach J. S. Taraporewala (tr.), *The Divine Songs of Zarathushtra*, Bombay, 1993, p. 118.

53. Kanoko Tanaka, *"The Life-Ethics of Yasna 30, 4 and its Educational Effects on the Zoroastrian Youth"*, Congress Proceedings of the 6th World Zoroastrian Congress, Tehran, June 19-22, 1996.

54. 'Mēnōg' in Pahlavi, Middle Persian language).

55. 'Gētig' in Pahlavi. Cf. "The gētīg existence is better than the previous mēnōg one, for in it Ahura Mazdā's perfect creation received the added good of solid and sentiment form." (Mary Boyce, *op. cit.*, p. 25).

56. Piloo Nanavutty Jungalwalla, *Fravarānē "I Believe" — A Zoroastrian Child's Confession of Faith —*, Delhi, 1987, p. i.

57. Zoroastrians put on *Sudreh* (a white muslin shirt with a V-shaped neck) and *Kušti* (a thread, woven of seventy-two strands of fine sheep's wool) all the time except when they bathe. Five times a day, they tie the Kushti thrice round their waist while reciting 'the Kušti prayers' (Padyap-Kušti); 'Ašəm Vohū', 'Yathā Ahū Vairyo', 'Kem-na Mazdā', 'Ahura Mazdā Khodāi' and 'Jasa-me Avangha-e-Mazdā' (Piloo Nanavutty Jungalwalla, *op. cit.*, pp. 11-14).

58. *Yasna* 27, 14. Jae Rustamji Vimadalal (tr. & ed.), *The Sacred Khordeh Avestā (Shahenshahi) — A Book of Zoroastrian Daily Prayers,* Bombay, 1984, p. 2.

59. M. Henning (tr.), *The Hymns of Zarathushtra,* London, 1992, p. 137.

60. Viraf Minocher Dhalla (ed.), *Symbolism in Zoroastrianism — The Religious Ceremonies and Customs of the Parsees,* Bombay, 1994, p. 16.

61. Cf. *Acts* 2 : 1 - 4.

62. Jal Rustamji Vimadalal (tr. & ed.), *op. cit.*, p. 72.

63. Viraf Minocher Dhalla (ed.). *op. cit.*, p. 24.

64. 'Boi' means 'scent', 'smell'. Priests called *bōywārās*, with the veil (*padān*) over their mouths, feed the Fire babul logs, sandalwood and frankincense. *Ditto*, p. 26.

65. Dastūr Khurshed S. Dabu, *Message of Zarathushtra,* Bombay, 1859, pp. 114-15.

66. The sacred Fires are classified into three ranks: (1) *Ātarš Bahrām* [Fire of (the divine being) Bahrām] owned by royal family, (2) *Ātarš Ādurān* (Fire of Fires) brought by priests, warriors, peasants, and artisans, and (3) *Ātarš Dādgāh,* a Fire from kitchen oven. The hierarchy of the sacred Fires reflects the monarchy of Iranian empires, the Achaemenians and the Sasanians.
67. The word 'Parsi' means "the people from Pars or Fars, a province in South Iran". In the early tenth century, some Zoroastrians fled their homeland where the rulers tried to convert them to Islām. In 936, they finally drifted ashore at Sanjān, a small fishing village in Gujarāt, the west coast of India. The Hindū rulers permitted to settle down there and embrace their own religion. Since then, Parsis of India have been forming the major stream of Zoroastrian communities (Anjuman).
68. Mary Boyce, *op. cit.*, p. 172.
69. Cf. Visuals, Plates.
70. Adil F. Rangoonwalla (tr. & ed.). *Meher Niyaesh*, Bombay, p. 1.
71. *Ditto,* p. 21.
72. The word 'Ahriman' in Middle Persian language (Pahlavi) became popular since the time of the Sasanian dynasty. The Sassanian rulers recognized Zurvanism, a heretical Zoroastrianism as the state religion. In Zurvanism, Ahura Mazdā and Ahriman are the Twins born from 'Time' (Zurvān). Both are the counterparts until the end of their battle. Zurvanism had influenced the views of Zoroastianism in later periods. It is not correct to understand that Zarathuštra revealed the battle between two Gods, repesentatives of good and evil, because this theory distorts his monotheism shown in the *Avestā* that Ahura Mazdā and His Bounteous Spirit (Spenta Mainyu) met with the Destructive Spirit (Angra Mainyu) and had started a battle together with His creation. Angra Mainyu cannot be called God, but can be regarded as the destroyer of God's creation. Therefore, we cannot identify 'Angra Mainyu' with 'Ahriman' if we consider the historical backgrounds behind these names. cf. " . . . evil is only a temporary phenomenon and goodness alone is the final thing. Thus, the dualism in Zoroastrianism is only relative and Ahura Mazdā remains the only Reality. Thus dualism is swallowed up in the Absolute monotheism of Zoroastrianism." (Y. Masih, *op. cit.*, p. 33).
73. This illuminator seems to play an important role of informing non-Zoroastrians that the ever-burning Fire is enshrined in the Temple, because they are not allowed to enter the Fire Temple in India. This taboo was put by the Parsi community when they sought refuge at the Sanjān village, the west-coast of India.
74. Mary Boyce, *op, cit.*, p. 29.
75. Cf. *Exodus* 20 : 7, *Deuteronomy* 5 : 11.
76. *Genesis* 18 : 2.
77. *Exodus* 3 : 4.
78. *Ibid.,* 13 : 21.
79. *Genesis* 1 : 28.
80. *I Kings* 3 : 2.
81. *Exodus.,* 20 : 24-26.

82. *Ibid*: 20 4-6, *Deuteronomy* 5 : 8-10.
83. *Ezekiel* 5 : 11, *Isaiah* 49 : 18, *Jeremiah* 22. 24, etc.
84. *Exodus* 34 : 1.
85. *Ibid.*, 35 : 12.
86. *Ibid.*, 40 : 2.
87. *Ibid.*, 40 : 34-35.
88. *Ibid.*, 33 : 20.
89. *Leviticus* 16 : 3.
90. *Ibid.*, 16 : 2.
91. *Exodus* 38 : 1.
92. *Leviticus* 17 : 18.
93. *I Kings* 1 : 50-51.
94. *Ibid.*, 6 : 1.
95. *I Kings* 8 : 4.
96. *Ibid.*, 8 : 6.
97. *Ibid.*, 8 : 22.
98. *Ibid.*, 8 : 27-29.
99. *Ibid.*, 8 : 29.
100. *II Chronicles* 6 : 32-33.
101. *I Kings* 8 : 11.
102. *Exodus* 25 : 31-40, 37 : 17-24.
103. *I Kings* 8 : 27.
104. *John* 20 : 29.
105. *Genesis* 22 : 1-14.
106. *Ibid.*, 48 : 11-20.
107. *Exodus* 3 : 2.
108. *Ibid.*, 34: 1-29.
109. *Ibid.*, 14: 4, 15.
110. *Ibid.*, 14 : 27-28.
111. *Ibid.*, 15 : 22, 29.
112. Cf. *Genesis* 35 : 22, 49 : 1-28.
113. Cf. *Exodus* 35 : 11.
114. Cf. *I Samuel* 4 : 17?
115. *Ibid.*, 5 : 1-5.
116. *I Kings* 17 : 10-24.
117. *Esther* 6 : 11.
118. *II Samuel* 5 : 3.
119. *Exodus* 2 : 1-10.

120. Cf. Chapter II, 3; *Fig.* 14 (5).
121. *Genesis* 1 : 27.
122. Cf. In Jewish tradition, the empty chair (Kise Reik) can be seen in a synagogue and a residence of rich family. This chair is prepared for the coming of the Prophet Elijah in the future. Cf. *II Kings* 2 : 11, *Mark* 15 : 35, etc.
123. This is why those who enter the synagogue must put a cap (kippā) on their heads to remember God's presence.
124. *Exodus* 34 : 33.
125. *Ibid.,* 34 : 34.
126. J.P. Migne, *Patrologia Cursus Completus*, Series Graeca, Paris, 1857 ff, III, 1320b, from John Meyendorff, *Christ in Eastern Christian Thought,* St. Vladimir's Seminary Press, New York, 1975, p. 179 (9. Vision of the Invisible; The Iconoclastic Crisis).
127. *Luke* 24 : 51, *Acts* 1 : 9.
128. *John* 14 : 16, *Acts* 2 : 1-4.
129. *John* 14 : 26.
130. André N. Grabar, *The Beginnings of Christian Art,* (E. tr.), London, 1967.
131. Cf. *I Corinthians* 15 : 26.
132. *Matthew* 28 : 6, *Mark* 16 : 6, *Luke* 24 : 6.
133. Cf. *I Corinthians* 15 : 12-26.
134. Cf. *John* 14 : 27, *I Corinthians* 12 : 6.
135. *John* 19 : 19.
136. *Revelation* 20 : 12.
137. Cf. *Isaiah* 6 : 1-3.
138. *Revelation* 21 : 8.
139. Cf. *Encyclopedia of World Art,* Vol; IV, McGraw-Hill, New York, 1963, p. 823.
140. Cf. *Psalm* 9 : 7, *II Corinthians* 5 : 10.
141. *Revelation* 20 : 14, 21 : 8.
142. *Luke* 22 : 19.
143. *Ibid.,* 22 : 20.
144. Cf. *I Corinthians* 12 : 3-11.
145. *John* 14 : 6-7.
146. *John* 14 : 9.
147. The Latin word 'ecclesia' is a female noun meaning 'the gathering'. It is often used as an equivalent of 'the church'.
148. *Matthew* 26 : 17-30.
149. *Luke* 2 : 7.
150. *The Catholic Encyclopedia* II, (J. tr.), Tokyo, 1971, p. 349.
151. Cf. *Luke* 24 : 30-32.
152. *Sūrah* XXX27,XLII 19, etc.

153. *Ibid.*, LVI.
154. *Ibid.* LV, LXXVI.
155. *Ibid.*, III. 19-20.
156. *Ibid.*, XXXIII. 40.
157. *Ibid.*, IV. 163.
158. *Ibid.*, IV. 163.
159. *Ibid.*, V. 15-16.
160. Cf. *Exodus* 20 : 7.
161. *Sūrah* XXXIII. 40.
162. It means the disorderly period (without the faith in Allāh).
163. *Sūrah* LIII. 19-23. *Allāt* (female form of Allāh), *Manāt*, and *al-'Uzzā* were some of the most popular gooddesses in those days. And the god Hubal might have been very powerful in the *Kā'ba*, although it is never mentioned in the *Qur'ān*.
164. 'Allāh' consists of the noun *'al ilāh'* meaning the god.
165. *Sūrah* XII. 40.
166. *Ibid.*, CV.13.
167. *Ibid.*, V. 97.
168. *Ibid.*, III. 96-97.
169. *Ibid.*, II. 125, III. 97.

     It recalls the purport of the horns on the Jewish altar. Cf. *I Kings* 2 : 28, 1 : 50. The *Kā'ba* is described as a tomb, too. "A series of prophets, numbering hundreds, is said to have been buried round the Kā'ba . . . (Because) every prophet belongs to Mecca."

     E. J. Brill's First Encyclopedia of Islām, Vol. V, 1913-36, p. 590.
170. *Sūrah* II 142-150. Jewish *ḳibla* is the direction of Jerusalem, the place of the Lord's House (*I Kings* 8 : 48). Formerly, Muslims also offered the ṣalāt toward Jerusalem.
171. 'Abraham' is called 'Ibrāhīm' in Arabic.
172. *Sūrah* III. 67 (cf. *The Meaning of the holy Qur'ān*, translated by Moḥammad Marimaduke Pickthall, Crescent Publishing Company, Delhi 1985).
173. *Ibid.*, II. 135, IV. 125.
174. *Ibid.*, II. 131.
175. Cf. *Genesis* 17 : 1-7 (1-3).
176. *Sūrah* III. 96.
177. *Ibid.*, II. 129-130.
178. Cf. *Matthew* 3 : 3, *Isaiah* 40 : 3.
179. *Sūrah* III 97.
180. From the historical viewpoint, the origin of the *Kā'ba* is too old to know. But it is sure that this edifice had been a centre of Arabic tribal religions. Muḥammad himself belonged to one of the most powerful tribes, the Quraish whose homeground was Mecca, the place of the *Kā'ba*.
181. It is called *'al-dīn al-qaiyim'* (the eternal religion).

182. E.J. Brill, *op, cit.*, p. 585.
183. We omit a reference to other acts of pilgrimage, the *Saai* (to go and return between two hills, *Marwa* and *Safā*), the *wukūf* in *Arafāt* (to repent of one's sin), and throwing seven stones to three devil's pillars (*jamlāt*) in *Minā*, because they are performed out of the precinct of the *Kā'ba*.
184. *Sūrah* CVIII. 2. Both in Buddhism and Christianity, the killing of living beings for religious purpose is prohibited.
185. E.J. Brill, *op. cit.*, p. 586.
186. "The introduction of the niche miḥrāb into the mosque is no doubt rightly ascribed to the Omaiyads, who were the first to build mosques of any size, under the influence of the Christian architecture of their lands. The simple Arabian and Persian village mosques have no niches even at the present day." E.J. Brill, *op. cit.*, p. 485.
187. E.J. Brill, *op. cit.*, p. 485.
188. The author is grateful to Miss Nagilaà Kamal Moḥammad Ali from Sūdan, Miss Ozra Nomani from Afghanistan, Miss Shahīda Khatun from Bangladesh, her friends of the University Hostel, and Prof. M.S. Ashraf, Head of the Arabic Department, University of Delhi, for their help.
189. Cf. *Sūrah* CXII. 1, 4.
190. Cf. *Ibid.*, XXXIII. 40, XLVIII. 29.
191. *Ibid.*, CXII.
192. *Ibid.*, III. 37. The words inside the parentheses are not written in the portion of 'd' but are helpful in knowing the context of the calligraphy.
193. *Ibid.*, III. 45, cf. *Luke* 1 : 26-55.
194. *Ibid.*, III. 39. cf. *Luke* 1 : 5-25. The phrase "a word from Allāh" points to Jesus the son of Mary.
195. *Ibid.*, XXXIII. 40.
196. In *Pl.* 28, the *makām* (the standing place) of the *imām* (the leader of the *ṣalāt*) during the *ṣalāt* can be seen on the floor, just under the *miḥrāb*.
197. E.J. Brill, *op. cit.*, p. 485.
198. *Sūrah* II. 177, In passing, we should confirm here the five basics of Islām (*Ibādat*), (1) *Kalema-i-Shahādat* (to accept that God is One and Muḥammad is His prophet), (2) *Ṣalāt* (to pray), (3) *Zakāt* (to donate), (4) *Saum* (to fast during the specified month every year), and (5) *Haj* (to make a pilgrimage to the *Kā'ba*).
199. This is the saying of Ibn al - 'Arabi (al-Futūḥāt al-Makkīya, i. 733). E.J. Brill, *op. cit.*, p. 588.
200. '*Granthī*' is used for a person who recites the *Ādi Granth*.
201. Harbans Singh Doabia (tr.), *Sacred Jap Jī — Translation & Transliteration containing some of the Fundamental Sermons of the Sikh Religion,* Amritsar, 1992, p. 18, *Jap Jī* (1).
202. *Ditto,* p. 19.
203. Harbans Singh Doabia (tr.) *Sacred Nitnem — Containing The Divine Hymns of the Daily Prayers by the Sikhs* Amritsar, 1993, pp. 252-253, from the verse of the *Ardās*: *"Ik Oṅkar*

wāhegurū jī kī fateh" [God is one; All victory is of the Wondrous Guru (Respected God)] is very often recited during the service in a Gurdwārā.

204. Gobind Singh Mansukani, *Introduction to Sikhism*, New Delhi, 1994, p. 65.
205. Act 2 : 2 - 4.
206. The word '*Rāgī*' comes from '*Rāga*', "a melodic composition in vocal music in classical Indian style . . . The Adi Granth is organized on the basis of 31 ragas". H. S. Singha, *Mini Encyclopedia of Sikhism (Illustrated)*, p. 85.
207. Harbans Singh Doabia (tr.) *Sacred Jap Jī*, p. 72.
208. Gurbachan Singh Talib (tr.), *Śrī Guru Granth Sāhib,* Vol. 2, Patiala, 1988, p. 937.
209. Cf. *John* 1 : 1 - 14. The Guru-trinity in Sikhism is: (1) The highest Guru is God Himself, (2) The ten Gurus explicated His Will in meditation, and (3) The Scripture, *Guru Granth Sāhib* is the last Guru for the future spiritual guidance of the Sikhs.
210. Gurbachan Singh Talib (tr.), *op. cit.*, p. 937.
211. Cf. Harbans Singh Doabia (tr.), *Sacred Jap Jī,* p. 72.
212. Gobind Singh Mansukani, *op. cit.*, p. 52.
213. Cf. *Revelation* 20 : 12, "The dead were judged according to what they had done as recorded in the books".
214. Harbans Singh Doabia (tr.), *Sacred Jap Jī,* p. 43, *Jap Jī* (20).
215. H. S. Singha, *op. cit.*, p. 62.
216. The saints include not only the Sikh Gurus but also Hindu *Bhaktas* and Muslim *Sūfīs*.
217. Gobind Singh Mansukani, *op. cit.*, p. 53.
218. Parkash Singh, *Community Kitchen of the Sikhs*, Amritsar, 1994, p. 101. The sweet dish is usually called '*Halwā*'. Guru Nānak started to run the community kitchen (*langar*) for the purpose of sharing food with others, irrespective of caste, race, and creed, which embodies the universal brotherhood (Khalsa).
219. As suggested by Mr. Budh Singh, a devout visitor to the Delhi Gurdwārās.
220. Harbans Singh Doabia (tr.), *Sacred Nitnem*, pp. 102-103, *Jap Sāhīb* (84).
221. *Ten Masters*, Diamond Comics Digest XLII, New Delhi, p. 31.
222. J.P. Suda, *Religions of India,* p. 253, quoted from the *Ādi Granth*.
223. It will be discussed again in this Chapter.
224. 'Borcan' imitates the pronunciation of 'Burhan' meaning 'Buddha' in Mongol.
225. Cf. Aldo Ricci, *The Travels of Marco Polo*, translated into English from the text of L.F. Benedetto, London 1931, chapter 6.
226. Cf. *I Corinthians* 8 : 6, 12 : 6, *Ephesians* 4 : 6.
227. *Sūrah* VI. 75, V. 104.
228. Cf. *I Kings* 16 : 13.
229. *II Kings* 23 : 5.
230. *Exodus* 20 :4.
231. Cf. *Acts* 17 : 28; *I Kings* 18 : 10.
232. *Acts* 17 : 29.

233. *Hosea* 13 : 2.
234. Cf. *I Kings* 18 : 26-29.
235. *Hosea* 3 : 1.
236. *Jeremiah* 7 : 9.
237. *Hosea* 3 : 18.
238. *Ezekiel* 20 : 31, 23 : 39.
239. *I Samuel* 15 : 23.
240. *Ezekiel* 14 : 3.
241. Cf. *Psalms* 131 : 1.
242. About this subject, please refer to one of the short stories of Isaac Bashevis Singer, *Fool's Paradise* (*Zlateh the Goat and Other Stories,* 1966). Singer is a Jewish writer who was born in Poland and awarded the Nobel Prize in 1978.
243. *Exodus* 20 : 6.
244. Cf. *Ezekiel* 20 : 39.

V

Conclusion

Our research does not end in a study of early Buddhist art but starts looking for something significant for the people of modern times. If ancient Buddhists of Bhārhut and Sāñcī could know about our discussions on early Buddhist art (Chapters II, III and IV), they would feel incompatibility with our way of seeing and thinking about their works of fine arts. What does it suggest? It seems to suggest the following points:

(1) The work of fine arts remains through the ages after the death of the artists, and various viewers try to derive different meanings from it through their own standpoints.

(2) Therefore, our study of fine arts is for our own good. Finally, the surest and the most important thing lies in finding out as to what is precious and meaningful to us in modern times rather than trying to work out one proper answer to explain the historical truth.

(3) The meaning of our study lies in the pursuit of more possibilities of seeing and thinking about the fine arts which is to be observed from different aspects. At the same time, it is for the sake of supposing how the same object should be observed by the people with different opinions. This is a general matter of concern applicable in our daily lives.

The object of our study is not only early Buddhist art but also other kinds of fine arts if they deserve to be considered. In this book, we have seen all kinds of discussing-points focus on early Buddhist art in an ideal process; basic (Chapter II), applied (Chapter III), and evolutional (Chapter IV) studies stem from an enquiry into the absence of the Buddha image in early Buddhist art.

Our research has just begun. There are a lot of problems awaiting further consideration in our discussions.

For instance, we did not arrange the sections for two Indian religions, Jainism and Hinduism. To understand the absence of Buddha images in early Buddhist art as thoroughly as possible, it is necessary for us to look into other kinds of spiritual inheritance alive in India.

Besides, we cannot forget to compare early Buddhist art with the art of the Buddha image in later periods in order that we may not become partial to the former but also reconsider the latter's significance.

An enquiry into the absence of the Buddha image in early Buddhist art becomes new whenever we see it (cf. *Illust.* 9) free from the former viewpoints, just as seen in Chapters II to IV. It may be compared to a thought flying from the earth to heaven. There we naturally shift our eyes from microscopic to macroscopic dimensions, away from the original point where we re-discovered that there is no Buddha image in early Buddhist art.

Such a thought as to search for more and more meanings of the same object from different distances is quite necessary not only for us dealing with the humanities but also for all kinds of other people living in the present age, because human beings are usually apt to seeing things only from their own standpoints. It is not easy for them to see afresh the same thing once they finish doing value judgement. In case they do not have any doubt about their thoughts, there naturally emerges a conflict among them; racial, linguistical, religious, political, economical or any other human activities are full of conflicting elements as we know very well.

However, thanks to the growth of international communications in our days, it is not difficult to take an extensive view of such a reality of this world. It means that modern people are fully able to cease adhering to their own standpoints for the good of mutual understanding. One of the best ways to carry it out is a discussion on the same or common object to be considered. It may not be easy to find an ideal object out of uncountable subjects. But at the same time, it is certain that any kind of object becomes ideal to discuss depending on ideas and methods.

After all, our effort in this book is aimed at realizing such a philosophy.

Appendix

What is the Purpose of Comparative Religion?

— A five-point ethics to be obtained through the field-work —

'What is the purpose of Comparative Religion?' This question arises whenever I have a chance to answer the question: 'What is your academic field?' It is sometimes good to say: 'Fine arts, above all, early Buddhist art', if the questioner is interested in the history of art. Then he/she can have a good time exchanging views with me and it would help me to increase my knowledge on fine arts. But I usually prefer to describe my field as 'Comparative Religion', so that the questioner can have a general idea of my research career.

Some people often ask me how many 'religions' I deal with for a comparative study. But the question dare not let me enumerate the 'names' of religions but reminds me of each 'personality' of my friends in India who lives a Zoroastrian, Jewish, Christian, Islamic, Sikh, Hindu, Jain or Buddhist life. They are not only scholars but also nuns, monks, priests, businessmen, merchants, journalists and school children. I remember how they chanted daily prayers, how they sang hymns, how they celebrated holy days, how they talked about their life, how they liked to eat and drink, and how they loved to make friendship with one another.

Some of these people became my friends before I got to know about their respective religious faith, because we liked to observe each other's personality first without a preconception about our own religions, nationalities, social backgrounds, etc.

Other people opened their minds to me only after coming to know that I sincerely studied and tried to understand their religions.

One day I was invited to participate in one of the Jewish festivals held in a synagogue. When a *rabbi* got to know that I was not a Jewish but a scholar of Comparative Religion, he asked me the reason why I was eager to study his religion and know about all other religions. I managed to answer as follows:

---

* This essay is based on the author's memorial lecture for the Lent Term at the University of Cambridge in February, 1996.

'First of all, I do not want to become your enemy but your good friend. To become a good friend of yours, I need to understand better how you live a life in this world. For the purpose, the best thing to do is to know about your own religion. Secondly, it is good for my soul to have a share of your blessing by the grace of the Absolute. His mercy covers the world all over and I can enjoy His blessing wherever I am in the world: in the synagogue, church, mosque, temple or any other holy places. Therefore, at least for myself, Comparative Religion is a tool of knowing about the variety of religious salvation; and for others, it is a medium of mutual understanding.'

I was not sure that I had made myself understood to the *rabbi,* but he kindly promised me that he would help me in my study of Judaism.

On the other hand, I have ever seen a lady take a firm attitude towards me in the work of Comparative Religion. She belonged to Jainism and liked to hear a sage (called *Muni-jī* in Hindi) preaching and answering his followers' questions. The *Muni-jī* and I were friendly with each other. Whenever he needed to converse with me on religious questions, he kindly asked one of his disciples to translate my words into his native language. On that day, the lady in question was asked to help her *Muni-jī* but she seemed troubled about how to translate my questions on a comparative view of Jainism and other Indian religions. She did her best, but finally refused to take her role. She said to me: 'I do not know why you are so curious about Jainism and want to compare it with other religions. I was born as a Jain and am completely satisfied with Jainism. Jainism is the best and everything to me. I am not concerned with other religions.'

Then I ceased talking to her so as not to confuse her any longer, but tried chanting a Jain prayer with other followers for a while. I am not sure whether my prayer could relieve her feelings, but she smiled at me and went away.

Since then, I have become more careful when an occasion to discuss religious topics presents itself. It is so painful to see one's feelings being hurt by scholarly carelessness.

I thank the lady for her frank attitude. Her firmness might have its source partially in the nature of Jainism. In Jainism, everyone has to rely on one's own efforts to purify the soul; one cannot pray for another because one's fate is produced only by one's own *kārmic* factors: thoughts, words, and deeds. Nevertheless, her sayings are fully understandable and can be seen in the case of all those who have faith in only one religion.

One loves one's own religion, language, nationality, birthplace, etc. best of all. Religion influences one's personality from birth to death. I have never known an example of a child choosing his/her own religion after knowing and comparing all the religions of the world. In most cases, it is natural for the child to take his/her parents' religion and follow it all of his/her life. Generally the people tend to refuse knowledge about other religions consciously or unconsciously, because it may bring about an identity-crisis and cause heresy in their religious community. Each religion is the best and perfect for its follower, and one can attain good humanity according to his/her daily religious practice. It is true that good humanity can be produced by every religion as long as one takes the path of righteousness.

In this context one's religion almost means one's way of life and an innate principle of life to be conveyed from the parents to the children. Therefore it may be said that Comparative Religion shows us many ways or possibilities of human life.

It is only one way of life that we can take in this world. No one can solve the mystery of the reason why some are born as Christians and others are born as Hindus. Anthropologists, ethnologists and historians may not regard it as a mystery but give some explanation. They do not need to evaluate the mystery as a starting point of a mutual respect among different people.

But a scholar of Comparative Religion is responsible for making peace with each religion and its followers. At least, the scholar must orient his/her subject to an ethical and moral way to avoid causing antipathy, disunity, misunderstanding and other negative feelings among the people. For the purpose, the scholar feels responsible for his/her own knowledge and attitude towards different religions. As far as my own experience is concerned, there are several human virtues helpful to heighten the purpose of Comparative Religion:

(1) Humility is the most important to get true and living knowledge of a religion from the person who has a faith in the religion concerned. Our humble attitude will open his/her mind and prepare a good situation in which he/she can tell us about his/her faith with calmness and frankness. It is also helpful for us to overcome 'our ignorance of others' step by step every time we have a chance to meet and talk with them.

(2) Patience tells us how to take more time to understand each religion and each religious personality, because we are not perfect to see through the nature and thought of others. It is natural that we may feel incompatible with those who have the faiths and cultures unknown to us. But if only we have patience to keep on observing their daily life without any preconceptual and self-centred viewpoints, we will certainly be able to go beyond a sense of 'difference' towards 'others' to reach true understanding of their good humanity.

(3) Flexibility is necessary to take the role of a mediater who helps the people to understand others and their religions. I used to play this role among my Hindu, Christian, Sikh and Muslim friends whenever they started to discuss religious topics.

It was possible for me to smooth their conversation by keeping a benevolent neutrality and flexible correspondence with each speaker. This small success seems to have been realized by the fact that I was a good friend to each speaker and we knew each other well. In this sense, good human relationship may be one of the best factors to make peace among different religions, as far as the individual level is concerned.

(4) Maturity can be acquired by a macroscopical view of the world's religions. It means that we finally finish discussing the different and common points to be found as the result of Comparative Religion, and start pursuing a possibility of grasping all the religious phenomena as a whole with a view to seeing how 'religion' can orient itself to new phases of the modern world. As it is also a work of seeing mankind at a certain distance, it is helpful and meaningful to derive a hint from the scientific fields: biology, anthropology and astronomy, etc.

(5) The final virtue is the Awe towards the Invisible Holiness (God, Law of the Eternal Truth, etc.). We can see the religions keep their sanctuaries empty. People use symbols at the holiest places, Cross, Scripture, Image, Sacred Fire, etc., as the reminders of their faiths. But their eyes are ultimately pointed to the Invisible One, and their own minds become the sanctuaries at the last stage of purification. We must not lose our respect and awe towards these sanctuaries and the Invisible to be enshrined there. Otherwise, Comparative Religion misleads us in our intellectual pursuit of knowledge.

It is desirable that a scholar of Comparative Religion is well versed in the world's religions. But if he/she approaches each religion and its followers without any awe and respect, his/her research work will not be ethical to make a contribution towards world peace, and may fall into a dead end just as known in the Greek myth of Icarus who fell into the ocean by losing his awe for the sun-god.

In this respect, it is reasonable to think that the scholars of Religious Studies had better establish their identity by means of their own religious faiths. A non-religious person cannot experience the reverential fear towards the Invisible, one of the most essential human feelings to understand 'religion'.

In this way, it is important to find and learn several human virtues in the process of working in Comparative Religion. It is easy to say: 'My field is Comparative Religion'. But it is not easy to make oneself responsible not only for discussing different religions but also for making peace with their followers. After all, it is better to have 'a faith in good humanity' common to all the human beings at any time and in any situation. One's responsibility for Comparative Religion may be a burden on one's life, but one's responsibility can produce one's love towards neighbours if one does not lose sight of good humanity to be derived from every religious faith.

The method of Comparative Religion has many possibilities according to the nature and character of the scholar. As for myself, I have been studying and doing a field-work on the relationship between 'Art and Religion'. 'Art' includes fine arts and music. During my study in India between 1991 and 1995, I was engaged in field-work at different asylums and sanctuaries of Zoroastrian, Jewish, Christian, Islamic, Sikh, Hindu, Jain and Buddhist people. The main topic is divided into two sections:

1. Religion and Fine Arts.
   * How is the sanctuary decorated?
   * What is the meaning of 'the object of worship' represented in a visual way with symbol or image?
   * Analysis of the criticism of idolatry.
2. Religion and Music.
   * Dictation and translation of hymns, chants, and recitation of holy words in the scriptures and the prayer-books.
   * What is the role of music for the understanding of religions?
   * Whether some element of the music has originality peculiar to the religion?
3. Reference to the scripture regarding (1) and (2).

This research was aimed at seeing the artistic environment of religious sanctuaries, and making the most of the experience to introduce one's religious life into others in modern society where everyone should make an effort to understand and get along with those who have different faiths and lifestyles.

Most of the people who cooperated with me belonged to India, where Zoroastrian, Jewish, Christian, Islamic, Sikh, Hindu, Jain, and Buddhist people naturally have a chance to know something about each other's religion in school days, and so many religious holy days offer the people a good chance to participate in the prayers and festivals at temples, churches, gurdwārās, mosques, etc. Accordingly, not a few of the Indian people are fond of discussing the variety of religions and like to attain a sort of generosity towards others' religions. Above all, Hindus, the majority of Indians, like to quote a verse from the *Ṛgveda* I, 164.46 mentioning how only one God is called by so many names, in order that they can come to a conclusion that the world's religions have different ways to reach the same goal.

In any case, Indian attitudes toward religions include good hints on how to introduce each religion to modern people, especially the children who are expected to recognize and appreciate this world with their impartial and friendly eyes. India is a very old country, but she can suggest to us a very modern way of world-recognition.

Finally, I finish my discussion with a quotation from the address of His Holiness Pope John Paul II to the leaders of non-Christian religions, at Rajaji Hall, Madras, on February 5, 1986:

> . . . The Indian rightly thinks that religion has a profound meaning for him. His very being experiences impulses, instincts, questions, longings and aspirations which testify to the greatest of all human quests: the quest for the Absolute, the quest for God. In my first Encyclical after being elected Pope, I made reference to the fact that the Second Vatican Council's Declaration on Non-Christian Religions "is filled with deep esteem for the great spiritual values, indeed for the primacy of the spiritual, which in the life of mankind finds expression in religion and them in morality, with direct effects on the whole of culture (*Redemptor Hominis,* 11).
>
> The Catholic Church recognizes the truths that are contained in the religious traditions of India. This recognition makes true dialogue possible. Here today the Church wishes to voice again her true appreciation of the great heritage of the religious spirit that is manifested in your cultural tradition. The Church's approach to other religions is one of genuine respect; with them she seeks mutual collaboration. This respect is twofold: respect for man in his quest for answers to the deepest questions of his life, and respect for the action of the Spirit in man. *(The Pope Speaks To India — All the addresses and homilies of the Holy Father duing his ten-day Visit to India,* St. Paul Publications, Bombay, 1986, p. 83).

A List of Visuals

Tables (Analyses)

Figures (Drawings)

a-4: *Ibid.*, Pl. 51, a Die-panel of the Eastern Gateway. Cf. *Illust.* 8c.

b-1: *Ibid.*, Pl. 46, a Pillar between the Top and Middle Lintels of the Eastern Gateway.

b-2: *Ibid.*, Pl. 38, the edge of the Lowest Lintel, the Eastern Gateway.

b-3: *Ibid.*, Pl. 53, a Capital of the Western Gateway. Cf. *Pl.* 7.

c: *Ibid.*, Pl. 49, the North Pillar of the Eastern Gateway.

Fig. 9 The extraction of Buddhist monuments (*caitya*) from the relief-scenes, the gateways of Sāñcī *Stūpa* 1.

a: *MS*,II, Pl. 34-a2, a Die-panel of the Northern Gateway (cf. *Ibid.*, *Pl.* 52-a, the South Pillar of the Eastern Gateway). Cf. *Illust.* 8b-1.

b-1: *Ibid.*, Pl. 40, the Lowest Lintel of the Eastern Gateway. Cf. *Illust.* 13a-3.

b-2: *Ibid.*, Pl. 61-3, the Lowest Lintel of the Western Gateway (back side). Cf. *Illust.* 12a-2.

c-1: *Ibid.*, Pl. 51a, the South Pillar of the Eastern Gateway. Cf. *Illust.* 8c.

c-2: *Ibid.*, Pl. 18b, the West Pillar of the Southern Gateway. Cf. *Illust.* 8a-1.

Fig. 10 The extraction of Buddhist monuments (the *Dharmacakra*-shrine) from the relief-scenes, the railing of Bhārhut *Stūpa*. Cf. a-1 is from *Illust.* 10a-1 and a-2 is from *Illust.* 10a-2.

Fig. 11 The extraction of Buddhist monuments (the Bodhimaṇḍa) from the relief-scene, the railing of Bhārhut *Stūpa*. Cf. *Illust.* 9.

Fig. 12 The extraction of altar-shaped motifs from Zoroastrian cultures.

a: A fragment of fire-holder discovered from Pasargadae, the capital city of Cyrus the Great (559-530, BC), founder of the Achaemenian dynasty. Cf. Mary Boyce, Yumiko Yamamoto (tr.), *Zoroastrians — Their Religious Beliefs and Practices* — Chikuma Shobou, Tokyo, 1983, p. 73.

b: A restored image of fire-holder (cf. Fig. 12a)

c: The crown worn by the Sassanian king, Shapur II (AD 309-379).

d: The crown worn by the Sassanian king, Peroz I (AD 459-484).

e: The crown worn by the Sassanian king, Khusraw II (AD 591-628).

f: A crenellated wall caving Persian guards, Persepolis, sixth-fifth century BC

g: A Soghdian sculpture discovered at Penjikent, Tadzhikistan.

Fig. 13 The main motifs of early Buddhist art. Cf. Chapter 2, Note No. 65.

Fig. 14 The main motifs of early Christian art. Cf. Chapter 2, 3: A Consideration of the Visible Facts; A reference to the motifs of early Christian art.

Illustrations (Monochromatic pictures)

Illust. 1 A survey of the motifs of Thrones, *Bodhi*-trees, *Dhamacakras* and *Stūpas*.

a: *MS*,II, Pl. 15-1, Back of the Southern Gateway; Top Lintel.

b: *Ibid.*, Pl. 55-2, Front of the Western Gateway; Middle Lintel.

c-1: *Ibid.*, Pl. 46-1, Back of the Eastern Gateway; Top Lintel.

c-2: *Ibid.*, Pl. 48, Back of the Eastern Gateway; North End of the Top Lintel.

c-3: *Ibid.*, Pl. 47, Back of the Eastern Gateway; South End of the Top Lintel.

Illust. 2 The motif of *Bodhi*-trees.

a-1: *MS*, II, Pl. 43, Front of the Eastern Gateway; Die-panel, North End of the Top and Middle Lintels.

a-2: *Ibid.*, Pl. 58, Front of the Western Gateway; South End of the Middle Lintel.

b-1: *Ibid.*, Pl. 31, Back of the Northern Gateway; Die-panel below the Capital, West End of the Lowest Lintel.

b-2: *Ibid.*, Pl. 17 a, Back of the Southern Gateway, West End of the Top and Middle Lintels.

b-3: *Ibid.*, ditto.

c: *Ibid.*, Pl. 36-c2, West Pillar of the Northern Gateway; Die-panel on the Inner Face.

Illust. 3 The motif of *Dharmacakras*.

a-1: *MS*, II, Pl.26-a, Front of the Northern Gateway; Die-panel, West End of the Top and Middle Lintels.

a-2: *Ibid.*, Pl. 42, Front of the Eastern Gateway; Die-panel , South End of the Lowest Lintel.

b: *Ibid.*, Pl. 18-a1, West Pillar of the Southern Gateway, Upper Panel on the Front Face.

Illust. 4 The motif of *Stūpas*.

a: *MS* II, Pl. 11-1, Front of the Southern Gateway; Middle Lintel.

b-1: *Ibid.*, Pl. 12, Front of the Southern Gateway; Die-panel, West End of the Middle and Lowest Lintels.

b-2: *Ibid.*, Pl. 32-3, Back of the Northern Gateway; Die-panel, East End of the Top and Middle Lintels.

c: *Ibid.*, Pl. 36-c1, West Pillar of the Northern Gateway on Inner Face.

Illust. 5 The scenes of *Bodhi*-trees (with Thrones) surrounded by devotees (in sitting posture).

a: *MS*, II, Pl. 34a, East Pillar of the Northern Gateway.

b-1: *Ibid.*, Pl. 35a, West Pillar of the Northern Gateway, Lowest Panels on the Front Face.

b-2: *Ibid.*, ditto.

c-1: *Ibid.*, Pl. 65-b2, South Pillar of the Western Gateway, Upper Panels on the North Face.

c-2: *Ibid.*, ditto.

Illust. 6 The scenes of *Bodhi*-trees (with Thrones) surrounded by devotees (in standing posture).

a: *MS*,II, Pl. 49-c, North Pillar of the Eastern Gateway, Upper Panels on the South Face.

b-1: *Ibid.*, Pl. 64-a-2. 3, South Pillar of the Western Gateway; Upper Panels on the Front Face.

b-2: *Ibid.*, ditto.

Illust. 7 The motifs of *Bodhi*-tree (with Throne), *Dharmacakra* and *Stūpa* along with a group of devotees in standing posture.

a: *MS*, III, Pl. 103-a, Southern Gateway of *Stūpa* III, West Pillar on the South Face.

b: *Ibid.*, Pl. 103-b, ditto, East Pillar on the South Face.

c: *Ibid.*, Pl. 103-c, *ditto*, West Pillar on the East Face.

Illust. 8 A collection of Buddhist shrines.

a-1, a-2 and a-3: *M.S.*,II, Pl. 18-b1, West Pillar of the Southern Gateway, Upper Panels on the East Face.

b-1 and b-2: *Ibid.*, Pl. 34a-2, East Pillar of the Northern Gateway on Front Face.

c: *Ibid.*, Pl. 51-a South Pillar of the Eastern Gateway; Upper Panel on the Front Face.

Illust. 9 A relief-scene of *Bodhimaṇḍa* from the railing of Bhārhut *Stūpa*.

B.M. Barua, *Bārhut Book II, Jātaka-Scenes*, Indian Research Institute,

Calcutta, 1934, Pl. XXX, 3, XIII, Scene 32, p. 5.

Illust. 10 The scenes of the *Dharmacakra*-shrine, from the railing of Bhārhut *Stūpa*.

a-1: 'King Prasenajit visiting the Buddha', Photo-section of the National Museum, New Delhi (Photo No. 340/61).

a-2: 'King Viḍūḍabha visiting the Buddha', Roy C. Craven, *Indian Art*, Thames and Hudson, London, 1974, pl. 32, p. 61.

Illust. 11 a: 'The *Deva-avatāra* at Sāṅkāsya'.

b: 'Indra's Visit'.

a-1 and b-1 (Bhārhut): Osamu Takata, *The Birth of the Buddha Image*, Iwanami Shoten, Tokyo, 1987, pl. 1-10 (p. 38), pl. 1-2 (p. 20).

a-2: *MS*, II, Pl 34c, West Pillar of the Northern Gateway on Front Face.

b-2; *Ibid.*, Pl. 35B1, East Pillar of the Northern Gateway, Upper Panel on West Face.

Illust. 12 'The temptation of Māras and the Perfect Enlightenment'.

a-1: *MS*, II, Pl. 29-2, Back of the Northern Gateway; Middle Lintel.

a-2: *Ibid.*, Pl. 61-3, Back of the Western Gateway; Lowest Lintel.

b: Roy C. Craven, *op. cit.*, Pl. 53, p. 89, Gāndhāra.

Illust. 13 Front of the Eastern Gateway; Middle Section of Lintels. *MS*, II, Pl. 40.

a-1: *Bodhi*-trees and *Stūpas*.

a-2: 'The Great Departure'

a-3: 'King Ashoka visiting the *Bodhimaṇḍa*'.

b-1 and b-2: Pillar-designs of *Bodhi*-trees, *Dharmacakras* and Aśokan Pillar.

Illust. 14 a: 'Indra's visit', Gāndhāra. Osamu Takata, *op. cit.*, pl. 1-3, p. 21.

b: 'The Great Departure', Gāndhāra photo-section of the National Museum, New Delhi (Photo No. 1605/56).

Illust. 15 The slab of *Stūpa* from Amarāvatī, ditto (photo No. 473/58).

Illust. 16 The slab of *Stūpa* from Nāgārjunakoṇḍa, ditto, (photo No. 58/1959).

Illust. 17 'The Buddha visiting Kapilavastu', Amarāvatī. *Encyclopedia of World Art*, Vol. 7, McGraw-Hill, London, 1953, Pl. 412.

Illust. 18 The Buddha image destroyed by Muslims, Bāmiyān, Afghanistan. Roy C. Craven, *op. cit.*, Pl. 61, p. 99.

Illust. 19 Wall-painting with representation of the Menorah and the Ark of the Covenant, late second-third century AD, Rome, Jewish Catacombs of Villa Torlonia, *Encyclopedia of World Art*, Vol. VII, p. 405.

Illust. 20 a-1: A general view of the Western Wall of the Synagogue at Dura-Europos, Syria, early third century AD. Andrè Grabar, Sahoko Tsuji (tr.), *The Beginnings of Christian Art*, Shinchosha, Tokyo, 1967, pl. 66.

a-2: 'A Prophet standing firm', a part of *Illust.* 20a-1. Andrè Grabar, *op. cit.*, p. 71.

Illust. 21 'Christ enthroned, between SS. Peter and Paul', early fifth century AD, Rome, Catacomb of SS. Pietro e Marcellino. Andrè Grabar, *op. cit.*, pl. 234.

Illust. 22 'The Empty Throne awaiting the Christ', a part of *Illust.* 23. Otto Pächt, Koichi Koshi (tr.), *Methodisches zur Kunsthistorichen Praxis*, Iwanami Shoten, Tokyo, 1982, pl. 50.

Illust. 23 Mosaic on the West Wall of the Cathedral of Torcello (Santa Maria Assunta) representing the Last Judgement, twelfth century AD. David Talbot Rice, *Art of the Byzantine Era*, Thames and Hudson, London, 1963, pl. 164.

Illust. 24 'The Dispùta', by Raffaello Sanzio (1483-1520). The Catholic Encyclopedia, vol. III, Fuzanbou, Tokyo, 1971, p. 216.

Illust. 25 Sancta Sophia, Constantinople, 532-37, AD. Interior, After Fossati, Aya Sophia, Constantinople, as recently restored by order of H.M. the Sultan Abdul Medjiel, London, 1852. David Talbot Rice, *op. cit.*, Pl. 35.

Plates (Coloured pictures)

Pl. 1 A distant view of the hill of Sāñcī.

Pl. 2 A close-up view of the hill of Sāñcī.

Pl. 3 A view of *Stūpa* 1 from east, Sāñcī.

Pl. 4 A view of *Stūpa* 1 from the Eastern Gateway, Sāñcī. A figure on the right side extracts 'the *vedikā* designs' from the *Stūpa* and the Gateway.

Pl. 5 The railings (*vedikā*) accompanying one's right-handed procession (*pradakṣiṇa*) around the *stūpa*.

Pl. 6 The image of the Buddha and his guardian gods destroyed by Muslims, *Stūpa* 1, Sāñcī, fifth century AD. The modelling of the round halo and the body of the Buddha show a Gupta style.

Pl. 7 A Capital of the Western Gateway, Stūpa 1, Sāñcī. It looks as if Yakṣas are supporting the architrave whose edge shows decorative patterns of stepped-pyramids.

Pl. 8 A *caitya*-roof and its side-motif of stepped-pyramids, Cave No. 10, Ajantā, second century BC.

Pl. 9 A Buddhist monk in meditation under the tree, Sārnāth.

Pl. 10 The *Vajra-āsana* of Bodh Gayā, third century BC.

Pl. 11 Two pilgrims beside the *Vajra-āsana* of Bodh Gayā.

Pl. 12 The Buddha images and the *Vajra-āsana* of Bodh Gayā.

Pl. 13 The Sārnāth Buddha in *Dharmacakra-mudrā*, fifth century AD.

Pl. 14 The relief from Sārnāth representing four phases of the Buddha's life: the Birth, the Enlightenment, the First Sermon and the Perfect Decease; fifth century AD.

Pl. 15 The empty niche lack of the Buddha image, Dhāmekh *Stūpa*, Sārnāth, fifth century AD.

Pl. 16 The image of *Śākyamuni* Buddha from Seiryōji, Kyoto, Japan, AD 987.

Pl. 17 The fire-altar (*vedi*) surrounded by four Paṇḍits: devout servants of Shiv Mandir (Hindū Temple), Delhi.

Pl. 18 Digambar Jain Temple, Delhi. On the wall of the temple-tower, a *svastika* (卐), an auspicious symbol can be seen inside the *vedī*-shaped frame. The same case arises also in Pl. 17 (See carefully the shrine's lintel behind the Paṇḍits).

Pl. 19 A series of *vedī*-shaped motifs found in the pattern of a sweater, Delhi.

Pl. 20 A series of *vedī*-shaped motifs from the festival-hall in the precinct of Chattarpur Mandir, New Delhi.

Pl. 21 A tree surrounded by the brick-railing, Sārnāth.

Pl. 22 A *Bodhi*-tree surrounded by the railing, with the decoration of garlands and umbrellas. This bas-relief is carved on the railing of a *stūpa*, Bodh Gayā, second century BC.

Pl. 23 Two empty thrones under the umbrellas arranged for male and female gods who are invisible to human eyes, Lakshmi Narayan Mandir, New Delhi.

Pl. 24 Fom left to right: 'Kai Lohrāsp' (The king of the Kayanian dynasty whose successor was Vīshtāsp, Zarathuštra's royal patron), 'Divine Radiance' (Fire Burning at the altar) and 'Ratu Zarathuštra' (The prophet of Ahura Mazdā). Minocheher Hormasji Toot, *Practical Metaphysics of Zoroastrianism*, Bombay, 1962, Frontispiece.

Pl. 25 A night view of the fire temple called 'Dar-e-Meher', Delhi Parsī Anjuman,

Delhi. The decorative illuminator on the roof takes the shape of the sacred fire buning in the Afarganyu: the fire holder (cf. *Pl.* 24).

Pl. 26 Mass on the night of Christmas Day, Vatican Embassy Chapel, New Delhi.

Pl. 27 Evening service at the Judah Hyām Synagogue, New Delhi.

Pl. 28 Miḥrāb, Sokullu Mehmet Pasha Mosque, Istanbul, AD 1571-72. Photo by Kokai & Shuon Tanaka.

Pls. 29-32 A process of '*Pārikarma*' around the *Pālkī*: the wooden stand with a roof used for supporting the holy scripture '*Guru Granth Sāhib*', Gurdwārā Singh Sabhā, Delhi.

Acknowledgements

Fuzanbou: *Illust.* 24; Indian Research Institute: *Illust.* 9; Iwanami Shoten: *Illust.* 22; McGraw-Hill: *Illusts.* 17, 19; Mr. R.S. Dhondy's Publisher: *Pl.* 24; National Museum, New Delhi: *Illusts.* 10a-1, 14b, 15, 16; Seiryo-ji: *Pl.* 16; Shinchosha: *Illusts.* 20, 21; Swati Publications: *Illusts.* 1-8, *Illusts.* 11a-2 & b-2, *Illusts.* 12a-1 & a-2, *Illust.* 13; Takata, Osamu: *Illusts.* 11a-1 & b-1, *Illust.* 14a; Tanaka, Kokai & Shuon: *Pl.* 28; Thames & Hudson: *Illusts.* 10a-2, 12b, 18, *Illusts.* 23, 25.

Visuals

A Guide to the Visuals

1. The word 'Visuals' is a coinage of the author and the publisher meaning that the visual (the visual objects whose perspectives open out to give a direct and intuitional impact on one's eyes) have priority over the literary sources and the texts of the Chapters all through the arguments of this book.
2. The Visuals consists of (1) Tables (Analyses), (2) Figures (Drawings), (3) Illustrations (Monochromatic quotations inserted among other Visuals) and (4) Plates (Coloured pictures).
3. The Visuals make a visual context as a whole, and place themselves separately from the whole text. This treatment enables you to grasp the visual logic of this book. It will release you from the standpoint of 'literalism' that tends to regard the Visuals (2) ~ (4) as supplementary to the literary sources and what is written in the Chapters. Please remember that (2) ~ (4) can directly show you their own visual messages without attaching any comments. On the other hand, (1) talks to you about some visual facts and key-concepts in connection with (2) ~ (4).
4. The author does not put any titles beside the Visuals (2) ~ (4) in order that you may not act as a visitor to art-galleries and museums who makes it a rule to read the titles of the exhibits first of all and soon pass away there without finding anything from the objects themselves.
5. The collective arrangement of the Visuals brings you the convenience of searching for one of them every time the author refers to the same in different contexts.

Tables

Table - 1
A Table of the Theories on Illust. 10 a-2 (1)

Points aimed at		Theories	1
			Barua, *Bharhut Book* II,1934,Plate XXXI, 2 (Scene 53) pp.48-51.
①		Subject	Viḍūḍabha's march on Kapilavastu. Non-violent attitude of the Śākyas. Buddha's intervention and its effect.
Left Side	②	The back view of an animal passing through the arch.	a richly caparisoned elephant
	③	The man whose face is seen over the arch.	——
	④	The elephant and the man on its back.	The mahout who sits down on the shoulder of the elephant is violently piercing the animal's head with a goad, causing an excruciating pain, which the elephant finds himself unable to bear. He grasps an outer branch of the tree with his trunk, while his body shrinks down and shrivels up.
Both Sides	⑤	The trees on both sides of the caitya-hall.	the tree
Centre	⑥	The caitya-hall.	a Dharmachakra-shrine
	⑦	The interior equipment (Especially, about the Dharmacakra).	A highly ornamented wheel is set up inside the hall, with an ornamented square seat below, over which it can revolve.
	⑧	Two standing males and two knee-ling females with their hands joining.	(1) a couple of man and woman is doing the worship and perambulation. (2) King Viḍūḍabha (?) (3) Śākyas, men and women, who are taking a strong vow to remain non-violent to the last.
Right side	⑨	The man who raises his right hand on a chariot.	King Viḍūḍabha
	⑩	The meaning of raising his hands⑨.	his right hand upraised in front seems to ask the charioteer to restrain the motion of the chariot.
	⑪	The man who holds the reins.	the charioteer
	⑫	(The person who should hold an umbrella behind⑨&⑪.)	a man, whose head remains concealed behind that of the charioteer ...
	⑬	The animal drawing a chariot.	two high-mattled horses.
Interpretation of the inscription	⑭	Original text	Atanā maramtā (pi),
	⑮	Translation	Even if they be dying,

Table - 1 (2)

Theories / Points aimed at	2 **Coomaraswamy, *La Sculpture de Bharhut*, 1956, Planche XXV, Figure 66, pp. 68-69.**	3 **Lüders, *Bharhut Inscriptions*, 1963, A 112 (880) Plate XIV, p. 56.**
①	. . . . . . événements immédiatement cońsécutifs à cette visite.	It presents the procession of King Prasenajit of Kosala around the Dharmaśālā erected as a memorial of Buddha's first preaching in the city of Śravāstī.
②	——	horse
③	——	a man on horse-back rides through the entrance gate.
④	——	In front of him (③) an elephant goes having a man on its back, shown in side-view in a very clumsy way. The elephant with its trunk gets hold of the branch of a tree hanging above.
⑤	——	a tree
⑥	Gandhakuṭi, la cellule (celle)	the edifice
⑦	L' édifice qui abrite le Bouddha,représenté come précédemment par l'autel la route et le parsol, est le même;	the wheel
⑧	Viḍūḍabha, son général et sa suite.	The standing figures are bigger than the representation of the kneeling women and this perhaps characterizes them as gods.
⑨	le roi Viḍūḍabha	To the right, a chariot on which two men are standing and which is drawn by two horses is seen.
⑩	——	
⑪	... son général Dīghakārāyana	
⑫	——	——
⑬	——	two horses
⑭	attanā maraṁtā'pi	(1) ...... (ka)sa dānaṁ(a)tanā (2) cha(ka) ta
⑮	Or ceux du clan du Pleinement Éveillé ne prennent pas la vie d'autrui, fussent-ils mourants eux-mêmes.	The gift of ...... (ka), and made by himself.

Table - 1 (3)

Theories / Points aimed at	4	5
	Lippe, *The Freer Indian Sculptures*, 1990, Plate 4, Figure 4, pp. 6-9.	**Craven, *Indian Art*, 1976, Plate 32, pp. 61-62.**
①	the scene is not, as had been thought previously, another version of King Prasenajit's visit, but depicts the subsequent visit of Viḍūḍabha.	The episode has been identified as the visit by King Viḍūḍabha to the Buddha in a story related to the history of the Shākya clan.
②	a caparisoned horse	a horse
③	the turbaned head of its (①) rider	——
④	we see the front part of a preceding elephant, his trunk grasping the branch of a tree while the mahout urges him on with a goad (cf. Barua④).	a mahout struggles to refrain his elephant from breaking a branch from a blossoming mango tree.
⑤	a tree	a blossoming mango tree
⑥	gandhakuṭi at Ulumpa (Medalumpa); a vihāra (residence) and at the same time, an actual Buddhist temple.	chaitya, shrine
⑦	The Wheel of the Law (dharma-cakra) represents the teaching Buddha.	the preaching Buddha who is here represented as a giant wheel.
⑧	(1) one couple in two stages of circumumbulatory worship. (2) the king and his consort, each represented twice.	four devotees pay homage to the preaching Buddha ......
⑨	King Viḍūḍabha	appears to be the King Viḍūḍabha.
⑩	his right hand in a gesture of command.	one hand in greeting, while with the other he steadies himself on the shoulder of the driver.
⑪	...... his (⑨) general, Dīghakārāyaṇa.	the driver
⑫	an invisible attendant who is concealed by the charioteer.	——
⑬	two caparisoned horses	two bullocks with raised hooves seems to be approaching at a fast trot.
⑭	attana maramta (pi)	The relief of the Buddha's sermon originally had such an inscription on the roof of the shrine, but most of the characters have now been lost through the stone's flaking.
⑮	Even though they be dying ...... Now the kinsmen of the Fully Awakened ...... One does not take the lives of others, even though they be dying (themselves)	

Table - 2
A Table of the Key-Concepts in Chapter IV, 2

Religion	(1) What is 'The Empty Throne' ?	(2) What is the emptiness of 'The Throne' ?	(3) What (or who) is enthroned there?
Buddhism	Monument of the seat of the Buddha where he attained the Enlightenment; the place where the Buddha-Dharma (the Eternal Law) was, is, and will ever be revealed.	Commemorative space to be shown to those who recall the Deceased Buddha, or the invisible presence of the Buddha-Dharma.	Invisible Dharma itself, or the spirituality of the Eternal Buddha as the embodiment of the Dharma.
Zoroastrianism	The altar (Khuān) of the sacred Fire (Ātarš) as the image of God.	The presence of invisible God and His living Word.	God (Ahura Mazdā), the Lord of Wisdom.
Yahwism/Judaism	*The altar set in the open air. *The tent of the congregation with the Holy Ark. *The house of the Lord built by Solomon. *The place where the Holy Ark (Oron Hakodesh) is enshrined in synagogue.	The presence of invisible God and His living Word.	God (Yahweh; YHWH), the Lord of Israel.
Christianity	*The empty tomb of Christ. *The empty throne of Christ to come for the Last Judgement. *The altar in the Church.	*The proof of Christ's resurrection. *The tence air in waiting for the Last Judgement. *The spiritual presence of Christ through the Eucharist and His Gospel (living Word).	Jesus Christ in the mistery of Trinity.
Islām	*Kā'ba: the house of God. *The miḥrāb niche of the Masjid set in the direction of Kā'ba (ḳibla).	The presence of invisible God and His living Word.	God (Allāh). the Lord of His people embracing Islām.
Sikhism	Āsana where the Ādi Granth is enshrined.	The presence of invisible God and His living Word.	God (Wāheguru), the Wondrous Master to be recognized through the tradition of Guruhood.

Table - 2

(4) Who pays reverence to 'The Empty Throne' ?	(5) What is performed on, before or around 'The Empty Throne' ?
Saṃgha: Buddha's disciples: bhikkhu, bhikkhunī, upāsaka, upāsikā: the people who devote themselves to Triratna: Buddha, Dharma and Saṃgha. *Accepters of the precepts.	Pūjā: offering of flowers, light, incense, food and water. *Recitation of the Sūtras and confession of faith in the Triratna (in Sanskrit, Pāli, Tibetan, Chinese, and one's own language).
Anjuman; Mazdāyasni Zarathustis: those who choose the righteous path of God by the guidance of Zarathuštra. *Accepters of the initiation of Sudresh-Kušti (Naōjōte).	Padyap-Kušti including the confession of faith (Fravarānē) and other prayers (Ātarš Niyāišn, etc.). Boi-Ceremony: maintenance of the sacred Fire. *Recitation of the Avestā (in Avestan).
The tribes of Israel selected by God. *Accepters of the circumcision.	Sacrifice of burnt and peace offerings: sheep and oxen. *Recitation and explanation of the Tôrâ, and T[e]fillā: prayer and confession of faith (in Hebrew).
Ecclesia: gathering of people called by God in the name of Jesus Christ; the members of Church. *Accepters of the baptism.	Eucharist (the Lord's Supper): taking the sacramental water and wine. *Reading of the Gospel, prayers and confession of faith (in Greek, Latin, and one's own language).
Ummah: community of Muslims; those who surrendered themselves to God by the guidance of Muḥammad. *Accepters of Islām.	Tawāf: left-handed circumambulation around the Kā'ba for seven times. Ṣalāt: prayer including the confession of faith (Shahāda). *Recitation and explanation of the Qur'ān (in Arabic).
Sarbat Khalsa (Sangat): Sikh society of universal brotherhood; Gurmukh: those who are oriented to 'the Word of Gurus' (Gurbāṇī). *Accepters of the baptism.	Pārikarma: right-handed circumambulation around the Āsana. *Recitation of the Ādi Granth (in Puñjābī). *Kīrtan: continuous singing Gurbāṇī from the Ādi Granth.

Figures

Fig. 1

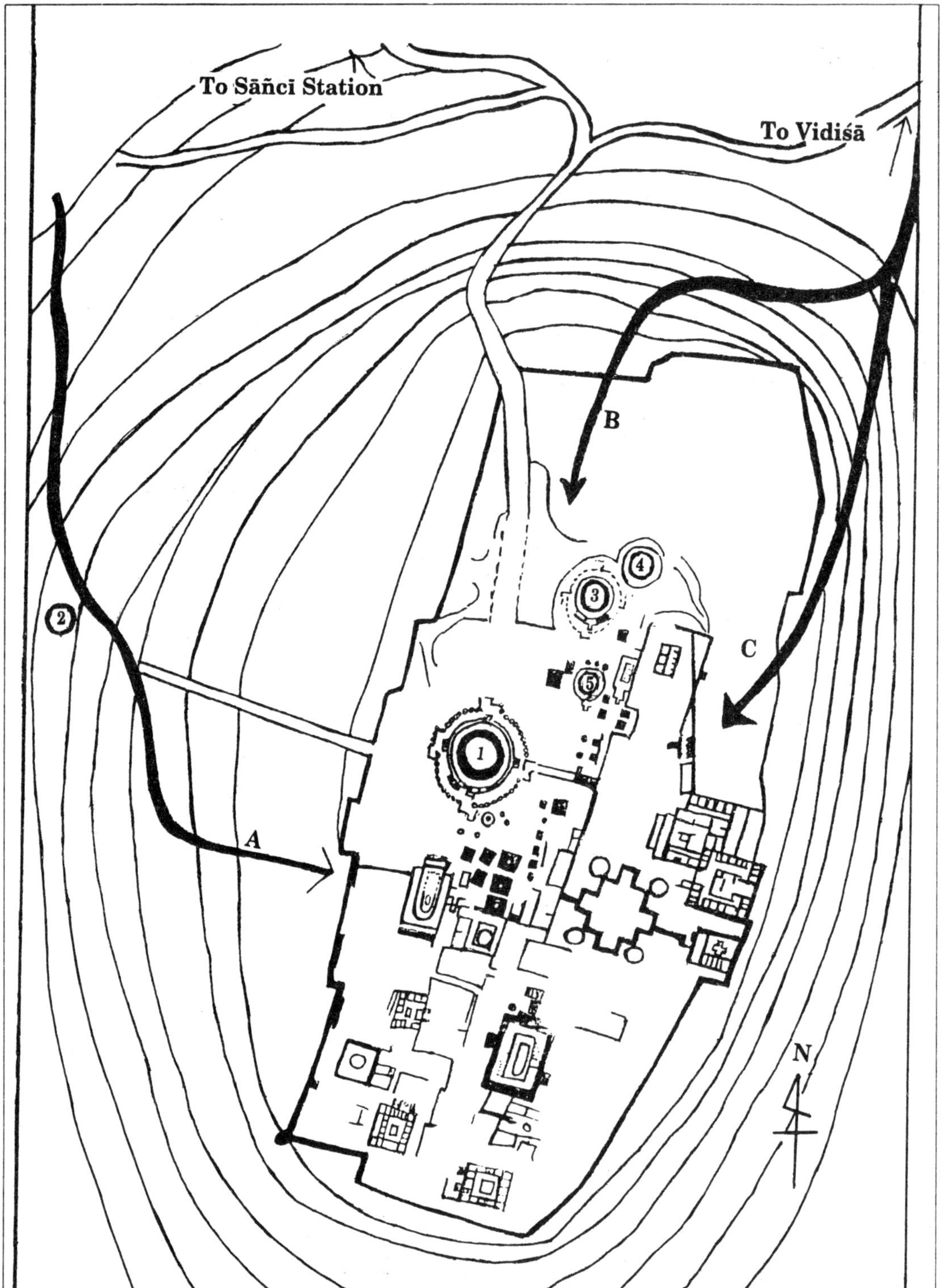

Fig. 2

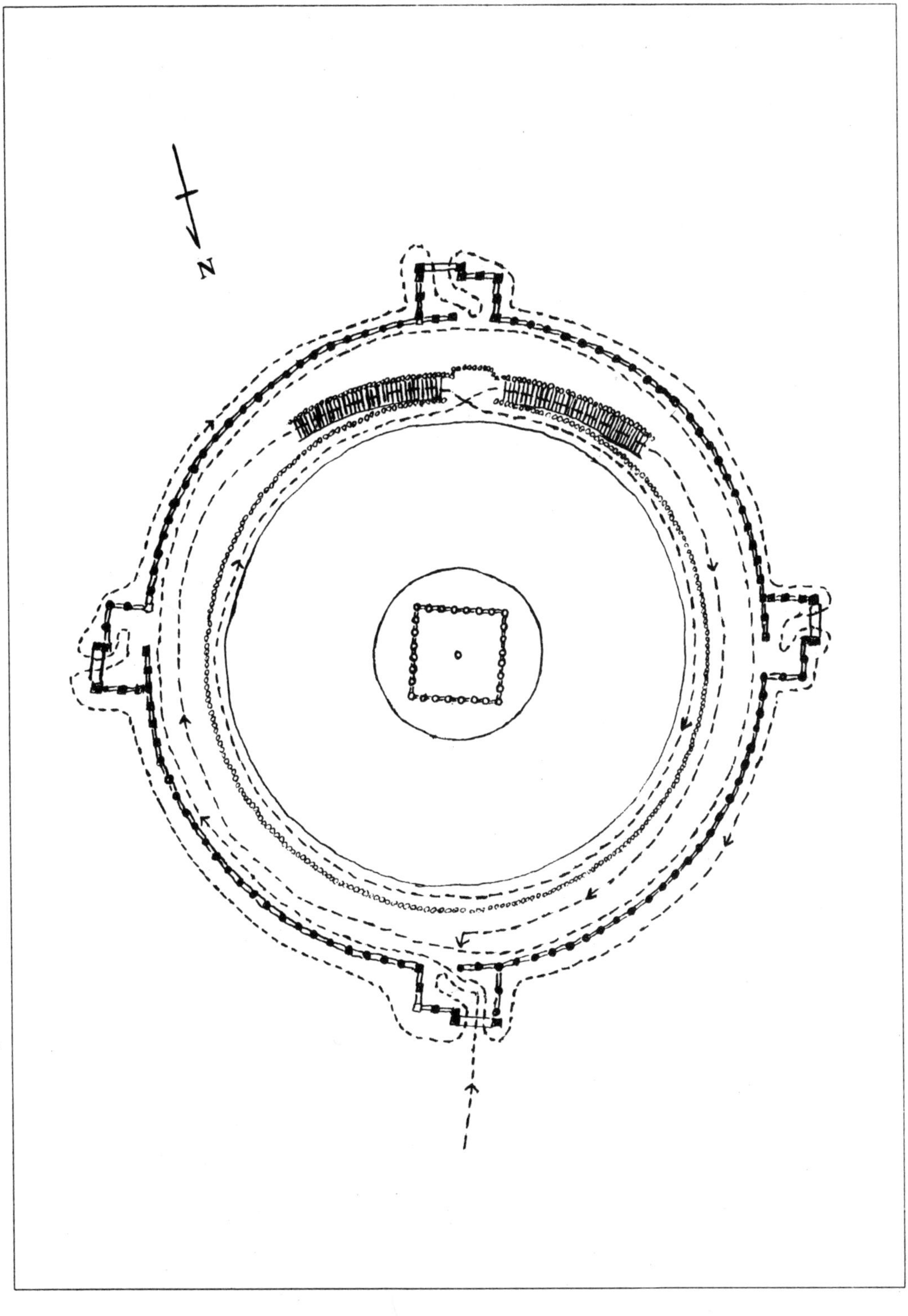

Fig. 3

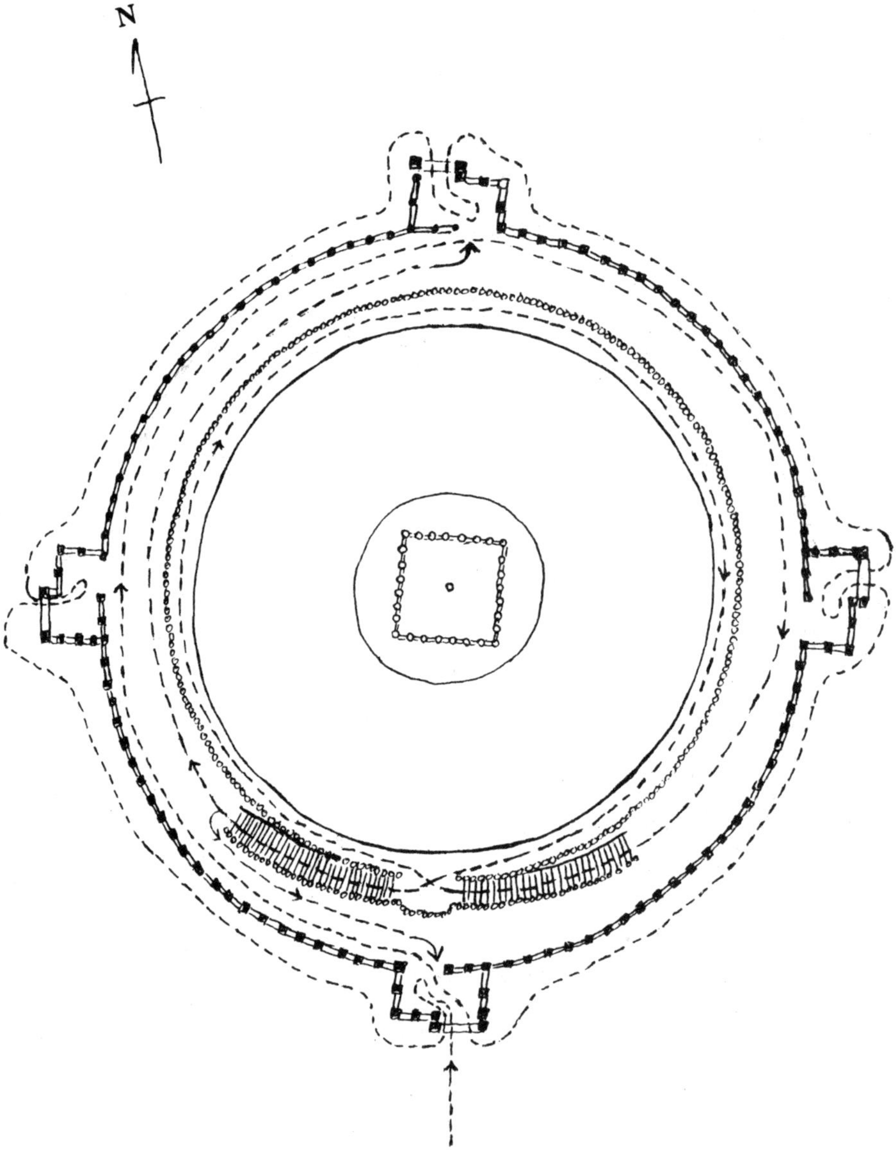

Fig.4

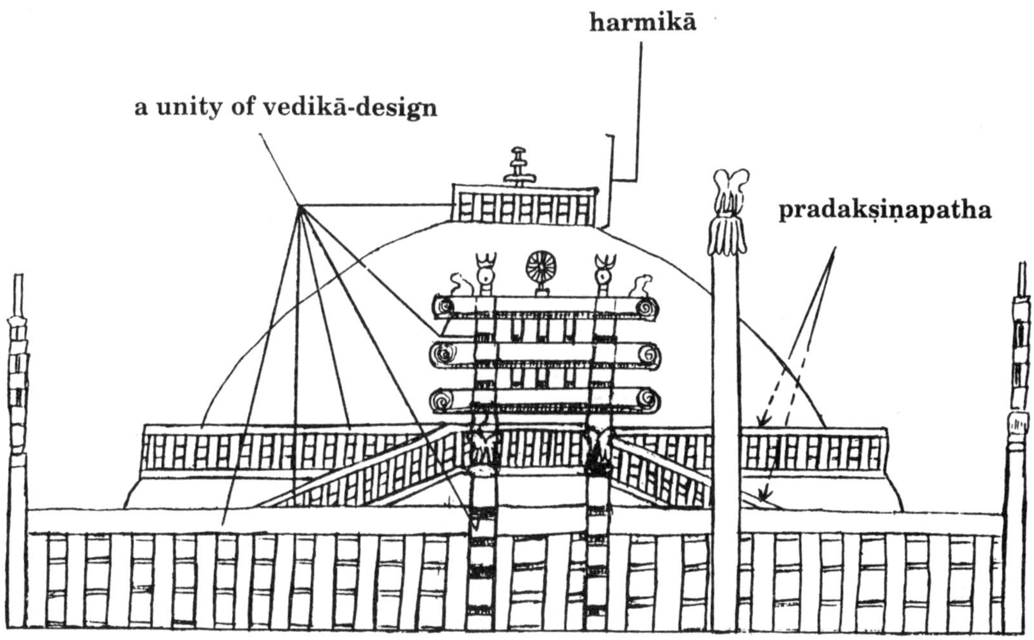

Fig. 5

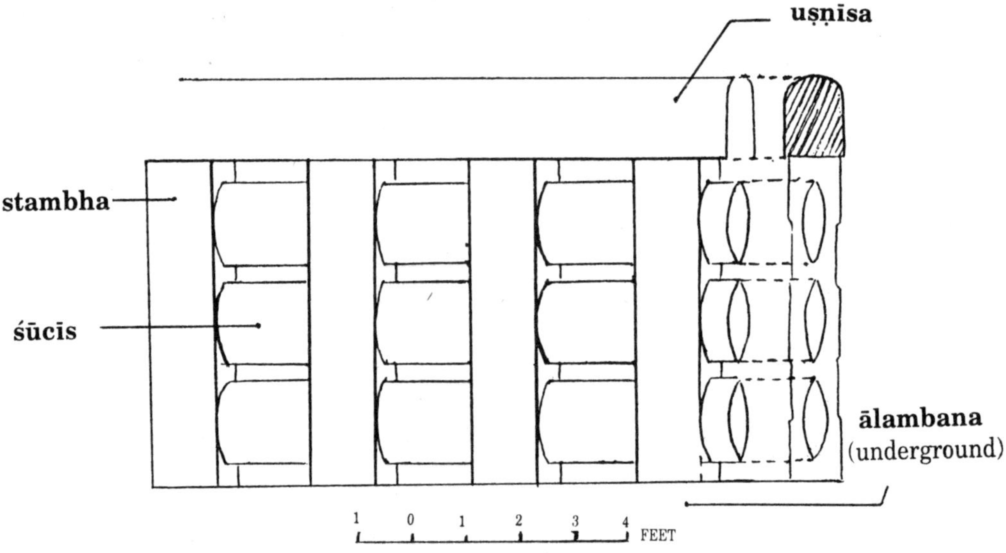
uṣṇīsa
stambha
śūcīs
ālambana
(underground)
1 0 1 2 3 4 FEET

a

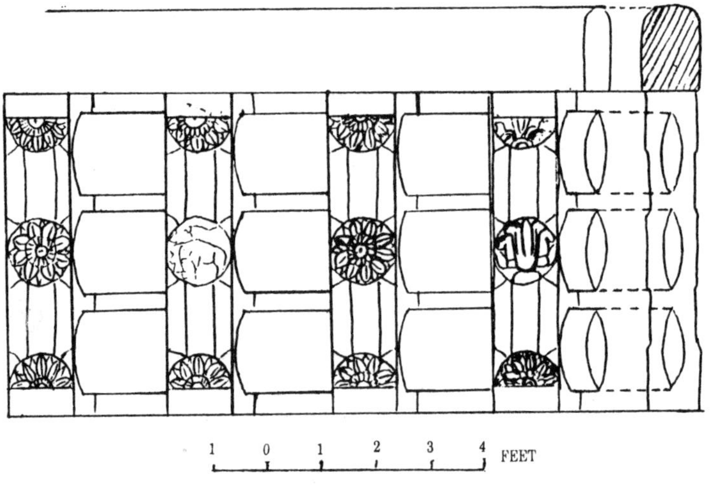
1 0 1 2 3 4 FEET

b

Fig. 6

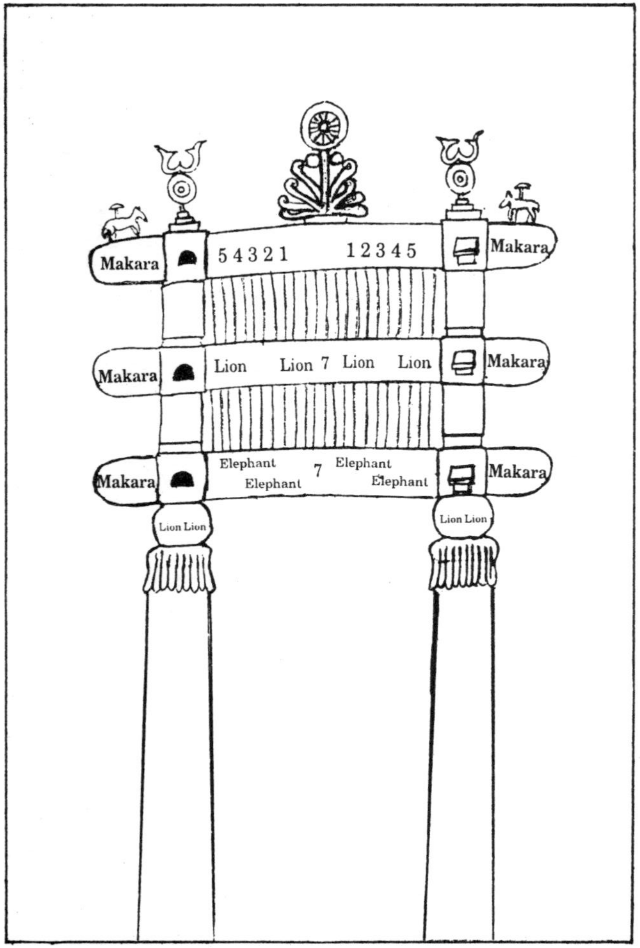
Makara
5 4 3 2 1
1 2 3 4 5
Makara
Makara
Lion
Lion 7 Lion
Lion
Makara
Makara
Elephant
Elephant
7
Elephant
Elephant
Makara
Lion Lion
Lion Lion

Fig. 7

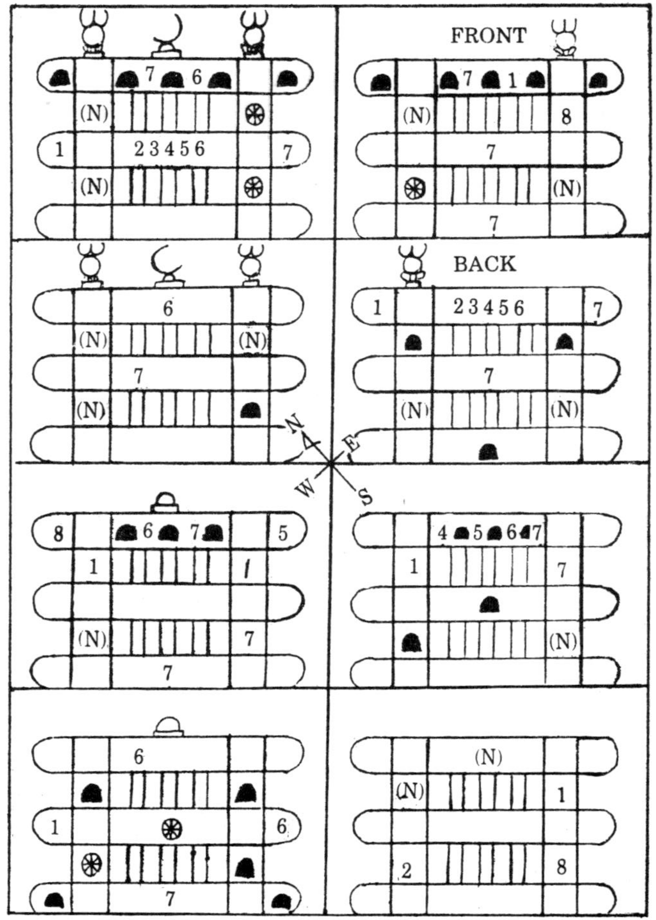
FRONT
BACK
N
E
W
S

Fig. 8

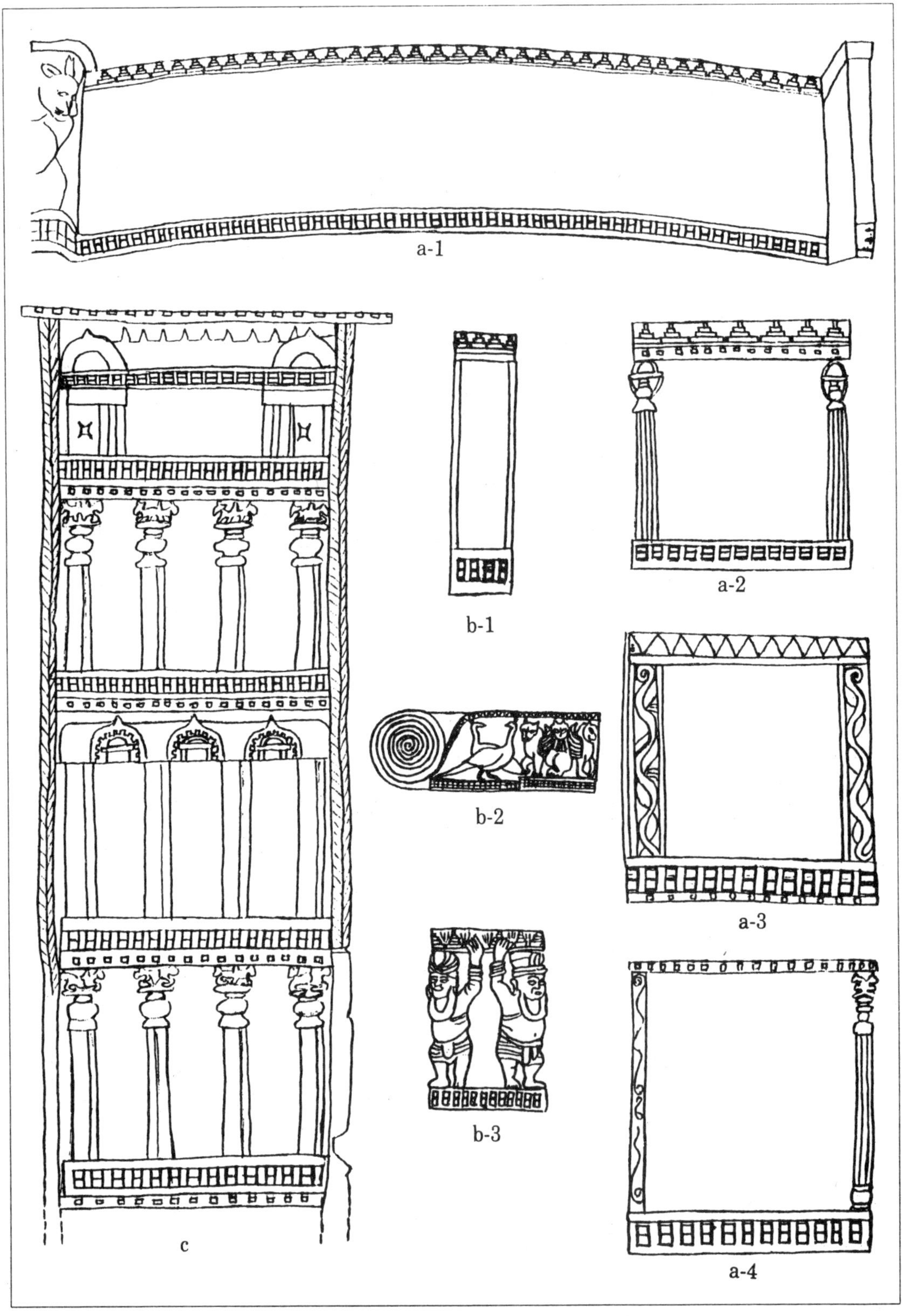

Fig. 9

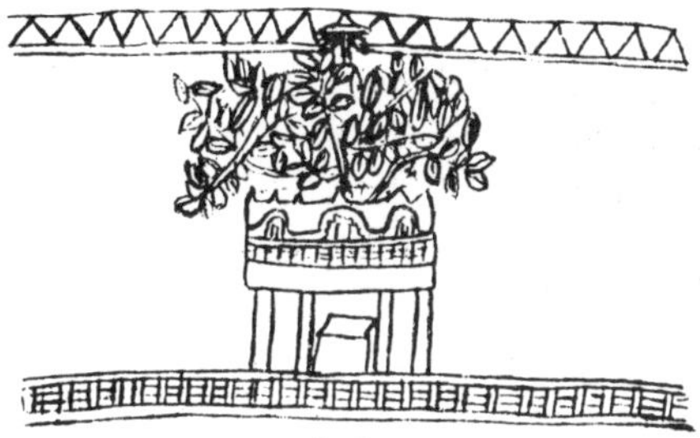

b-1

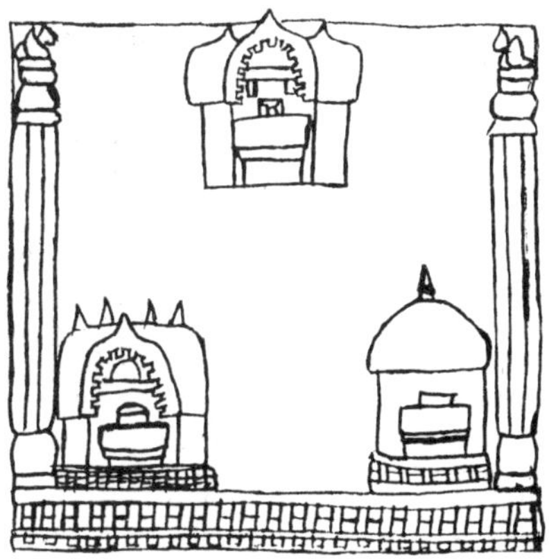

a

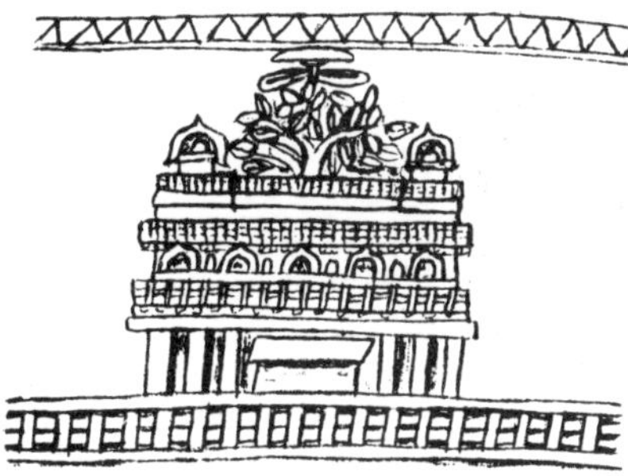

b-2

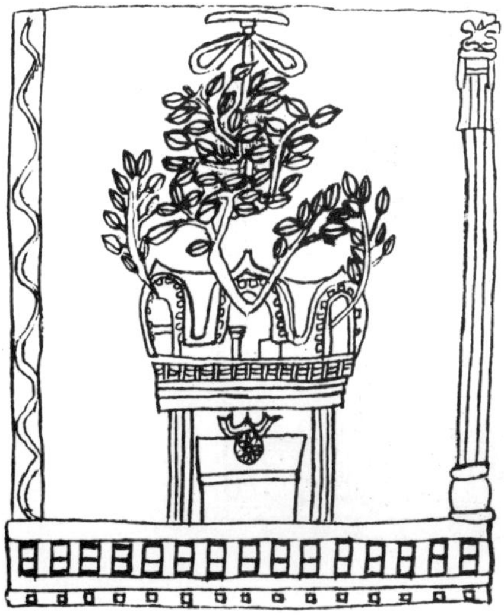

c-1

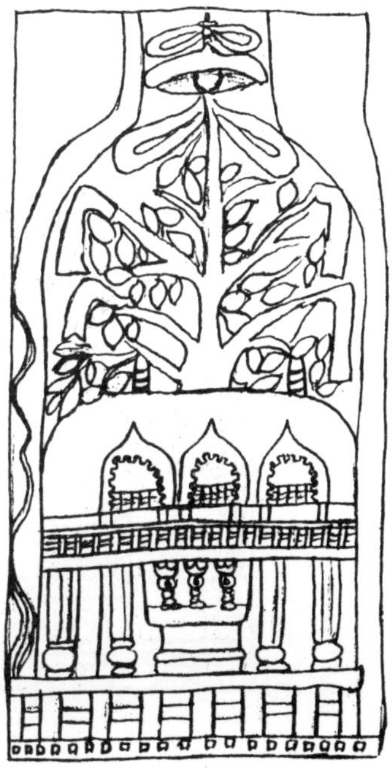

c-2

Fig. 10 (Cf. Illust. 10)

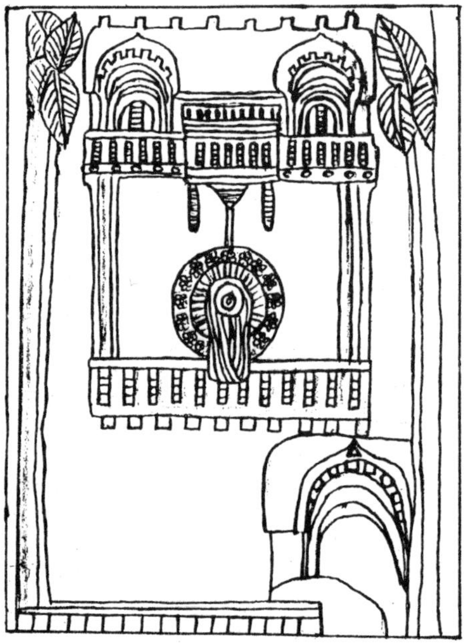

a-1

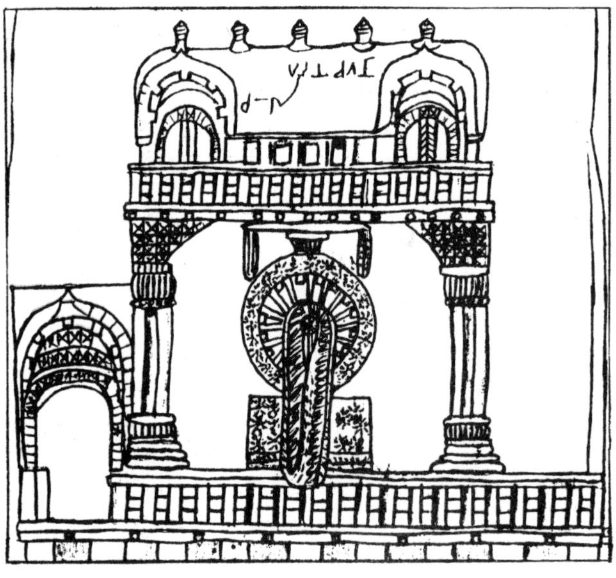

a-2

Fig. 11 (Cf. Illust. 9)

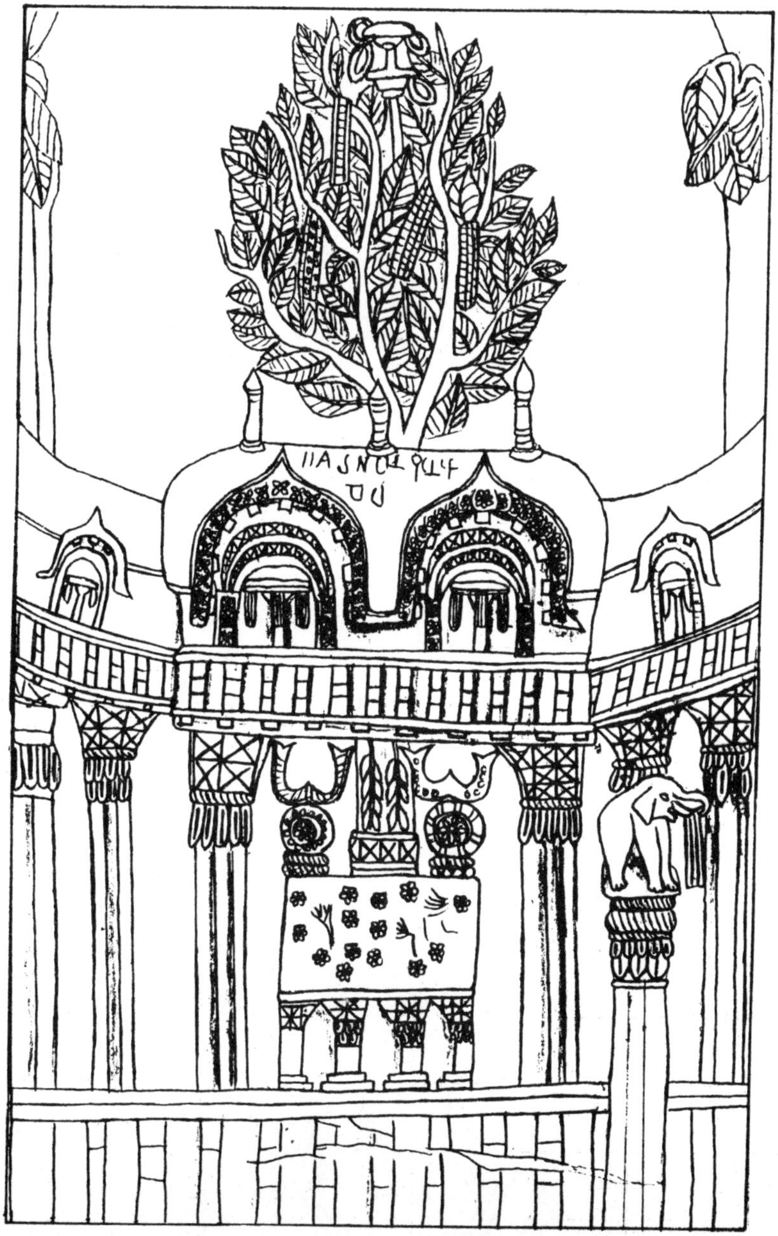

Fig. 12

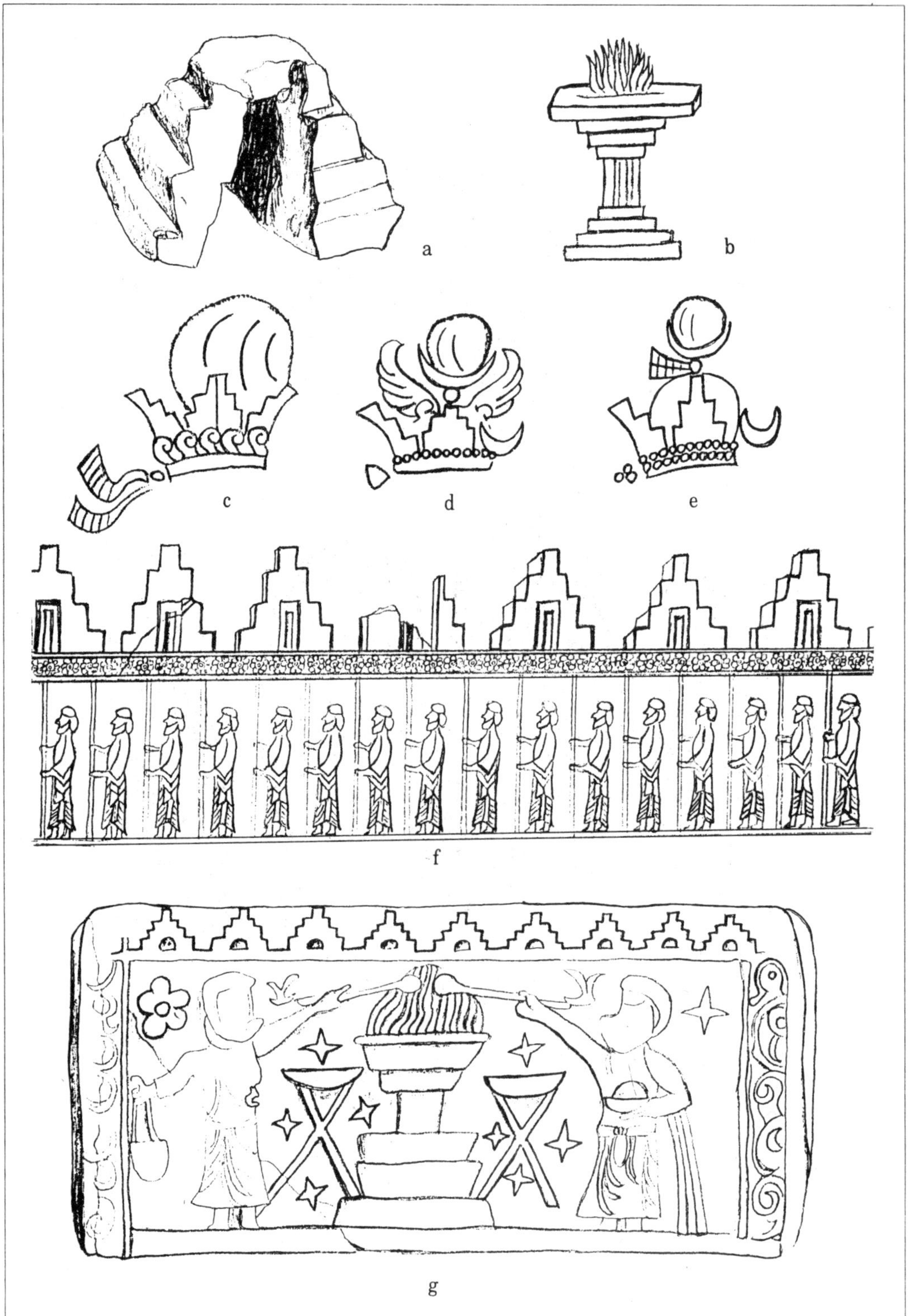

Fig. 13

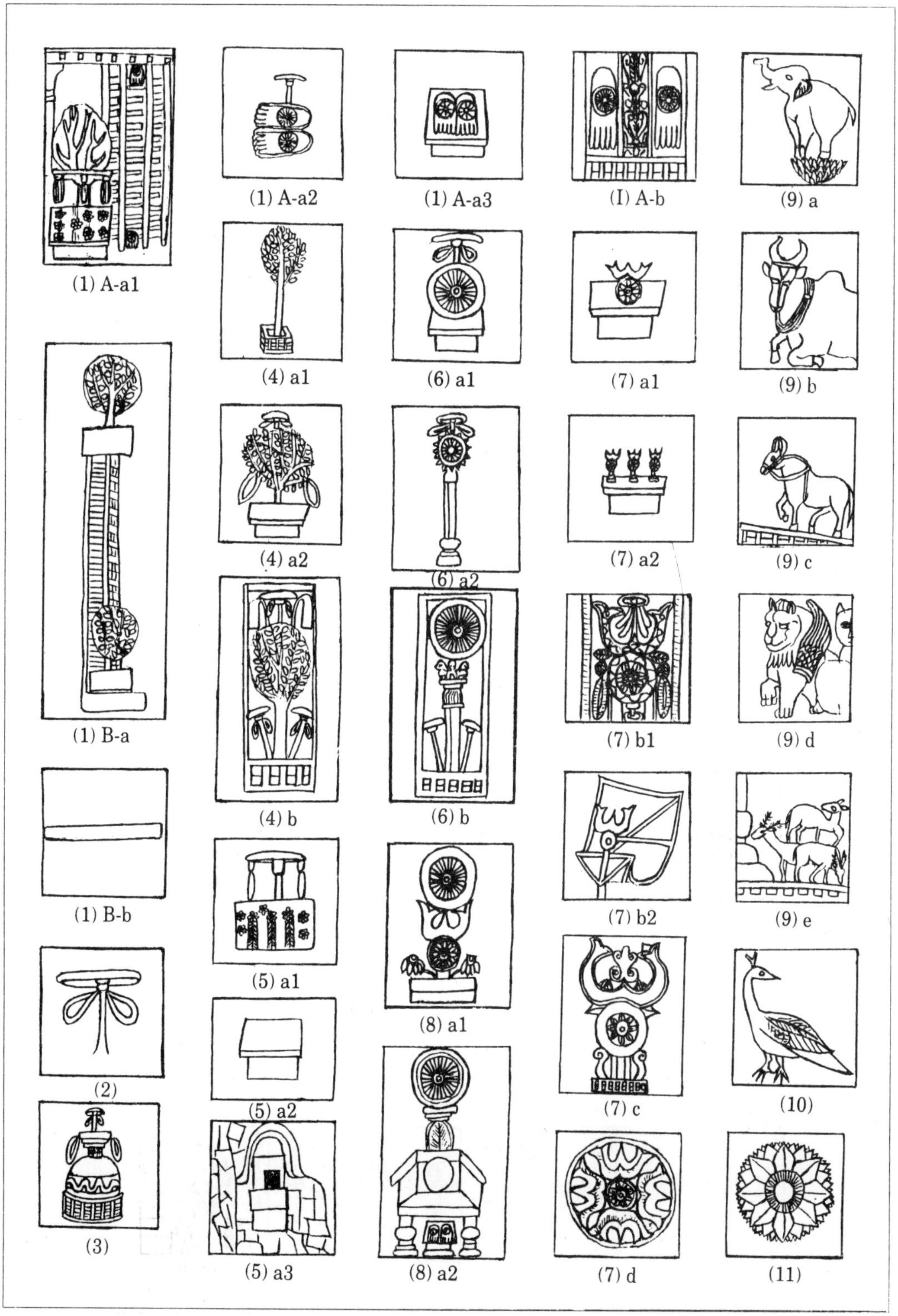

(1) A-a1
(1) A-a2
(1) A-a3
(I) A-b
(9) a
(4) a1
(6) a1
(7) a1
(9) b
(1) B-a
(4) a2
(6) a2
(7) a2
(9) c
(7) b1
(9) d
(4) b
(6) b
(1) B-b
(7) b2
(9) e
(5) a1
(8) a1
(2)
(5) a2
(7) c
(10)
(3)
(5) a3
(8) a2
(7) d
(11)

Fig. 14

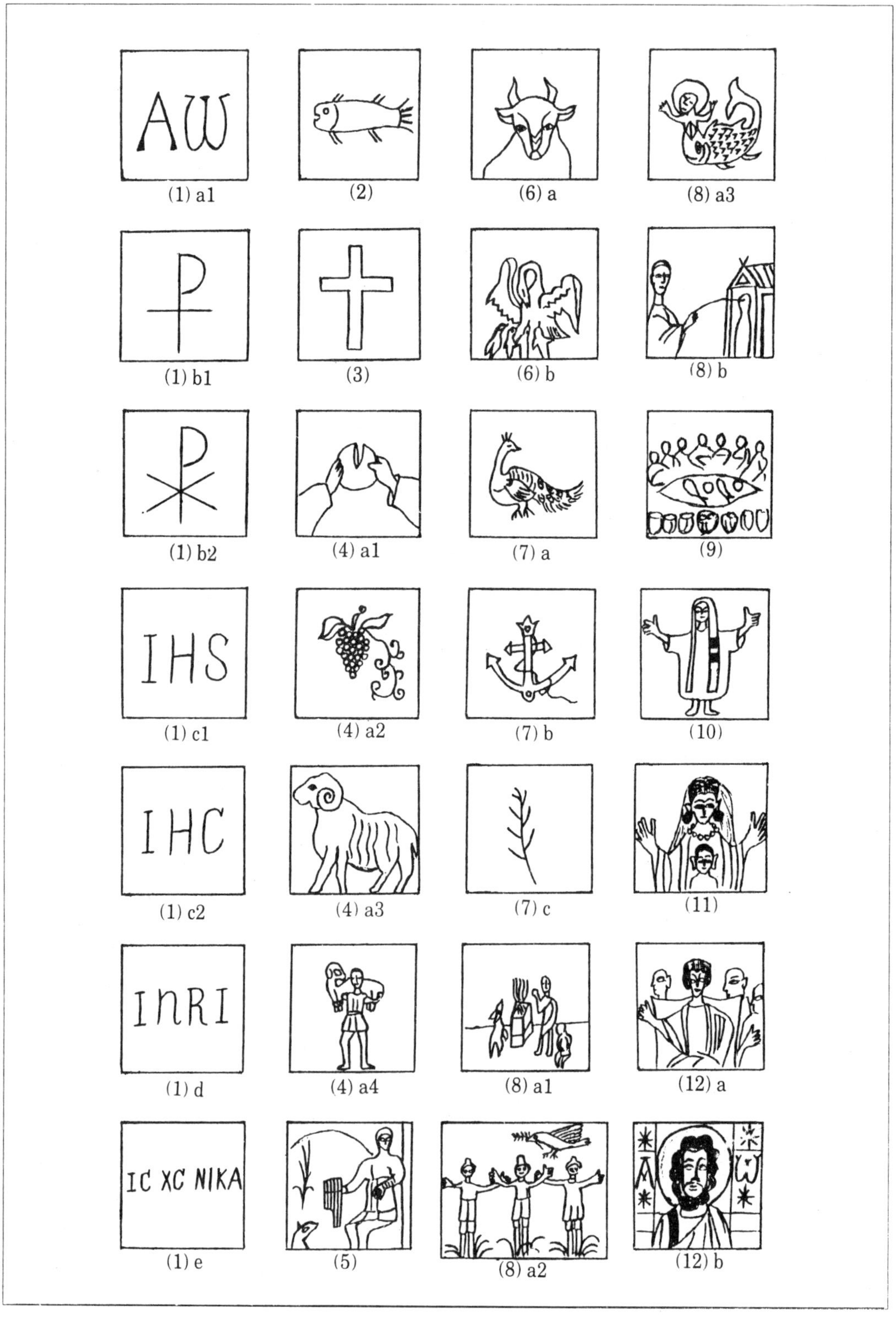
AW
(1) a1
(2)
(6) a
(8) a3
(1) b1
(3)
(6) b
(8) b
(1) b2
(4) a1
(7) a
(9)
IHS
(1) c1
(4) a2
(7) b
(10)
IHC
(1) c2
(4) a3
(7) c
(11)
INRI
(1) d
(4) a4
(8) a1
(12) a
IC XC NIKA
(1) e
(5)
(8) a2
(12) b

Illustrations

Illust. 1

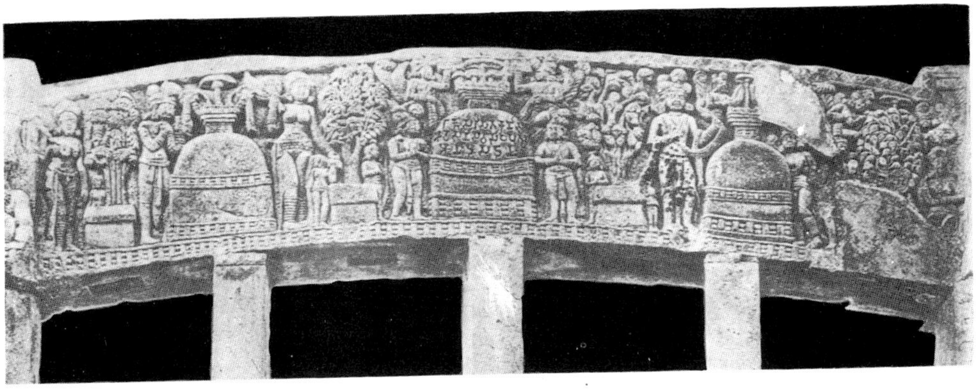

a

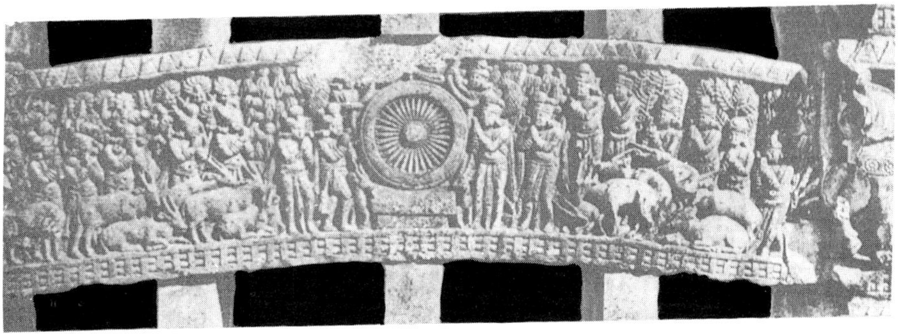

b

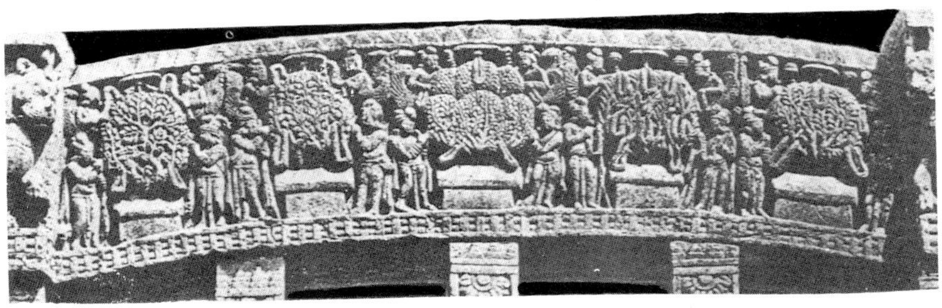

c - 1

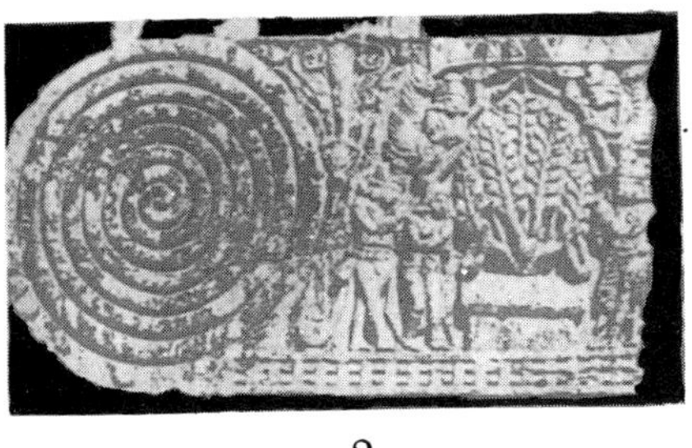

c - 2

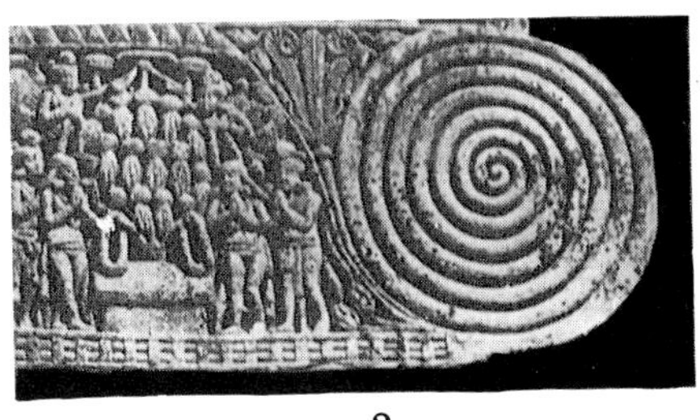

c - 3

Illust. 2

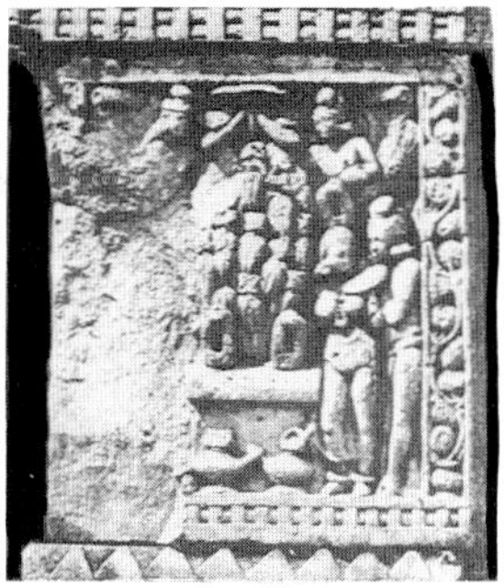

a - 1

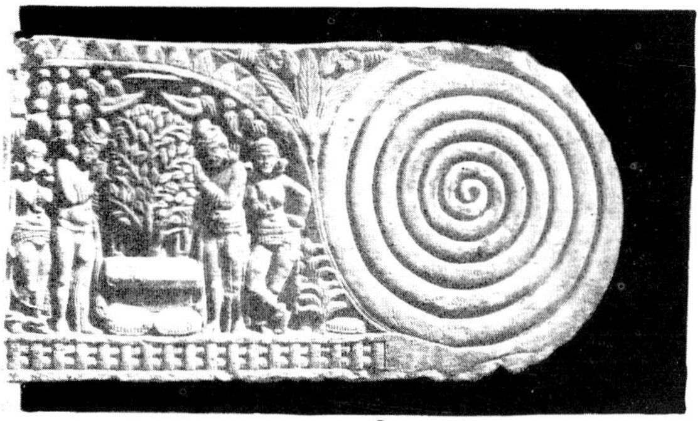

a - 2

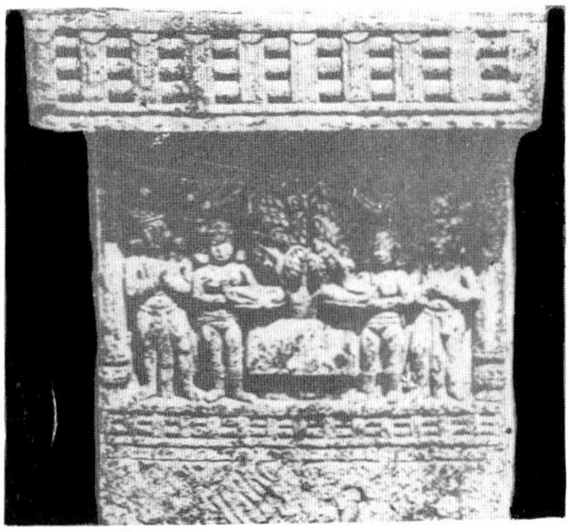

b - 1

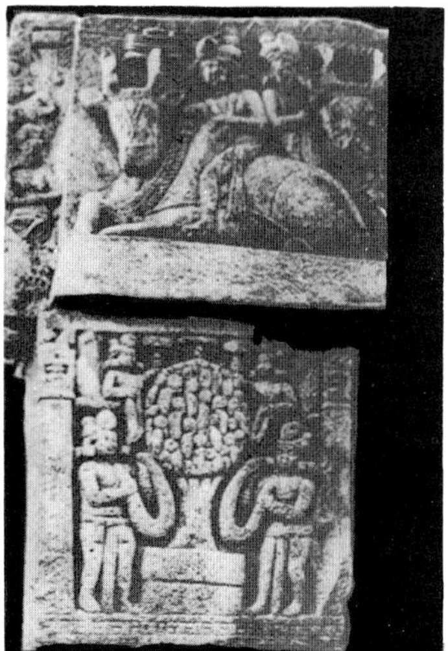

b - 2

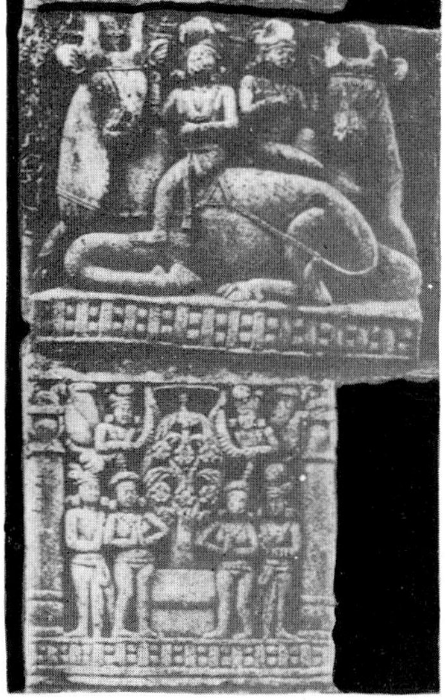

b - 3

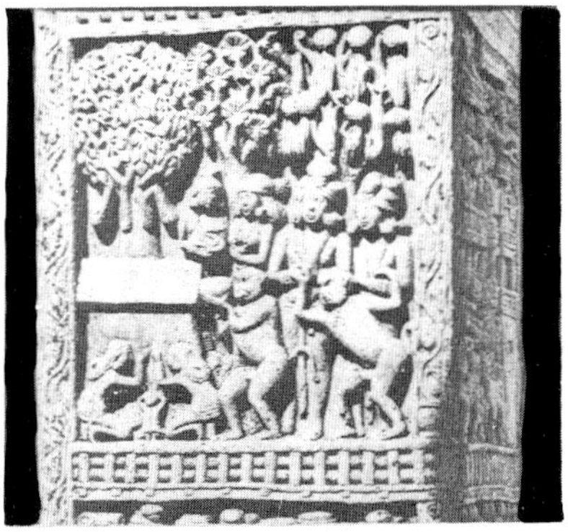

c

Illust. 3

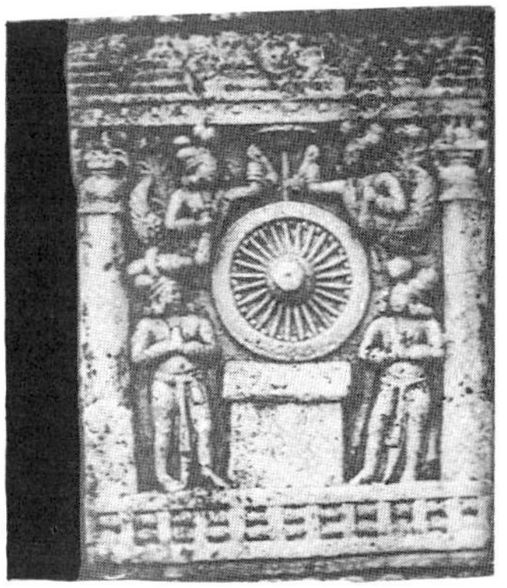

a - 1

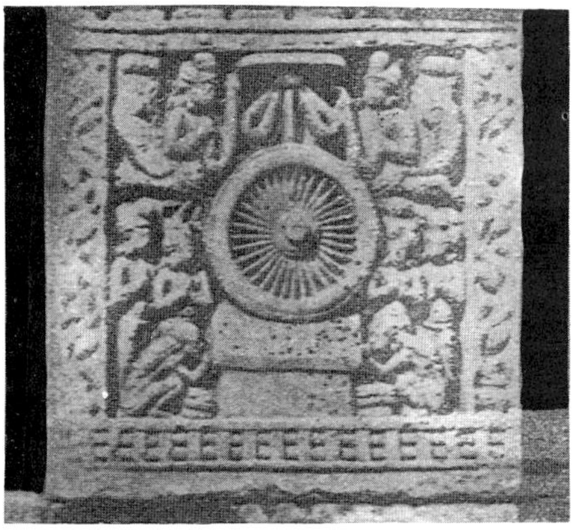

a - 2

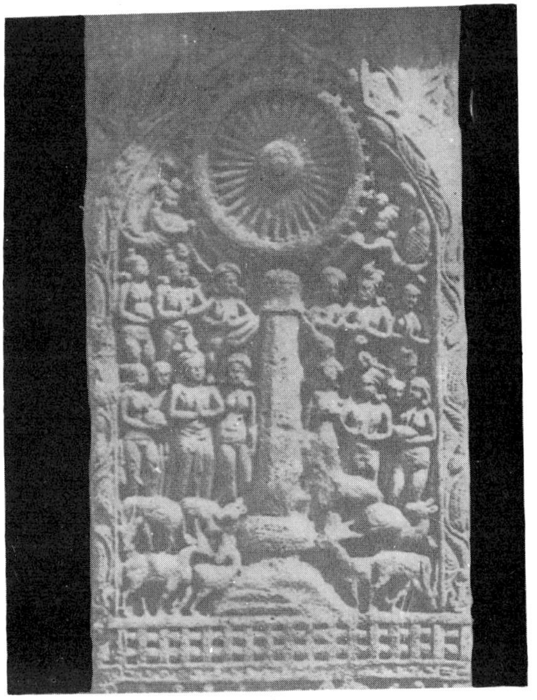

b

Illust. 4

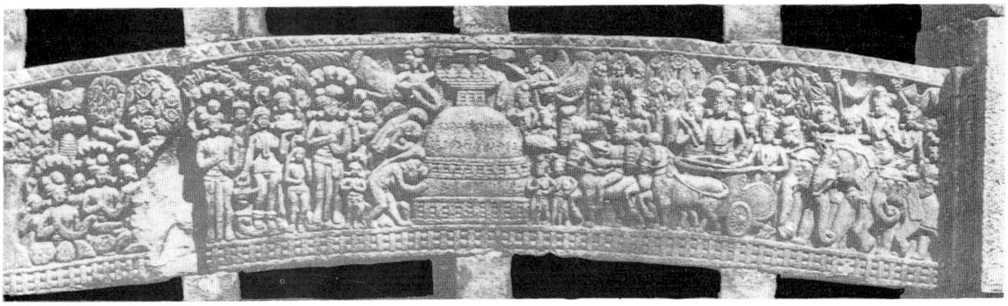

a

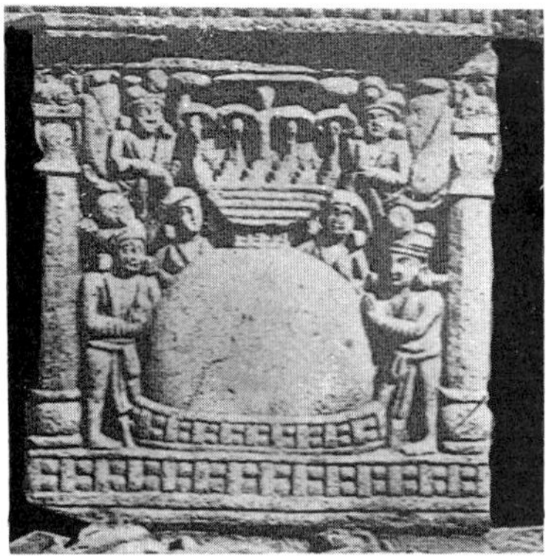

b - 1

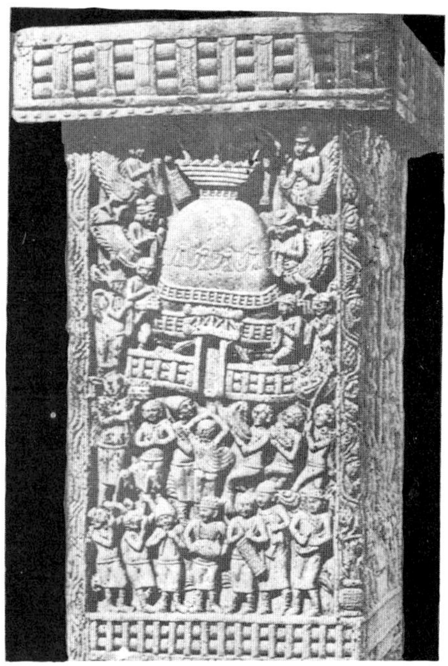

c

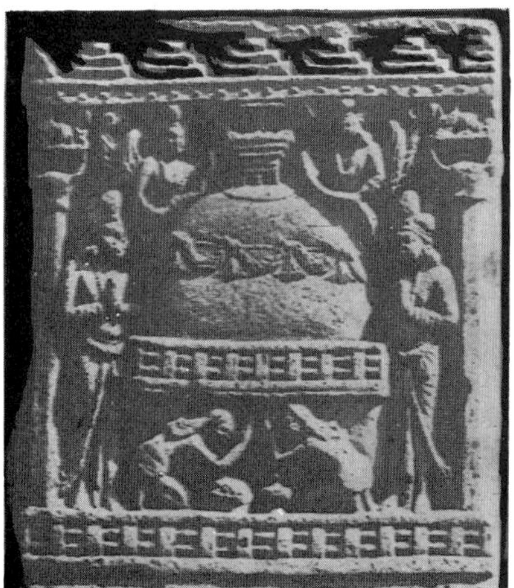

b - 2

Illust. 5

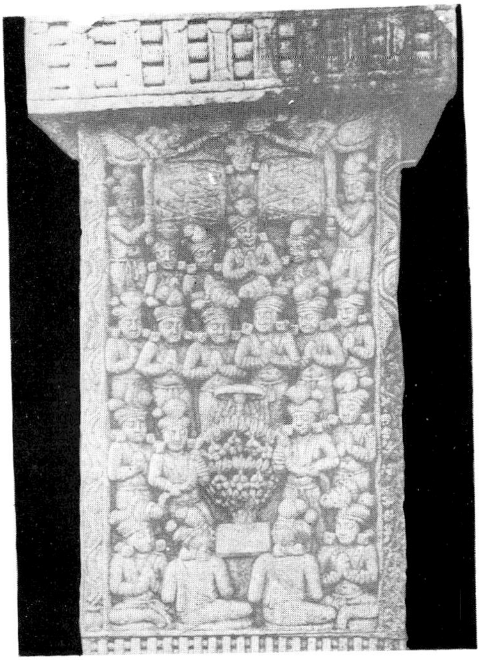

a

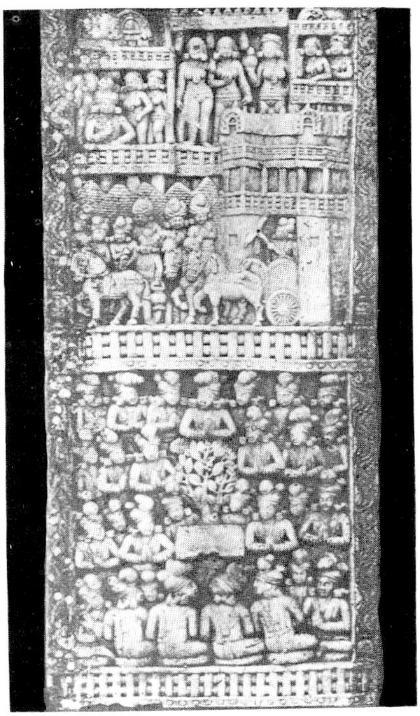

b - 1

b - 2

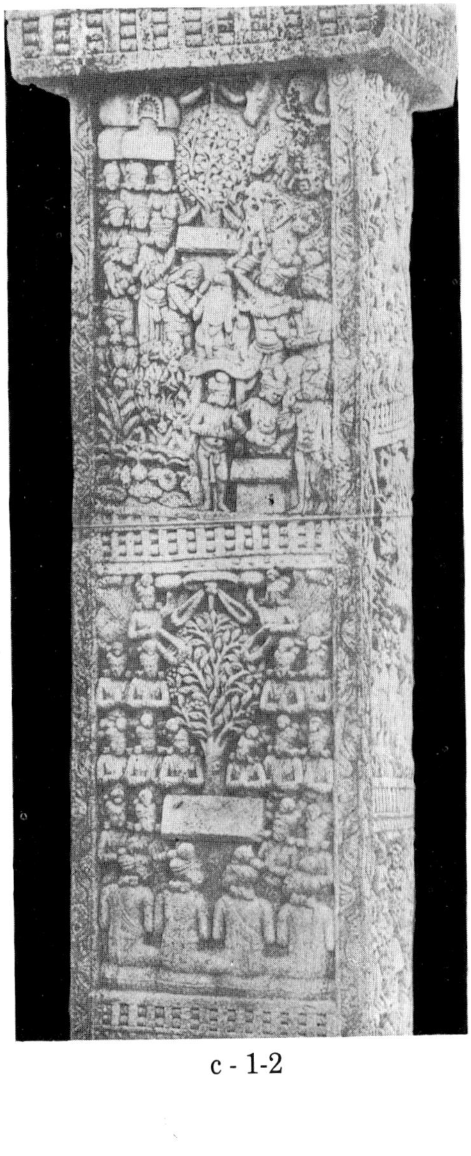

c - 1-2

Illust. 6

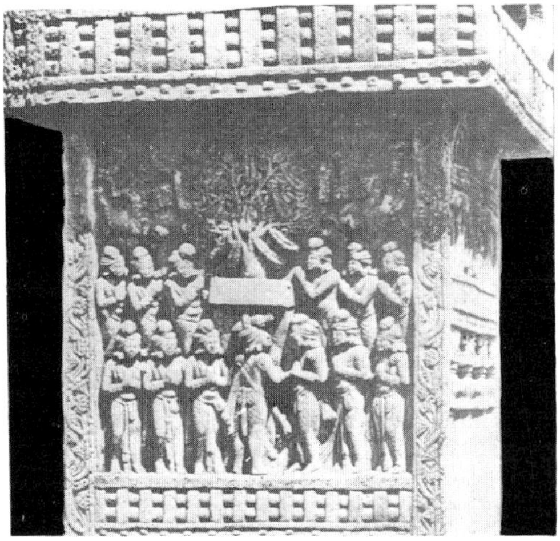

a

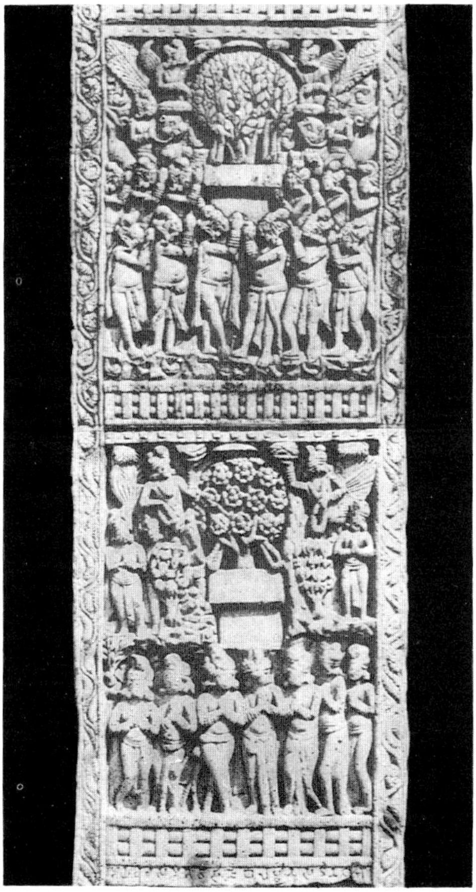

b - 1

b - 2

Illust. 7

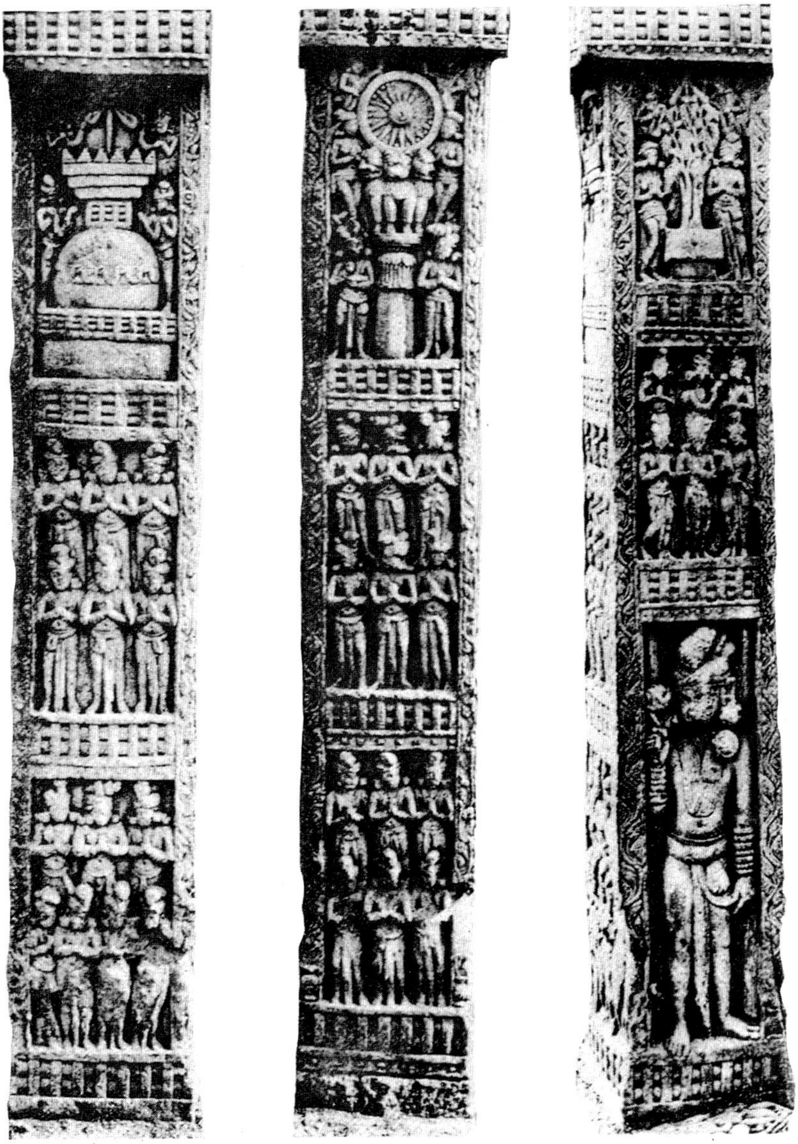

a b c

Illust. 8

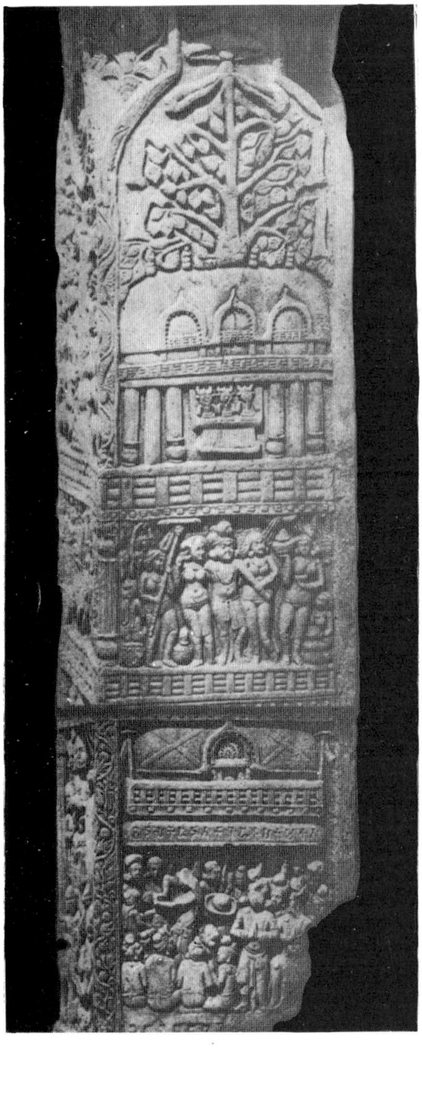

a - 1

a - 2

a - 3

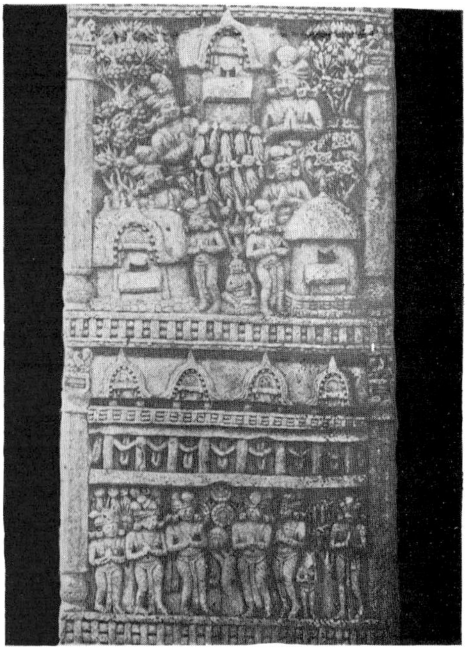

b - 1

b - 2

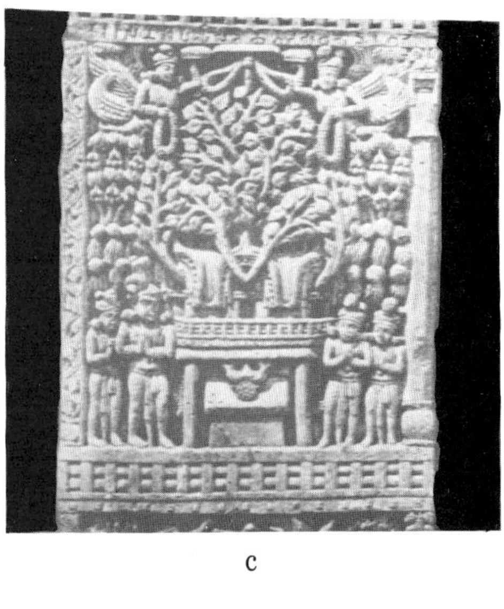

c

Illust. 9 (Cf. Fig. 11)

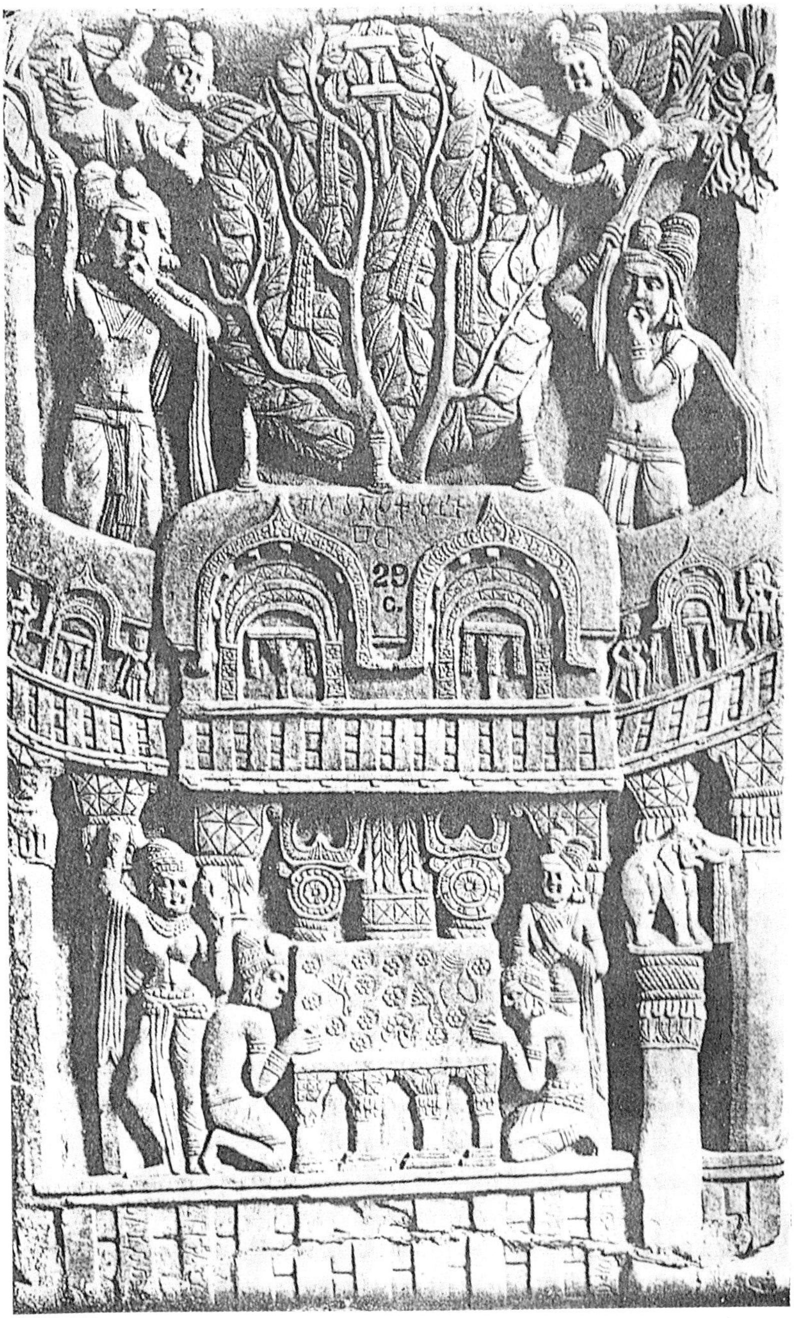

Illust. 10 (Cf. Fig. 10)

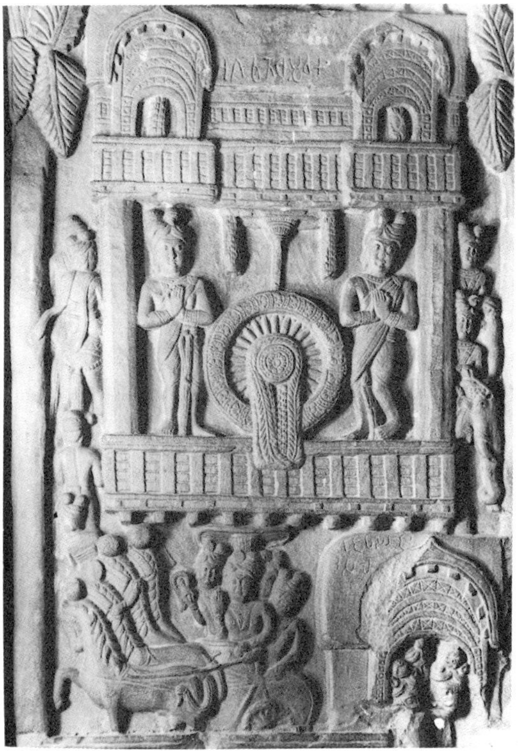

a - 1

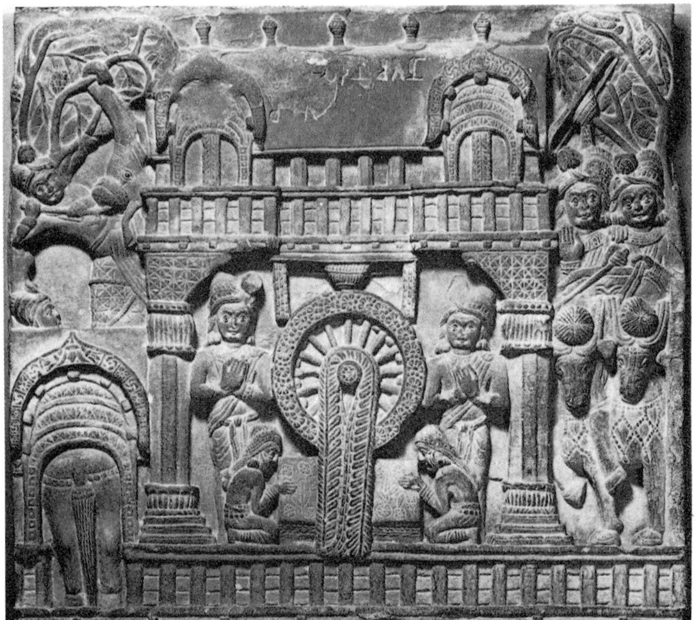

a - 2

Illust. 11

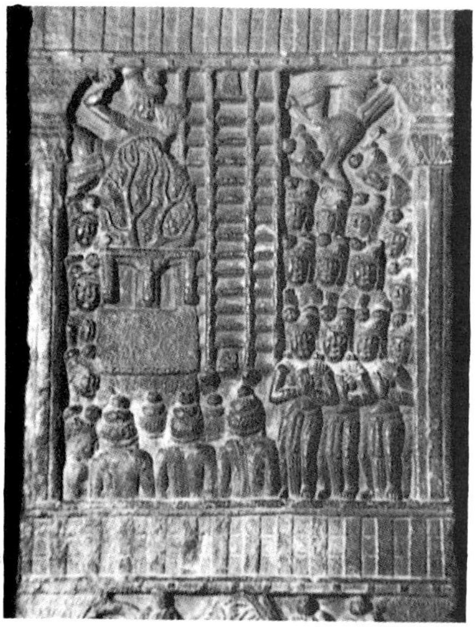

a - 1

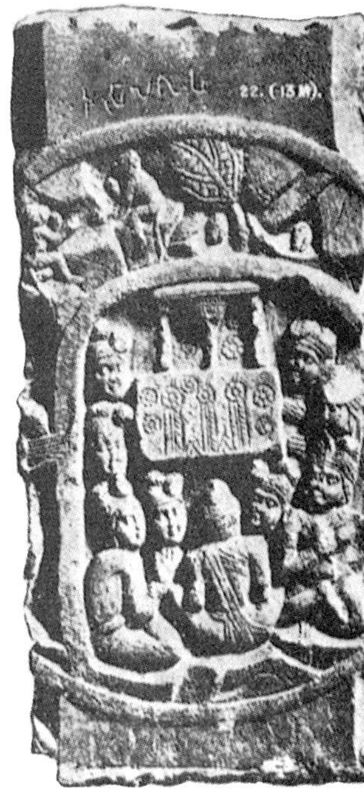

b - 1

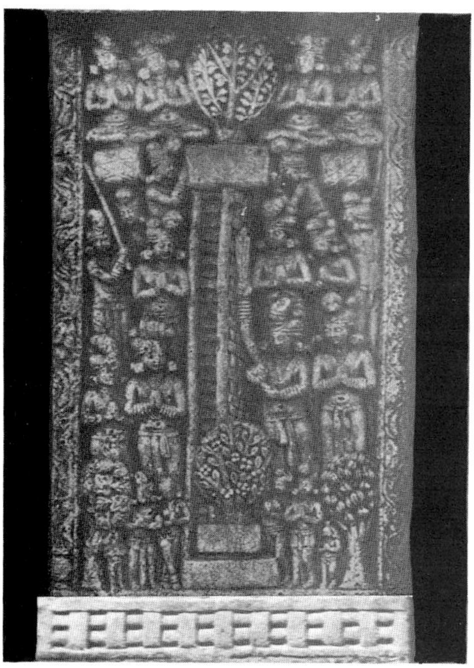

a - 2

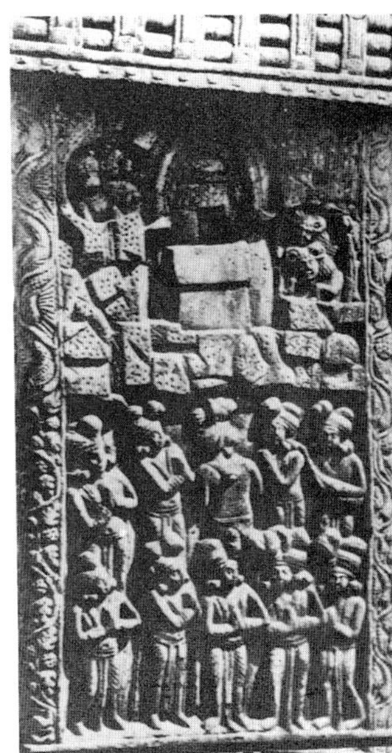

b - 2

Illust. 12

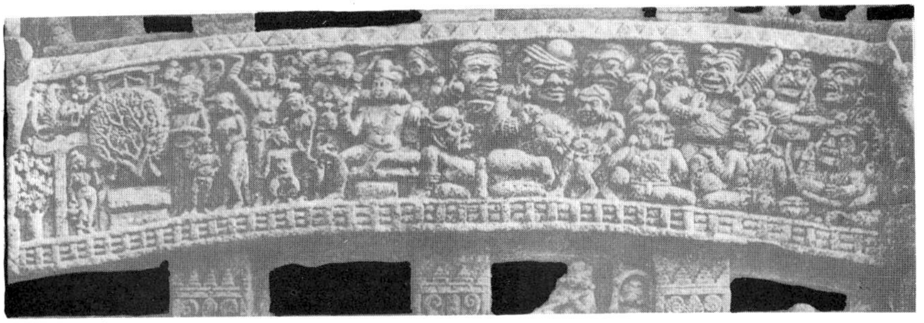

a - 1

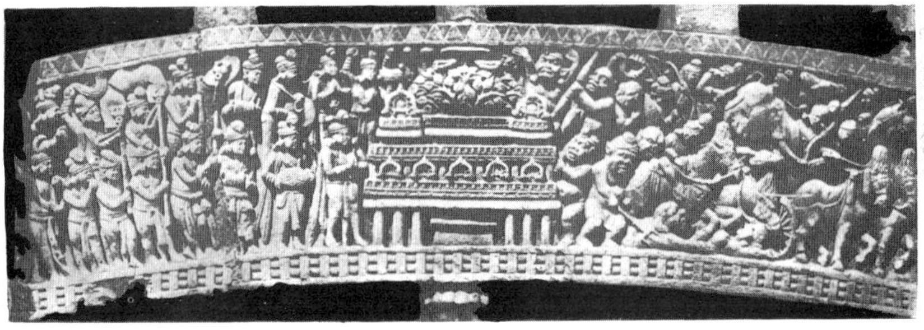

a - 2

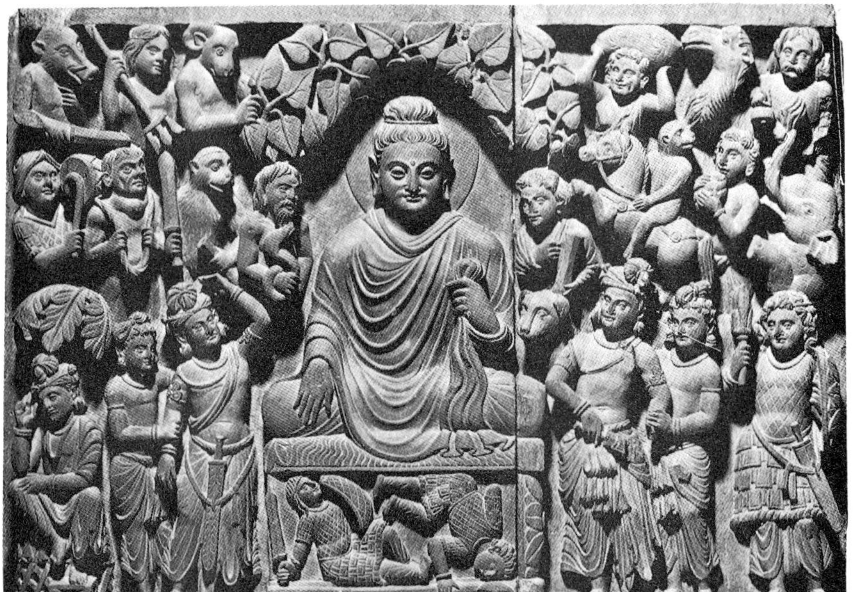

b

Illust. 13

a - 1

b - 1

a - 2

b - 2

a - 3

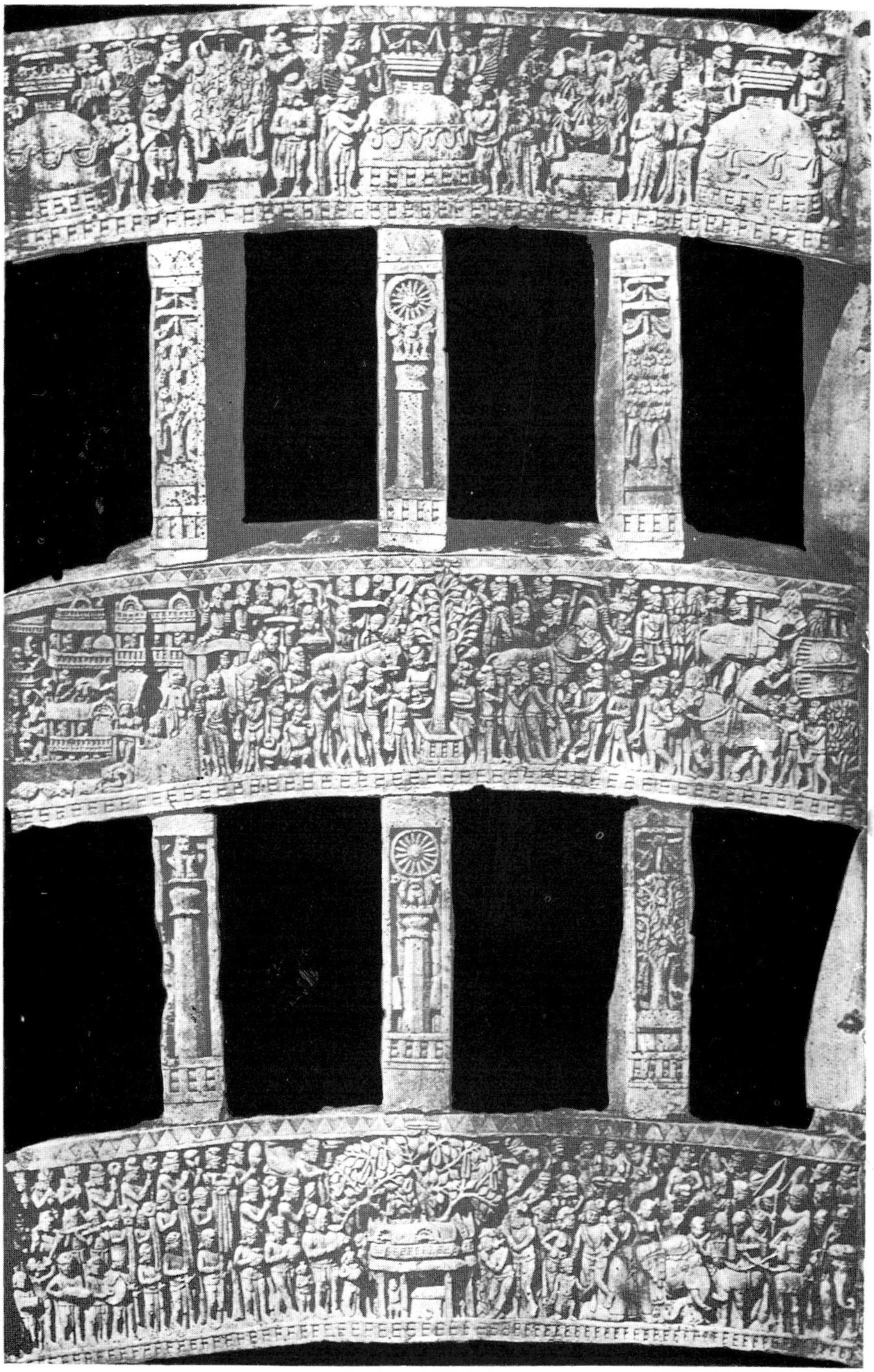

Illust. 14

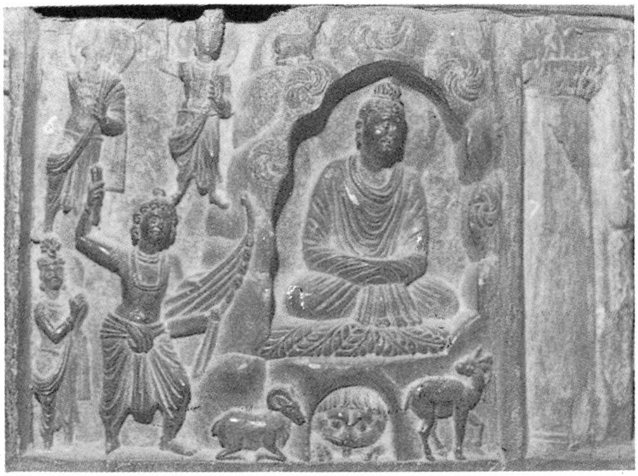

a

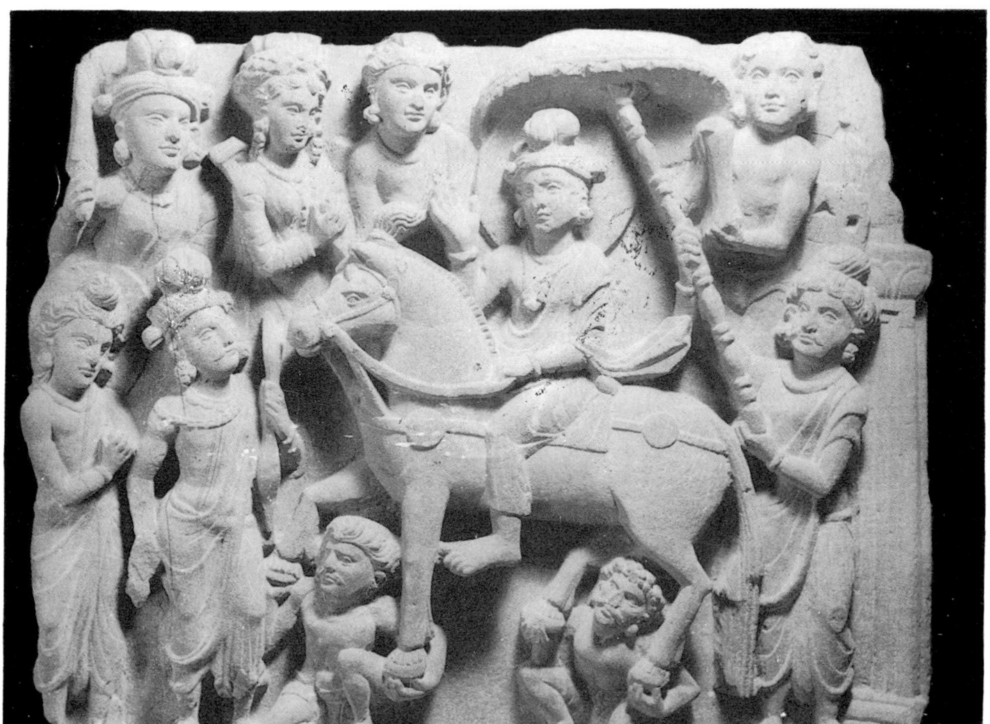

b

Illust. 15

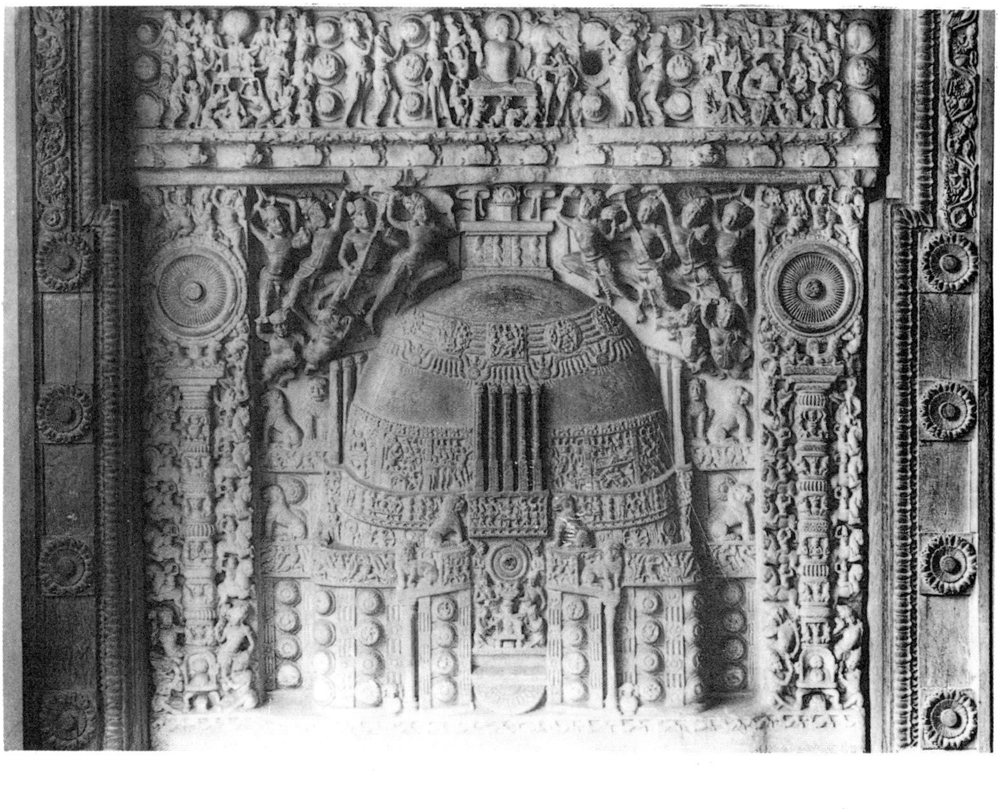

Illust. 16

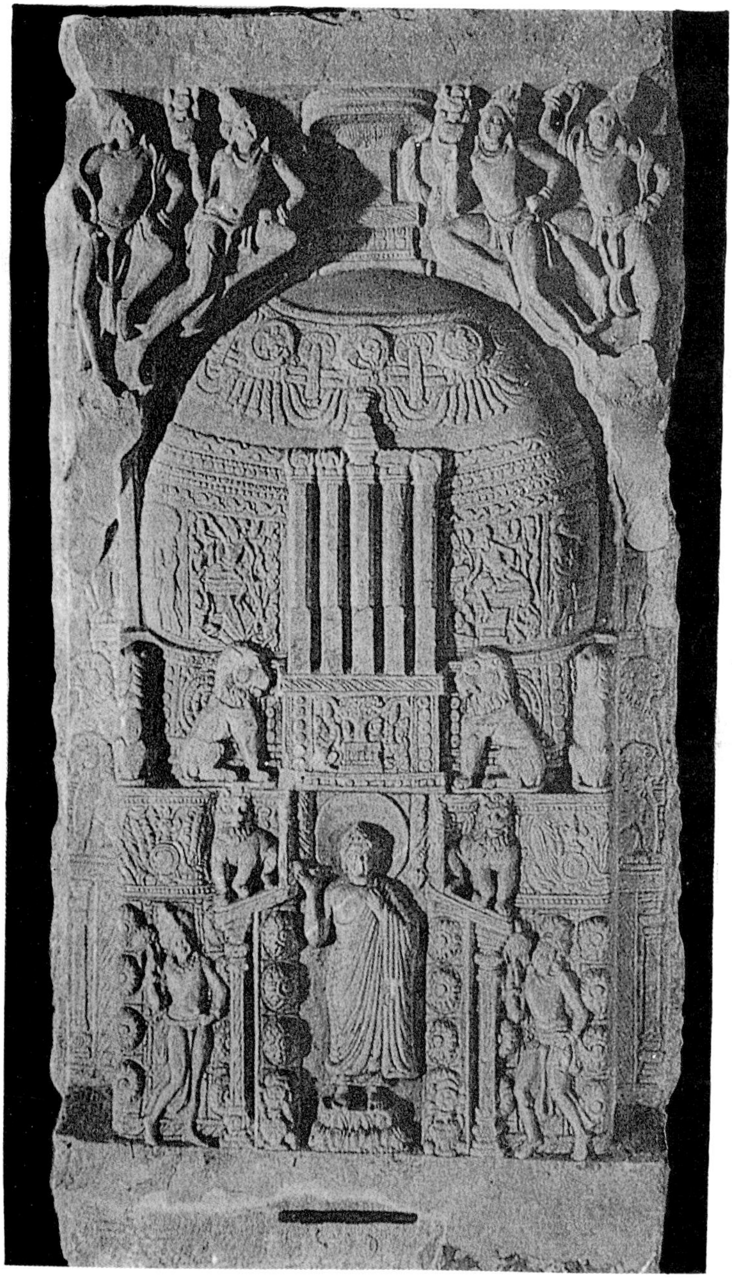

Illust. 17

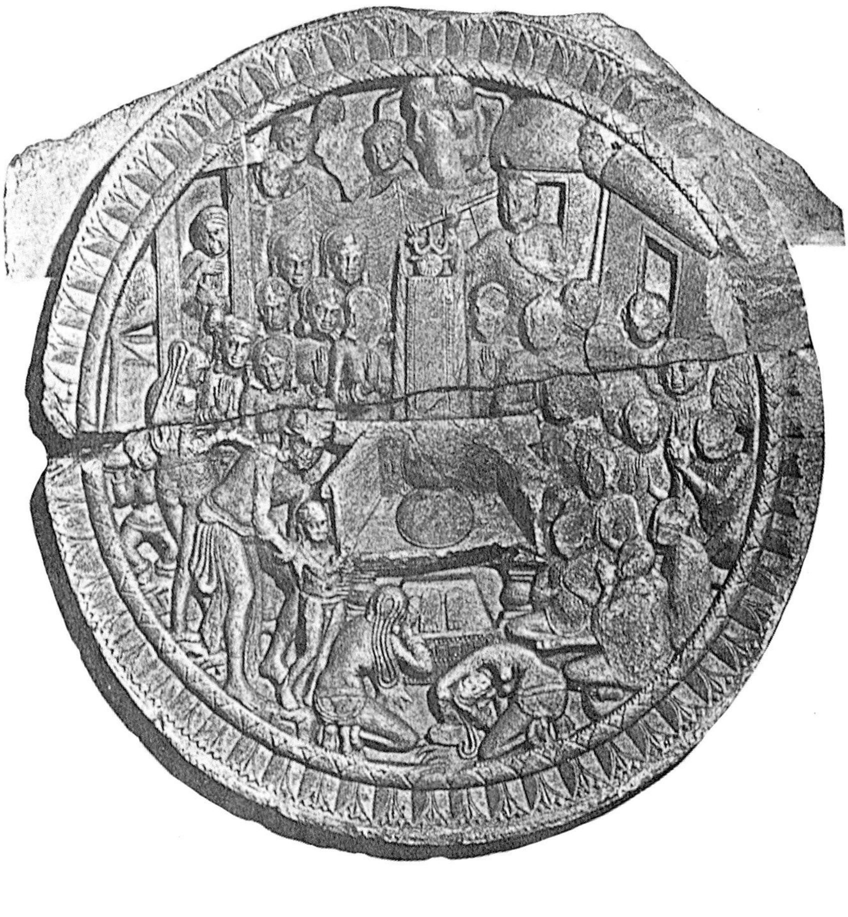

Illust. 18

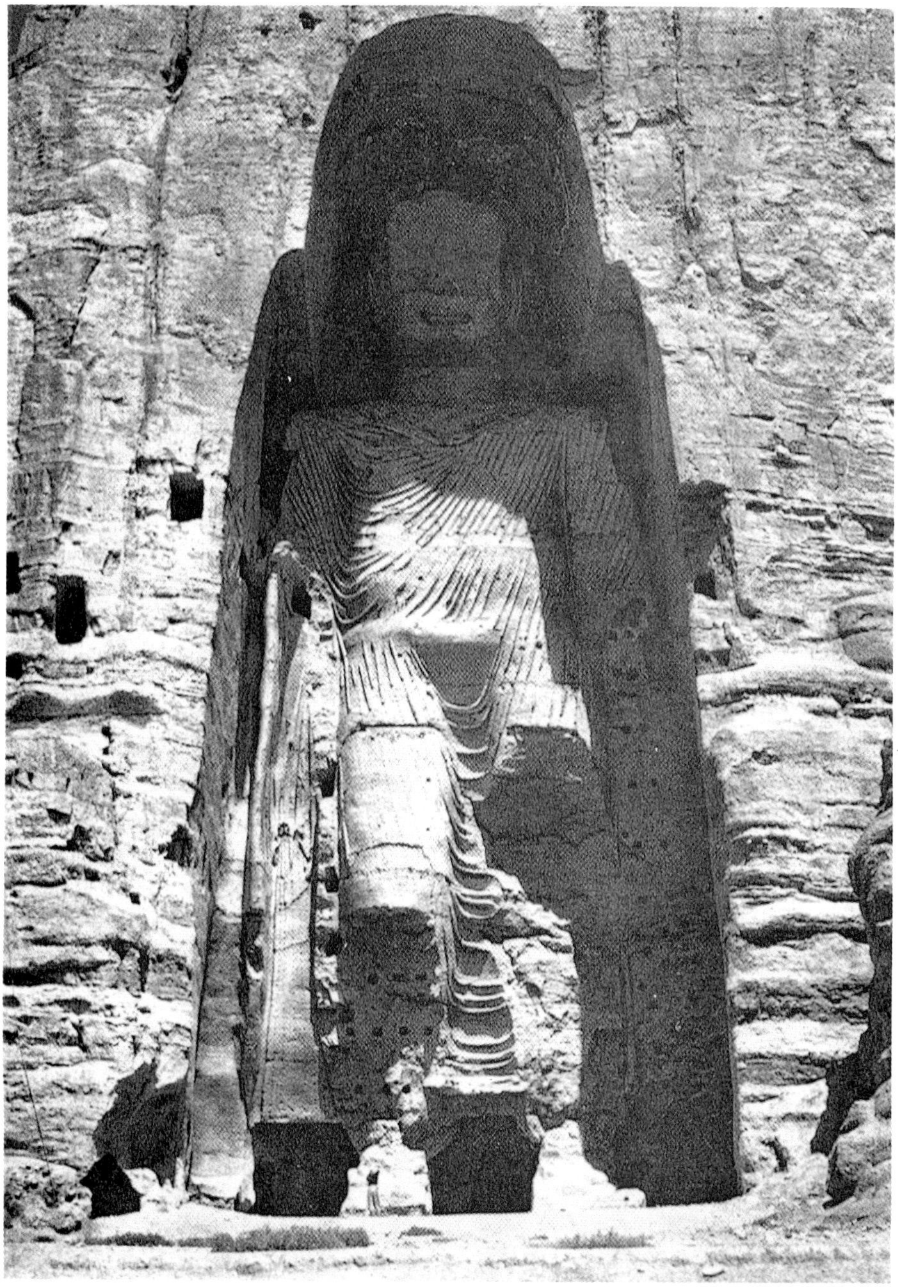

Illust. 19

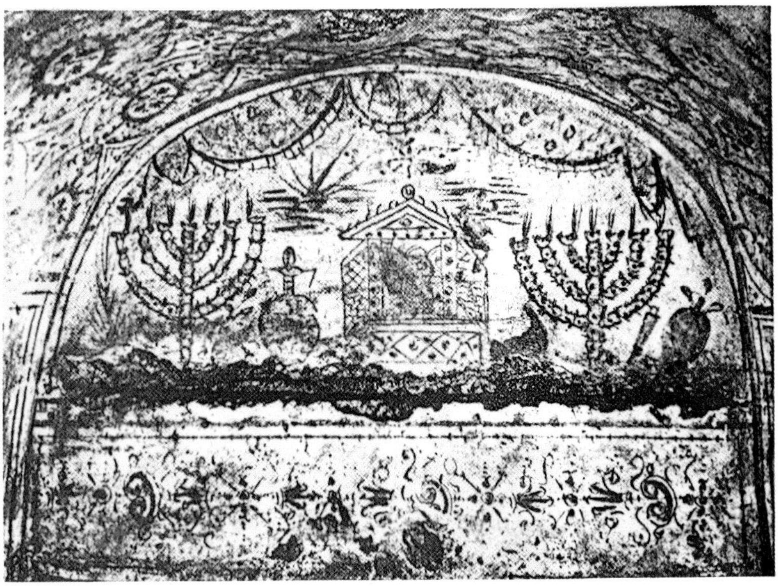

Illust. 20

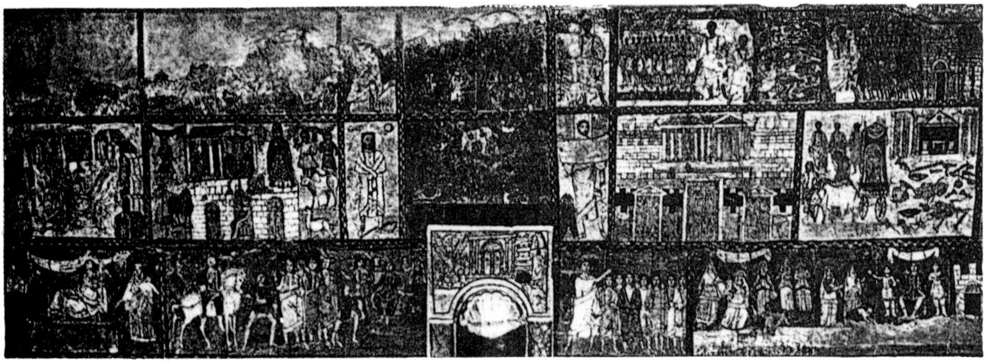

a - 1

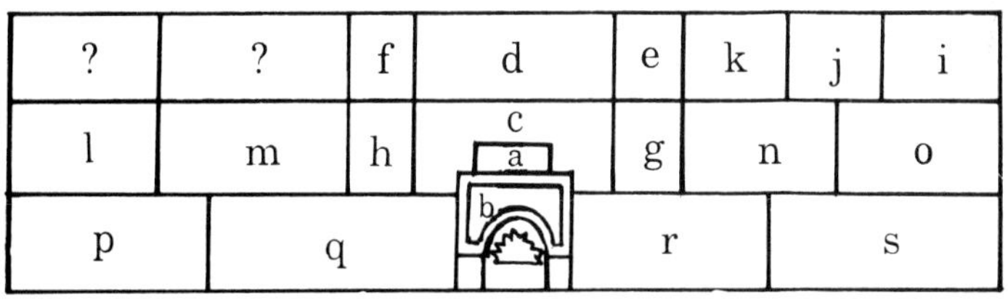

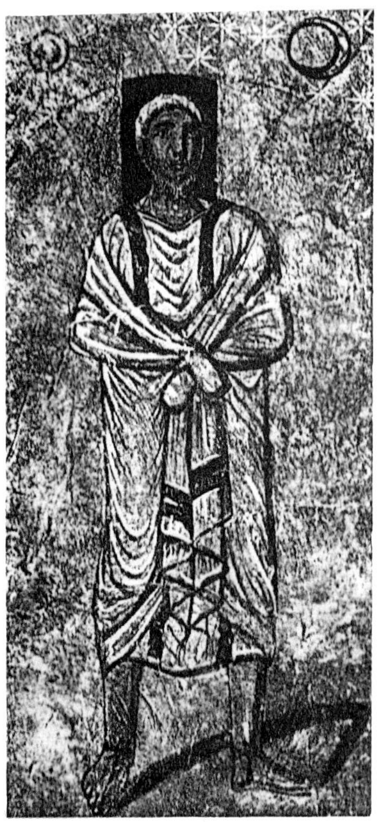

a - 2

Illust. 21

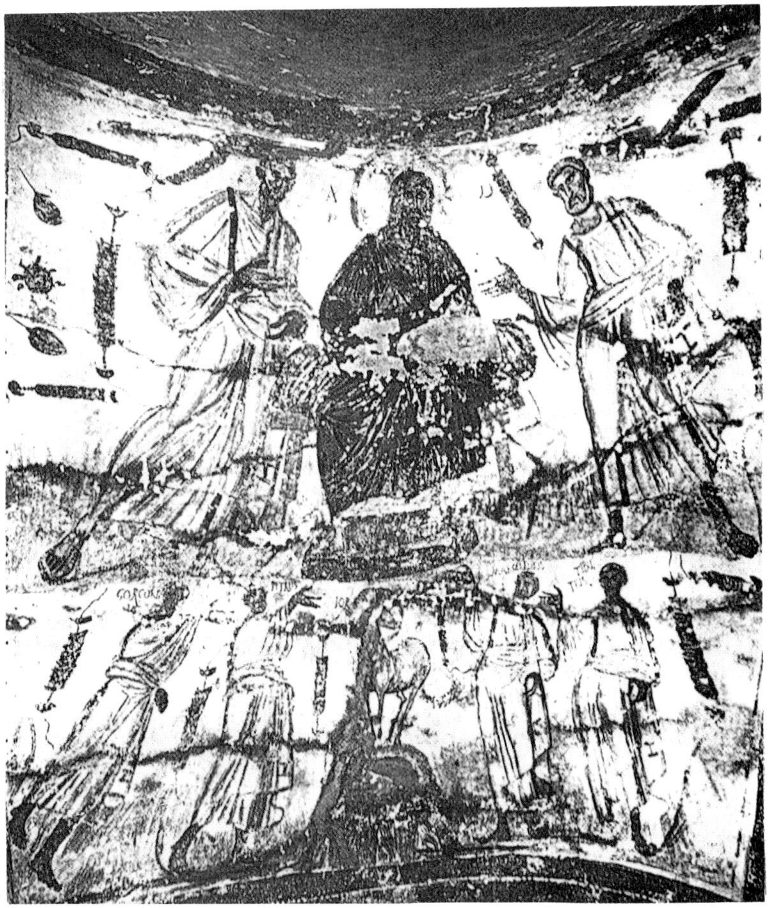

Illust. 22

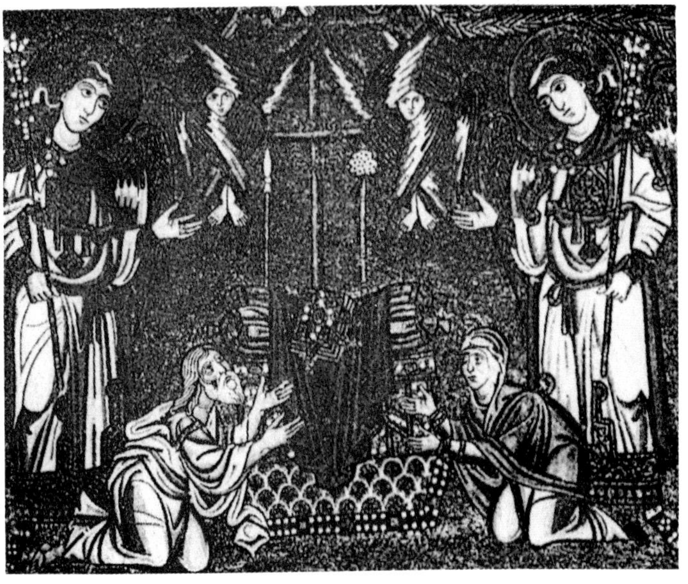

Illust. 23

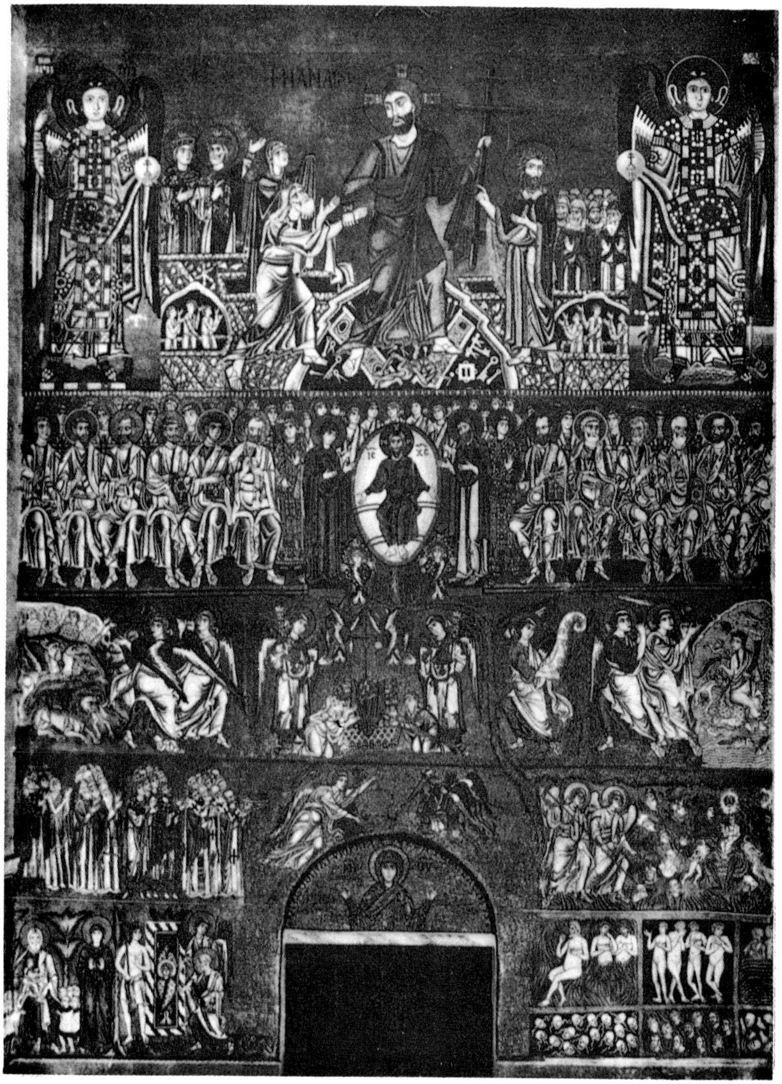

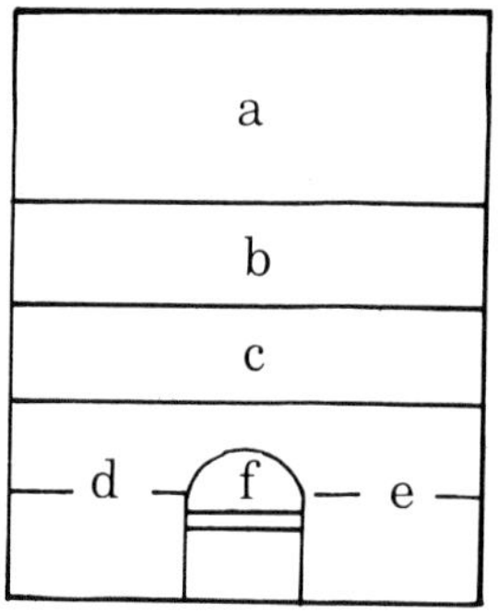

Illust. 24

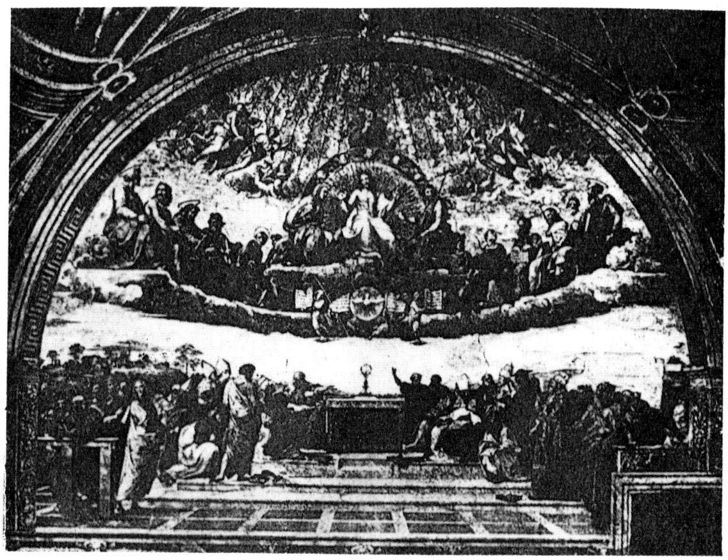

Pl. 3

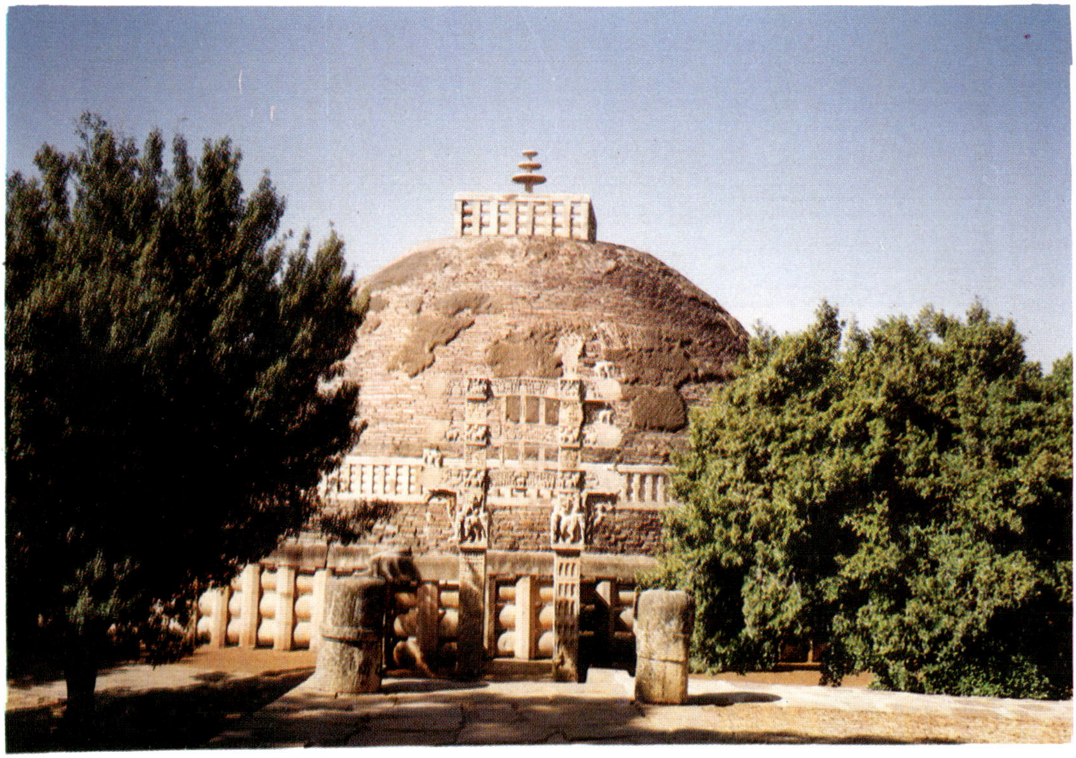

Illust. 24

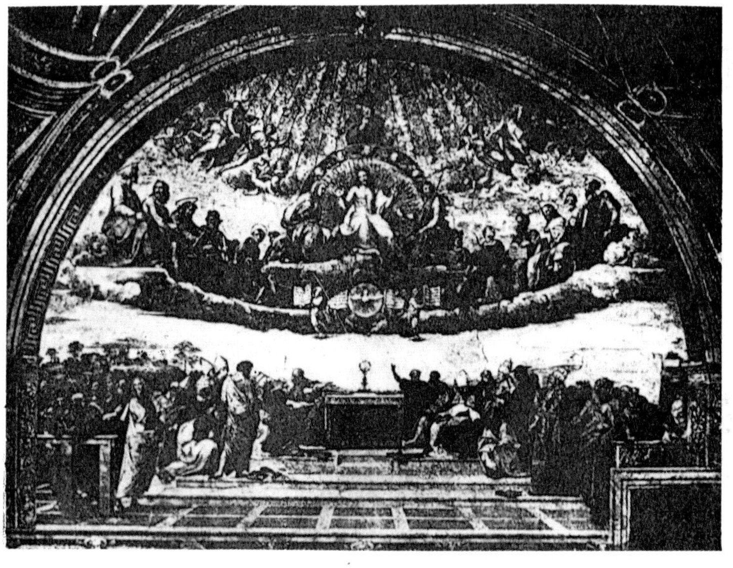

Illust. 25

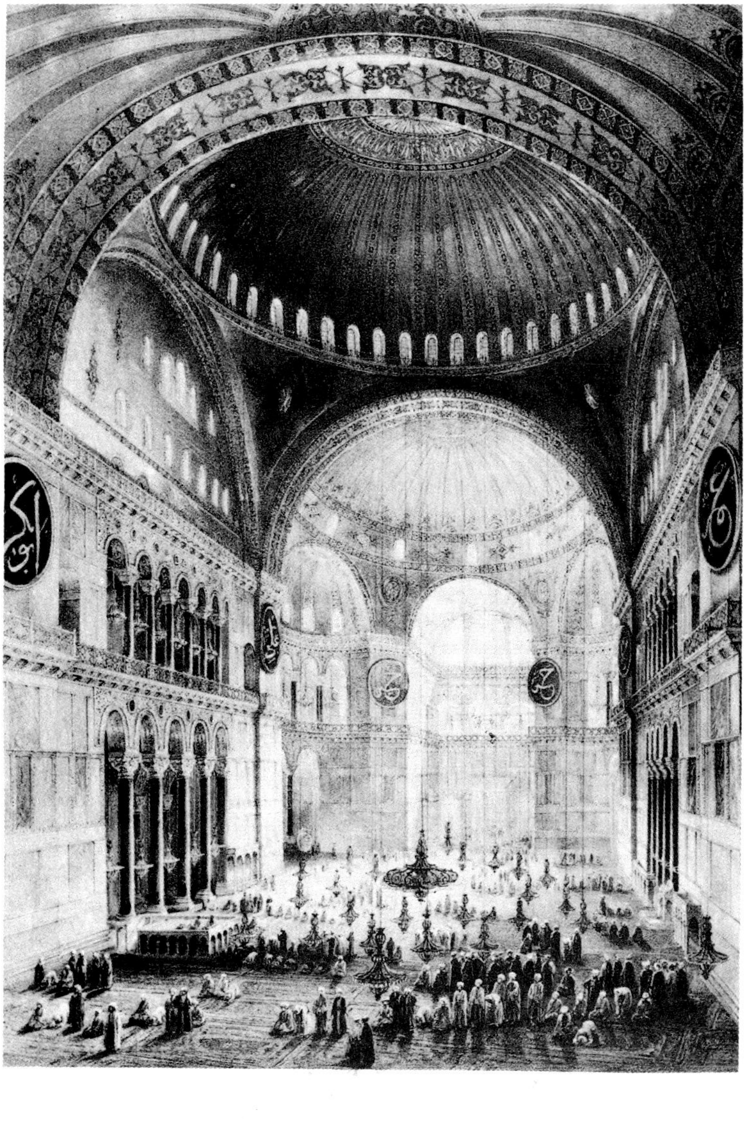

Plates

Pl. 1

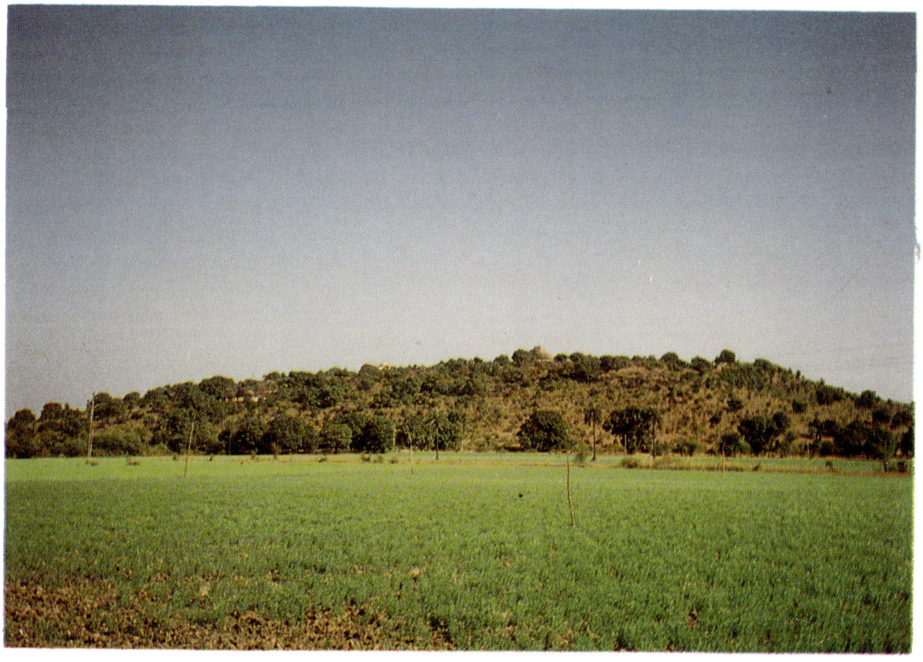

Pl. 2

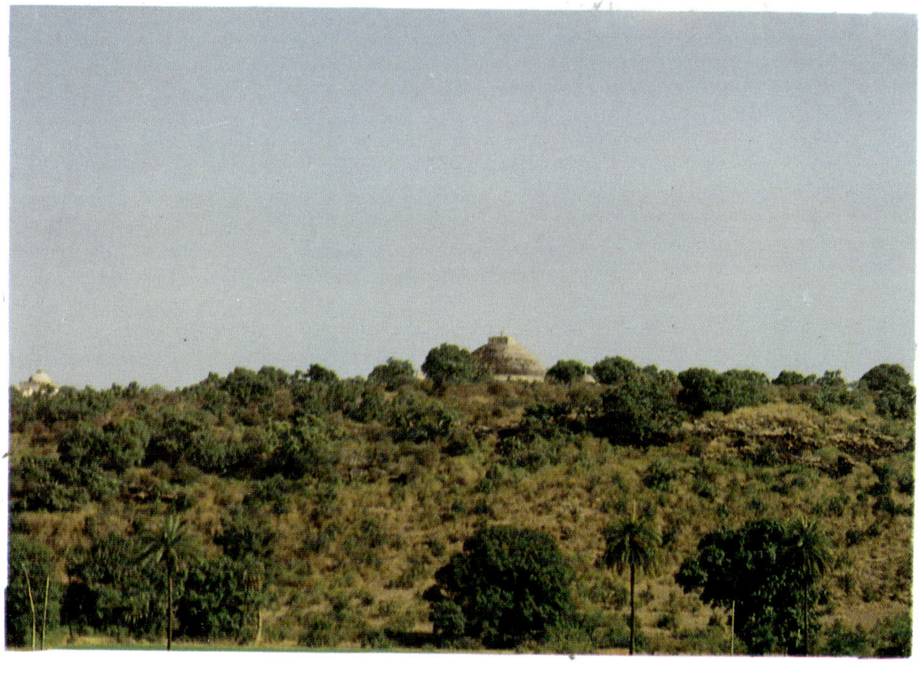

Pl. 3

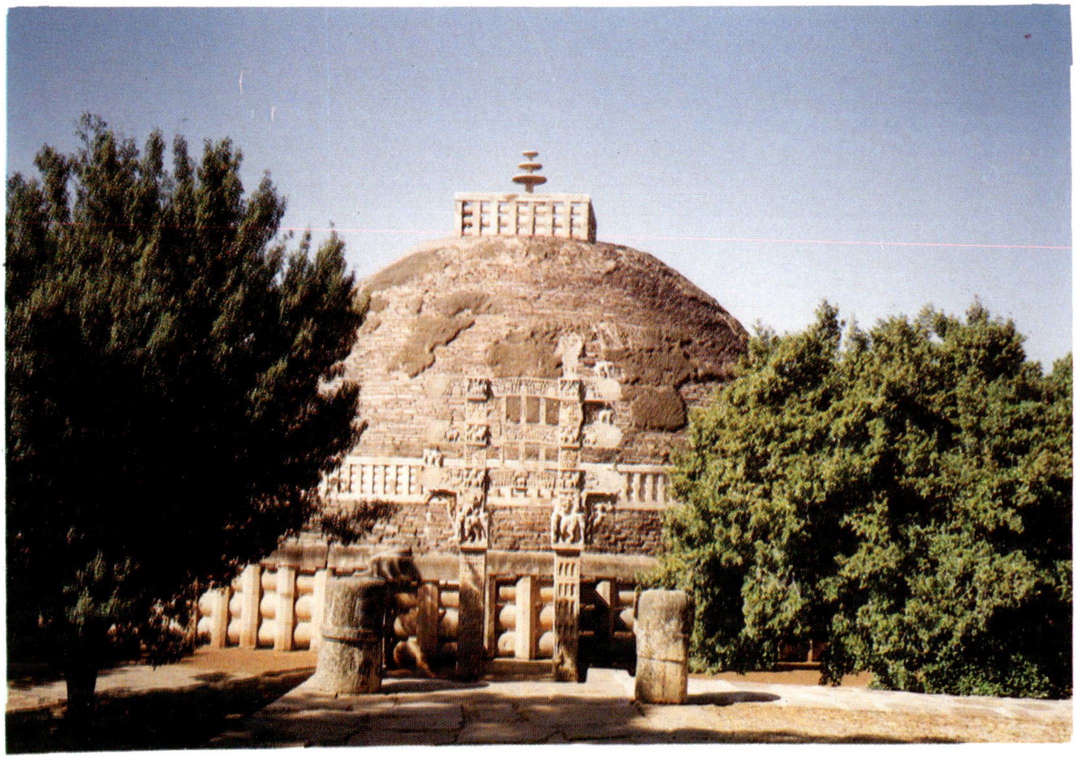

Pl. 4

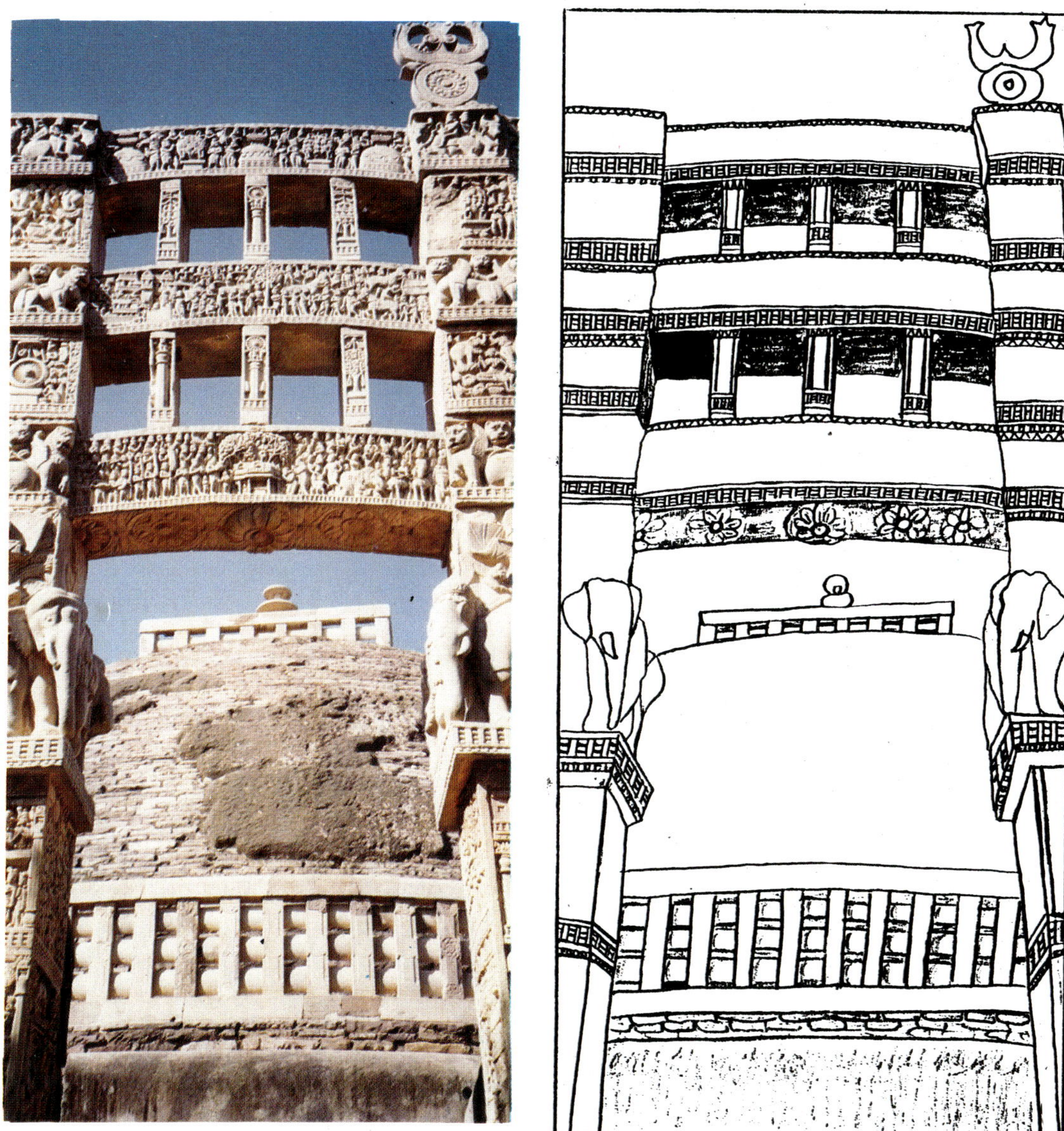

Pl. 5

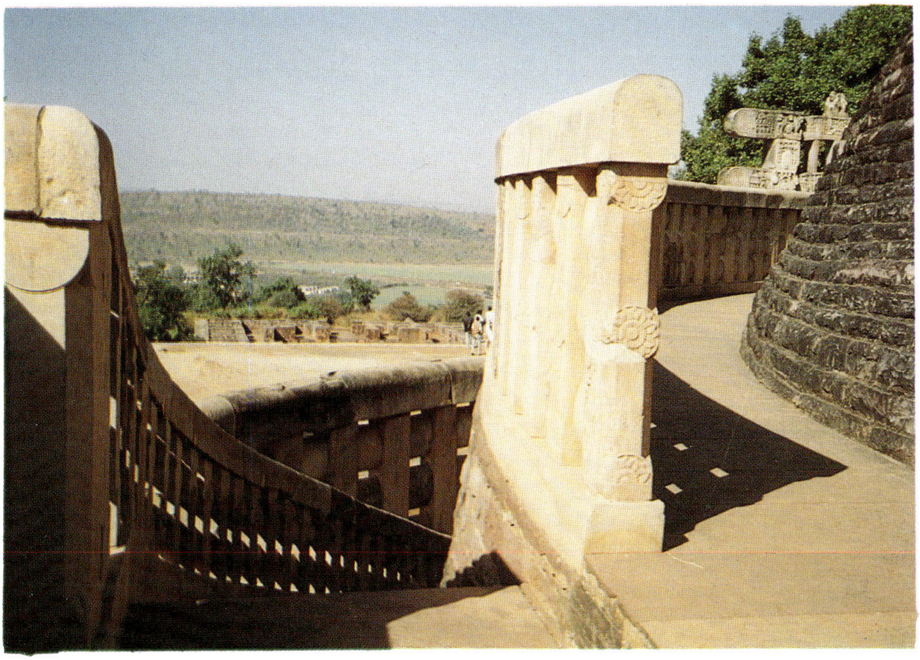

Pl. 6

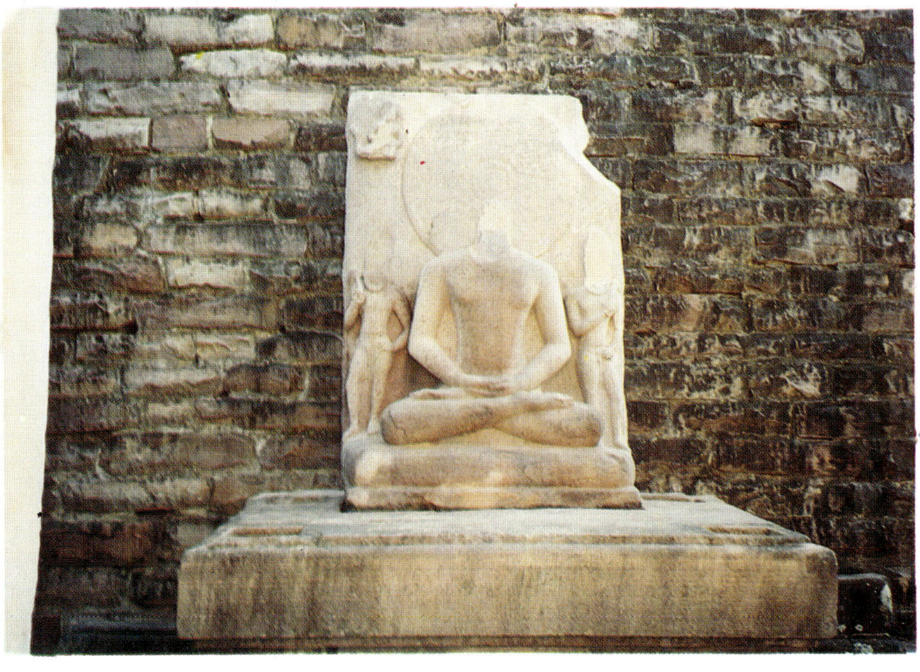

Pl. 7

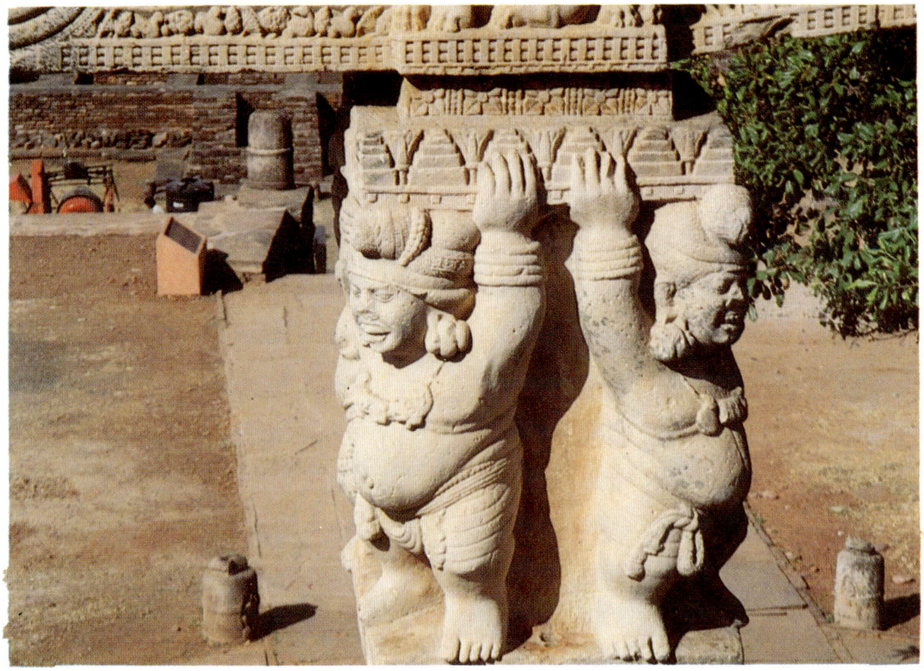

Pl. 8

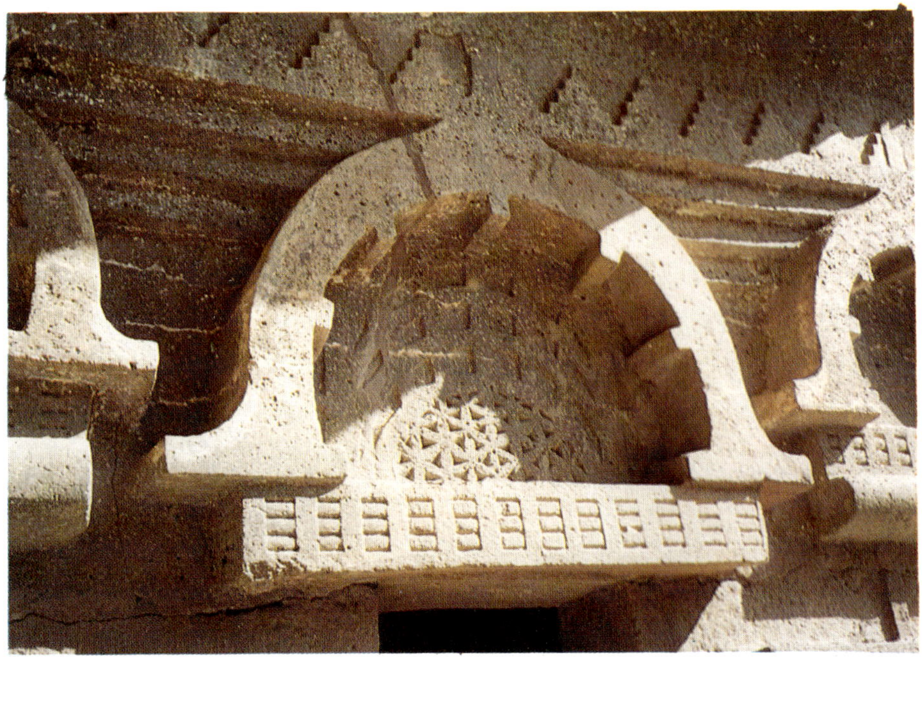

Pl. 9

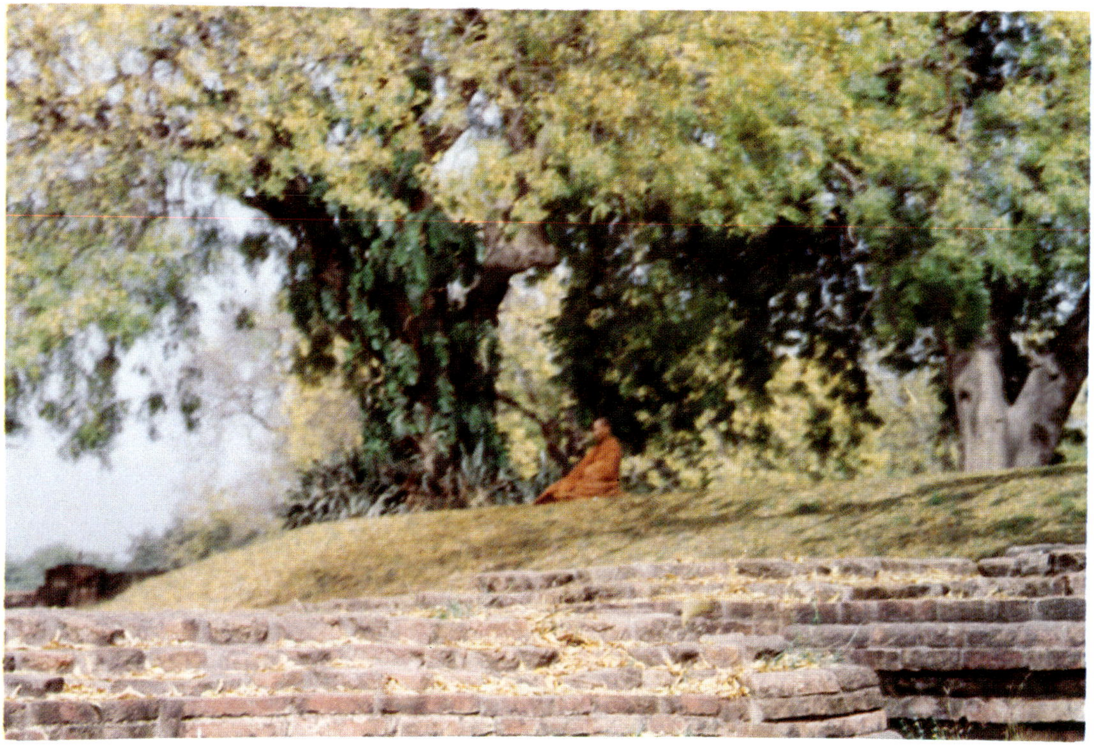

Pl. 10

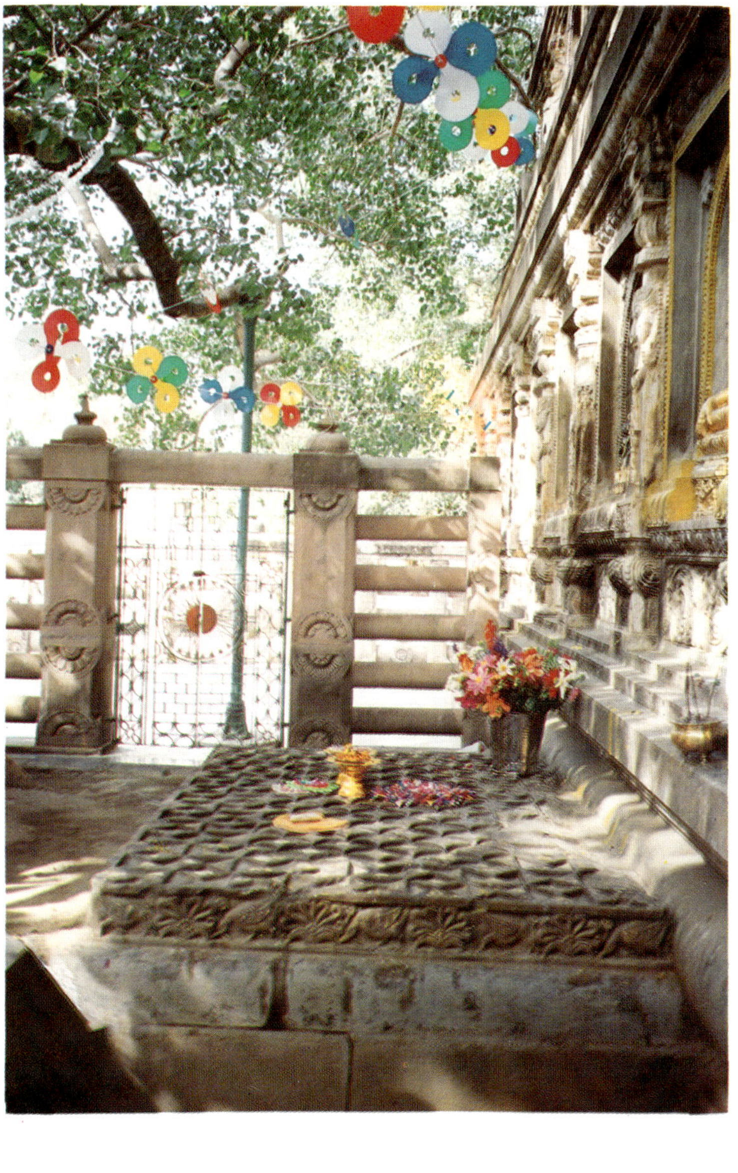

Pl. 11

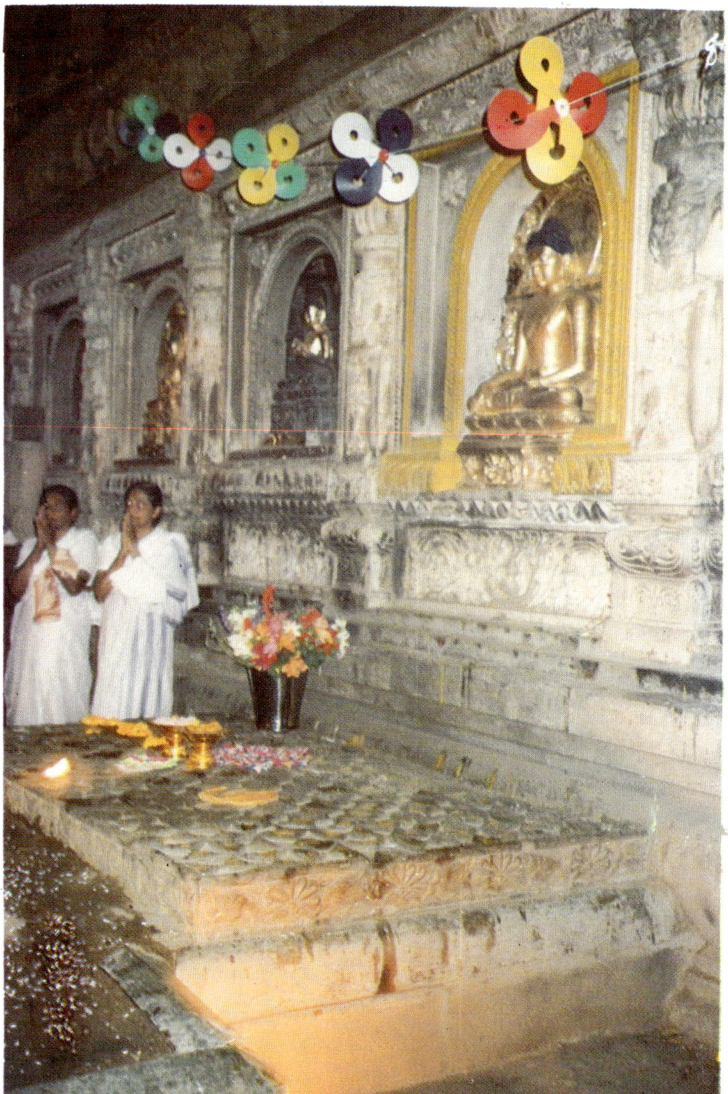

Pl. 12

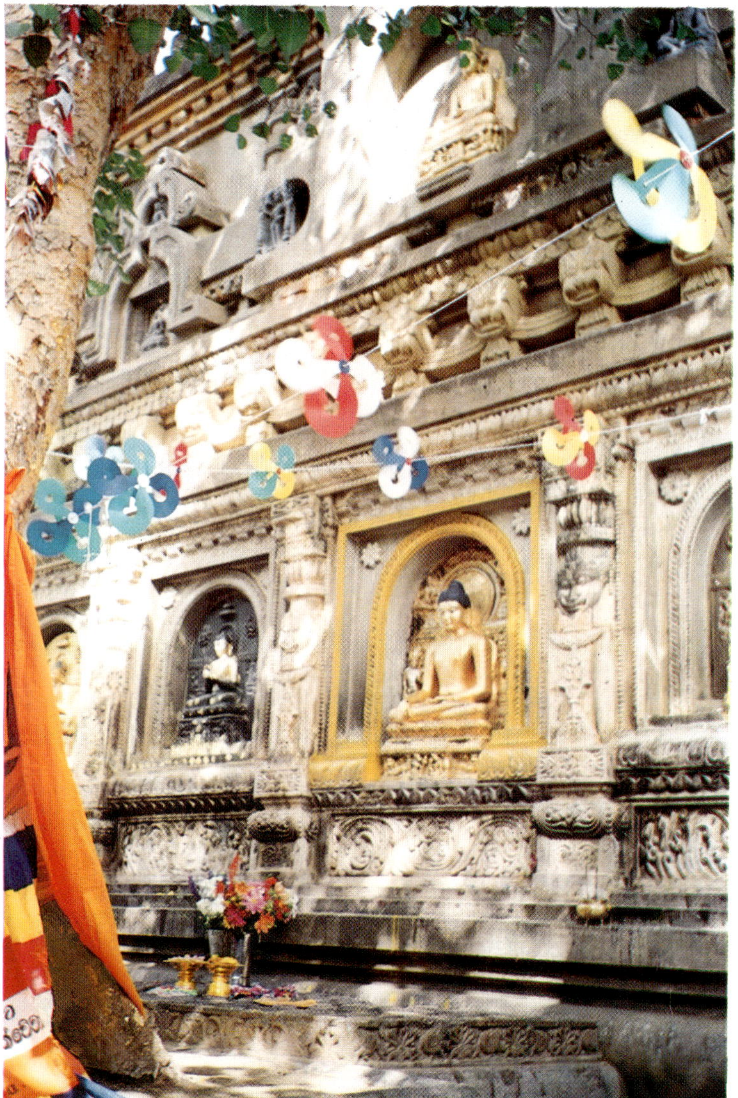

Pl. 13

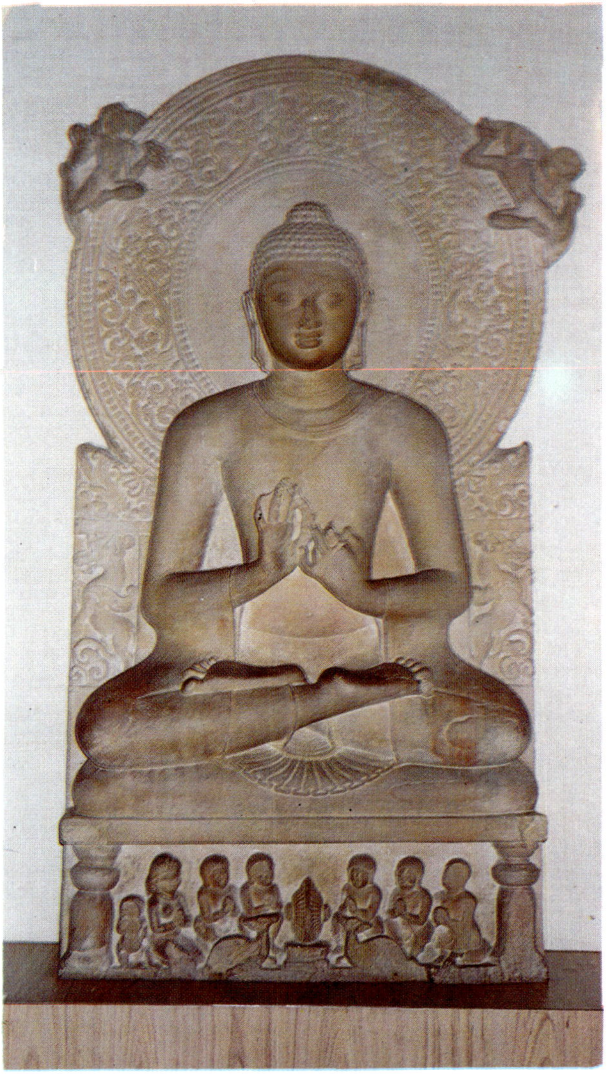

Pl. 14

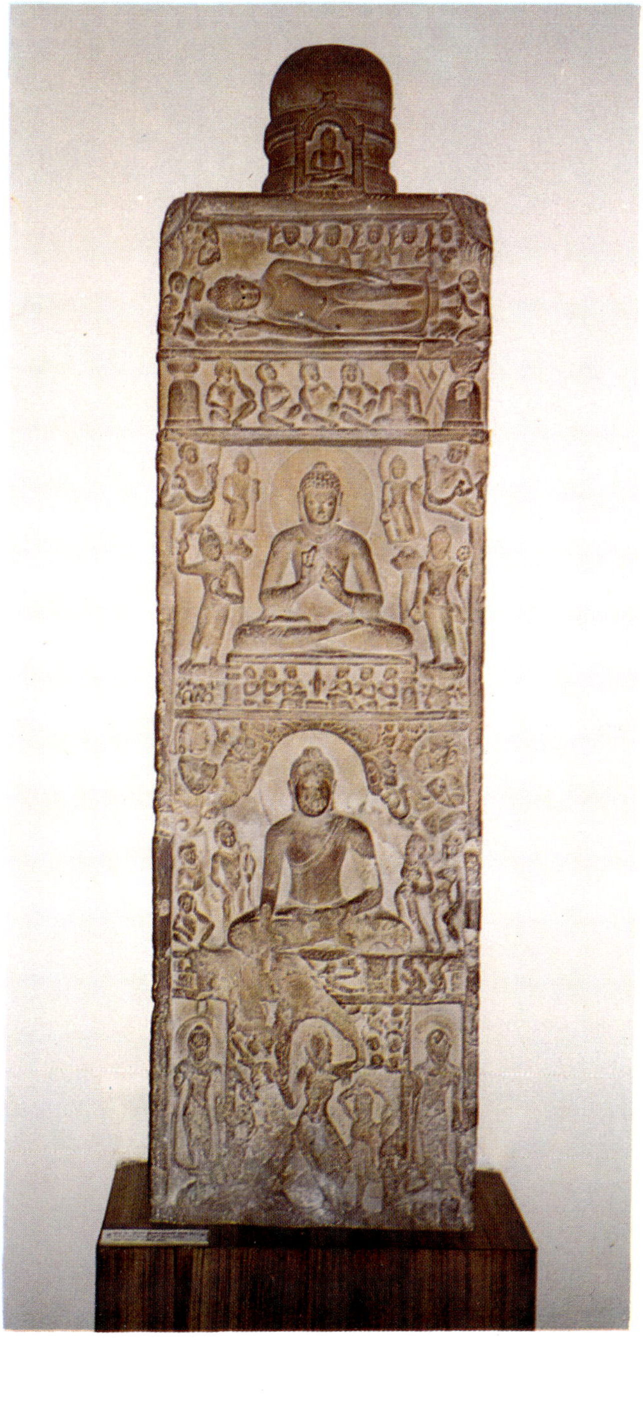

Pl. 15

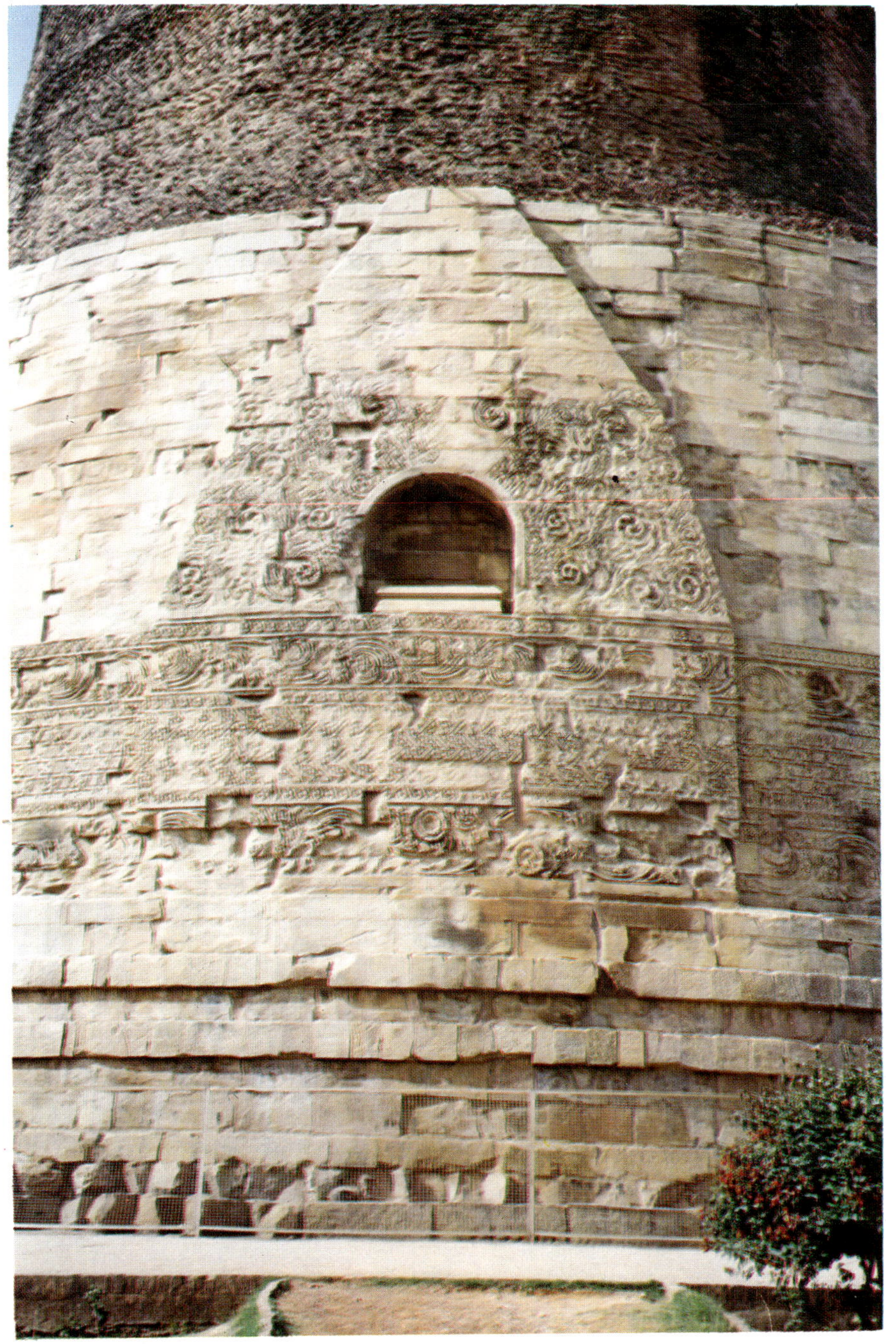

Pl. 16

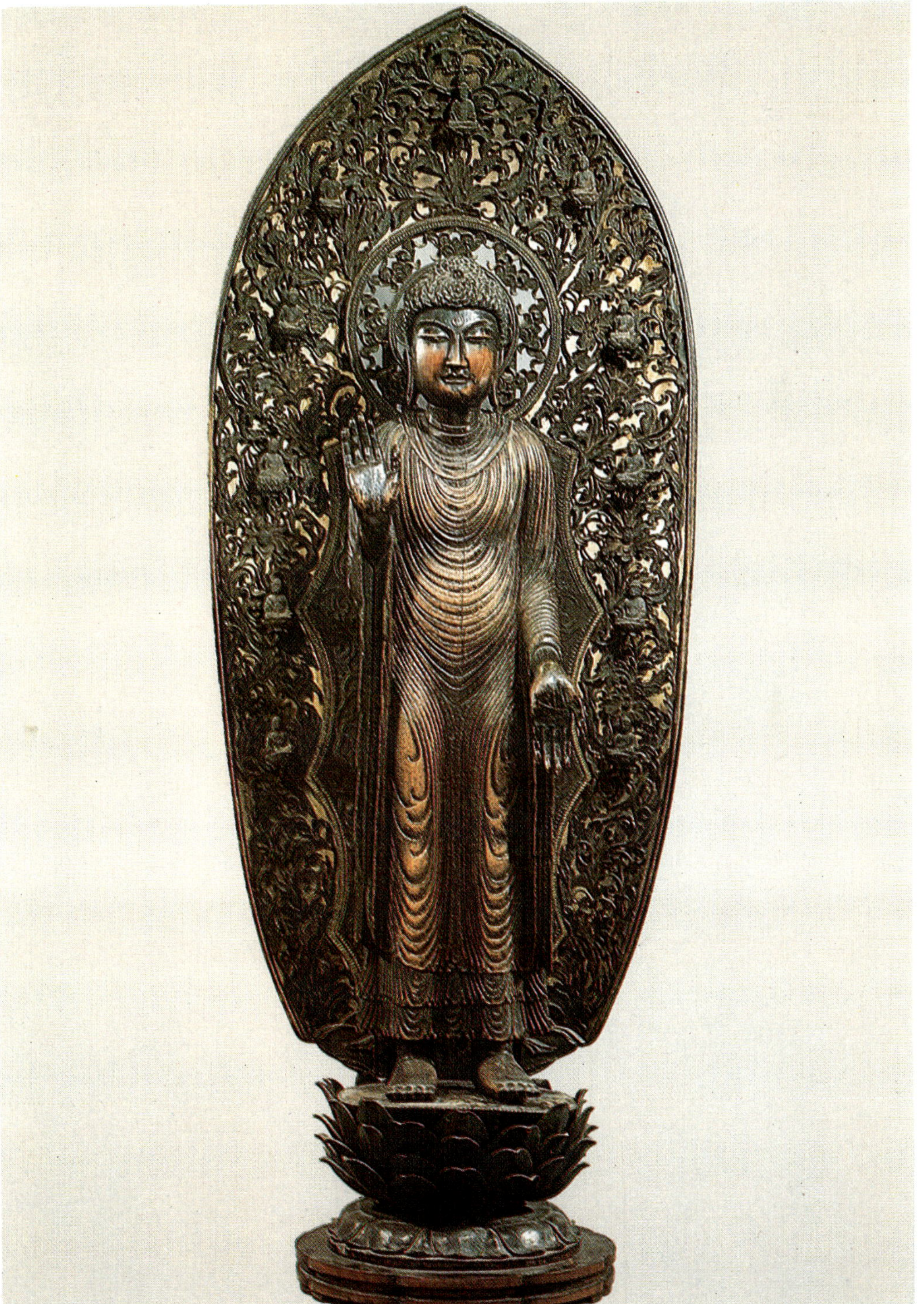

Pl. 17

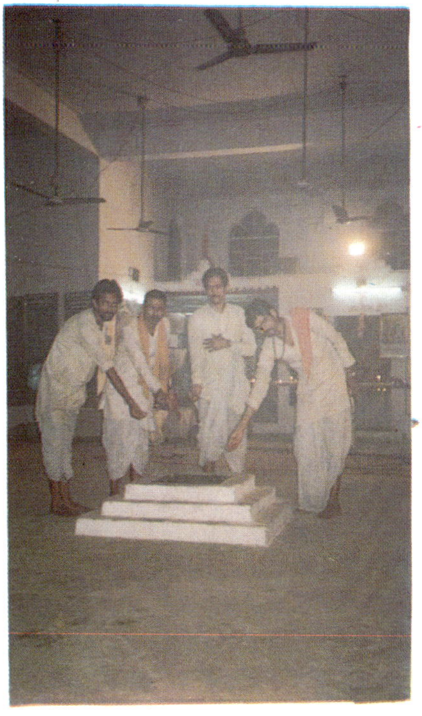

Pl. 18

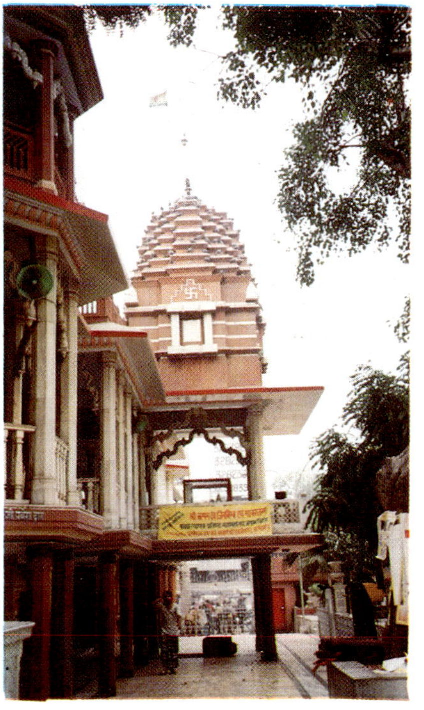

Pl. 19

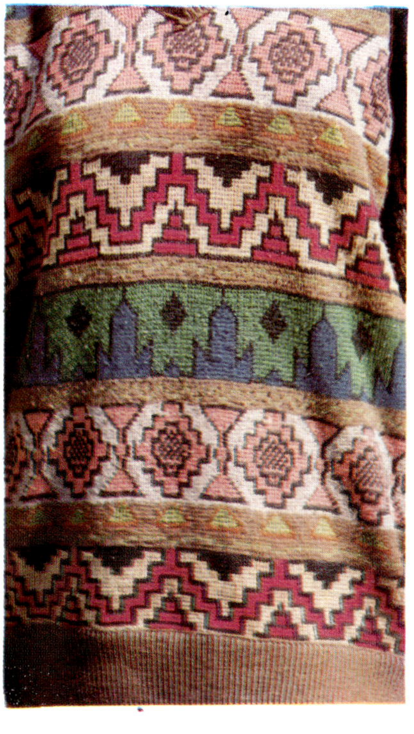

Pl. 20

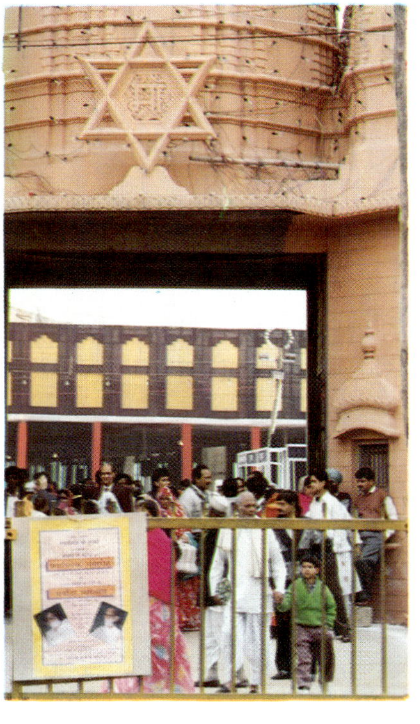

Pl. 21

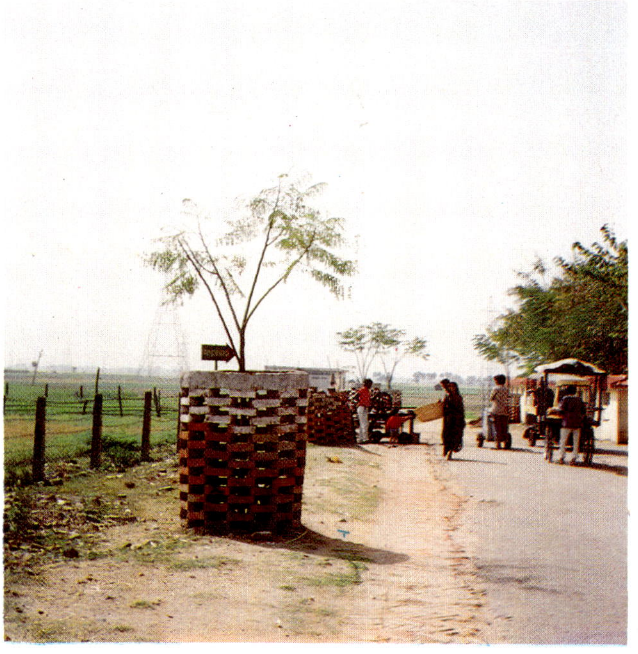

Pl. 22

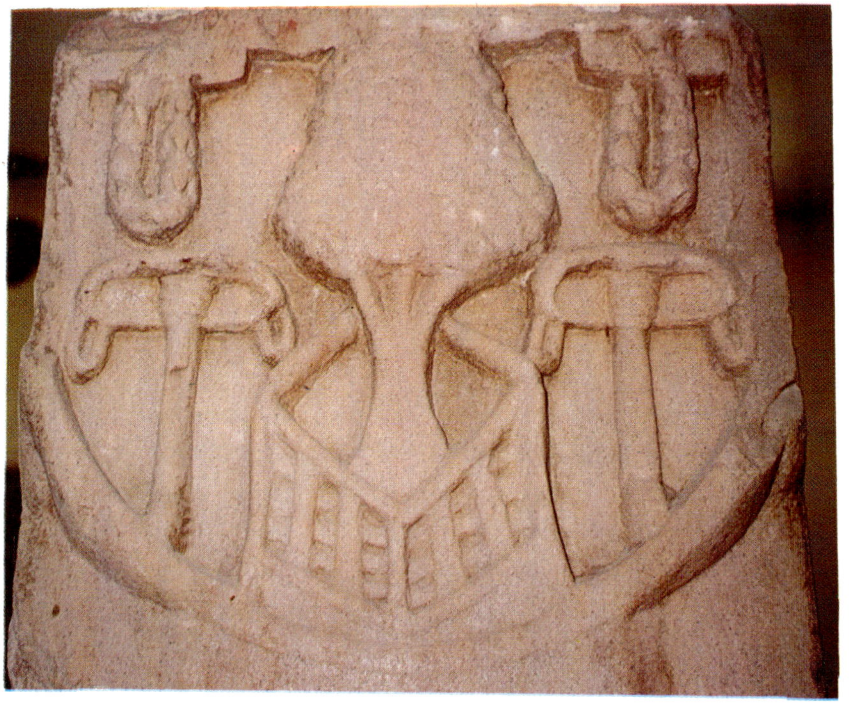

Pl. 23

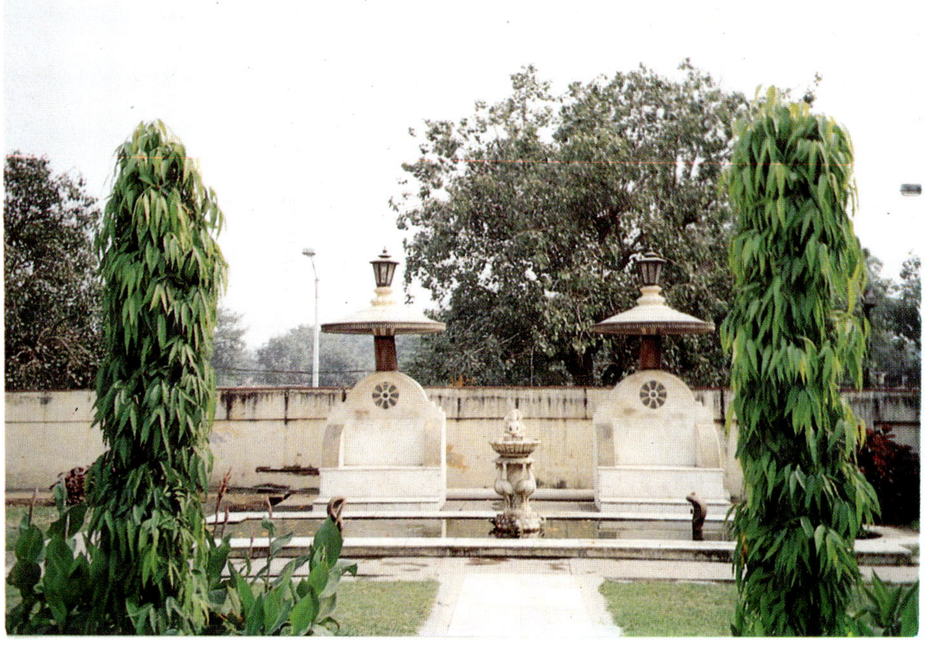

"They call Him (one God) Indra, Mitra, Agni, and He is heavenly able winged Garutman. Are Rāma, Kṛṣṇa, Śiva and Viṣṇu so many Names of One?"

Ṛg Veda I, 164.46

Pl. 24

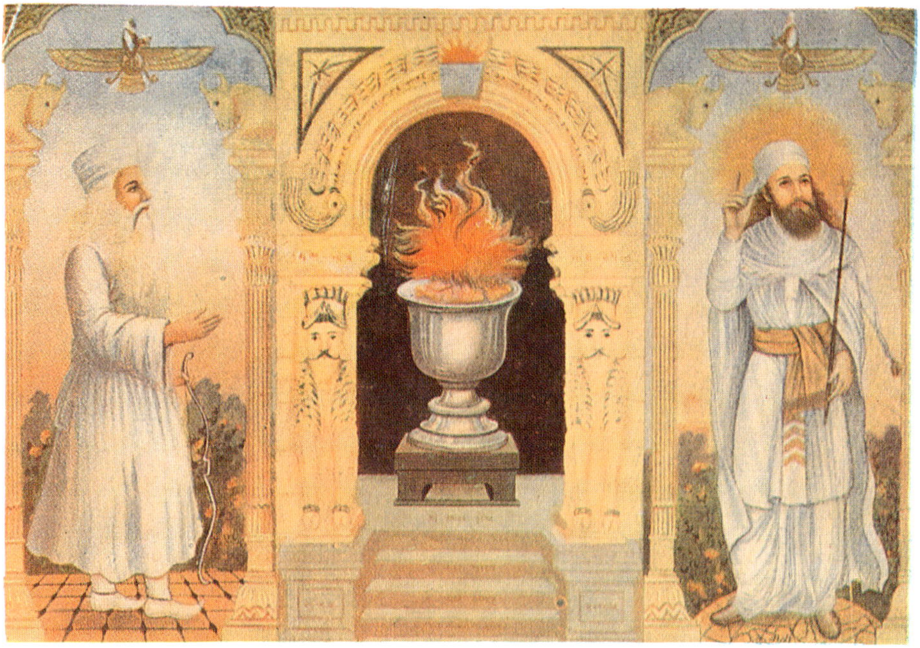

Pl. 25

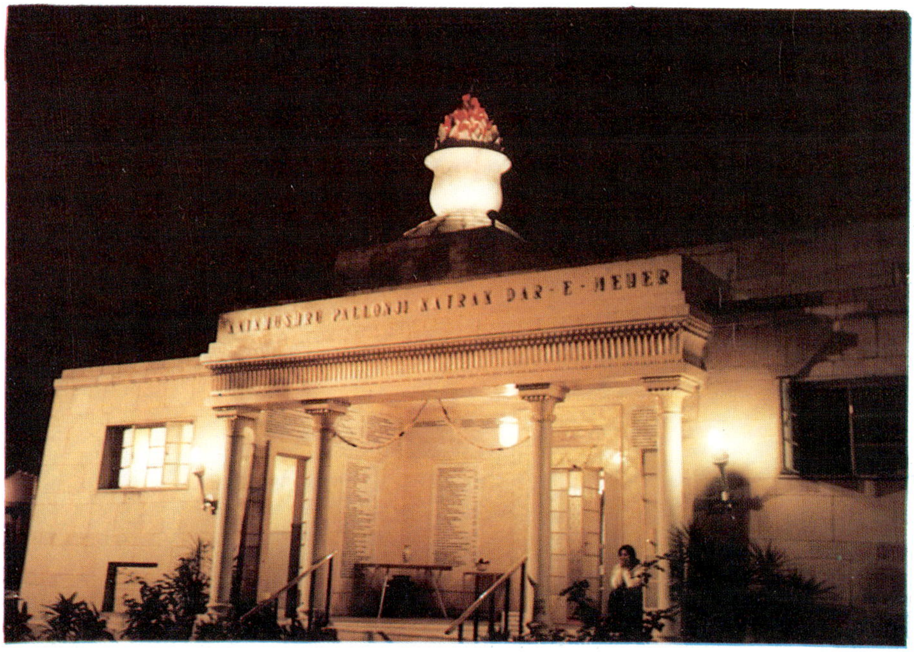

Pl. 26

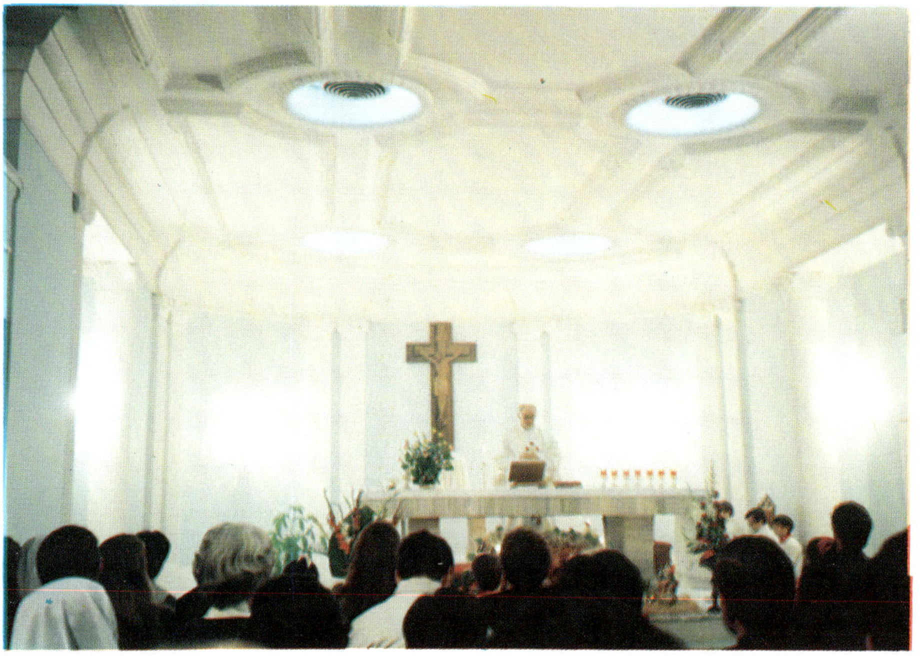

Pl. 27

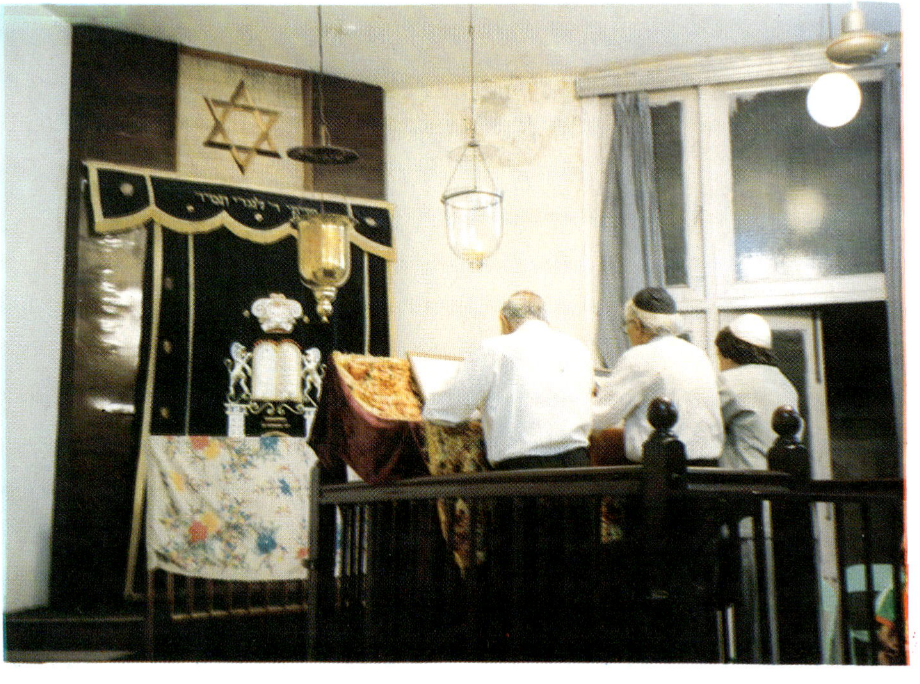

Pl. 28

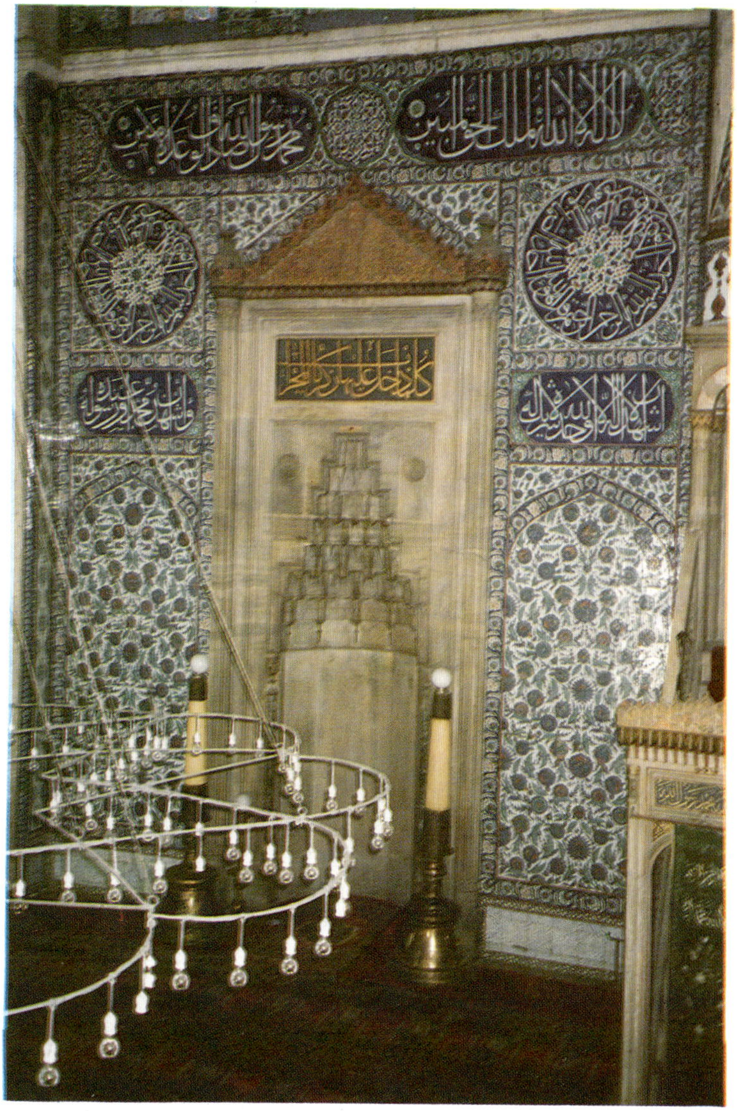

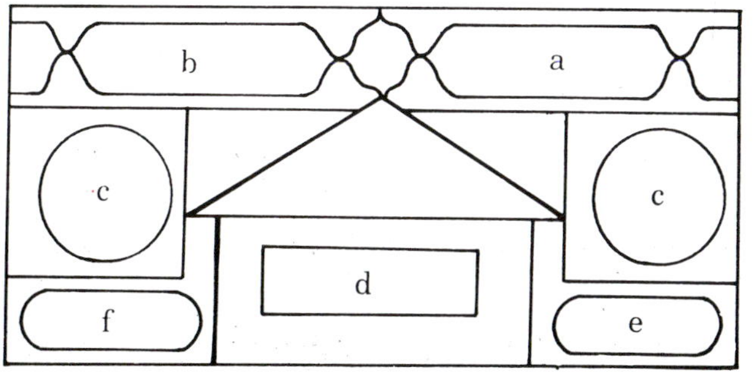

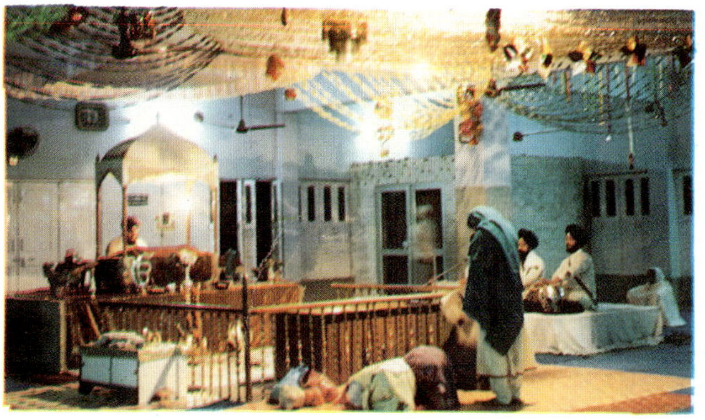

Pl. 29

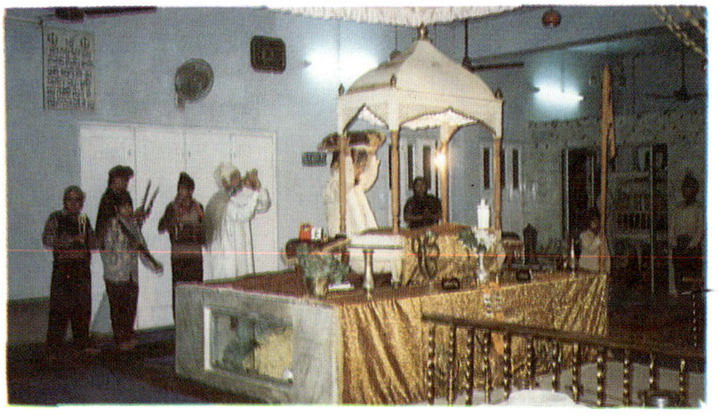

Pl. 30

Pl. 31

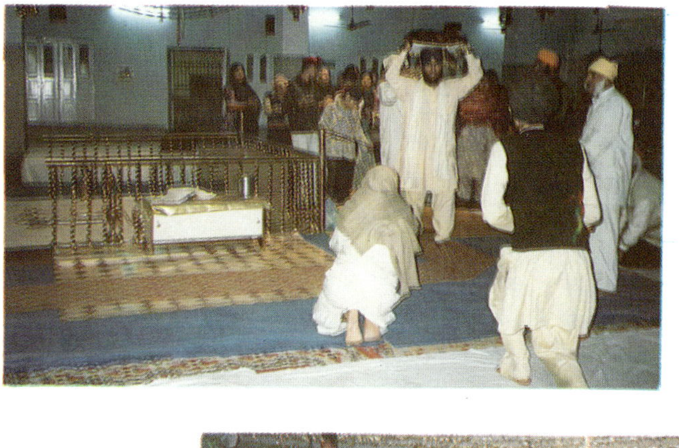

Pl. 32

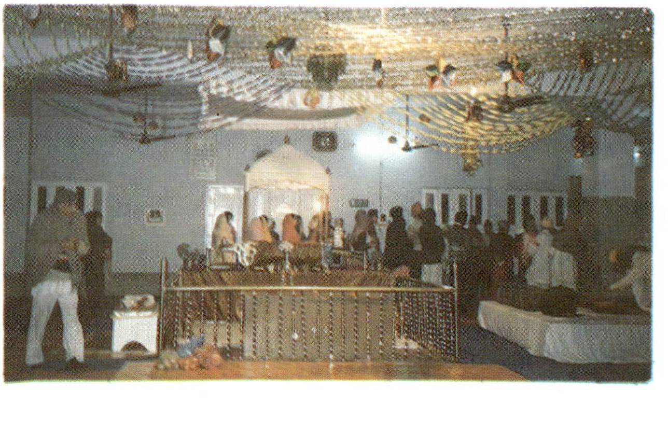

Select Bibliography

Fine Arts

(A) BUDDHIST ART

Auboyer, Jeannine, *Daily life in Ancient India from appoximately 200 BC to 700 AD*, London, 1965.

Barua, B.M., *Bārhut Book II, Jātaka-Scenes*, Calcutta, 1934.

Coomaraswamy, A.K., *Transformation of Nature in Art,* New York, 1934.

———, *Elements of Buddhist Iconography,* New York, 1935.

———, *La Sculpture de Bhārhut*, Paris, 1956.

———, *Introduction to Indian Art,* Delhi, 1969.

Craven, Roy C., *Indian Art*, London, 1974.

Cunningham, Alexander, *Bhilsa Topes or Buddhist Monuments of Central India*, London, 1854.

———, *The Stūpa of Bhārhut*, London, 1879.

Dhavalikar, M.K., *Sāñchī, A Cultural Study*, Poona, 1965.

Government of India, Ministry of Information and Broadcasting, *The Way of Buddha* (published on the occasion of the 2500th anniversary of the *Mahāparinirvāṇa* of Buddha), 1956.

Grünwedel, Albert, *Buddhist Art in India*, Delhi, 1901.

Kala, S.C., *Bhārhut Vedikā*, Allahabad, 1951.

Lippe, A., *The Freer Indian Sculptures* (Oriental Studies No. 8), Freer Gallery of Art, Smithsonian Institution, Washington, D.C., 1970.

Lüders, H., *Bhārhut Inscriptions* (*Corpus Inscriptionum Indicarum*), Government Epigraphist for India, Ootacamund, 1963.

Maisey, F.C., *Sāñchī and its Remains*, Varanasi, 1972.

Marshall, Sir John, *A Guide to Sāñchī,* The Government of India, Calcutta, 1955.

Marshall, Sir John & Foucher, Alfred, *The Monuments of Sāñchī*, Vols. 1-3, Delhi, 1982.

Mitra, Debala, *Buddhist Monuments*, Calcutta, 1980.

Murthy, K.K., *Material Culture of Sāñchī*, Delhi, 1983.

Rao, P.R. Ramachandra, *The Art of Nāgārjunikoṇḍa*, Madras, 1956.

Ray, N.R., *Maurya and Śuṇga Art*, Calcutta, 1965.

Rowland Jr., Benjamin, *The Evolution of the Buddha Image*, New York, 1976.

———, *The Art and Architectures of India — Buddhist, Hindu, Jain,* London, 1984.

Sarkar, H.B. and Nainar, S.P., *Amarāvatī,* New Delhi, 1972.

Sen Gupta, Sankar, *Sacred Trees across Cultures and Nations,* Calcutta, 1980.

Sinha, B.C., *Glorious Art of the Śuṇga Age,* Delhi, 1985.

Snellgrove, David L., *The Image of the Buddha*, Tokyo, 1978.

Srivastava, A.L., *Life in Sāñchī Sculpture*, New Delhi, 1983.

Subramaniam, V. (ed.), *The Sacred and the Secular in India's Performing Arts — Ananda K. Coomaraswamy Centenary essays*, New Delhi, 1980.

Vijayatunga, J., *Nāgārjunakoṇḍa*, Delhi, 1956.

Werner, Karel (ed.), *Symbols in Art and Religion — The Indian and the Comparative Perspectives*, Delhi, 1991.

Zimmar, Heinrich, *Myths and Symbols in Indian Art and Civilization,* New York, 1946.

(B) CHRISTIAN ART

Aringhi, Paolo, *Roma Subterranea Novissima*, Luteriae Parisiorum, 1659, (Collegium Graphicum, PSWA, Vols. 15-16, 1972).

Ferguson, George, *Signs and Symbols in Christian Art*, New York, 1954.

Grabar, Andrè, *The Beginnings of Christian Art* (E. tr.), 1966, (J. tr.) by Sahoko Tsuji, Shincho-Sha, Tokyo, 1967.

Rice, David Talbot, *Art of the Byzantine Era*, London, 1981.

Stevenson, J., *The Catacombs — Rediscovered Monuments of Early Christianity* London, 1978.

(C) ISLAMIC ART

Nath, R. Jharokha, *An Illustrated Glossary of Indo-Muslim Architecture,* Jaipur, 1986.

Rice, David Talbot, *Islamic Art,* London, 1984.

(D) SIKH ART

McLeod, W.H., *Popular Sikh Art*, Delhi, 1991.

Art-Philosophy

Dovořák, Max, *Kunstgeschichte als Geistesgeschichte,* 1921, (J. tr.) by Shigeo Nakamura, Tokyo, 1966.

Frey, Dagobert, *Grundlegung zu einer vergleichenden Kunstwissenschaft,* 1949, (J. tr.) by Kenjirō Yoshioka, Tokyo, 1961.

Leeuw, Gerardus Van Der, *Vom Heiligen in de Kunst*, David E. Green (tr.) *Sacred and Profane Beauty. The Holy in Art*, 1963.

Pächt, Otto, *Methodisches zur kunsthistorichen Praxis*. Ausgewählte Schriften, München, 1977.

Philosophy

Huizinga, John, *Homo Ludens — Proeve eener bepaling van het spel — element der cultuur,* Haarlem, 1958.

Raju, P.T. & Radhakrishnan, S., *The Concept of Man — A Study in Comparative Philosophy*, Delhi, 1992.

Scriptures

(A) INDIAN AND BUDDHIST SCRIPTURES

Aṅguttara Nikāya (*The Book of the Gradual Sayings*, tr. by F.L. Woodward and E.M. Hare, 5 vols., P.T.S. Translation Series, nos. 22, 24-27, London, 1932-36). (*Taisho* vol. 2).

Arthaśāstra (*The Kauṭilīya Arthaśāstra,* ed. by R.P. Kangle, 3 vols. Bombay, 1963-65).

Aśokāvadāna (*The Aśokāvadāna,* ed. by Sujitkumar Mukhopadhyaya, New Delhi, 1963).

Dhammapada (*The Dammapada, A Collection of Verses*. ed. by Friedrich Max Müller, *SBE*, vol. 10, Oxford, 1881).

Dīgha Nikāya (ed. by Friedrich Max Müller, *SBB*, vol. 2, P.T.S., Oxford, 1992).

Mahāparinibbānasuttanta (*The Dīgha Nikāya*, ed. by T.W. Rhys Davids and J. Eslin Carpenter, vol. 2, P.T.S., London, 1947).

Mahāvastu (*The Mahāvastu,* tr. by J.J. Jones, 3 vols., *SBB*, vols. 16, 18-19, P.T.S., London, 1949-56).

Majjhima Nikāya (*The Middle Length Sayings*, tr. by I.B. Horner, 3 vols., P.T.S. Translation Series, nos. 29-31, London, 1954-59).

Prajñāpāramitā-sūtra (tr. by Friedrich Max Müller, London, 1894, *SBE*, vol. 49).

唐三藏法師玄奘 (譯)　『般若波羅蜜多心經』, Taisho vol. 8

Ṛg-Veda (*Gedichte aus dem Ṛg-Veda*, tr. by P. Thieme, Reclam Nr. 8930, Stuttgart, 1964).

Saddharmapuṇḍarīka (*Saddharmapuṇḍarīka Sūtra,* eds. by Hendik Kern and Bunyū Nanjō, *Bibliotheca Buddhica*, No. 10, St. Petersburg, 1962).

鳩摩羅什 (譯)　『妙法蓮華經』七卷, *Taisho* vol. 9.

Saṃyutta Nikāya (*The Book of the Kindred Sayings,* tr. by C.A.F. Rhys Davids, 5 Vols., P.T.S. Translation Series nos. 7, 10, 13, 14, 16, London, 1917-30).

Sutta-Nipāta (tr. by V. Fausboll, *SBĖ*, vol. 10, Delhi, 1992).

The Amitāyur-dhyāna-sūtra (tr. by Junjiro Takakusu, *Buddhist Mahāyāna Texts*, Part II, pp. 159-204, London, 1894, *SBE*, vol. 49).

畺良耶舍 (譯)　『觀無量壽經』, *Taisho* vol. 12.

The Larger Sukhāvatīvyūha (tr. by Friedrich Max Müller, *SBE*, vol. 49, Part II, Oxford, 1894).

康僧鎧 (譯)　『佛說無量壽經』, *Taisho* vol. 12.

The Smaller Sukhāvatīvyūha (tr. by Friedrich Max Müller, *SBE*, vol. 49, 1894).

鳩摩羅什 (譯)　『佛說阿弥陀經』, *Taisho* vol. 12.

Theragātha (*Psalms of the Brethren,* tr. by Rhys Davids, . . . S., 137).

Therīgātha (Psalms of the Sisters, tr. by Rhys Davids, P.T.S., 1909, 1949).

Udānavarga (tr. by William Woodville Rockhill, Trübner, London, 1883).

Vajracchedikā-prajñāpāramitā (tr. Friedrich Max Müller, in "Buddhist Mahāyāna Sūtras", *SBE*, vol., 49, pf. 2, 1894).

鳩摩羅什 (譯)　『金剛般若波羅蜜經』一卷,　*Taisho* vol. 13.

(B) ZOROASTRIAN SCRIPTURES

Henning, M.(tr.), *The Hymns of Zarathushtra,* London, 1992.

Homji, Homi B. Minocher (tr. & ed.), *Pocket Avestā,* Toronto, 1993.

Humbach, Helmut & Pallan Ichaporia (tr.), *The Heritage of Zarathushtra — A New Translation of His Gāthās*, Heidelberg, 1994.

Kanga, Ervad Manek Furdoonji, *Khordeh Avestā*, Bombay, 1976.

Rangoonwalla, Adil F.(tr. & ed.), *Meher Niyaesh,* Bombay.

Taraporewala, Irach J.S. (tr.), *The Divine Songs of Zarathushtra*, Bombay, 1993.

Vimadalal, Jai Rustamji (tr.), *The Sacred Khordeh Avestā (Shahenshahi) — A Book of*

Zoroastrian Daily Prayers, Bombay, 1984.

(C) JEWISH AND CHRISTIAN SCRIPTURES

New Testament — English New International Version & Japanese Colloquial Version, The International Gideon Society, Tokyo, 1984.

Seisho (The reference Bible in Japanese edition, Nihon Seisho Kankokai, Tokyo, 1973).

The Holy Bible, Containing the Old and New Testament, King James Version, World Bible Publishers, Australia.

(D) ISLAMIC SCRIPTURES

Eliasii, M.A. Ḥaleem (tr. in Roman Script) and Mohammed Marmaduke Pickthall (tr.), *The Holy Qur'ān*, Arish Company, New Delhi, 1993.

Izutsu, Toshihiko (tr.), *Kōran*, vols. 1-3, Iwanami Shoten, Tokyo, 1957-58.

Maududi, Maulana Syed Abul A'la (tr.), *The Meaning of the Qur'ān*, vols. 1-2, Board of Islamic Publications, Delhi, 1973 (1982).

Pickthall, Mohammad Marmaduke (tr.), *The Meaning of the holy Qur'ān*, Crescent Publishing Company, New Delhi, 1985.

Shakir, M.H. (tr.), *Holy Qur'ān*, Ansarian Publications, Islamic Republic of Iran.

(E) SIKH SCRIPTURES

Doabia, Harbans Singh (tr.), *Sacred Japjī — Translation & Transliteration containing some of the Fundamental Sermons of the Sikh Religion,* Amritsar, 1992.

——— (tr.), *Sacred Nitnem — Containing the Divine Hymns of the Daily Prayers by the Sikhs,* Amritsar, 1993.

——— (tr.), *Sacred Sukhmani*, Amritsar, 1993.

Mansukhani, Gobind Singh (ed.), *Hymns from Guru Granth Sahib*, New Delhi, 1975.

Singh, Gopal (tr.), *Sri Guru Granth Sahib* (vols. 1-4), New Delhi, 1993.

Singh, Manmohan (tr.), *Sri Guru Granth Sahib* (Vols. 1-8), Amritsar, 1987-92.

Talib, Gurbachan Singh (tr.), *Si Guru Granth Sahib* (Vols. 1-3), Patiala, 1988-91.

Religious Thoughts

(A) BUDDHISM

Bapat, P.V., *2500 Years of Buddhism*, Ministry of Information and Broadcasting, Government of India, Delhi, 1959.

Beal, Samuel (tr.), *Buddhist Records of the Western World*, 2 vols., New York, 1968.

Cowell, E.B. (ed.), *The Jātaka or Stories of the Buddha's Former Births*, Cambridge, 1901.

Jha, D.N., *Ancient India — An Introductory Outline*, New Delhi, 1977.

Johnston, E.H., *The Buddhacarita or Acts of the Buddha*, Delhi, 1992.

Legge, James (tr. and ed.), *A Record of Buddhistic Kingdoms*, New York, 1965.

Mookerji, Radhakumud, *Aśoka*, Delhi, 1989.

Pathak, V., *History of Kosala*, Delhi, 1983.

Sinha, B.C., *History of the Śuṅga Dynasty*, Delhi, 1977.

Srivastava, K.M., *Discovery of Kapilavastu*, New Delhi, 1986.

Strong, John S., *The Legend of King Aśoka — A Study and Translation of the Aśokāvadāna*, Delhi, 1989.

(B) ZOROASTRIANISM

Boyce, Mary, *Zoroastrians — Their Religious Beliefs and Practices*, London, 1979.

———, *A Persian Stronghold of Zoroastrianism*, London, 1989.

Dabu, Dastūr Khurshed S., *Zarathushtra and His Teachings (A Manual for Young Students)*, Bombay.

———, *Message of Zarathushtra*, Bombay, 1959.

Dastoor, Ervad K.N., *The Divine Science of Navjote and Sudreh-Kushti*, California, 1993.

Dhalla, Maneckji Nusservanji, *History of Zoroastrianism*, Bombay, 1963.

Dhalla, Viraf Minocher (ed.), *Symbolism in Zoroastrianism — The Religious Ceremonies and Customs of the Parsees*, Bombay, 1994.

Dipanjali, Journal of Delhi Parsi Anjuman, June-December, Delhi, 1994.

Eduljee, H.E., *Kisseh-i-Sanjān*, Bombay, 1991.

Gershevitch, Ilya, *Approaches to Zoroaster's Gāthās*, IRAN XXXIII, The British Institute of Persian Studies, 1995.

Hinnells, John R., *Persian Mythology*, London, 1988.

International Congress Proceedings (5th to 8th January 1995), K.R. Cama Oriental Institute, Bombay, 1995.

Irani, D.J., *Introduction to the Holy Gāthās* (P.D. Maker Avestan Series Vol. 1), Bombay, 1927.

Ito, Gikyo, *Zoroaster Kenkyū* (Japanese edition), Tokyo, 1979.

Jehanian, Ardeshir, Jehanbaksh D. Daruwala (tr.), *The Religion of the Achaemenians*, Bombay, 1971.

Journal of the K.R. Cama Oriental Institute, No. 59, Bombay, 1994.

Jungalwalla, Piloo Nanavutty, *Fravarānē "I Believe" — A Zoroastrian Child's Confession of Faith*, Delhi, 1987.

———, *The Parsis*, New Delhi, 1977.

Mistree, Khojeste P., *Zoroastrianism — An Ethnic Perspective*, Bombay, 1982.

Motafram, Ervad Ratanshah R., *History of Ancient Iran*, Bombay, 1993.

Parsiana, Vol. 17, No. 4, Bombay, 1994.

Rustomjee, Framroz, *The Life of Holy Zarathushtra*, Bombay, 1984.

Toot, Minocheher Hormasji, *Practical Metaphysics of Zoroastrianism*, Bombay, 1957.

Tunel, Ervad N.E. (ed.), *1251st Anniversary of Installation of Sacred Iranshah Atash Bahram*, Bombay, 1972.

World Wide Fund For Nature - India, Annual Report, New Delhi, 1993-94.

WWF - India Quarterly "25 Years", Newsletter Vol. 5, Nos. 3 & 4, July-December, New Delhi, 1994.

(C) CHRISTIANITY

Enchiridon Symbolorum Definitionum of Declarationum de Rebus Fidei et Morum, edited by Debzinger & Schönmetzer, Editio XXXVI, Freiburg in Breisgau, 1965.

Meyendorff, John, *Christ in Eastern Christian Thought*, New York, 1975.

The Catholic Catechism (Japanese edition), Tokyo, 1972.

The Catholic Encyclopedia, vol. 2 (Japanese edition), Tokyo, 1971.

The Orthodox Catechism (Japanese edition), Tokyo, 1980.

(D) ISLĀM

Ahmad, Syed Barakat, *Introduction to Qur'ānic Script*, New Delhi, 1984.

Houtsma, M. TH., A.J. Wensinck, H.A.R. Gibb, W. Heffning and E.Levi-Provençal (ed.), *E.J. Brill's First Encyclopedia of Islām 1913-36*, Photomechanical Reprint Vol. 7, E.J. Brill, Leiden, New York, København, Köln, 1987.

Muḥammad, Shaykh & Ibn' Abd al Wahhāb, *Kitāb al Tawhīd*, Delhi, 1988.

Penrice, John, *A Dictionary and Glossary of the Koran*, Delhi, 1873 (1990).

(E) SIKHISM

Delhi Sikh Gurudwara Management Committee (ed.), *Historical Sikh Shrines in Delhi*, Delhi, 1993.

Duggal, K.S., *Sikh Gurus — Their Lives and Teachings*, New Delhi, 1993.

———, *The Sikh People, Yesterday & Today*, New Delhi, 1994.

Kohli, Surindar Singh, *Guru Granth Sahib — An Analytical Study*, Amritsar, 1992.

Mansukhani, Gobind Singh, *Introduction to Sikhism*, New Delhi, 1994.

Oberoi, Mridula, *Life and Times: The Sikh Guru,* New Delhi, 1993.

Safeer, Pritam, Singh, *The Ten Holy Gurus And Their Commandments,* Delhi, 1988.

Singh, B. Chattar Singh Jiwan, *Ardas*, Amritsar, 1993.

Singh, Bhai Sahib Sirdar Kapur, *An Incomparable Prophet Guru Amar Dass,* Delhi, 1983.

Singh, Daljeet, *Sikhism —A Comparative Study of its Theology and Mysticism,* Amritsar, 1994.

Singh, Ganda, *A Brief Account of the Sikh People*, Delhi, 1988.

Singh, Kulmohan, *Shahadat Naama —Brief Account of Sikh Martyrs*, Delhi, 1994.

Singh, Parkash, *Community Kitchen of the Sikhs*, Amritsar, 1994.

Singh, Singh Sahib Darshan & Jathedar Akal Takhat Sahib (ed.), *The Primary Introduction of Sikh Religion & Sikh History,* Delhi, 1990.

Singh, Teja, *The Sikh Religion, An Outline of its Doctrines,* Delhi, 1993.

Singha, H.S., *Mini Encyclopaedia of Sikhism* (Illustrated), New Delhi, 1989.

Ten Masters, Diamond Comics Digest XLII, New Delhi.

Religious Studies

Durkheim, Émile, *Les Formes élémentaires de la Vie religieuse, Le Système totémique on Australie*, Paris, 1912.

Eliade, Mircea & Kitagawa, Joseph M. (ed.), *The History of Religions — Essays in Methodology*, London, 1959.

Hastings, James (ed.), *Encyclopedia of Religion and Ethics*, New York, 1914-64.

Lapide, Pinchas & Moltmann, Jürgen, Jüdische *Monotheismus—Christliche Trinitätslehre*, München, 1979.

Masih, Y.A., *Comparative Study of Religions*, Delhi, 1990.

Smith, Wilfred Cantwell, *The Meaning and End of Religion*, New York, 1962.

Söderblom, Nathan, *Das Werden des Gottesglaubens*, 2 Aufl., 1926.

Tiwari, Kedar Nath, *Comparative Religion*, Delhi, 1983.

Index

Abbreviations

Ara.	Arabic	Jpn.	Japanese
Av.	Avestan	Lat.	Latin
Eng.	English	Mon.	Mongol
Fre.	French	Pah.	Pahlavi
Gre.	Greek	Pāl.	Pāli
Guj.	Gujarati	Per.	Persian
Heb.	Hebrew	Puñ.	Puñjābī
Hin.	Hindī	Skt.	Sanskrit
Ita.	Italian	Yid.	Yiddish

Note: Both 'ś' in Sanskrit and 'š' in Avestan, Pahlavi and Persian are pronounced 'sh'.